I Cannot Tell A Lie

I CANNOT TELL A LIE

The True Story of George Washington's African American Descendants

Linda Allen Bryant

iUniverse Star

New York Lincoln Shanghai

I Cannot Tell A Lie
The True Story of George Washington's African American Descendants

Copyright © 2001, 2004 by Linda Allen Bryant

iUniverse Star
an iUniverse, Inc. imprint

iUniverse books may be ordered through booksellers or by contacting:

iUniverse
2021 Pine Lake Road, Suite 100
Lincoln, NE 68512
www.iuniverse.com
1-800-Authors (1-800-288-4677)

ISBN: 0-595-31899-1 (Pbk)
ISBN: 0-595-66442-3 (Cloth)

Printed in the United States of America

Dedication

This book is dedicated to the descendants of West Ford—**Stand Proud, Stand Tall!**

I also wish to offer a special dedication to my parents, Elise and James O. Allen. Thank you mother; you taught me how to reason and to stand up for what is right. And in loving memory of my father, James O. Allen (1918–2000), who taught me how to dream and to reach for the unreachable.

Once in a lifetime a story is revealed that changes the face of history.

James O. Allen

Contents

Foreword

A critic advises not to write on controversial subjects like freedom or murder, but to treat universal themes and timeless symbols like the white unicorn.

Dudley Randall

For most of her adult life, my mother, Elise Ford Allen, was the Ford family's official chronicler, passing on the legacy of West Ford within our extended family at annual reunions. The responsibility of transmitting our centuries-old family secret—that we were the descendants of George Washington—weighed profoundly on her heart.

In 1994, she decided that the American populace might be ready to accept our story. To me she handed the task of becoming the next official chronicler and of "carrying the charge" beyond our immediate family. With a great deal of help from my sister, Janet, and our cousin, Dr. Judith Saunders-Burton, I have developed a website, made multiple appearances on television, and am publishing *I Cannot Tell A Lie* to preserve our family legacy.

Many biographies have been written about George Washington, from his life as a Virginia planter, to his military exploits in the

Revolutionary War, to his role as a statesman, and as the nation's first president. *I Cannot Tell A Lie* was written to introduce his son, West Ford, and his descendants. The sections of this book depicting Washington were integral to the Ford history and have not been introduced before in any other bibliography on him. I have also dissected and digested Washington's personal diaries and letters with the intent to share a certain intimacy with him, to better understand him as one of my great grandfathers.

The book addresses many questions that arise in response to the Ford family's claim, such as how the reputedly childless George Washington could have met the slave Venus and fathered her child, and why she chose to reveal the father's identity to her son. *I Cannot Tell A Lie* brings to life the extraordinary story that my family has hidden from the public for the past two hundred years.

I Cannot Tell A Lie was written as narrative history for a variety of reasons. This format allowed me to relay my heritage in the way it was passed down through the generations by the Ford chroniclers. The book is written in a style that allows the reader full glimpses into the workings of the minds of my ancestors, with all the nuances of their character and the events that shaped the lives of their descendants. It is an accessible format through which the Ford family history might be considered, while offering a compelling exposure to the many sociopolitical issues surrounding the claim to the Washington bloodline.

The text is supported and enhanced by actual historical accounts, placing Ford family members with prominent figures such as General George Custer, W.E.B. Dubois and another American President, Teddy Roosevelt. I have also added an extensive reference section that will be of great interest to anyone wanting "proof" of my family's claim to the Washington family tree. This and other authentic letters and excerpts from last wills and testaments, land grants, journals, newspaper articles, tax records, and national archives are peppered throughout *I Cannot Tell A Lie* and add to the depth of this intriguing story. This original material was presented to the Mount Vernon Ladies' Association at a historic 2000 meeting as documentation of our heritage.

The story of the Ford legacy begins with the birth of West Ford and traces his lineage through his children to subsequent generations of Fords; each faced with the emotional and political challenges of their shared secret identity and respective eras in which they lived. The book traces my family's ironic tale from its beginnings in post-colonial Virginia to current times. In essence, the story covers factual incidents supported by personal anecdotes and excerpts from numerous historical records and archival documents. However, the names of some of the people cited in this work have been changed to protect their privacy.

The lineage information presented in this book can be documented, but with one central exception: who was West Ford's father? No living person can testify to the act that conceived West Ford, but the testimony of Venus, the woman who contributed one half of his genes, is available to the public for the first time in *I Cannot Tell A Lie*. Venus revealed the identity of the father to the son, who in turn told his son. Thus, the Ford family's origins were preserved in an oral document that has endured for over two centuries. And consequently, the Ford descendants have carried on the traditions of patriotism and family pride, despite being unable to lay claim to a famous grandfather known for those self-same traits.

The Washingtons never openly claimed a blood relationship to West Ford. And alas, many historians wish to place the onus of West Ford's birth on his nephews, Bushrod or Corbin Washington. But we, the African American heirs of West Ford, know of our heritage. There are no Bushrods or Corbins in the Ford family tree of names.

I am fully aware that a book depicting George Washington as anything but honorable will elicit some controversy, causing debates among historians and pundits for many years to come. But American history must be recounted, challenged, and kept accessible. The Ford family wants to claim its legacy and this book serves as documentation of our heritage. The descendants of West Ford by no means wish to denigrate George Washington, but merely desire the validation and vindication of who we are in American history for our children and our children's children.

As you turn the pages of this book, you will gain a closer understanding about the descendants of George Washington, his African American heirs—his blood heirs.

Let us share our story with you because our story must be told.

Linda Allen Bryant

Acknowledgements

I first wish to thank and honor God, who makes all things possible.

I would like to acknowledge my sister, Janet Allen, for her diligence in keeping the history of West Ford and the Ford family oral history alive. As one of the Ford family chroniclers, Janet gave me the creative energy and the moral support needed to tell our story. Without her help this book would have never been completed. I would like to give a special thank you to my parents, James and Elise Allen, who all those years ago gave me the encouragement to convey the family story in written format. I have always relied on their love and guidance. I am most appreciative to Cousin Judy, whose doctoral dissertation on the history of West Ford and Gum Springs, Virginia, was invaluable in supporting many facts in this book. Judy is a historian who has dedicated a great deal of time and effort in researching West Ford and his descendants. Judy established the West Ford Museum in Gum Springs and was instrumental in the refurbishing of the Mount Vernon Slave Memorial.

I want to acknowledge Russell Phillip Bryant for his support and to my sons, Julian, Russell III, and Ian who knew that Mom could do it. I appreciate all my other siblings, Carol, Jim, Joy, Angela, Barbara, Norman, Gregory, and Tim, who helped in gathering historical data and pictures. I want to offer many thanks to the Fords all over the country, especially Uncle Harrison, Aunt Florence, Aunt Delores, Cousin Harriet, and Cousin Ruby, who responded to the call for oral history and family memorabilia. I would also like to render a special thank you to my good friend and mentor, Emerson Hollis.

I wish to extend a special thank you to my editor, Wendy Robinson, who has literally been my right arm. Wendy has given me direction and guidance from the conception of this project until its completion. Wendy and her husband, Eli, created the Ford Family official website, which has won a place of distinction on the Internet. My gratitude also goes out to Jack Bolts, Mary Lynn Hanley, Geraldine Mitchell, Billie Caldwell, Thelma Craig, Damaris Rowland, Durthy Washington, and Michelle McFalls, who assisted in critiquing the many drafts of my work. Michelle went the extra mile when she accompanied me on a trip to Mount Vernon to collect data on West Ford. I give a special thank you to J. Madama for his rendition of Venus. I am very thankful to Dr. Eugene Foster for helping me to decipher the intricacies of DNA and Annette Gordon-Reed for her words of encouragement. Many thanks to my friends for their support—Helen Margaret Jackson, Millie Hall, Shelly Hodge, Elma Hairston, Diane Sykes, Lynne Mullins, Paula Kolen, Alison Needham, Jeanine Fletcher, Thomas Wolfe, Gina and Mike Townsie, and to all my friends at Cephalon, Inc. and John Phillips Printing Company. And lastly, thanks to the news reporters, Robert Jackson (*Rocky Mountain News*), Bill Briggs (*Denver Post*), Jeremy Manier (*Chicago Tribune*), Nicolas Wade (*New York Times*), Pam Adams, Christopher Williams, and Christopher Thorne (*The Peoria Journal Star*), Jon Jeter (*Washington Post*) and Amanda Milkovits (*Foster's Daily Democrat*) for their shared interest in the story of our heritage.

I CANNOT TELL A LIE

George Washington—25 years *West Ford—21 years*

A PORTRAIT COMPARISON

A portrait of George Washington and a sketch of West Ford at similar ages illustrate a resemblance between the two men.

George Washington   *Venus—mother of West Ford*

A PARABLE OF ANCESTORS

An influential leader in post-colonial Virginia and a mulatto maid owned by his sister-in-law. Their fateful union produced a son, West Ford.

PART ONE

The Beginning

Along this road of stress and strain,
I journey on despite the pain,
advancing onward toward my goal,
where human chains can't bind my soul.

Janet Allen

Prologue

...all the past is but the beginning of a beginning...

H. G. Wells

The small, dark room smelled of sickness and impending death. It seeped into and permeated the area with insidious intent. It was eerily quiet except for the laborious breathing of the old man lying in his bed. He was resigned to his fate. He wasn't afraid to die, because he had been a God-fearing man and had lived an exemplary life. In fact, he was curious as to what lay ahead of him once he passed his earthly realm. But it was becoming more difficult for him to draw a decent breath. It was as if a ton of bricks were stacked upon his frail upper body, crushing his chest.

A number of his family members stood vigil around his bedside—his wife, three sons, three daughters, and several of his grandchildren. But his thoughts were focused on the petite, teenaged girl with eyes the color of warmed brandy who knelt beside him. She clenched one of his gaunt hands. Once in a while, when it became difficult for him to grasp a breath, she would grip his hand, forcing him to alertness.

But he was tired, so very tired.

"Don't die, Big Papa! Please don't die and leave us!" the young girl cried out in anguish. She could sense that her grandfather was slipping away and she couldn't bear the thought of it.

"Everybody dies," he rasped. "It's...a part of life. D-don't cry f-for me, Lesey." He sighed and spoke gently, patting her hand.

"You still have a lot of years left, Big Papa. We need you. Please, I know you can get over this sickness. You just have to!"

Expelling a weary breath, the old man turned towards his grand-daughter and said in a soothing voice, "Lesey...i-it w-will be all right."

His sight was leaving him. It was as if he saw her through a veil, but he needed to look into her eyes and remind her of the task ahead before his voice left him also. He noted that Lesey's eyes were shiny with tears. They pooled in the corners, clinging to her long lashes like raindrops on a leaf before slipping onto her cheeks. She sniffled and rubbed her free hand under her nose.

"C-come c-closer Lesey."

The grief-stricken girl rose and leaned over the bed, resting her hands beside his damp pillow. His hands were skeletal as he gathered his last ounce of strength to frame her face, bringing her closer. He wanted to look into his granddaughter's eyes, needed to see what he knew lurked behind them—strength and fortitude—characteristics she would require for her life-long task. His probing gaze was prolonged and intense. A hint of relief etched his features, as if measuring her and liking what he saw. Then his hands dropped.

A moment later his voice rang out with a surprising burst of strength, "You are the chronicler. The charge is now yours."

He began to cough then gasped for breath. It became a battle for him to regain control from the relentless rattling sound emanating from his overburdened lungs. His will was strong because he couldn't let death claim him yet, not until he finished what he needed to say.

In a much weaker voice he went on, "L-Lesey, d-don't let our h-heritage die."

"I won't Big Papa. I promise."

*   *   *

Present Day

A shout of laughter broke the trance of Elise Ford Allen's thoughts from the past. She had been looking through a lace-curtained window in her bedroom into the backyard of her Midwest home. She was alone. Perhaps forgotten for awhile, with all of the activities to celebrate her birthday and yet another family reunion. Later they would all gather to hear the family story. It was a ritual as old as she could remember, one that started over two hundred years ago. That is why her thoughts had been on her beloved grandfather, George Ford. She always thought about him this time of the year and the charge he had given her on his deathbed.

Stepping away from the window, Elise glanced into the ornate, gold-framed mirror over the cherrywood dresser. The reflection staring back at her had changed as much as her life these past several years. Time had left its traces on her face, in the small lines next to her mouth, on her neck and brow, and the creases in the corners of her eyes.

Patting the brownish-gray curls on the side of her head, she said aloud, "Not bad for seventy-nine." She didn't feel her age—at least, not every day.

Elise walked away from the mirror and sat in the rocker next to her bed, and picked up a dog-eared scrapbook from an end table. This book contained parts of her family's heritage, handed down through the years. Lost in memories once again, she flipped through the old newspaper articles, obituaries, letters and yellowed photographs of her ancestors.

Pressing her head back against the rocker, she was overcome by nostalgia. Time was on her mind this day. Today was her birthday, but it was not only that. Today she would choose the special ones, those of her offspring who would continue the legacy of the family. They would carry the charge forward into their generation. For sixty years she had been the family chronicler, and the duty weighed heavily upon her shoulders. So many times during her lifetime she wanted to let the past be just that—the past. It would have been so much easier just to forget about the responsibility handed over to her by her grandfather to keep their family's secret legacy alive. But then she would remember her grandfather and the other generations of Fords who were designated chroniclers—they had not given up. Each had been admonished to stand proud, stand tall during life's hardships and triumphs, and for that reason she had continued. With a new resolve, Elise rose and slowly went outside.

Today she would once again tell the family story from the beginning, starting with her fourth great grandparents, George Washington and Venus.

Chapter 1

Bushfield Plantation, Virginia—1785

I cannot tell how the truth may be;
I say the tale as 'twas said to me.

Sir Walter Scott

The girl had turned into a raving maniac. Her blood-curdling scream shook the rafters.

"Mammy, I can't push no more!"

"Hush now. You ain't doin' nothin' no other woman ain't done before. Now push." Her mother gently wiped clammy perspiration from her daughter's brow with a cool cloth and said with quiet intensity, "Venus, you hush now. You know how Miz Hannah don't like no loud noises."

"I don't care if'n the whole plantation hears. This be the worsest feelin'. Awhouch!" Venus gasped in shock as another strong contraction rolled over her small frame.

"Ooooh! Jes let me die, jes let me die!" she wailed.

If Jenny hadn't been so tired and exasperated helping Venus cope with the birthing of her first grandchild, she might have been tempted to laugh at her daughter's theatrics. Even as a little girl, Venus never could withstand pain of any kind. A scratch on her finger would cause her to carry on so much that one would have thought it had been cut off.

Jenny studied her daughter's pain-wracked face. Even the struggle of childbirth could not disguise her exotic beauty. Venus' cat-like eyes were wide-spaced and framed with long, curly lashes; their color a mixture of gold and brown. When she smiled, two deep dimples graced her cheeks. These features were set in an oval face with high cheekbones and a slightly flared nose. The girl's crown of glory was her wavy, dark brown hair. That hair was now sweat soaked and plastered over her straw pallet as she thrashed in the final stages of childbirth.

A tremendous pressure gripped Venus' belly. Her body suddenly went rigid and she began to whimper. "M-Mammy! Help me!"

"Venus, you gots to push now. The babe is comin'. Push. Push hard, chile!" her mother urged her.

Moments later, with a screech loud enough to wake the dead, Venus gave birth in a hot, airless room on the Bushfield Plantation. Jenny turned the newborn upside down to drain its nostrils and gave it a light spank on the rump. The child's piercing screams replaced those of his mother.

"Venus, you got yourself a fine boy chile," Jenny said, holding the squirming, bawling baby. "And he's a-kickin' his arms and legs every which ways."

"A little boy? Let me see him."

Venus' tawny eyes glittered and she smiled for the first time in hours. Suddenly the smile vanished and her face contorted in pain as her body expelled the afterbirth. This time the pain didn't last long.

"L-let m-me see him," she murmured again.

"Jes let me clean him up a bit first," her mother said as she examined her grandson. The infant's nose was flattened somewhat and his head was a little elongated from his travel through the birth canal. He had all his toes and fingers, the proud grandmother noted as she wiped the birth fluids from his tiny body. With lighting speed, she tied off the umbilical cord with thread, cut it, and swaddled the child in a piece of coarse linen.

Jenny placed the baby boy into the young mother's waiting arms and watched the look of disbelief that crossed her daughter's pallid face. Venus was dismayed. The baby was whiter than she was. He was milk white—massa white.

Venus watched as her newborn tried to focus on her face. His half-closed eyes were not golden like her own, but a striking blue-gray, and a thatch of red-brown hair covered his tiny head. The baby's hair was not curly, but stick straight. She gently touched the mane of damp hair and found it soft as cotton.

Venus' son did not have the appearance of a slave child. He looked like—a massa. It was going to be difficult for him to fit into the life of a slave with white skin, red hair and blue-gray eyes.

A rush of emotion overcame the young mother's dismay as she studied her precious baby. At that moment she felt so much love for him that she thought she would burst.

"Lawsy, that sure be the whitest slave baby I ever done seen," remarked Jenny as she took the child from her daughter. "Them Washingtons ain't gonna like this one bit, but don't you worry, little one, you gots me and your mammy to love you," she cooed to the baby. Her voice took on a wistful note. "I sure do wish your pappy could 'of seen this here chile."

Venus lay back on her pallet, exhausted. The twenty-one hours of labor overpowered her. Closing her eyes, she remembered the events that led to her present predicament.

Master John Washington had been grieving over the recent death of his seventeen-year-old son, Augustine. The youngest of his three sons had been killed while away at Delaman's Academy. A fellow student had been playing with a loaded gun when the weapon discharged. Augustine, who had been sitting nearby, took the bullet in the chest and died a few minutes later.

Mistress Hannah, Master John's wife, had fallen into a strong convulsion when she learned of her son's death. The shock was too great for her frail frame to bear, and she remained bedridden. Bushrod and Corbin, the two remaining sons, had been notified and were on their way home.

The big house was in deep mourning because young Augustine was well liked by all of the house slaves. He had been a personable young man. Venus and her mother cried together when they learned of his death. Jenny doted on the young man—she had been his mammy until he was twelve, and he remained close to her and Venus as he matured.

Venus was also the playmate of his little sister, Mildred. Whenever Augustine returned to Bushfield between school breaks, he would bring Mildred a piece of chocolate or hard candy and there was always a piece for her and her mother as well. Oh, how she had looked forward to those special times.

Venus would never forget how Master Augustine had taught her the letters of the alphabet and how to spell her name when she was around ten. He was forever trying to teach her to speak "The king's good English."

"Venus, the word is 'you' not 'you's,'" he would patiently correct her diction.

"Yas'm, Massa Augustine, ahs try harder," she replied.

"Not 'ahs,' Venus, the word is 'I,'" he would say, smiling.

Augustine had been a handsome boy, tall and lanky, with brown hair and gray eyes. He was forever smiling, but now that warm smile would never grace the rooms of Bushfield again.

A letter had been dispatched to Master John's favorite brother, George, with the dire news. Master George owned the Mount Vernon plantation, one-or-two day's ride from Bushfield. Mount Vernon was a bachelor hall until Master John married Hannah Bushrod and brought her to his brother's home. Master John had managed Mount Vernon while his brother was away, fighting in the French and Indian War. When George married Martha Custis in 1759, John Augustine and Hannah relocated to her family's estate at Bushfield. Since then, the brothers often visited each other's plantations by horseback or schooner.

Venus mentally shuddered as she recalled the night she was asked to comfort George Washington. Master John had stopped her on the stairs leading up to the tiny room where she and her mother slept.

"Venus, you get yourself to Master George's room. He...ah...needs comforting and has asked for you," Master John said.

She noticed that his face was flushed and he seemed distracted. She watched as he ran a large hand through his auburn hair, displacing the curl on the side of his face. She could sense a vague discomfort in him. *Poor massa, he all red with his grieving,* she thought sympathetically.

"Yassuh, Massa John. I jes go and light the fire and warm some bricks for his bed," Venus replied.

"No...Venus..."

She could sense him groping for the phrasing of his next words.

"Ah...Master George needs warming of another kind," he elaborated, looking pointedly at her.

Long seconds ticked by before Venus realized what he wanted her to do. She couldn't seem to catch her breath. Her cheeks grew hot. She had heard about what went on between a man and a woman, but she had never lain with a man before. Yet that didn't stop her master from ordering her to sleep with his brother. Her honey-gold-colored eyes stared with anguish at his face.

"Don't look at me that way, girl. You just do as I say and get to his room, now!" Master John's angry gray eyes blazed in the light of the candelabrum.

When she still didn't move or answer, he took her arm in a firm grasp and half-dragged her up the stairs toward his brother's bedchamber. Venus forced her legs to move, dumfounded by his request. She had never witnessed this side of her master before. She was truly frightened.

Master John's family had always treated her and her parents favorably. Her father, Billey, was his 'waiting man' and had been indispensable to him. It was even rumored that Billey had Washington blood. Venus' father also managed the house slaves, and her mother, Jenny, was the plantation's head seamstress. When Billey died the past year, John Augustine had even allowed Bible words spoken over his grave. Later, a wooden cross was fashioned by one of the carpenters to grace Billey's final resting-place. No other grave in the slave cemetery had a cross.

Billey had not only been Venus' father, he had been her protector, her shield, her fortress. No man would have dared molest her with her father nearby. He'd put on his bulldog expression, his gray eyes flashing a warning, and stare down the bolder field hands who had the audacity to glance her way.

But her father was dead and couldn't protect her that night. She wasn't even allowed to see her mother before going to Maser George. For the first time in her short life she felt alone. For the first time she realized what it meant to be a slave.

Master John stopped in front of the guest bedchamber door a few moments later, still gripping Venus' arm in a steel vise. With his free hand, he softly knocked on the wood panel. A few seconds later they heard his brother's deep voice bidding her to enter.

Venus turned from the door and gazed into her master's cold, gray eyes, and in their depths saw the finality of her situation. She knew that no amount of crying or stalling would stay his command. Hers was the lot of the slave woman. They were at the whim of any white man who wanted them sexually. Both her mother and father had been conceived in such a fashion. Somehow, she never imagined finding herself in a similar circumstance.

Master John still held Venus' arm in his tight grasp when an uncontrollable anger surged within her breast. She yanked it from his embrace, shocking him and herself with her boldness. *Go on ahead and whup me, I don't care!* she thought. But he stared at her with utter disbelief. She could sense his surprise at her uncharacteristic disobedience.

Venus glared at him steadily, her eyes sparking golden fire. Then, her small chin tilted in a pose she hoped looked dignified, she turned and entered the bedchamber.

Venus' mind snapped back to the present. She rubbed a tired hand over her eyes, trying to block out the memory of that scene. She would not allow her reminiscing to dredge up the shadows of what transpired in that room. No, she had them too well hidden in her consciousness. So, she let her thoughts drift to when she first encountered Master George Washington.

Venus knew Master George because he visited Bushfield many times in the past when she was a child. Several years later, when she was around twelve, she accompanied her mistress to Mount Vernon. During that visit, she had been slightly afraid of Master George, who was taller than most men and had pits on his face from a bout with smallpox. He also hardly ever smiled. Instead, his thin lips straightened until the wistful quirk at the corners of his mouth disappeared into a straight line. Venus had heard the other house slaves talking about how his teeth were made of some kind of 'white bones.' She remembered staring at his mouth, wondering how he kept those bones from falling out when he spoke. But not once had she seen a single bone.

Venus never thought that Master George took much notice of her. But how could he not? Everyone who came into Venus' presence would remark about how pretty she was.

She remembered once when she was taking a tray of tea and cakes into the parlor at Bushfield. One of Miz Hannah's lady friends remarked in amazement, "Why Hannah, this little servant girl of yours is lovely. My goodness…she's so white looking! And I've never seen such an eye color on a Negress before."

The woman gave Hannah a bemused look, and then smiled slightly behind a white hanky she brought to her mouth.

Miz Hannah had stared at her maid after her friend's observation. Venus could tell by her mistress's demeanor that she was displeased that someone had commented on her beauty. Miz Hannah had always intimidated her. She could still feel that cold gaze on her back as she left the room.

Now Venus had matured into a beautiful young woman—the epitome of her namesake.

After that fateful night, Venus was made available for George Washington's *comfort* whenever he visited Bushfield. However, their union didn't end there. When Venus accompanied her mistress to Mount Vernon that fall after Augustine's death, she had laid with him under his own roof. She became his personal bed partner, and only he could touch her sexually. Master Washington never knew that Venus didn't come to him of her own free will. And she never told him. He treated her very gently during his visits and she came to care for him in a fashion. And only when it was obvious that she was with child, was she finally left alone.

When Venus could no longer hide her pregnant state, Miz Hannah confronted her while she was changing the bed linens in her mistress's room. Her back was aching and as she reached around to rub the offending area, the small bulge of her stomach became obvious.

"My God!" Her mistress almost screeched the words. "Venus, you are obviously with child and I want to know who the father is!" Her voice was imperious.

Mistress Hannah was a chaste woman and could not abide loose behavior—not even in her slaves. She was also a stern mistress and was not above banishing her house slaves to the fields if they displeased her. She was small, with light brown hair, a large, beak-like nose, and closely-spaced brown eyes. Those eyes were now full of suppressed ire as she awaited Venus' response.

Venus thanked God almost every day that Massa John ordered her to comfort his brother, George, that night and not himself or his remaining two sons. A shiver ran through her at the thought of what the consequences would have been if one of Miz Hannah's menfolk had fathered her child! Evidently, that is what her mistress was thinking, as she waited for her servant's answer.

Venus was unsure whether to tell the truth about the paternity of her unborn child, but Miz Hannah didn't countenance lying, so she simply stated, "The Ole General be its sire, mistress."

If she hadn't been so exhausted, Venus would have smiled, remembering the incredulity in the old woman's lined face after the pronouncement. But she was just too worn out. Tears swelled in her eyes as she thought about her present circumstances. *"Oh Lord, what I gonna do with a white baby? What gonna happin' to him?"*

Usually, when a child of a prominent plantation owner was born, the beaming father accepted congratulations from the county's bluebloods and other plantation owners. Fine wines would flow and expensive cigars would be given out. The proud father would introduce his son or daughter to the countryside at an extravagant gathering as soon as his wife regained her strength. Style, breeding, and class distinction were all-important to the southern gentry.

There were no such celebrations on the day Venus' child was born. There were no soirees held on the plantation grounds, no gala parties to announce the child's birth, no guests coming by to congratulate the proud father, because Master George's child was born of a slave and not to his wife, Martha.

Master George Washington had finally fathered a son. How fickle the fates were that allowed him to sire a son with the forbidden Venus and not with Martha. He had no natural children with his wife, but raised her two children by a previous marriage as his own. It was rumored in Masonic circles that Martha had needed corrective surgery to conceive after the birth of her daughter, Patsy.

Venus vowed at that moment that even if Massa George never acknowledged his child, she had enough pride and love to shower on her newborn son. His sire didn't matter.

Her meandering recollections were interrupted when her mother asked, "Whats you gonna name this here fine boy?"

Slaves usually selected names that linked them to one of their relatives, friends or a geographical area. Most times slaves took the surname of their masters or fathers. Venus remembered the day she answered Miz Hannah's query about the father of her child. She had been instructed that she could not name the child after its father or any other name that would connect him with his father. No, no. They couldn't have the tongues wagging about the paternity of this child! It was against the law for whites and blacks to mix. Besides, Master George Washington was too politically important to have scandal attached to his name.

Venus thought about the word Mistress Hannah had uttered on the stairs the day she told her that she was increasing. Now what was it? Missing…miscen…miscegenation. Yes, that was the word. Some kind of law that didn't allow white folks to mix with slaves.

But white and black blood had commingled, and Venus' son was the living proof.

Venus' tawny eyes glowed with fierce love, pride, and…a *secret* as she watched her mother cuddling her child. She answered a few seconds later:

"West. I gonna call him West."

Venus' last conscious thought before she fell into a much-needed sleep was, *"What the Ole General gonna say?"*

Jenny walked over to the one window in the spartan room and placed her grandchild into an ornate wooden cradle beneath it. Scrolls and birds adorned the sides in intricate detail. Her husband had lovingly carved the cradle for Venus. Now Venus' child would sleep within it.

Watching her sleeping daughter, Jenny was amazed that Billey and she had created such a beautiful girl. Venus possessed a beauty as rare as a rose in winter. The physical attributes Venus acquired from her were golden-hued eyes, dimples and a short stature. Venus inherited her slightly flared nose, light-brown skin, and hair texture from her father, Billey.

Jenny let her thoughts stray to George Washington and how she, Phyllis, Jeremy and Joe had been his playmates as children. He was different then—kinder, more willing to smile. She could remember how avid he had been about horse racing and hunting in his early teens. As he matured, he became a man about the town, making the social rounds expected of a well-to-do Virginia planter.

But that was a long time ago.

As George became older, his temperament changed and he was easily riled. When he didn't get his way, he became moody and stubborn. Now, alas, the responsibilities of commanding an army had made him sterner, almost unapproachable.

Jenny wondered what he would think about his slave son.

She leaned and kissed her daughter's still-damp brow and whispered, "Sleep now, chile, the hard part is jes gettin' ready to happen."

Chapter 2

Appearances deceive,
and this one maxim is a standing rule:
Men are not what they seem.

Harvard

Venus and her mother were in their room in the attic space in the big house. It was several days after the birth of Venus' child when Hannah Washington waltzed in.

"Mornin' Miz Hannah," Jenny said. Two dimples framed her bright smile. She was putting the finishing touches on several slaves' jackets she had made from the plantation's home-grown cotton.

Venus was sitting on a pine chair and had just finished nursing her baby. Her mistress came over to her and stared at the infant as it nestled against her breast.

"My God! This child is white!"

"Yas'm, he is," Venus said warily.

Hannah scrutinized the infant's light eyes and red-brown hair. Reaching, she pulled the baby's tiny hand into her pudgy, blue-veined one and examined his fingernails. Her assessing glance then moved to the rim of the child's ears.

Venus knew what her mistress was searching for: the darkened skin that usually appeared below the fingernails and along the tips of the ears of a mixed-race child. That darker shade usually denoted what color the child would turn after the first few months of birth. Her mother had told her that mixed children always came out "half-baked."

Venus' child did not possess the darkened skin around his fingernails or ears. He was white all over. Her baby probably would not darken much.

"This won't do. This won't do at all," Hannah said to no one in particular. She glanced again at the baby, then turned and left the room.

"What you think she gonna do, Mammy?" Venus asked, unable to mask the fear.

"I don't know, chile. I jes don't know." Jenny's brow was furrowed with worry. She knew that Miz Hannah could be unpredictable in her actions with her slaves.

"Well, one thing's for sure, she ain't gonna send my boy away. I jes run away, that's jes what I do," Venus declared as she hugged her baby close.

Venus knew that a white-skinned slave child on the Bushfield plantation could cause problems for the Washingtons. Certain rules were to be followed in regard to slave/master offspring in the South. Most slave children fathered by white fathers were sold or fostered on a relative's plantation. Crueler masters had their illegitimate children taken from their mothers and killed.

Venus had seen first-hand what could happen to those children when she was around ten. Once a slave trader came to Bushfield and called out to a girl named Sinah who was working in the yard near the big house. Sinah had born a child by one of the white overseers named Otus Bowes.

"Girl, go git that chile of your'n and git it in this here wagon. I done bought it this mornin," the slave trader commanded.

Not one to disobey a direct order from a massa, Sinah went over to where old Abigail, the mammy for the slave children, sat holding her little daughter. Venus was helping Abigail with the older children. She watched as Sinah took the light-brown child, Jany, from Abigail's arms. Kissing the child's forehead, she hugged Jany so tight that the child cried out in discomfort. Silent tears streaming down her round, black face, Sinah walked toward the slave trader.

The overseer, the child's sire, was standing by the wagon. Otus Bowes was a young, slightly built man with unkempt, dirty, dark blonde hair. His constant companion, a black whip, was hanging from his leather belt.

Stopping in front of Bowes, Sinah implored, "Don' let'em take my baby Massa! Please! She so little! She all ah's gots! Please!"

"Naw! Now hush up and git that pickininny in that wagon," he replied. "I ain't got no time for your cryin' and carryin' on."

Sinah began to shake her head from side to side and started to back away from the two angry men. Bowes had to pry her fingers from the child's body. Then he pushed her so hard she fell. Sinah pulled at her short hair and pounded the ground in agony.

The overseer walked to the rear of the wagon and handed the child to a shackled man who also had been sold. The man's dark eyes showed no emotion as he settled the crying infant in strong black arms.

As the slave trader drove off with her child, Sinah began to make keening cries like those of a wounded animal. Venus covered her ears with her hands to shut out the heart-wrenching sobbing. She remembered crying herself, fearing the slave trader might come back and seize her too. Sinah finally fainted from the trauma and had to be carried back to her cabin.

Master Bowes didn't bat an eyelid at the pandemonium occurring around him. He snapped his whip at the slaves who had gathered to witness the event and shouted, "You niggers git on back to work 'fore you get sold."

Old Abigail muttered something about "dirty nigger traders and mean massas."

Venus had been unable to fall asleep that night. She relived the scene of Sinah's torment. The memory of the anguished woman's cries echoed in her mind, and raised gooseflesh on her neck. She would never forget Sinah's grief.

The next morning Venus heard the house slaves talking about how Massa Bowes had gone to Sinah's cabin that same evening for a little pleasuring. But Sinah was still distraught about the selling of her child and had tried to kill the man with one of cook's chopping knives. She slashed Bowes across his face and arms before he was able to subdue her. In retribution, the overseer arranged to have her stripped, whipped and sold for daring to mar his person. Master John didn't like to use the whip on his slaves unless it was extremely necessary. In this case he believed Sinah's punishment was justified.

All slaves on the plantation had to be present to witness what happened to troublesome slaves. Sinah was led forward and her arms were stretched over her head and bound to a metal loop that had been embedded in an oak tree. She was not tall, and once her hands were tied, she was forced to stand on the tips of her toes. This done, Bowes took a knife from his boot and slit the back of her dress from neck to waist. He then tore the material away to lay bare her back. Stepping away from the young girl's bound form, Bowes took the black whip from his belt loop. As he shook it from its coils, it slithered along the ground near his feet like a deadly black serpent. His cold dark eyes focused on his fleshy target, he drew back his arm and flicked his whip into action.

Venus' golden-hued eyes widened and then teared as she watched Sinah being whipped. When the slave was finally cut away from the tree, her back was a mass of blood and gashes, and the coarse rope around her wrists had torn deep channels through skin and muscle. Then, without her wounds being treated, the same slave trader came back the next day and hauled her unconscious form into his wagon.

The Bushfield slaves talked of nothing else for the next several days. The whipping left a powerful and lasting impression on any other slave who might feel rebellious. They were subdued.

Whupping or not, no one, no one will be takin' my baby from me. Never! Venus vowed as she held her infant son. She would protect him with her life.

Venus didn't have to worry much about Hannah Washington sending her son away. After her initial visit, Hannah came to Venus' room every day to spend time with the child.

"What did you name your son, Venus?" she inquired on the second visit. Miz Hannah was sitting in a rocking chair that she had one of the servants bring up from the nursery. She had held her own children in the same rocker.

"West," Venus answered nervously.

"Where in the world did you come up with the name *West?*"

"I jes thought it nice soundin.'" Venus turned her face away from her mistress's probing look, not wanting to meet her calculating brown eyes.

Hannah stared intensely at the young girl's profile, the lines in her face tightening as if trying to decipher what she was sure Venus was hiding. The young woman kept her features schooled. She refused to let her mistress read what was going on inside of her head.

Shrugging, Miz Hannah told her, "I want to take this baby outside with me on the verandah for awhile. You get on with your sewing now."

Helpless to protest her mistress's action, Venus watched as Miz Hannah carried her baby from the room.

It became a daily ritual for her mistress to take West from his mother for longer and longer periods of time. It was as if the child belonged to her and not to her house slave. Jenny told Venus that Miz Hannah was substituting West in the place of her dead son, Augustine. Venus did not sympathize. She wanted to spend time with her child, not watch another woman take her place.

Venus was not the only one who was concerned with her mistress's doting behavior towards the baby. Hannah and her husband were in the parlor of the big house. It was a spacious, well-proportioned room, fitted with a pair of massive mahogany bookcases on one wall and a stone fireplace with a corniced mantle on another. The walls were painted a delicate shade of green and trimmed with elegant, but restrained cornices of creamy white. Carpets in rich hues of burgundy, cream, and green covered the wood floor.

"You're spending too much time with that child, Hannah! It is unseemly. Have you considered what our neighbors would think if they saw you with it? It's a slave child for God sakes!" A flustered John Washington commented as he poured a hefty snifter of French cognac from a row of neat, crystal decanters on a mahogany sideboard. He breathed in the rich fumes before sipping. As the brandy burned down his throat, his determination to stop Hannah from coddling the slave child increased. The snifter in hand, he turned to face his wife and ordered, "You must cease this madness at once!"

Hannah sat on a green brocade sofa with West cradled in her arms. "Now John, calm down. I promise not to let our neighbors see me with him." Smiling at the cooing infant, she said, "Besides, he comforts me."

"Bushrod is getting married in a few short weeks. Soon you'll have your own grandchildren to comfort you," he countered.

Directing a penetrating gaze towards her exasperated husband, Hannah replied wryly, "That may be the case; however, we both know who fathered this child."

John Augustine winced and looked away from his wife's censoring face. He was surprised and slightly chagrined that she would mention his brother's indiscretion and that she might know about the role he played in it. He downed the rest of the brandy. A bright shade of red infused his face as he turned back to the sideboard and poured another drink. He drained his second snifter without further comment, but his mind was spinning with plans on what to do with the bastard child.

He had to get rid of it, and soon, before his wife became more attached.

Chapter 3

Freedom hath a thousand charms to show,
that slaves, however contented never know.

Cowper

The pre-dawn sounds of the waking plantation drifted up to the attic room where Venus, her mother, and infant son slept. Outside, slave gangs were already on their way to work in the fields. In the colonial planting system a slave gang consisted of a dozen slaves. No slave remained idle on the Bushfield plantation. Everyone, including the children and expectant and nursing mothers, had tasks to perform. They were expected to work from sunup to sundown, and only on Sunday were they given a respite from their labors. The Bushfield slaves referred to their labors as *'cain't to cain't'*—you work 'till you cain't see in the morning 'till you cain't see at night.

As house slaves, Venus and her mother had better accommodations than the slaves who worked in the fields. They were encouraged to give themselves a few airs and graces and this personification created a distinction between them and the field hands. The house slaves also dressed better, wearing uniforms or the discarded clothing of Massa John and Mistress Hannah.

But better accommodations or not, all were beholden to their owners.

Venus yawned and stretched, then stared at wooden support beams in the ceiling. Several large cobwebs were attached to an area near where she slept. *Spiders!* Just the thought of those creepy, crawly things living over her bed made her shiver. She'd have to get out a broom and remove them before one of the despicable bugs bit her two-month-old son.

Venus' gaze then traveled towards the room's window to assess the morning. The faint, silvery glow of dawn was washing the darkness from the sky. Hearing her baby stir, she rose from her pallet. She glanced toward her mother's empty bed. Jenny sometimes helped out in the cookhouse, and Venus assumed that she was there now. West continued to make whimpering sounds and she went to his cradle. She lifted him out and sat in the confiscated rocking chair next to the window. He gazed up at her, his lower lip quivering.

"Ahh, my baby boy, you be hungry now?" she whispered softly.

Would she ever look at him without thinking he was the most beautiful baby in the world? He stared back with anxious eyes, pursed a rosebud mouth, and made sucking noises. West waved a chubby fist, building up to a scream for his breakfast.

"Hold on now, chile," Venus said, placing him gently at her breast.

An hour later, she took her little one to the plantation nursery.

Venus was on her way to the spinning room to work on the slaves' winter wardrobe when Suck, the downstairs servant, stopped her near the dining room. Mahogany-skinned, Suck was Venus' best friend and confidant. Suck was a tall, buxom girl with a short cap of springy, black hair that hugged her scalp. She was several years older than Venus.

"Venus, Miz Hannah be wantin' you to go and get her gloves she done left in the carriage yesterday. She say to bring them to her in the parlor. She in there with old Miz Peake." Her hands on her ample hips, Suck continued, "That old Miz Peake's face be so full of wrinkles, ah almost got out my flat iron to see if ah could press some of them out."

Suck had an infectious sense of humor. She was also the eyes and ears for news concerning the Bushfield servants. That's because she was nosey and had to be in the center of everybody's business, and that included her white masters.

Doing her best imitation of Miz Hannah, Suck said, "Tell that lazy Venus to make sure she cleans them properly before bringing them to me." Holding her head and nose high in the air, Suck returned to the sideboard where she had been folding table linens.

Venus giggled and glanced around the dining room. If Miz Hannah witnessed her and Suck mimicking her or maligning her friends, they would suffer. Seeing that they were alone, Venus raised the hem of her coarse cotton dress and curtsied to her friend. Both girls laughed.

In a serious moment, Suck warned, "Venus, you best be keepin' West away from Massa John. Ahs think he hate that baby 'cause Miz Hannah dotes on him so much."

"How you know that?" Alarm raced through Venus' spine.

"'Cause theys be fussin' all the time 'bout it. A body cain't help but hear them, they be so loud sometimes." Shrugging, she continued, "But as long as Miz Hannah be 'round, your boy be all right."

"Thanks for tellin' me, Suck. I be sure to keep West away from Miz Hannah when Massa be around, if'n I can."

"It be too bad she don't feel the same way 'bout you," Suck added. Her eyes grew large.

Wrinkling her nose, Venus replied, "Miz Hannah, ain't never liked me none since I growed up. I think it's 'cause she wants West all to herself. She don't never let me be 'round him too much during the day no more. She always be tellin' me I be ig'norent and don't no how to take care of no child. Humph! The old bat, she just be jealous 'cause I gots a babe and she don't."

"You right about that. And she don't like me none neither."

"That's 'cause she knows you be sippin' her ladanum."

"Thats 'cause ahs gots pain from all the work theys be makin' me do 'round here."

Venus raised one eyebrow. Suck had the easiest chores assigned to her and most of the time she only served the meals. Venus said, "Well, I best be gettin' on down to fetch her gloves then for she have a fit."

In a daze of dread, Venus headed to the stables to fetch her mistress's gloves. She couldn't help but wonder if her worst fears would come true. Would Massa John send her boy away?

As she neared the stables down a long curving path behind the house, she spotted a tall, lean, black man standing near the unhitched carriage. She recognized him as one of the stable hands. She saw him sometimes as he brought Massa John's horse or carriage to the front of the big house. He would nod his head in greeting and smile.

But Venus never acknowledged him; she'd just turn her head and glance away. He was a field hand and in plantation hierarchy, beneath her. He was now leaning against the building's wall, his arms crossed over a muscled chest. He was shirtless and she realized he must have taken it off while working.

"Mornin' Venus," the man said as she approached the carriage.

She ignored him as usual and bent, looking into the carriage for the gloves. She could see that he was looking at her in obvious appreciation. She had no idea how the sunlight caught the brown highlights in her hair or how the coffee-colored dress she wore made her eyes as bright as newly minted gold pieces. She stood and turned, catching him in his blatant perusal.

The man was taken aback with her loveliness. Never in all of his born days had he seen such a beautiful creature. He continued to appraise her, his eyes heavy-lidded.

Hers narrowing with umbrage, she told him, "Don't you be a lookin' at me that way!"

"What way dat be, Miss Venus?" he answered softly and walked toward her.

"You know, like I be somethin' you could gobble up."

He laughed, his teeth flashing in a roguish smile.

When he stopped a few feet away she asked, "How you know my name anyhow?"

"Why, ah knows everythin' about ya. Ah know you be the prettiest gal ah ever done seen," he said, his assessing gaze once again settling on her delicate features. "Ah guess since ah knows your name, you best as well know mine." He smiled before saying, "My name be Prince, but Massa Washington change it to Fortune."

When she didn't say anything more, he went on to elaborate, "Massa Washington give me that name 'cause he say ahs cost him a fortune to buy. Ahs be a horse man. Ahs knows horses better than most horses knows themselves."

Fortune glanced behind her, then bent and retrieved the white gloves from the floorboard of the carriage. Venus, noticing them in his hands, reached to take them. But he held the gloves high over his head, intentionally out of her grasp. After several feeble attempts, she snatched them from his large hands, a movement that brought her close against the solid wall of his chest.

This was Fortune's goal in the first place. He was tired of her uppity ways just because she worked in the big house. He was going to make sure that Venus took notice of him this time.

And she did. She felt the heat from his muscled chest. A thrill ripped through her, and she was overwhelmed by the sight, sound, and smell of the virile young man.

Looking directly into her light eyes, he said silkily, "Ahs also knows, Miz house gal…that, you ain't got no man."

Venus stared at Fortune's handsome face for a few seconds, shocked into silence by his bold statement and his closeness. Stepping back, she turned away, determined to walk off without responding.

But before she could take her first step, Fortune put his hands firmly on her shoulders and turned her back around to face him. Venus tried not to flinch. No man had touched her since the Ole General.

"Now don' get all scared now. Ah don't mean you no bother," he said gently. When she didn't answer, but glanced at his hands on her shoulders, he sensed her uneasiness and removed them.

He continued to smile warmly and said, "Cain't we be friends?"

Venus knew at that moment that she wanted to be his friend. She needed a friend. She had been lonely since Suck married Jonas, Massa John's waiting man, a few months ago. Sometimes she was so miserably lonesome and forlorn that the sharp ache of it lay deeply within her chest. This man, Fortune, was very good-looking. Venus realized she had ignored him in the past because she was attracted to him, and it was obvious that he was attracted to her as well.

Venus couldn't help but be secretly pleased that her breasts were full, her waist tiny, and her hips softly rounded. She felt beautiful in his eyes. Her reserve of unfriendliness vanished in an instant. Glancing at Fortune through thick, black lashes, she smiled showing small, even white teeth. Her beauty made Fortune catch his breath. Nodding, Venus turned and walked back to the big house with Miz Hannah's gloves.

After that day, whenever Fortune was out in front of the big house with the horses, Venus would find an excuse to come outside to visit. Fortune filled an empty space within her. He made her feel free and light-hearted.

During the next several months, Fortune lavished attention on Venus and she soaked up every drop. He would tell her how pretty she was when in his presence. He had the cook give her a bouquet of wild flowers he had picked. On Sundays, Fortune would take long walks with Venus and West down by the river. He treated West like he was his own son.

Fortune's ardent attention brought the sun into Venus' lonely existence and eventually they decided to 'jump the broom.' This was the marriage ceremony of the day for slaves. Many slave owners discouraged permanent marriages among them because it caused complications in the mobility of the individual slave. If a slave was sold and he or she claimed to have a spouse, that spouse was not permitted to go with the sale as a matched set. They were separated—forever. So why let them marry?

When Venus became pregnant with her second child, Miz Hannah was again irate. She stopped Venus on her way to the spinning room and looked down her long nose at Venus' protruding belly.

In a frigid voice she asked, "Who got you with child this time?" Grabbing Venus by her arm and shaking it, she said, "Don't lie to me, girl!"

"It be Fortune. He's my man now, We's married," Venus proudly answered.

The relief on her mistress's face was evident. She apparently thought that the second child would also prove to be her brother-in-law's.

Letting go of Venus' arm, she said grudgingly, "Well, I'll have a cabin set aside for you and Fortune."

Venus smiled her appreciation and waited for her mistress to dismiss her. "Venus," Miz Hannah added, "I still want West brought up to see me daily. You may go now." Miz Hannah waved her hand at Venus with a gesture of dismissal, a circlet of lace swaying from her dress sleeve.

When Venus' daughter, Bettey, was born, Hannah had Venus bring the child up to the big house to see her. Bettey was a beautiful, mahogany-skinned baby, but she was clearly sired by Fortune.

Mistress Hannah didn't take any interest in this child. Bettey wasn't white-skinned and didn't have Washington blood.

Chapter 4

Lend thy serious hearing to what I shall unfold.

Shakespeare

Once again the Bushfield plantation was in mourning. Master John Augustine Washington had died suddenly almost a week before with what doctors said was a fit of gout in the head. Miz Hannah was still carrying on something terrible from the shock of her husband's death. Venus didn't really know how she felt about her master's passing. Their relationship had been strained ever since he'd ordered her to his brother's bed. But with him gone, the threat of him selling West was finally over.

Venus' son, sensing all the turmoil around him, had become fretful. She decided that they needed to leave the house for a while. She dressed West in an extra layer of clothing and went downstairs. Before going out of the front door, she came across her mother carrying a tray of food.

"Mammy, I jes gonna go on down and visit Fortune for a bit. I be takin' West with me. Bettey, she be down with Mammy Abigail."

"You jes do that, chile. Ah's gonna take some tea and biscuits up to Miz Hannah." Shaking her head, she said worriedly, "Po' woman ain't ate nothin' since yesterday when the doctah gib her them powders."

Venus watched her mother mount stairs to the second floor. She seemed to be walking a little slower these days. A deep sadness overcame Venus. Her mother was old. Jenny's once-black hair was streaked with gray and she seemed to have lost height in the last couple of years. *Please Lord, don't let Mammy up and die on me too,* she prayed as she made her way to the stables.

Venus had gone a few yards when she heard the approaching sound of a horse's hooves, pounding along the dirt road, which made up the curving entrance to the big house. The rider was Master George. The household had been expecting his arrival, as Master Bushrod had dispatched a message to him about the death of his father.

Washington trotted a spirited gray stallion to where Venus stood, reined his horse and dismounted. Long plumes of mist shot from the horse's nostrils as it exhaled in the frigid air. Master George looked older and haggard, his grief plainly written over his face.

Tossing the horse's reins to Fortune, who had silently approached the couple unawares, he said, "He's had a long day. See that he's rubbed down."

Then George Washington turned the full force of his blue-gray gaze upon Venus. Their eyes locked and she found herself unable to pull away from his riveting perusal. He surveyed her slender frame for a few more seconds and then turned to the child in her arms. The air seemed charged and oppressive, as if a storm were about to break. Venus hugged her son tighter. Master George had never been this close to his child before.

West was a happy, outgoing toddler and when he saw the stranger staring at him he smiled. Master George appeared startled by the boy's response, but then he did something Venus didn't expect. He smiled back. His smile was slightly crooked, not perfect or polished, as if he were not used to the act. Looking at his mouth, Venus reflected, *where be the 'bones' everybody be whispering 'bout?* All she could see were large, brownish-white teeth.

His gaze was cool as he continued to watch Venus. She saw a slight flicking of something in his eyes before he masked whatever it was he was thinking. He then said to Fortune, "Be sure to give my horse an extra portion of grain." Then he brushed quickly past them and headed into the house.

"Well, hello to you too," Venus piped at his retreating back. She was somewhat vexed that he didn't even speak to her or ask about the boy. He had to know that the child was his.

Fortune walked up to Venus and kissed her on the forehead. He always seemed to know what was on her mind. No one had ever seen all the way inside of her being as Fortune did.

"Now gal, you knows dat he ain't gonna say nothin' 'bout your boy."

"I know, it's jes that, he smile at him and didn't even ask me his name."

"Well dat da way it be with white folks. Now get on up to da big house woman. Ah'll take West down to old Abigail."

"Yesuh, Massa Fortune, suh," Venus teased in her best servant voice, laughing at the dumfounded look on his handsome face that her comment had elicited. Still chuckling, she turned and headed back toward the big house.

Master John was buried a few hours later on that brisk January afternoon. The air was cold, the sky cloudless. Master John's friends from neighboring plantations and the Bushfield slaves attended the funeral. After the ceremony, Mistress Hannah became so distraught that her sons Bushrod and Corbin had to carry her back up to the big house for the reading of old Master John's will. Throughout the remainder of the day, the servants whispered among themselves as they listened to the wailing of their mistress. The next morning after breakfast, Master George returned to Mount Vernon.

Two weeks later, Venus was surprised when George Washington returned to Bushfield. She didn't' witness his arrival. She had just put the children down for the night when Suck poked her head into the dimly lit cabin.

The one-room dwelling was extremely small for a family of four. A stone fireplace dominated the center of the room and a small blue cabinet that held utensils for cooking, a couple of cups, and a teapot were located next to it. A small wooden table, two chairs, and two straw pallets took up most of the room on a hard-packed, dirt floor. Most slave couples slept on a single straw pallet. Any children slept on the ground. Mistess Hannah wanted to make sure that West had a pallet of his own.

"Venus, ahs come to get West for Miz Hannah and bring him up to the big house," said Suck.

"What do she be wantin' him for this time of the night?" Venus' eyes held a questioning look.

"Ah was a pouring the tea for Miz Hannah and the Ole Gen'ral, and he ask her to see the boy," Suck said as she went to West and Bettey's pallet in one dim corner of the cabin.

"That boy sure do look like his pappy," Suck remarked as she pulled back the bed linen covering his small body. The sleeping toddler woke as she lifted him into her arms. He was startled from his slumber and started to protest by softly crying.

"Hush, boy, befo' you wake your little sister," Suck quietly admonished. After bundling him up with a blanket, she left.

Venus was perplexed by an onslaught of contrary emotions. Why all of a sudden was the Ole General interested in West? Why now? Just when she thought that West was safe from Massa John, a new threat arose from Massa George.

Fortune took Venus in his arms and quietly held her. "It be all right, gal."

"How you know that, Fortune?" Venus looked steadily at him, worry etched on her facial features.

Fortune had no answer. All he could do was to continue to reassure her until West was back safely in the cabin. He clutched her tightly against his chest.

When Suck brought the boy back an hour later, Venus was relieved. "What they do with him?" She asked her friend as she took the sleeping West into her arms. Anxiety knitted Venus' delicate brow.

"Waall...the Ole Gen'ral jes look at that boy when ahs bring him into the parlor. Miz Hannah told me to lay West on the sofa. Then she tell me to go and close the door. Ahs tried to listen, but ah couldn't hear everythin', only bits and pieces of words. They was talkin' real quiet like." Suck paused for a moment, her fingers massaging an ear. "My po' ear. Ahs pressed it so hard to that door it made a poppin' sound when ah stood up."

Noting the questioning look still registering on Venus' face, Suck sighed and continued, "Miz Hannah was a tellin' the Ole Gen'ral how good a baby West be. Then Miz Hannah call for me to bring the boy back to you."

Venus thanked Suck for the information and watched as Fortune closed the door behind her when she left the cabin. Then she looked down at the sweet face of her son. Oh, God, how she loved him!

Fortune took West from her, walked over to the pallet, and laid him down next to Bettey. He saw Venus' stricken face, and they stared at each other for long seconds before she threw herself into his strong embrace. He held her close, rubbing a soothing hand along her back. *Everythin' is gonna be all right,* she thought. *It gotta be. Please Lord, don't be lettin' them send my chile from me!*

Venus walked on pins and needles for the next several days after Master George's visit. Every time a wagon pulled up to the mansion house she would visibly shake, thinking it was a slave trader come to take her son. Several weeks passed before Venus was able to relax. It seemed that West wasn't going to be sent away.

A couple of months later, Hannah Washington asked to buy West from Bushrod and Corbin, but they made a gift of him to her instead. Hannah told her sons that she was going to put a stipulation in her will, freeing West when he reached twenty-one. She also wanted the lad to be inoculated as soon as possible for smallpox and be taught a trade.

Venus was very surprised when she was informed about her son's eventual freedom. Miz Hannah had never freed a slave before and West was the only slave to be freed in her will. Venus felt hope for once in her life. *Freedom.* Her son would be a free man. He would be able to choose his own destiny. Then the elation left her when she thought about her own circumstances. There would be no freedom for her, her mother or her young daughter, Bettey.

West continued to be singled out of the pack of slave children that roamed the yard of the Bushfield plantation. At first it was Mistress Hannah, but then Master George took special interest in the boy. West accompanied him on wagon rides around the countryside and was even allowed to go to Christ Church with him where he was provided a private pew. At the age of four, West became the personal attendant for George Washington. The boy would fetch and carry and do all kinds of small errands for him when he came to visit at Bushfield.

One day after spending time in Master George's company, West asked, "Mama, is the Old General my papa?"

Venus grabbed the boy by his arm and ushered him quickly outside and away from the big house towards the woods. As soon as she made sure they were alone she asked him, "Who done told you that?"

"I heard the cook and her helpers sayin' that he be my papa. They say I look just like him. What they mean?" West added, "Fortune be Bettey's papa, is he mine too?"

Even though the Washingtons didn't want the Fairfax populace to know of West's paternity, the slave population at Bushfield and Mount Vernon knew. No news could escape the slave telegraph. Massas and Missys would have discussions around their slaves as if they didn't exist, treating them as if they were deaf and dumb. So, they were privy to many a private conversation.

Venus studied her son's small, solemn face. She noted his startling eye color and chestnut-colored hair. Her son's features mirrored those of his sire's.

Few slave mothers told their children anything of their origins. Most slaves learned about their fathers as West did, in bits and pieces from older slaves, mammies and white people's conversations. Venus knew that if West was to be free one day, he should at least know who fathered him.

Kneeling so that she was eye level with him, she said quietly, "The Ole General be your papa." Venus watched as West's eyes lit with wonder. She quickly added, "But don't you be tellin' no one, 'cause you ain't 'posed to know. One day you can tell your children, but for now it be our secret. So you stand proud, stand tall, 'till then, you hear me?"

West nodded his red-brown head. He would keep the secret for now. Then he smiled at his mother in camaraderie. He loved no one more than her, but now he could also love his father.

Even though life was tranquil on the Bushfield and Mount Vernon plantations, the thirteen colonies of America were not experiencing the same idyll. The government was floundering because it was politically unstable. The country needed a leader who could develop a cohesive, working federal government. The country needed George Washington. The American public had enormous confidence in General Washington's abilities because of his exploits in the Revolutionary War.

On April 30, 1789, George Washington was on his way to the ceremonies that would make him the first president. He rode in a cream-colored carriage drawn by six spirited white horses, accompanied by four spiritless black slaves wearing red collars and cuffs. That day he ceased to be a private person and became a public man. No longer could he ride around the countryside accompanied by a small mulatto boy named West, given that each of his actions would be recorded for all time in prosperity.

But it was already too late for secrecy, because now that small boy knew who his father was. And one day so would the world.

Chapter 5

True dignity is never gained by place,
And never lost when honors are withdrawn.

Massinger

The Old General left his beloved Mount Vernon to take up the reins of the presidency. During his two terms, George Washington visited Mount Vernon as many as fifteen times. West had seen him on only a couple of those infrequent visits. Not many days would pass without West asking his mother, "Where is the Old General? When's he comin' to see me, Mama?"

At first Venus would make up excuses about his absence. "Honey, the man be too busy and right now he be too far away to come callin' on us. Maybe he'll come in the springtime."

"How far be far?" West's eyes were large and assessing as he waited for her answer. He had always been an inquisitive child.

"It be far. I don't know how much. Now get on with you so's I can get to my chores 'round here before Miz Hannah come hollerin' on me."

But West continued to pester her and she finally decided to tell him the truth. He had run her down while she was dumping the chamber pots from the upstairs' bedrooms. Her nose was still wrinkled from the smell of the one she just emptied from her mistress's room.

She put her hand on her hips and said, "West, Massa George be an im'portant man. He can't spend no time with you now. Jes 'cause you be white-lookin' don't mean nothin'. You be a slave and he be a massa— and thats jes the way it be."

West's eyes teared, but he didn't cry. He looked at his mother for a moment, then turned and headed back down the stairs.

Venus knew that her son was hurting emotionally from Master George's rejection, but she never regretted telling him who his father was. Unfortunately, West still missed the Old General and loved his absentee father.

As a young boy, West couldn't comprehend the role of a slave because he was treated so well by the Washingtons, especially Mistress Hannah. He was close to her and she was forever making sure that he wanted for nothing. Venus knew he would have problems adjusting to the life of a slave because he wasn't being treated like one.

Even though West was saddened by the desertion of Master George from his life, Venus had never felt better. She had bloomed into an even lovelier young woman under the gentleness of Fortune's love.

Venus' beauty wasn't lost on one of the white overseers. He'd been watching Venus from afar for several years, but that black buck of hers had been around whenever he got close enough to catch her alone. The overseer was watching Venus now, as she took her children to the slave mammy's cabin. *She's a high yella one; almost white-lookin' with that long brown hair and those golden-colored eyes,* he mused.

The overseer continued his covert assessment as Venus kissed her children before leaving them in the old mammy's care. He decided then and there that he wanted those full, pouty lips on him. He wanted a taste of lighter meat, as all he had for years was the darker slave women who worked in the fields. No white woman in the county would spend any time with him, except an occasional whore. Even they didn't want to lie with him, as he was one mean son of a bitch.

He enjoyed inflicting pain.

The slave women couldn't complain to anyone about his cruel treatment, and even the married ones had no protection against him. *One day soon*, he pondered; *I'll have Venus in the position all slave women belong—underneath a white man.*

Several days later, Venus decided to take her baby daughter for a short visit with Fortune in the stables. It was a lovely summer day, the kind that made you want to sit in the sun and enjoy its warmth playing over your skin. Venus smiled broadly as she paused in the yard and watched West playing with the rest of the slave children. The children were under the guidance of old Abigail and Fann, her eventual replacement. Abigail wasn't as spry as she used to be. Now she sat in a wooden chair with a long willow switch by her side. The switch must have been twenty feet in length. She used it to lightly tap the rumps of the unruly children as they played in the yard. Venus' smile deepened as she watched West eyeing the switch in Abigail's hand. *If his eyes be gettin' any wider, they'll pop out of his head*, she thought amusedly. West wouldn't be getting into mischief anytime soon.

Venus was in good spirits when she stepped inside the stable. The smells of animals, hay, and fresh manure assailed her nostrils. She paused for a moment, waiting for her eyes to adjust to the semi-darkness. She didn't see Fortune, so she called out to him. She received no answer and several seconds later a man stepped out from the shadows. In the dim light she couldn't immediately identify him. She just knew it wasn't Fortune.

"Don't look like your nigger buck is here to meet you," the man said, his breathing as loud as the snorts the horses were making in the stalls. "I sent him on down to the boat landing to bring back some bushels of grain."

The overseer had been scrutinizing Venus' movements and he knew that she came to the stables before suppertime. He had sent Fortune on a bogus errand earlier so that he could catch her alone. He was thinking that today would be his lucky day.

"He ain't my buck. Fortune be my husband," Venus replied hotly as she adjusted her daughter on her hip.

"You call that heathen broom business a marriage?" he laughed harshly, as he slowly advanced towards her. "You niggers ain't really married."

Venus recognized this particular overseer as he stepped into the light. It was Massa Bowes, the one who had Sinah whipped and sold when she was a child. He had lost hair since the last time she'd seen him and was about thirty pounds heavier. The scar that ran from his left eyebrow down along his jaw line stood out with stark relief. But she noticed his eyes more than his scar.

The overseer's eyes were dull, flat and black. They looked like the eyes of a dead slave Venus had once seen when she helped prepare his body for burial. Rachal, the cook's assistant, usually helped her mother clean and dress the slaves when they died, but she was not available that day as she was pregnant. Slaves were superstitious and believed that an unborn child could be marked by witnessing a traumatic event. Rachal didn't want to mark her unborn child, so Jenny had asked Venus to bring old cotton rags from the big house to help her clean the embedded dirt from the man's body. Venus remembered watching her mother whisk the cloths over his rigid form. The man's eyes had been open and they couldn't close them. They pulled on his eyelids, pressed down on his forehead and pushed up on his cheekbones, but the dead man's eyes kept sliding open. Venus' mother finally had to stitch his eyelids shut with yarn.

Venus had wondered how eyes that had reflected light during life could absorb it so utterly upon the soul's departure. After that day, she never wanted to view another dead person, preferring to remember them as they were when they were alive rather than the lifeless, shell they became.

Massa Bowes had those kind of eyes—dead eyes.

"I only want to be your friend," Bowes said, and brushed against her, touching her breast with a grimy hand. Venus flinched and twisted her upper body away from his grasp.

He chuckled at her reaction. "Aw, come on now. I only want to be your friend, a real good friend."

His breath was so rank that Venus' nose twitched and her eyes watered. She chewed nervously at her bottom lip, wondering what to do. He was, after all, a massa.

"I needs to go back to the big house now. Miz Hannah be lookin'—"

"Be still!" he interrupted tersely. Reaching out and grabbing her chin in his sweaty hand he said hoarsely, "I need some pleasurin' and you be just what I want to do it with."

Venus wrenched her chin out of his grasp and backed away, clasping her young infant in her arms. She was frightened not only for herself, but for Bettey who had begun to cry, sensing her mother's panic. Silently, Venus debated whether to scream or to run. Before she could do either, Bowes wrested Bettey from her, holding her carelessly by her tiny arms. As Venus watched in horror, he flung her child casually to one side like a rag doll. The infant smacked into the wall of the stable with tremendous force and lay where she landed in a pile of hay, motionless, not making a sound.

Rage and fear coursed through Venus as she tried to run to her baby, but Bowes grabbed and detained her. Venus turned into a wildcat. She kicked, bit, and clawed, raking fingernails down the side of his face that wasn't scarred.

"You bitch!" he swore and threw her against the stable wall where she struck her shoulder, then her head.

A sharp pain shot through her arm, but the blow to her head dazed her just enough to dull its intensity. Her legs gave out, and white sparks shot behind her eyelids as she slumped to the dirt of the stable floor. Bowes fell on her then, ripping her dress down the front.

"You get off my mama!" a child's frantic voice shouted.

Five-year-old West had come into the stable looking for his mother and had witnessed the man striking her. West pummeled him with his little fists, but the man ignored his futile attempts. Desperate to help his mother, he leaned down, biting hard on the overseer's shoulder. The enraged man howled in pain, turned and back-handed West across his face, knocking him almost senseless to the stable floor. West landed hard and lay struggling to bring air into his lungs.

Noting that the boy was immobile, Bowes turned and bent back over a dazed Venus.

"Massa Bowes, you'd best be gettin' away from my wife." Fortune had returned.

Though Venus hadn't noticed the overseer's covert interest in her, Fortune had. He had gone down to the boat landing for the grain and found the pier empty. He knew in his gut that something was wrong and hurried back to the stables.

Rage rose in Fortune like a thick, black tide. Cords in his neck stood out like the roots of an oak. The overseer dared to manhandle his Venus and he would kill him for it! His blood boiled with fury.

Bowes froze, then spat out a nasty curse and lurched to his feet, reaching for the whip at his belt loop. "Well, nigger, what do you think you're goin' to do?" Bowes wanted to whip the skin off the young man and then he'd have Venus to himself.

Fortune was a dead man and he knew it, because he'd decided to kill the overseer for touching his wife. It wasn't a black or white thing; it was a man thing, something only a man could understand when another man encroaches on what is his.

Fortune had faced indignities to his person almost from the day he was born into slavery. He had been sold from his mother at the age of six, whipped, fondled, and even spit upon. The treatment he received from the hands of his masters had made him feel less than a man.

But today he would die like one.

Fortune slowly approached Bowes, his large hands tightly curled. He was going to choke the overseer to death with his bare hands.

Bowes was ready. He released his long black whip, striking Fortune on the neck and face, staggering him. But Fortune kept coming. The whip lashed again and again with terrible accuracy along the man's face and head. It was a cruel weapon that whip. Blood ran freely down the slave's face and into his eyes, temporarily blinding him.

Keeping one arm up to protect his face, Fortune used his other to wipe the blood from his eyes. Finally, the blows forced him towards one of the open stalls. The continued whine of the whip caused the horses in the stable to fret and kick.

The overseer purposely whipped one of the horses along its head, spooking and enraging it. The stallion reared high on its hind legs and lunged with its forefeet. Fortune was caught on the side of his head, and knocked under the crazed animal's thrashing hooves.

"Fortune!" screamed Venus as she saw him go down.

Venus' face was pale, her hair tangled, and an enormous lump was swelling on the side of her head. She had run to Bettey as soon as Fortune entered the stable, but the child was still unconscious. When Venus saw the horse trample her husband she knew it was too late to help him. She stood by, helplessly crying out his name.

Occupants in the barn were not aware that West had regained consciousness and had run to the big house. "Miz Hanna! Miz Hannah!" he screamed as he raced into the parlor where she was working on correspondence.

"What *is* it, child?" The old lady was so startled from his piercing cries that she was visibly trembling.

"The man…he be killin' my mama in the stable!" the boy shouted, his breaths in short gasps.

Hearing West's frenzied screams, several of the house slaves came running into the parlor, including Suck's husband.

"Jonas, you get down to the stables and see what is going on!" commanded Miz Hannah. Seeing the tears in West's large blue-gray eyes, she shouted at his retreating back, "Hurry, Jonas! Hurry!"

When the house servant arrived at the stables, the overseer was off to the side of a bloodied stall, calming one of the stallions. Bowes smiled as he watched Venus soothing what Jonas thought was a piece of raw meat.

"Oh Fortune, Fortune! You ain't gonna die, you hear me! You can't die. I won't let you!" Venus whispered against the mass of crushed bones and blood. The anguished woman was working her hands over the top part of Fortune's head, trying to recover the gray matter of his demolished brain. Bettey lay unconscious in a pile of straw near her.

Moments later, Mistress Hannah entered the stable. When she saw what remained of Fortune's head, she turned and vomited. Jonas grasped the old lady's arm and helped her to a bale of hay.

Finally, when Hannah was able to compose herself, she directed her horrified attention to the overseer, "What happened in here?"

"That nigger attacked me and I whipped him. He got too close to the horse's stall and it trampled him, and I say good riddance." Bowes spat in the straw for emphasis.

"That be a lie!" Venus shrieked. Her eyes were slivers of bright fury. Had they been arrows, they'd have pierced Bowes' evil heart a thousand times. "You try and lay with me, and he stop you. That be why you whup him."

"You lying whore! You asked for it," Bowes said menacingly and approached Venus to strike her with the handle of his whip.

"That will be enough, Mr. Bowes!" Miz Hannah said in a voice that demanded acquiescence. "Mr. Bowes, clean yourself up and meet me at the big house." She directed her attention to Venus. She was cradling her dead husband's head in her arms. She said a moment later, "Jonas, you stay here and help Venus with Fortune."

Miz Hannah went to Venus, Suck close behind her. "Give Bettey to Suck, Venus. She'll take her to the big house and clean her up."

Venus watched Suck pick up her unconscious daughter. "Take my chile to my mammy. She take care of her for me." Gazing around for her son she inquired anxiously, "Where be West? He be hurt too."

"He's already up at the house. I told him to stay in the parlor. Don't you worry about him. He's all right," answered Miz Hannah.

Venus nodded. Realizing they could do no more for her at that moment, Miz Hannah and Suck turned and left the stable.

Venus returned her attention to Fortune's face. His glazed eyes were wide open—the horror of the last moments of his life imprinted on them for all to view. Everything that hurt arose in Venus. At first tears, blinding in intensity and burning, filled her eyes and coursed down her cheeks. And then came the sobs—gut wrenching gulps for air that wouldn't let go.

Venus tried to clean Fortune's battered face with her torn bodice, but there was too much blood. Softly she whispered through her tears, "You done gone and left me. You done gone and left me. You done *gone*."

Venus carefully lifted her husband's head from her blood-soaked lap and rose to her feet. Suck's husband was wiping tears from his eyes.

"P-please take care of Fortune for me, Jonas. He done gone and I, I gots to go see about my babies." Shakily she left the stable, dreading to see Bowes, dreading to face the world without her beloved husband.

The fates smiled for a short time on Venus because she never had to look upon the face of Bowes again after that tragic day in the stables; he was dismissed from his overseer's position. Hannah Washington had an uncanny knack for deciphering when a person was lying. And she knew that the overseer had tried to rape Venus. But she released the man from her service because he dared to strike West. One of the small boy's eyes turned puffy and black, and he had suffered a deep cut above the left corner of his mouth. The doctor treated it and told Miz Hannah the wound would leave a scar.

The slave community was buzzing with the news about Master Bowes' release from Bushfield. The field slaves were joyous and celebrating in their own fashion. "No more whippings from him," they shouted as they danced in jubilee around the plantation grounds. It was as if God had answered their prayers for deliverance.

But for Venus, it was a time for mourning her one true love. Fortune was laid to rest next to Venus' father in the Bushfield slave cemetery. Another piece of her heart had died. It was difficult for her to accept that her husband, her world as she had known and loved it, could never be again. But Venus knew she would persevere. Two children depended on her.

She would survive.

But Venus had made an enemy for life, because Otus Bowes was not the type to take an offense lightly. He vowed to take revenge on the yella bitch someday, somehow.

Chapter 6

Oh you much partial gods! Why gave ye men affections, and not power to govern them?

Ludovick Barry

Hannah Washington allowed Venus and her children to move back into the big house after Fortune's death. West was inconsolable for many a day when he learned that Fortune was dead. He had come to care for the kind man who had treated him like his own son.

West and Venus had not only lost a man who loved them without reservation, but also Bettey in a way. The toddler didn't die from the severe injuries she received and eventually regained consciousness, but her eyes remained blank, like a body without a soul. Mistress Hannah had a physician come and examine the child. He explained that the blunt blow to the head had damaged her brain. Bettey would forever live in a vegetative state, never to awaken.

The doctor's assessment proved accurate as the weeks passed. The infant moved when they roused her and she ate if they put food into her mouth. But she did not speak. She never smiled, never laughed and never even cried. Venus prayed for her return to good health, but as the weeks passed into months and with no change in her condition, her hopes withered and died.

West became very protective of his mother after Fortune's death. He couldn't lose her too, and he began to follow her around the big house as she carried out her duties. Whenever she went outdoors, he tagged along.

Venus became concerned. The young boy hardly smiled anymore. He didn't want to play with the other children on the plantation. And he didn't want to visit with Mistress Hannah overlong when his mother wasn't within his sight. Venus knew that he feared for her safety. Finally she spoke with him about his apprehension.

"West, you best go and play now, bein' it's Sunday," she urged. "Tomorrow you gots to hoe the garden next to the cookhouse."

"I don't want to play right now, Mama. I just gonna sit here and watch you sew that shirt." His gaze was intent as he observed Venus stitch a sleeve onto a garment. His rapt expression didn't fool her.

"West, I know you be scared for me. But that mean man ain't never gonna hurt you, your sister, or me again." She leaned forward. "He gone. And he ain't never comin' back here."

"You sure, Mama?" The boy's brow was furrowed with doubt and anxiety.

"I be sure. Go on along with you now," she said gently.

West rose and walked to the door, but before he left he ran back to his mother, hugged her tightly and said, "I love you, mama."

"I love you too, West," Venus replied softly, rubbing the top of his head in affection.

Shortly thereafter, Hannah Washington began to have West taught the rudiments of reading and writing. He again became the inquisitive young boy he had been before Fortune's death.

Over the next few years, several deaths occurred in the Washington family. Mistress Hannah's two daughters died, Jane in 1791 and Mildred in 1797. Venus remembered hearing her mistress say, "How could God let me outlive my own children?"

*   *   *

West was around twelve when he was taught a trade under the guidance of Basco, the master carpenter at Bushfield. Sitting next to Basco on a wooden stool in front of the stable, West could have passed for a son of the plantation, except for the cut of his clothes. His brown shirt was too small for his growing frame and his pants were full of holes and tears. Fortunately, they were his work clothes and his mother allowed him to wear his fancy ones only on Sunday.

Basco was a gritty old man with a shiny, black, bald head. He had rheumy eyes, the whites so congested and yellow that it was a wonder the man could see. He was also missing over half his teeth. His mouth was always working in a chewing motion, like a cow chewing its cud. And when he conversed, spittle flew in every direction, usually over the person's face he was talking to.

"Boy, ya gots ta tak' yo' time when you's makin' somfin'. You's got ta think 'bout what you's tryin' ta do," the old man said as he worked on the chair they were repairing for the big house. Basco's hands were so arthritic it was astonishing that he could manipulate the tiny tools it took to carve the wondrous wooden pieces he made for Bushfield.

West tried not to wipe the spit from his face as the old man reprimanded him. His face felt wet. When he was sure not to be noticed, he used the sleeve of his shirt to dry the offended area.

Today West was making a plough, but it more resembled a hoe. "Lordy boy! You's be the worsest carpenter ah ever don' seen!" the old man said in exasperation.

West shrugged. He was trying to focus on his carpentry work, but he couldn't concentrate. Suck had told him early that morning that she'd overheard Massa Bushrod saying to Miz Hannah that Massa George was coming back to Mount Vernon for good. Now all he could think of was that his father was coming home. All manner of scenarios played through his young mind. His father would finally claim him or his father would ask him to come live at Mount Vernon. The images were endless and all with happy outcomes. No, he couldn't concentrate today. His father was coming home!

West couldn't help but be disappointed when he learned that the retired president went straight home to Mount Vernon, by-passing Bushfield. West couldn't fault the Old General, as he had been away from Mount Vernon for several years. Of course he would want to see his home first.

George Washington had been back at his plantation for several weeks and his nephew, Bushrod, was going to visit him. West was not allowed to accompany him, though he pestered Mistress Hannah and Master Bushrod for an invitation. When his master returned from his visit to Mount Vernon, West asked him how the Old General was. Bushrod told him that he was as vigorous as ever.

Weeks passed into months, but the retired president never made a trip to Bushfield. West was feeling melancholy. It had been too many years since he had seen his father, and he didn't know how much longer he could wait. *Maybe I should just up and take a horse and ride to see him,* he thought one day. But he had to dash that plan when he realized that he didn't know the way to Mount Vernon.

A week later, West learned from Suck that one of Master George's slaves, Hercules, the family cook, had run off, and Billy Lee, Washington's personal attendant, was now crippled. Billy Lee had broken his knee in a fall and could not function as a valet. Washington was looking for another personal attendant and cook.

"Mama, the Old General be needin' a new waitin' man, and I'm gonna ask Massa Bushrod if I can be given to him," an excited West announced to his mother. She had her arms full of clean linens and was taking them upstairs to change the sheets on Mistress Hannah's bed.

Venus saw the hopeful look on her son's smiling face. She noted the lines and features that made up his face. The blending of his two races had marked his appearance undeniably. She concluded that the Washingtons would never allow West to attend Master George. He was almost the splitting image of his father.

Most southern slaveholders seemed to take for granted the connubial arrangements masters took with slave women and turned a blind eye from the hybrid children that resulted. Usually northern visitors detected similarities of the mulatto offspring to their masters when they weren't fostered elsewhere.

Venus knew her son was going to be hurt once again. How could she explain to him that he could never become Master George's personal attendant?

"West, you looks too much like him. Why, Miz Martha would up and have another stroke if'n she saw you. And all them other white folks that be visitin' him will also know he be your papa. No, them Washingtons ain't gonna let you 'round him." In a much firmer voice she continued, "I told you that you got to forget he be your papa."

"He be askin' for me, you see," a confident West replied as he turned away. He didn't want to hear what his mother was saying. He didn't want to believe it.

West waited for the Old General to request his services, but he never did. Instead, the retired president wrote to one of his overseers, requesting that a young slave named Cyrus be prepared for the position of his waiting man. Suck later told West of Cyrus' placement and watched as the young boy squared his shoulders, and walked out of the big house to lick his wounds in private.

George Washington's latest rejection hurt West to the core of his being. He would study his facial reflection in the large mirror in the parlor, noting the similarities between his father and himself. West thought that he looked like the general. Granted, his hair was curlier than his sire's, but it was the same chestnut color. His nose was slightly more flared at the nostrils, but shaped the same way as his father's. His eyes were blue-gray and his skin white.

But he wasn't white.

He was a slave. And all slaves were indoctrinated from birth with the ideology that whites ruled from God and that to question this divine theory was to incur the wrath of heaven. A slave was told that his condition was the fulfillment of the will of the Master on high.

Venus continued in her efforts not to let West harbor any false dreams, wishes or ambitions that George Washington would acknowledge an open kinship with him. As the years passed, West came to accept his role in plantation society. He was a slave and illegitimate. It didn't matter to anyone that his skin was white or that he had Washington blood ties.

His black blood was the major defining factor.

Chapter 7

At well at the moment, and you have performed a good action to all eternity.

Lavater

"He dead, he dead. The Ole Gen'ral be dead!" A harried Suck told Venus as she dusted the drapes in the dining room.

"You sure, Suck?" Venus' heart leaped into her throat at what she'd heard.

"Ahs heard Massa Bushrod when he read a note sent by Miz Martha. The Ole Gen'ral was riding 'round his farms and took sick. The doctah come and bleed him, but he up and die anyways."

Venus sat slowly in a nearby chair. She was numb with shock. Massa George was dead. Some vague feeling flittered near her heart. She realized that she cared for him in a special way because West was his son. But how was West going to take the news? *I got to be the one to tell him,* she thought anxiously as she brushed past Suck on her way out of the big house to find her son. She had to tell him about Massa George before he heard it from someone else.

Venus found West by the stable, chatting with Basco. The two were smiling as they examined the plow that West had made.

She said, "West, I needs to talk to you for a second." Her expression was guarded and she tried to calm her racing heart while waiting for West to come with her.

"Sure, Mama." To Basco he said, "Don't you be tryin' out the plow 'till I get back. Okay?"

The old man nodded, never looking up. He was impressed that West had finally mastered the skill of carpentry.

As West followed his mother into the woods, a fission of alarm raced up his spine. This was the spot where they had all their serious discussions.

"West, there be no easy way to say this. The Ole General be dead."

Shaking his head, his eyes bright with unshed tears, West shouted, "No! He can't be dead! I didn't get to see him yet!" West choked out more words: "D-Did he ask to see me?"

"I don't know. I jes know he gone."

Venus held out her arms to West in comfort and he came to her. They stood, hugging, crying and being close to one another. West cried for something he never truly had, but wanted so badly in his life. And his mother cried because she felt his pain and could do nothing about it.

"It hurts *so* much, Mama. I just wanted to get to know him. I wouldna' told nobody I be his son. I just wanted to be 'round him sometimes."

"West, it be all right to grieve. Lord knows I have. I done had so much grief in my life, I could jes crawl up and die." Venus looked into her son's reddened eyes. "But I be knowin' that you jes got to let your heart heal, and you gots to be strong and go on."

Mother and son returned to the mansion house. She had chores to complete and West, well he needed to find peace within himself. Like her mammy always told her, 'Ain't nothin' so big that the Lord can't handle.'

George Washington's funeral was a simple affair, with only his family members and some neighbors in attendance. West was not allowed to attend the memorial service, though it was his greatest desire. So, West grieved—alone. Only Venus understood the loss he suffered. George Washington was his father and he was dead, yet West could not share his grief with the legitimate Washington family members. The nation had lost its first hero. West had lost his father, his paternal link to who he was. A man he was never able to openly claim.

The countryside was in awe of George Washington's last will and testament. Upon his death, Washington had taken a stance on slavery. In his twenty-eight-page will, the retired president had made arrangements for all his hundred and twenty-six slaves to be freed upon the death of his wife, Martha. Aged and sick slaves were to be fed and clothed by his heirs. In addition, George Washington reinforced his determination about the freedom of his slaves by adding a clause ordering the executors of his will to carry out his wishes "religiously…without evasion, neglect, or delay." The hundred and seventy-five-plus slaves who belonged to Martha Washington, which she inherited from her first husband and brought to Mount Vernon, were not freed. These slaves were referred to as 'dower' slaves, and by Virginia law, entailed to the estate.

It appeared that Washington experienced a deeper change of heart concerning his perspectives on slavery during the latter portions of his life. It seemed he had finally questioned his own moral character when it came to buying and selling human beings.

Why this change of heart? Could it have been that his only son, the lad called West, was a slave?

George Washington's will also offered Billy Lee, his old valet, a choice of immediate or deferred freedom, plus an annuity of thirty dollars a year for his devoted service. Washington left the bulk of his estate to Martha Washington until her death, and then Mount Vernon was to go to his favorite nephew, Bushrod Washington. Bushrod was also to receive his uncle's personal papers and library.

Washington's will methodically mentioned every member of his immediate family.

But, there was no mention of West Ford.

Venus knew it was to be expected. The Ole General hadn't changed to the degree that would damage his reputation by claiming a slave as his son. She decided that it was time divulge to West the secret she had kept since the day she named him. She explained to her son how Augustine Washington had made an effort to teach her the proper way to speak and how to write, even though his parents would have frowned on it. Augustine was a natural teacher, and he liked to share his knowledge with those who would listen.

"Venus, do you know that your name comes from a legend of a mythical civilization?" said Augustine during one of his elocution lessons. He was home on a break from school, and as usual, he was trying to correct her grammar while giving her a history lesson.

"Why's I named for a legend?" Venus asked him. Her facial expression showed that she didn't really know what a legend was.

Augustine smiled, "It's an honor to have such a noble and intriguing name, Venus. You are named after the goddess of beauty and love. Of all the goddesses who lived on Mount Olympus, Venus was the fairest of them all." Taking out a sheet of paper he said, "Here, let me show you how to spell your name."

Master Augustine also told her about other names and places and how to spell them. During one of his history lessons he conveyed to her that the name Washington was once known as de Wessyngton when his ancestors lived in England. When his family settled in Westmoreland County, they changed the spelling of their last name to Washington. So, Venus came up with the abbreviated name of West, taken from Westmoreland County and the original spelling of the Ole General's last name.

After finishing the description of how West received his name, Venus continued, "I be around twelve years when he done told me that story.

The peoples that theys come from was some kind of nights or somethin' like that, and theys used long knifes to fight with. That be why I 'member it so good." Her voice gentled and she added, "I know it don't be much, but one day you be able to name your first boy, George, after the Ole General. Miz Hannah be dead and buried then, and it won't make no never mind."

West forced a tremulous smile at his mother. "It be enough for now Mama, it be enough for now." She had given him a piece of the Washington heritage, even if it was in a roundabout fashion.

The Bushfield slaves were somber when they heard about the freeing of George Washington's slaves. They had been slaves all of their lives. Would Master Bushrod, the executor of George Washington's estate, follow in his uncle's footsteps and free them someday? What was going to happen to them when their master took over Mount Vernon? But nothing changed for the Bushfield slaves. Bushrod and his mother continued to operate the plantation with a firm hand.

George Washington was not the only Washington to die in 1799. His younger brother, Charles, and his nephew, Corbin, died that same year.

Two years later, in 1801, Hannah Washington died. West was at her bedside when she passed away. She looked shockingly old, her pale cheeks sunken and her closed eyelids laced by spidery blue veins. Her shallow breathing barely stirred the quilted counterpane until finally it stopped completely. Hannah Washington had requested that they not bury her for at least three days after her death. She harbored the fear that she would wake up in her coffin, buried alive, with no one the wiser.

West took Mistress Hannah's death extremely hard. He had respected her, even loved her, and was grateful for all she had done for him over the years. West could now read and write when others of his race couldn't, and it was all due to Hannah Washington. She had always treated him special and he would miss her.

Venus on the other hand felt differently about the old woman's death. As she watched her mistress's coffin being lowered into a freshly dug grave, she realized that she still harbored animosity towards the dead woman. Miz Hannah had never been very pleasant to her and Venus could only reciprocate. And it had always bothered her that Miz Hannah had demanded so much of West's time. Venus knew that she was being ungracious, especially after all her mistress had done for her son, but she couldn't help it.

Besides, Miz Hannah was still exerting her wishes from the grave when it came to her and Suck. Venus learned just before the funeral that the old woman had stipulated in her will that she and Suck were only to be given her 'most indifferent' things from her wardrobe. But what shocked Venus to the depth of her soul and left her cold, was that she was to be a gift to Miz Hannah's grandson, Richard Henry Lee.

Venus watched dry-eyed as the dirt was being thrown into the grave. She would shed no tears for Miz Hannah.

She had to figure a way not to become separated from West.

Chapter 8

Whatever natural right men have to freedom and independence, it is manifest that some men have a natural ascendancy over others.

Greville

Death was making its rounds once again in the Washington family, as Martha Washington, the Ole General's wife, died in 1802. Bushrod Washington was now master of two plantations, Mount Vernon and Bushfield. Washington's favorite nephew had acted as his uncle's attorney on many occasions, and the two had been very close, except in their looks. Bushrod was not as tall as his uncle, and carried more flesh on his body. He had inherited his mother's brown hair and dark eyes. When angry, those eyes could shrivel a person in their tracks. It was a look he wore most of the time since becoming a member of the legal profession.

He and his wife, Ann, were taking several of the Bushfield slaves with them to the Mount Vernon estate. West, Venus, Bettey, and Jenny were the only house slaves chosen to make the move. Mistress Hannah's wish of separating Venus from West never came to fruition, as John Augustine Washington's will had stipulated that Venus and her mother could be given only to his children. It said nothing about grandchildren.

The fates it seemed were on Venus' side in this instance.

"Ah's gonna miss you, Venus. You know we ain't never gonna see each other no mo," cried Suck as she clutched the younger woman to her breast.

"I gonna miss you, too. Maybe the massa let me come sometimes when he and the missy visit Bushfield," Venus said as she wiped the tears from her red-rimmed eyes.

Both women knew that was wishful thinking.

Suck was eight months pregnant with her sixth child. Every one of her offspring had sickened and died during their first week of life. She was praying that this one would survive.

Suck took her huge, swollen belly into her two hands and said, "My babe be comin' soon and ahs shore' wish your mammy would be here to help with the birthin'." Rolling her black eyes, she went on, "We both knows old Abigail ain't the best with birthin' no chile. She jes put that big hand of hers on your mouth so's she cain't hear a body scream. Ahs tell you, if'n she do that to me, ah's gonna bite that old hand like a leech at dinner time."

The women burst out laughing. Leave it to Suck to make their parting less painful.

The wagon that was to carry Venus and her family to Mount Vernon was waiting outside the big house. It was time to say goodbye. Venus hugged the dearest friend she had in the world and then climbed into the wagon.

As they left for their new home, West thought with anticipation that finally he would live on the plantation that once belonged to his father. There was so much to look forward to. Venus was thinking about all she was leaving behind. What did she have to look forward to?

Upon their arrival at Mount Vernon, they found that the estate was in poor condition and many buildings needed repairs. The whitewash on the mansion house and outbuildings was peeling and one of the white pillars that graced the piazza in back of the house had rotted.

George Washington's pride and glory, the elaborate flower and vegetable gardens, were overrun with weeds. Master Bushrod immediately set out looking for the main overseer to start on the necessary repairs.

West didn't notice the peeling paint or garden weeds. He was in awe of the once-majestic mansion house. It was much more impressive than Bushfield. Why, this was where he would have expected the first president of the United States to reside!

He helped his family from the wagon and entered the house behind Mistress Ann, his mother, and his grandmother. Jenny and Venus followed their mistress up the curving staircase that led to the second-floor bedrooms.

West decided on a sightseeing tour, and began roaming from one room to the next on the first level. Most of the rooms' original contents were gone. Few pieces of furniture were left for the new occupants.

The front parlor of the house was painted Prussian blue from the baseboard to intricate molding that framed the ceiling and doorways. West examined portraits that adorned the brightly painted walls. He studied pictures of Martha's two children and lingered a long moment in front of the portrait of the Old General.

West then entered the dining room and stood in wonder. It was a magnificent room. The walls were painted verdigris green and the molding a bright white. A rich, burgundy rug covered the wooden floor. The room sported a Palladian window with white dimity curtains framed with deep festoons of green satin. West counted more than twenty chairs along the walls. A marble fireplace dominated one side of the room.

West exhaled deeply, fortifying himself before entering the wood-paneled study. It was a masculine room, darkly conservative. This is where he felt the Old General's presence most. West took in the large globe that dominated the center of the room and the glassed bookshelves. His eyes stopped their visual tour at a sculpted bust of George Washington. West went to it and stood a moment, admiring the quality of the work. The artist had captured the Old General's features to perfection.

He placed one hand on the bust and the other on his own face. Closing his eyes, he traced the bust with his hand, feeling the similarities between the cold, white plaster and his own warm skin. He opened them to find Bushrod staring intently at him, his obsidian eyes narrowed and a frown furrowing his brow.

West was startled, but he held his ground. Master Bushrod walked to where the boy was standing and said, "West, your mother is looking for you. She's in the cookhouse out back, being introduced to the other servants. Go and join her now."

"Thank you, suh. I just get to her right away." He started to leave, but before going out he saw his master examining the bust of George Washington.

West walked through the back hall, past the pantry and out under the vine-covered colonnade. There he paused, hypnotized by the panorama before him. A long, sloping lawn dipped into a wooded glen. Beyond was the Potomac River, a small steamship cutting through a ford in its placid waters.

West could scarcely believe he was going to live here, the home of his father. Remembering Master Bushrod's order, he headed towards the cookhouse, a separate building set back from the mansion.

Entering the large, sunlit room, West went to his mother and grandmother.

"Lawsy, dis be your son?" one extremely heavy-set woman exclaimed.

"Yeh, he be West," Venus stated. She couldn't help noting the servants reactons. Some were whispering, others were staring with their mouths hanging open.

"Well, ah be Doll, de head cook," the heavy-set woman said. Pointing to a fair-skinned black man, she continued, "Dis be Moses and his helper, Jacob." Jacob was the younger man with dark brown skin. "Theys help with the horses."

"Ah be Mima," a cocoa-colored woman with a bright red kerchief tied around her head stepped forward. "Ah wash and do the ironing."

Another very thin young girl murmured, "Ah be Lucy. Ah helps Doll."

Lucy pointed to a medium-height young man with curly black hair and said, "This be Frank. He be de butler and my husband."

The last person to be introduced stepped forward. "Ah be Cate. Ah take care of the sick." Cate was a tall, stately, black-skinned woman.

"We alls be free," Doll stated. "Most the other house and field hands left the plantation when we was freed by Missy Washington. We stayed 'cause we ain't got nowheres else to go."

Venus glanced around the room at the servants. Her jaw tensed as she said, "We still be slaves, 'ceptin' for West. He to be free when he reach twenty-one."

Shrugging, she said, "Well, free or not, we gots work to do before the new missy start complainin', so ah guess we best get to it," said Doll.

Doll went to a work table laden with food, picked up a plate filled with biscuits and meat, and handed it to West.

"West, you do me a favor, boy, and take dis here food to old Billy Lee."

Noting the questioning look on West's face, she continued, "Billy Lee was de old massa's waiting man. He be down at his cabin, way back behind the big house. He be crippled now and cain't walk so good no more. His cabin be off by itself."

Nodding, West took the plate and went down the white column piazza where he followed the path to the slave cabins. At one dilapidated cabin he saw an elderly black man, sitting on a wooden bench beneath an elm tree. His eyes were shut and his wooden, walking stick was lying next to his shoeless feet.

Not knowing whether to wake the sleeping man or place the plate beside him, West stood for several seconds contemplating the matter.

"How long you gonna stand there, boy?" a raspy voice demanded.

"I just didn't want to be disturbin' your sleep," West replied.

Opening bloodshot, brown eyes, Billy Lee said, "Well, bring the food on over, or do you wish for me to starve?"

West handed him the plate. The man took several bites of the victuals while he watched. Shortly the man said, "You be West."

West nodded .

Billy Lee continued. "I 'members you when you were jes a little youngin'."

West's light eyes lit up at this declaration.

Chewing, Billy Lee said with his mouth full, "You might nots 'member me, but I 'member how the old massa took you with him to church."

West searched his memory for a few seconds and realized he did recognize his father's elderly waiting man.

"I 'member. You'd be waitin' by the coach while we went in. How's come you didn't go in?"

"He never ask me," Billy Lee said.

West glanced away and surveyed the other slave cabins. They were in no better condition than the ones at Bushfield, he thought.

"You been down to the tomb where the old Massa be buried?"

"No. I don't know where it is."

Taking a chicken bone from his mouth and using it like a pointer, Billy Lee said, "Follow the path past the stables and fruit orchard. It be off to the left of the path. Go on down, the door ain't too hard to open. There be a lamp next to the door on the ground."

Taking the old man's advice, West went to the tomb. Dark, turbulent feelings emerged from where they had been locked in his soul. The deep yearnings for the Old General to accept him as his son gushed into his heart like a rising river.

The tomb wasn't what he expected. It was built into a small hill and the outside was brick, with a wooden door. A metal rod had been pushed between two metal loops, keeping it closed. A dilapidated wooden fence enclosed the area. West opened the gate and approached the tomb. He clenched and unclenched his hands before removing the rod holding the tomb door closed. He then opened the door, and placed a large rock next to it so that it would not close. Picking up the kerosene lamp, he lit it and entered the dark enclosure.

The tomb was dank and musty. The air smelled like death. He waited for his eyes to adjust to the darkness before going to the ornately carved wooden casket. West said a short prayer and left.

After that day, West spent his spare time at the Old General's tomb. He didn't go inside anymore, but sat near the tomb's entrance. He made himself a wooden, three-legged stool and sat and spoke to his father in death the way he never could in life, telling him about all his dreams and regrets.

"I be hurtin' when you stopped visitin' me, and I didn't get to see you no more. I hated you then. I hated you 'cause you didn't want me for your son. You didn't want nobody to know. I used to wish that you be carin' for me a little, bein' I was your flesh and blood." He continued, "I understand now that you couldn't be claimin' me. That, that was the way it had to be. I just wish we had more time together, and I just want you to know that I don't hate you no more."

Several months after their move to Mount Vernon, Master Bushrod sent for West. His master was sitting at his desk in the library, a stack of legal documents piled high on one side. He motioned for his servant to come in and take a seat. West tried not to squirm in the chair. He wondered what he had done to cause Master Bushrod to send for him.

After a moment, Bushrod glanced up from a book he was reading and said, "West, along with your jobs of carpenter and gardener, I also want you to guard George Washington's tomb. Too many visitors are coming here, wanting to see where he's buried. You think you can manage that?"

"Yassum, Master Bushrod. I be sure to keep the tomb area picked up and won't let no one come and bother the old master's grave," replied West.

Bushrod was once again absorbed in his paperwork and waved a dismissing hand towards West.

Venus didn't share West's enthusiasm for wanting to guard George Washington's tomb. "I don't know why you be wantin' to be 'round dead folks. It ain't right."

"Dead folks can't hurt you none, Mama. Anyways, I like to talk to the Old General sometimes."

"Boy, now I know you be needin' some help! The man be dead—you be alive—and you can't change that," a concerned Venus said.

"Mama, don't worry about me. I couldn't be around him when he be livin', but now I can. It be hard to explain."

Blue eyes begging for understanding, he added, "It may not be much, but somehow, I feel like he be listenin' to me, and that in his own way, he cared about me. And Mama, can't nobody take away the feelin's that live on in my mind."

Venus studied her handsome son. He had grown into a noble-looking young man. George Washington was dead, but his son would have his strength, his character. West assured Washington his immortality because they shared a blood bond, the bond of a father and son, even if no one else acknowledged it.

Venus never again spoke against West guarding the tomb.

West also spent an enormous amount of time with Billy Lee. Billy Lee had been with George Washington during the Revolutionary War, and West would listen for long periods of time about the Old General's military exploits.

"I 'member once when the first free Negroes tried to enlist in the war. The massa, he almost have a fit. He didn't want no Negroes in his army. He say that it cause too much dis'ruption.

Billy Lee held a jug containing some sort of questionable beverage and would take swallows from it as he recounted the story. It was a well-known fact that Billy Lee had developed a drinking problem. It was the only thing that dulled the pain in his knees.

Billy Lee continued, "But them British was lettin' the Negroes in their army and they was a whippin' our boys. So, Massa George figured he'd better let them free Negroes help, because we needed men and theys be good fighters. He had several join his command. Them Negro troops fought so good that the old massa wanted more."

Taking another long drink, he elaborated, "Massa Washington then say that any slaves who help in the fightin' should get their freedom. Well, I say to massa, I's fight-I want to be free! The general say he need me too much, but that he free me someday."

Billy's eyes held a faraway look as he continued. "Some of the massas changed their minds 'bout freeing their slaves who fought and took them back to their plantations when the war be over. Some slaves ran and many was caught, but some got away with the British."

Finishing the bottle, he said, "Well, massa finally free me, but now I too sick and broken to be free." Closing his bloodshot eyes, he said, "Leave me alone now, boy."

West continued to visit the old man every day, trying to get him to eat and to take better care of himself. Being around Billy Lee was like sharing a piece of George Washington's life.

Several more years passed uneventfully and in 1805, West was finally freed as stated in the terms of Hannah Washington's will. He decided that now that he was twenty-one and free, he needed two names. West knew he couldn't take the last name of Washington, so he chose the name Ford. There was a ford in the Potomac River back of the Mount Vernon plantation. He had sat for hours at a time gazing at that particular spot. And just like the word, he would ford his way through the river of life.

An artist was commissioned to sketch West's picture in commemoration of the event of his freedom. West was impeccably groomed and his chestnut hair was pulled back tightly against his head with no curls at the sides. This was the way Billy Lee said he had combed George Washington's hair when he was alive.

West went to Billy Lee's cabin the day his portrait was to be drawn. The old man was relaxing on a wooden stool near the front yard when West approached.

Whistling, Billy said, "You sure do look like your sire, boy."

"I do?" West answered, his light eyes sparkling with delight.

"Yesuhree. The old massa was a little taller, but you gots his eyes, mouth and forehead."

"Did, did he ever talk 'bout me?" West's voice held a hopeful note.

"Once. I heard him talkin' to Massa Bushrod, sayin' that he couldn't be seen with you no more after he became the president. Seeing the smile leave the young man's face, Billy Lee added, "You know that's the way it had to be, don't ya?"

"Yeah, I know," West said resignedly.

"I know he cared for you, boy. The eyes don't lie. I could tell by the way he looked at you when he thought no one was a watchin'. Anyways, you gonna get your picture drawn today. Someday *everybody* gonna know that the old massa was your father."

West nodded and turned to head back to the mansion house. After he had taken a couple of steps Billy Lee shouted, "West, I think the old massa be proud of the man you have become."

West turned and flashed a brilliant smile. His step was lighter as he went to pose for his drawing.

When the sketch was finished, West remembered how Massa Bushrod studied the image, his brown eyes pensive. "West, I'll keep this sketch for you in a safe place," he said. "We wouldn't want it to get damaged."

West was disappointed. He wanted to hang the picture in the spinning room where his family stayed. Having his likeness sketched was a great honor and he wanted to keep it safe and in his possession. West never saw the portrait again.

Later that evening, a simple party was held down by Billy Lee's cabin to celebrate West's freedom. Doll made a pound cake with sugar icing for the festivities. Billy Lee, Lucy, Frank, Mima, Jacob and Cate also attended.

Venus watched as her son was welcomed into the realm of the free. A place she could only dream about. A place she would never know. *West has been born for better things,* she thought. A smile tugged the corners of her mouth as Jacob began playing a lively tune on a fiddle. Now the group was stamping their feet and clapping their hands in harmony with the rhythm.

West, noting that his mother was not among the revelers, scanned the area around Billy Lee's cabin. His saw her sitting under an elm tree with a wistful smile. *She be an outsider, the only slave among us,* he thought. And here he was laughing and carrying on, celebrating being a free man. Going to his mother, he knelt in front of her and took one of her work-worn hands in his.

"Mama, you want some of Doll's cake? It's mighty tasty."

"No, son, I not too hungry right now."

She touched his smooth cheek, tracing each contour and angle. He had such distinctive features. Destiny had written freedom into the lines of his face. His father's blue-gray eyes, thin lips and high forehead would tell the story for generations to come.

Venus said in a soft tone, "Son, you be free now. This be the most im'portant day of your life. Nobody can own you no more." Her golden colored eyes glowed with love. "You stand proud, you stand tall," Venus continued in an impassioned voice.

"Mama, I promise." Swallowing audibly, West said, "And Mama, someday you gonna be free too. I'll find a way—"

"Shh." Venus put her finger to his lips. "Don't you be worrin' about me none, 'specially today. This be a time for celebratin'." Standing, she grasped his hand and said, "Let's go get some of Doll's cake 'fore Frank eats it all up."

A law was passed by the Virginia legislature on May 1, 1805, the year West was granted his freedom, requiring all slaves freed thereafter to leave the state. In 1806, the Virginia Slave Code was amended and it stated that all manumitted slaves who did not leave the state within one year were to be seized and sold.

Massa Bushrod asked if West wanted to leave Mount Vernon and move North. West told him no. The only family he had ever known was here—his mama and his grandmamma.

Besides, who would take care of the Old General's tomb the way he did?

Chapter 9

The heart will break, yet brokenly live on.

Bryon

A couple of months after West gained his freedom, his younger sister, Bettey, died in her sleep. Bettey had never grown much in height or weight, so her stature was that of a child instead of a young woman.

"Why did God have to take her, Mama?" West cried out to Venus as he watched his mother prepare his sister for burial. Reaching out a trembling hand, he straightened a strand of coarse hair from her sweet face. "She ain't never got to smile or to laugh, or to even play like other children. Why?" His eyes emitted tangible raw pain.

Venus didn't know how to answer her son's question. She couldn't reason at the moment. Her daughter, her little girl was dead. She wanted to ask God the same question as West. Why? Venus wanted to run and hide, to scream with the agony of losing her child. But she had to place her pain aside, though it was eating her up within. She had to be strong for her son. She would comfort him and then she would find a quiet place to grieve and hope to God she would survive for another day.

"West, we don't be knowin' the Lord's plan. Maybe in heaven Bettey be able to do all them things," she said as she continued to gaze at her daughter. Bettey appeared to be sleeping, her dark lashes resting on high cheekbones. *Thank God her eyes be closed,* Venus thought thankfully. She didn't think she could bear it if her child's eyes had stared sightlessly at her.

Bettey was buried in the slave cemetery at Mount Vernon. It was about thirty feet from George Washington's tomb and enclosed by a clump of trees and bushes. West made a large wooden cross and placed some of the flowers on Bettey's grave that were brought to grace the tomb of the retired president. Venus held one arm around West and the other around her mother, supporting both as the simple pine box was lowered into the ground.

She couldn't cry, not yet, not until she was alone.

Later that evening, Venus went into a wooded area away from the mansion house and the slave cabins. Once she was deep into the woods, grief such as she'd never known swept through her. Grief so overpowering, that thoughts of any kind ceased to exist, only an unbearable, empty ache.

Billy Lee had seen her walk into the woods and had followed discreetly. He stopped a ways from Venus and watched as her shoulders shook with the force of her tears. Then he heard her scream. It had no beginning and no end, as if it had always existed in its own pain. It was a shriek of agony so profound that it burned his soul. He remained hidden, but stood guard until finally she lay on the ground as if dead.

Billy Lee hobbled to her prone body and even with his bad knees, picked up her slight form and carried her back to the mansion house. There he met an anxious West who took her to the third floor bedroom she shared with her mother. Again, West became his mother's watch-dog. He made her eat when she didn't want food. He made sure that she rested if she looked over-tired. And every night he crept into her bedroom to make sure she was sleeping peacefully.

And thus Venus began the slow process of healing from the death of her daughter and was beginning to rally. But the winds of impartial fate wound its tethers once more into her existence.

"I be joinin' Bettey soon," Jenny told Venus a couple months after Bettey's death. They were in their bedroom. Jenny was still lying on her pallet, an unusual sight this time of the morning.

"Mammy don't you be sayin' that. You all I got!" Venus was distraught. Her eyes misted at the thought of her mother dying. She went to the bed. Jenny looked worn. The dark smudges lodged beneath her lower lids seemed more pronounced. She was so frail. Her neck, thrusting from the vee of her nightdress, appeared scrawny.

"Chile, you gots West. And I be old and plum tired. A body knows when it be time for them to die." Tapping a hand over her heart she elaborated, "It be a feelin' you get and you jes got to 'cept it. 'Sides, these old eyes done seen too much sorrow. I want to go where I can be free."

Two days later, Jenny's heart quit beating while she was repairing a tear in one of Mistress Ann's day dresses. She just slumped over and died in her chair. She was laid to rest next to her granddaughter in the Mount Vernon slave cemetery. Venus wondered if people ever died from grief. *And so I live,* thought Venus a few days later. *My heart be beatin', I be feedin' my stomach, I be breathin' air, and all of these things make me be livin' so that I can 'member my pain today, tomorrow, and forever.* Her tears came then, in great, moaning torrents.

A wounded, haunted look possessed Venus after the death of her mother. Her eyes mirrored a grief West had never seen in them. Watching his once-vivacious mother overtaken by melancholy frightened him. He began to spend his free time with her, trying to bring life back into her golden-colored eyes.

Walking to the slave cemetery, West saw his mother sitting, with her legs curled under her, between her mother's and daughter's graves. She seemed lost in a world of her own. He watched for a moment while she picked dandelions, growing near the grass-covered mounds. He approached her and lightly touched her shoulder.

"I loved them too," he told her.

"I be knowin' that, son," she murmured.

"Nothin' is ever gonna be the same again, is it Mama?" Before she could answer West continued, "I don't want nothin' more to change in our lives. Why can't time just stop? Why can't it stay just the way it is so you'd never grow old and we'd be together always? Why does God let us be lovin' somebody and then snatch them away?" In a quieter voice, he said, "It's just best not to love nobody."

Her eyes red and swollen, her face stained with tears, she took her son's strong hand in hers and pulled him down next to her.

"West, it be hurtin' somethin' awful to lose the ones we love, but God gave us the gift to love and that be a true blessin' 'cause there be some folks in this here world who don't got nobody to love'm. We had your grandma, your little sister, and Fortune with us for a time, and they be always alive in our hearts."

Venus sniffed and wiped the tears from under her eyes with her fingertips. She firmed up her chin and said, "And West, everythin' must change. If'n time never changed you'd still be a slave. You be free now." Waving her hands around she continued, "Someday you can leave this here plantation. One day you can tell your chillen 'bout your papa and that they be somebody more than a slave."

"Mama, I ain't never gonna leave you. *Never*. And I'm gonna tell my children who their grandpapa was," he said.

West rose to his feet and reached down to help his mother to hers. They walked arm-in-arm to the mansion house. In that moment, Venus decided it was time to remember the living and make peace with the dead.

Venus was assigned as personal maid to Master Bushrod's wife now that her mother was dead. Mistress Ann was a quiet woman and a semi-invalid. She reminded Venus of a little brown sparrow. She was not very verbal and left management of the estate to her husband who wasn't home much. Every morning Venus would bring her mistress pots de crème, a chocolate drink, and then curl her brown hair with a heated rod.

As West passed through his young manhood on the Mount Vernon plantation, he carried himself with a noble air. He was allowed to travel to Alexandria on errands with and for Bushrod Washington. He also continued to attend church on Sundays with the Washingtons. It was highly unusual for a freed slave to attend a white church because the Virginia legislature, notorious for trying to keep blacks and whites separated, forbade slaves or free blacks from receiving formal religious instruction.

Working outdoors in the hot Virginia sunshine had tanned West's milk-white skin to a light honey-brown. He had a whipcord build, not overly muscular, but far from skinny.

One summer day, while on business in Alexandria for Massa Bushrod, West met his one true love. The young woman was black-haired and had clear green eyes. She was almost as white-looking as he was. She was carrying several packages and strolling along King Street in one direction and he in the other when a carriage almost ran her down. Parcels flew everywhere. West went to help gather her belongings.

"That be all right massa sir, I can get them," the girl said when the aristocratic young man bent to help her.

"I be no one's massa," a deep, rich voice replied.

The girl was startled by the man's sensual voice and his reply that he was not a massa. She studied the stranger who was retrieving her belongings. In profile, his features were sharp and lean; a study in angles framed by thick, chestnut hair.

Sensing her perusal, West's eyes met hers and the young girl lost herself in his, mesmerized by their cool blue-gray depths. He looked white, she thought, but something about his manner proclaimed a mixed heritage. Also, his large hands were scarred and work-worn, not the hands of the average white man. She wondered who he was.

Helping the woman to her feet, West smiled and said, "I'll just help you with these packages Miz—"

"My name be Priscella, Priscella McPherson. I be a seamstress for Miss Josephine's Dress Shop." She hesitated and added, "I be free. You be a free man or some fancy-dressed slave?" Priscella was forever speaking her mind.

Taken aback, West paused, then responded, "I be free. My name's West Ford." He stood tall and added, "I be Massa Bushrod Washington's man over at the Mount Vernon plantation."

Her beautiful smile made his heart do strange things. Slowly, they went around the corner to Duke Street towards the dress shop. West's arms were full with packages. Their walk was interrupted when they noticed a gang of slaves being herded down the road to be sold at auction. When West turned back to Priscella, he couldn't hide his disgust and pain. They continued towards Miss Josephine's shop. Each was lost in deep thought.

Slave trading had become a big business in Virginia, and cities like Alexandria were mistresses to it. At times its major streets became open market places with a fair-like quality; any type of black person could be purchased. Long-established business houses that normally specialized in farming tools and animals, introduced a 'line' of slaves. These same merchants handled flesh along with tobacco, groceries, and real estate.

Fear that the slave supply would shortly be exhausted encouraged systematic breeding and rearing of slaves. Virginia, Kentucky, and Maryland were first to become known as the "Negro-raising states." Experiments in slave breeding often were as thorough as experiments to discover new medicines to cure diseases. A slave girl was expected to be a mother by the time she was fifteen. Prizes such as suckling pigs were given to every woman who had ten children or more.

Both West and Priscella realized how lucky they were to be free.

The couple continued in silence until they reached the dress shop. "I got to get back to my wagon and business now, Miz Priscella." West handed the packages to her. "I'd like to see you again, if'n you don't be mindin' that"

"That be fine, West. You can find me most days here, at the shop."

He smiled and headed back toward his wagon. Unfortunately, it was close to where the auction was being held. As West took in the appearance of the slaves, he noticed that they were manacled and dirty. Most of the women were bare-breasted and wore only tights or one-piece gowns fastened at the neck with draw-cords. The older men had on worn, tattered shirts and the younger ones were bare-chested.

West wore high black boots made of the finest leather and a tailored black jacket with a white lawn shirt tucked into black breeches. He wore the clothes of a master, not a slave. He couldn't help feeling guilty.

The auctioneer was crying out bids in a sing-song voice. "What you all give me for this handsome buck? He be prime stock and a good breeder! Why, he's already bred his previous owner twenty-five pickininies."

Loosing the drawstring on the slave's pants, the auctioneer exposed the man's genitals for the prospective buyers. The slave stood quietly, trying to maintain some semblance of dignity.

"I'll bid $500," one buyer called out. Another topped his price and the bidding continued.

A scarlet haze descended over West, blinding him with rage at the indignity the bound man suffered. West wondered how a person could show no emotion, though standing half-naked before hundreds of curious eyes. He didn't think he could. The anger still with him, he clenched his fists, climbed into his wagon, and left the city.

As West drove back to Mount Vernon he thought about his future. He was free, yet he wasn't truly free. Every time he saw a slave in bondage he realized that a trick of birth gave him privileges over others in his race.

Yet, he was free and he would take advantage of the opportunities given to him.

And, if he could help others less fortunate, he swore he would do so. He would also make sure that his children were not born into slavery. The woman he married had to be a free woman, as the status of the children took on the status of their mother. He knew he wanted Priscella to be that woman.

During the next several months, West visited Priscella in Alexandria whenever time permitted. On one Sunday afternoon, the couple was alone in the back room of the dress shop. Priscella was stitching lace onto one of the dresses being delivered the following day.

"I wants to tell you somethin', but you gots to keep it between us," West said in a conspiratorial voice.

"What that be?" she murmured. She was concentrating on sewing on the last bit of lace on the cuff of the dress sleeve.

"My papa be George Washington, he the first president of this here whole country!" He couldn't keep the pride out of his voice.

The statement garnered her attention. "I done heard he had a slave son!" She began to examine his features.

West began to chuckle at her awed expression and shrugged. "He never claimed me, but them Washingtons treat me right fine."

"My papa be an important man too. He owns a big plantation outside of Alexandria," Priscella informed him. "My mama was his mistress after his wife up and died. She loved him real good and he free my mama then. He be married again now, but he still sneak to my mama's bed every night." Priscella bit off a piece of thread and said, "I maked up my mind that I wasn't gonna live on the plantation no more and left. Miz Josephine hired me right soon enough when she saw how good I sews."

West wasn't used to such forthright language from a woman. And sometimes Priscella's comments caught him off guard. But it was this characteristic about her that intrigued him so.

The first person he told about his feelings for Priscella was Billy Lee. Billy was sitting on his bench and West was lounging on a tree stump converted into a stool.

"Billy, I be a little nervous about marryin' Priscella."

"You loves her, don' you boy?"

"Yeah, I do." His face took on a wistful look, "She sure be one fine lookin' woman. But I ain't had no chance to meet many gals, you know. All the young ones on this here plantation, well, they be slaves. Priscella be free."

"I be married to a free woman back during the war. Her name was Margaret Thomas."

"Where she be now?" West was amazed that the old man had a wife.

"The old massa and my Margaret didn't get along much. She was hired to help wash clothes and whatnot. It didn't sit too well with Margaret takin' orders, being she was free and all. The old massa thought Margaret be too uppity and they had words many a time. I was a slave, and couldn't say nothin'."

With a sad, faraway look Billy Lee paused then continued in a strained voice, "I ask massa to bring her back to Virginia and he said he would. But she wouldn't come. Now I don't know if'n she be dead or alive." Billy Lee's eyes were stark with pain.

West didn't know how to comfort his friend. "I-I be sorry, Billy Lee."

"Don't be sorry for me, boy. I was too proud. I thought that Margaret didn't love me enough when she told me she wasn't comin' with me. So, I jes left her and never looked back. Now that I be older, I reckin' she loved me too much and she jes couldn't watch me be a slave."

Looking into West's bright eyes, he ventured, "But you gots a chance to be happy. Because all we have in this here life is right now." He patted his chest in emphasis.

He grasped West's forearms, and said tersely, "Don't never let nothin' come between you and Priscella. Don't never be too prideful. 'Cause if'n you do, you could wind up like me—old and alone."

Billy dropped his hands from West's arms and walked back towards his cabin, but not before grabbing the bottle that had been lying next to the bench.

West and Priscella had a very short courtship and decided they wanted something more permanent. They were married in Alexandria on August 14, 1812. Master Bushrod made arrangements for the nuptials to be performed by Reverend Muir who was the pastor of the First Presbyterian Church of Alexandria, District of Columbia. West and Priscella were given permission to live above the spinning room, a building set-aside for the weavers.

A year later their first child was born. West gave his newborn son the Old General's middle name, William. When William first opened his blue-gray eyes to the world they held a serious expression. He didn't cry, only stared into the faces of his parents as if he were filled with questions he couldn't yet ask. West gazed into his son's eyes and it was like looking into a mirror. He loved him so much, this child of his flesh and blood and bone.

William also had light skin. He looked white. His parents now had to prepare themselves to deal with the problems William would experience as another white Negro living in the slave-infested south.

Chapter 10

I cannot draw a cart, nor eat dried oats; if it be man's work, I will do it.

Shakespeare

West and Priscella had three more children during the next several years—Jane, Daniel, and Julia. All had their father's milk-white skin and their eye colors ranged from blue to gray to green. The free black family flourished on the Mount Vernon plantation. Bushrod Washington made West one of the main overseers for the estate, a prestigious position that only white men had held previously. West couldn't help but revel in the life that fate had dealt him; he was living the life of a free man with all the amenities. The Washingtons, however, had yet to claim him as a blood relative. Instead, they treated him like a privileged servant.

This was not the case with other free blacks throughout the country. They presented the nation with an awkward situation. The South feared and distrusted them, and the North didn't want any more migration. The question of what to do with free blacks, who were daily becoming more articulate in their efforts to enter the national scene mystified nearly every white American leader.

"The free Negroes should be sent back to Africa," Bushrod Washington stated crisply. He was a judge now and was speaking to several men gathered for a meeting in his library.

"Hear, hear," said a tall, white-haired gentleman. "As Thomas Jefferson often said, 'the Negroes can never be integrated into American life,' and I am in total agreement."

The conversation paused when West entered the room and placed a box of cigars next to the brandy decanter. He quickly turned to leave, but before he reached the doors he heard one of the gentlemen remark, "The resemblance is uncanny."

Bushrod replied sharply, "Suh, it's something we don't discuss openly."

West heard no more as he closed the door and the dialogue was cut off. He later learned that the meeting in the library that evening evolved into the American Colonization Society, an organization for the purpose of sending free Negroes back to Africa. Bushrod Washington became the president. Other members of the society were Francis Scott Key and John Randolph.

The Society established a newspaper called the *African Repository* to educate the public with its aims. So convincing were the plans of the Society for transporting Negroes out of America, that President James Monroe had Congress authorize the purchase of a territory in Africa near the Senegal River on the West Coast for the settlements. The site was called Liberia, and in honor of the president the capital was called Monrovia.

Whenever he had the opportunity, West would read the copies of the *African Repository* that were scattered on Master Bushrod's desk. He perused one article that claimed that sending Negroes to Africa was an effort for the benefit of the blacks in which all parts of the country could join. He frowned, wondering if other free Negroes felt as he did, that America was their home, not a land far away and foreign.

West was twenty-seven when the first ship sailed to Liberia. Several weeks before that momentous day, Bushrod requested his presence in the library.

"You call for me, Massa Bushrod?" West said as he entered the quiet room. He took off his hat, and held it in two hands in front of his thighs.

"Yes, I did. Come in and sit down." He waved a hand to a chair in front of his desk.

"Glancing up from his papers he said, "West, you know I have been making arrangements for ships to take free Negroes to Liberia." Clearing his throat he said, "I wanted you to know that I can also make arrangements for you and your family to travel there. Once in Liberia, you can stake out a new life with people of your own race."

West didn't hesitate formulating a response. "I don't want to be leavin' Mount Vernon, Massa Bushrod. My people be born here, this land be my home. I don't know nothin' else."

"You don't have to make up your mind so soon, West. There will be plenty of ships leaving the country in the future. If you change your mind, I'll make sure that passage is made available for you."

"Thank you suh, but I won't be changin' my mind none too soon."

"Well, I just wanted to make the prospect known to you." A rare smile came to Bushrod's lips and he said, "But I must say I am relieved. I don't know what I would do around here without your services."

"I thank ya for that massa, suh. I guess I best be headin' over to the stables and check on the new foal if you be done with me now."

"You do that. Give me a report later on how it's faring." He bent over a document he had been scanning earlier.

West paused outside the office. This was his home; he would not leave it. *Africa.* He didn't even know where it was. For most free blacks, Africa was a distant memory, an ancestral alliance. It was not a place they wanted to return to as they had set down ties and families in America. No, he would not leave.

Besides, he could never leave his mother.

*   *   *

Though West was a free man and held some status on the Mount Vernon plantation, living within the 'color line' would sometimes intrude. The plantation system of house and field slaves created distrust of those with a mixed heritage by others of a darker complexion. In the southern socioeconomic order, lighter-hued blacks occupied a privileged, middling position between whites and darker blacks. Many southern whites preferred light-skinned blacks as house slaves and provided them better opportunities in slavery and freedom. In many cases, the house servants had blood ties with the family.

Southern white supremacy also theorized that the lighter-skinned blacks were genetically superior because of their white blood, and therefore more intelligent. Newspaper advertisements seeking the capture of runaway slaves were more likely to describe darker runaways as docile and loyal. Lighter-skinned blacks were seen as dangerous and violent. Many of the darker-skinned blacks perceived the half-white ones of having divided loyalties because of their ancestry.

West never condoned the attitudes of those who declared one segment of the Negro race superior to another because of differing shades of skin. He believed it was a divisive and destructive practice, especially considering the many tribulations that Negroes already faced.

West had come to terms with his white skin, but it was difficult for his firstborn son, William. William lived on the cusp of two worlds, one black and the other white. Though he had white skin, the Washingtons would never claim him as one of their own. And his free status separated him from the majority of slaves who now lived on the plantation. The slaves worked in the fields, while he had the privileged position of caring for a tomb and doing light carpentry work. William was allowed to use the front door at the mansion house, while others of his race used the back entrance.

William's elite status caused conflicts with the slave children, who would tease him about his white skin and how he talked like a massa.

It wasn't fair, thought William. There were other free slaves on Mount Vernon, but they weren't treated like him. Would the whiteness of his skin forever separate him from his race?

"I wish I were darker, papa, then them boys would play with me," William wistfully told West one day after being rebuffed again by the slave children. They were sitting at a small table in their cabin.

West took his son's pointed chin in his hands, raising the boy's face so they could look each other in the eye.

"William, people ain't got no choice on who their parents be or what color skin they be born with. To God, all people be the same color. Now I know you be havin' it hard, wantin' them boys to play with you. But they got to play with you the color that you are as God knows it ain't gonna rub off and one day you gonna wake up blacker, 'cause son, you be already black. No matter how white your skin be, you always gonna be black here in the South. If you act like you're better 'cause your skin be lighter, then them boys gonna know that and they gonna stay away from you. 'Member, just 'cause your skin be lighter, it don't make you better."

William sat quietly for a few seconds and said, "Papa, I know we are free, but why do we get to do things that the other free slaves don't get to do? And why are we so white looking?"

West knew it was time to tell his son of his heritage. Straightening his shoulders and taking a deep breath, he said, "Son, my papa was a white man. He be a Washington, George Washington. Now I know that you've heard his name spoken 'round here before. He be Massa Bushrod's uncle. He be the gentleman in the picture in the small parlor. Massa George also was a great general and he be the first president of this here country."

Noting the questions forming on his son's face, West continued, "You must never tell this to no white person, 'cause they wouldn't like it much that we be of Washington blood. Them Washingtons up in the mansion house don't even want to be a claimin' us that way. We be servants to them—privileged servants. Now you can tell your children someday, 'cause it be important. But don't tell no one else, you hear me boy?" West warned.

"Yes, sir, I promise," said William. The knowledge of his heritage made him stand a little prouder—a little taller. He would keep the secret until he could pass it on to his own offspring.

Several days after his heart-to-heart talk with his father, William stood behind the trunk of a large oak tree. He watched and laughed at the antics of several slave boys playing with a ball made up of rags. The boys were kicking the ball towards a line they drew in the dirt. Evidently, the winner of the game was the one who could kick the rounded ball closest to the line. One of the bigger boys was winning game after game.

Oh, how William wished he could join in. Why, he'd kick that ball farther than anyone. Then he decided, why not? His father said those boys had to play with him only if they wanted to. With a determined look on his face, William sauntered over to the boys.

"What you want, *mu-lot-toe*," the largest of the children said.

"I just want to play—"

"Play? Why does you wish ta play wif' us fo'? Ain't you scared you might git dose white hands dirty?" The other boys laughed at their leader's remarks.

"I ain't scared to get dirty," William replied, and because he was tired of the taunting and teasing, he added firmly, "And I ain't scared of you, neither."

The boy bristled at William's bold words. Wanting to maintain his elite status with the others he said, "Why we don't know if yo' scared 'cause you'd jes run up to da big house an' git the overseer to whip us."

The other boys all nodded and spoke in agreement.

"I'll fight you and if you win, I won't run and tell," William told their leader.

The larger boy was wary at first, but decided if the crazy mulatto wanted to fight him, he'd oblige. He nodded, his black eyes flashing. Then he balled his fists and came at William, arms swinging.

Fists were flying, feet were kicking, and when it was all over, William was still standing, barely. His nose was bloody and scratches and scrapes covered his body, but it had been a good fight.

The boy held his hand out in friendship and grinned, "You shore' don' fight like no mu-lot-toe. My name be Little Tom."

William smiled, grasped Little Tom's hand and said, "My name's not mulatto, it's William. William Ford."

Some of the other boys clapped William's shoulders, and they went back to playing kick the rag ball. This time William was one of them; he was included in the game.

William and Little Tom became best friends after their fight and were virtually inseparable. Little Tom topped William by about ten inches and had the whitest, straightest teeth William had ever seen. He was a handsome, ebony lad and told William that his family's ancestors had come from the Koromanti tribe in Africa.

The boys became very close, and to show their brotherhood, they borrowed one of the blacksmith's hot pokers and burned matching marks on their forearms. William winced when Little Tom touched the red tip of the hot metal first on his own forearm. When it was William's turn he almost passed out as he felt the searing pain and watched his skin turn black and then crinkle up.

"Now, we be brothers fo'ever," Little Tom told William as he put the juice of a crushed onion on his burn so it wouldn't become infected.

The burn hurt something awful, but William was determined not to cry. He was a Koromanti warrior now.

"Brothers forever," replied William. Then as he watched Little Tom apply the juice to his own burn William said, "Little Tom, you don't have but one name." He paused for a moment and continued, "I would like to give you my last name, Ford."

Tears misted in Little Tom's coal black eyes at William's caring gesture. "It be somethin' I want, little brother." They clasped their hands in friendship.

Living on the Mount Vernon plantation and having the privilege of being educated unlocked a world of knowledge for William and his siblings. Through books, William was introduced to cultures and societies he never knew existed, such as ancient Greece and Rome, and the empires of China and Africa.

And he soaked up the knowledge.

Through education, William saw the ludicrousness of the notions that one human being was better than another—that an accident of birth made one person more deserving of respect than one with a darker skin color. There was an insanity in the concept that black blood made one a slave and in the fact that it was so readily accepted by the South.

William knew there was so much more to the world than the Mount Vernon plantation, the South, and its prejudices. He wanted to leave Mount Vernon and make a new life in the North, maybe New York. William had never been to New York, but he knew opportunities abounded there for free Negroes. When he had enough money to free Little Tom, they would make their way there and open a carpentry business.

It was a scorching, Sunday afternoon and William was on his way to meet Tom. He and his friend were going swimming in the river to cool off. William was near the front of the mansion house when several wagons pulled up at the circular entrance. He watched as four armed men piled out of the three wagons and headed to the slave cabins.

Master Bushrod came out of the house a few seconds later and said to him, "William, I want you to go down and fetch your father from Billy Lee's cabin. Tell him the traders are here." He then turned and went back into the mansion house.

A frisson of unease struck a cord in William's mind. He ran along the dirt path towards Billy Lee's cabin, but his father was already on his way to the house. They met near the stables.

"Papa, Master Bushrod said the traders are here. Why would traders come here to Mount Vernon?" asked an anxious William. His light eyes were wide with concern.

"Son, I be wantin' you to go to our cabin and wait there with your mama and the others." He placed a hand on William's thin shoulder and squeezed it.

"Why, Papa? What's going on?"

Before he could answer his son, they saw one of the overseers herding several of the Bushfield slaves, including Little Tom, towards the wagons like cattle to a slaughterhouse. The women and children of the group were crying openly. A few of the armed traders were prodding some of the larger black men with shotguns.

Spying William, Little Tom hollered, "Lil' brother. Will! William!"

William's chest tightened and he could not breathe. He started shaking uncontrollably when the slave traders forced Little Tom into one of the wagons.

"Papa, where are they taking Little Tom and the others?" William's voice shook with alarm.

"William, son, Massa Bushrod, he be sellin' his slaves." The tone of his father's voice was sad, but matter-of-fact.

"Noooo! He can't sell Little Tom," William cried in outrage. Turning to his father he entreated, "Please, Papa! Please don't let him sell Little Tom."

"William, there be nothin' I can do. I already ask Massa Bushrod if'n he could keep Little Tom, seein' how he be like a brother to you. But he say that all of them got to go. He tell me that he done sold them to two Louisiana planters and the sale be final. Son, we got to thank the Lord that he didn't sell your grandma."

So that's why his father had been quiet and contemplative for the last several days, thought William. His father knew the sale was eminent. William stared in abject horror as Little Tom sat crying in the wagon with the others. A moment later he tried to run after the conveyance as it started to pull away, but his father grabbed him from behind, holding his arms.

"Let me go! Let me go, Papa!" cried a struggling William.

"I can't, son." His father's voice cracked with pain.

William continued to thrash about, but couldn't break his father's iron grip. He started yelling then, begging someone, anyone to stop the wagon. But no one came forward.

William's tear-blurred eyes met his friend's briefly, and he knew that they would never see each other again. With strength he didn't know he possessed, William broke free and began to run. William heard someone call his name, but he couldn't stop running any more than he could halt the nausea from rolling in his stomach. Finally he dropped to his knees behind one of the slave cabins and vomited. He then lay on his back on the hard earth and drew deep, slow draughts of air, staring at the sky.

West Ford found his son like that.

He sat next to the distraught boy until William was able to return to their cabin. When they entered, Priscella embraced her son. William was eleven, and this was just the beginning of the difficult lessons he would experience in his life.

His grandmother, Venus, was relaxing in a rocker, holding his little brother in her arms, and his two sisters huddled on the bed they shared, embracing each other.

"How could he do it, Papa? How could he do it?" William questioned, his voice wracked with grief. Tears coursed down his cheeks.

Sighing, his eyes full of entreaty, West replied, "Son, I don't know why one man be sellin' slaves and another don't. I ask Massa Bushrod how could he sell his slaves when the Old General free all his? He say to me that I be oversteppin' my place. He then go on to say that he ain't the Old General and that the slaves belonged to him, and he could do anything he be wantin' with them."

"I hate him. I'll always hate him," William murmured. His lips were clenched and his brow was creased in anger.

Venus got up from her chair by the fireplace and handed Daniel to his mother. Then she walked over to her grandson.

Once she gained his full attention she said, "Hate will eat at you everyday you be alive, if'n you let it. You gots to be stronger than hate. Let your heart heal and forgive, 'cause a heart that can't forgive will die."

William knew she had more reason to hate than anyone. He made up his mind that he would forgive Master Bushrod Washington.

But not today.

Today the pain was too raw.

Chapter 11

The best portion of a good man's life, are his little, nameless, unremembered acts of kindness.

Wordsworth

Days passed into weeks and William continued to feel betrayed by Master Bushrod. He had developed ties of loyalty to the Washington family and he had always believed that Bushrod was different somehow from the other southern plantation masters. But William knew now that he wasn't concerned about slaves. Their feelings were irrelevant to him.

"What's wrong with that son of yours, that William?" a disturbed Bushrod asked West several weeks after the sale of his slaves. William had avoided any contact with the master of Mount Vernon, and when forced into conversation, he answered Bushrod's questions in monosyllables.

West didn't know how to respond. Even now William remained upset over the selling of Little Tom. He decided that his master needed to hear the truth.

"Massa, William be still upset 'bout what happened to Little Tom. It gonna take some time, but he come 'round right soon enough," West explained.

Bushrod looked stunned. It never occurred to him that one of his servants would harbor animosity towards him, especially one of the Fords. He was contemplative before he responded, "That will be all, West," and went back into the library where he poured a large snifter of brandy.

It had taken time, but William eventually mastered the task of being polite in Bushrod's company. William grew, not just in breadth and height, but also in spirit and humanity that year. He was given more tasks of responsibility by Bushrod and began to adjust once again to plantation life.

The seasons faded one into another for several years without significant life-altering changes to the Ford family. It was a Sunday morning and the Ford offspring were in their cabin, sitting on stools pulled to a wooden table, engrossed in their Bible lesson. These lessons were usually conducted by William. He was now seventeen and the scholar of the family.

"Finish reading, Daniel," an exasperated William told his little brother.

"The Lord spoke unto Moses, go unto Pharaoh, and say unto him, thus saith the Lord, let my people go, that they may serve me." Closing the careworn Bible, young Daniel stated rebelliously, "I don't want to read no more."

"The word is "anymore," William corrected. He had been listening to his little brother read from the Good Book for the past several minutes. Daniel was eleven and the youngest of the Ford clan. He had gray eyes, a thin, straight nose, and curly black hair. Daniel's mind had been on fishing instead of how Moses was going to lead his people out of Egypt.

"William, we're all tired of reading," said chestnut-haired Jane. She was sixteen and favored William in looks—they both had their father's blue-gray eyes. The only sibling who wanted to read was little fourteen-year-old Julia. She enjoyed hearing stories from the Bible. Julia looked like a porcelain doll with her brown hair and grass-green eyes. She was almost the spitting image of her Grandmother Venus.

William released a long overdo sigh. For the last several months he had been helping them with their reading, even though they were taught by a tutor at the plantation school house a couple of times a week. He couldn't understand why his brother and sisters weren't interested in learning as much as he was. Resigned, he gave in.

"All right, we'll take a break."

Jumping up, Daniel grabbed his fishing pole. He flew past West on his way out. "Hi Papa, bye Papa!" Daniel hollered.

"Papa!" the girls screamed and ran to embrace their father. "Can you take us into Alexandria?" said Jane. "Mama needs to deliver the dresses she finished for Miss Josephine and she promised to buy some cloth for us while we're there."

"Baby girl, I can't be takin' you today 'cause Massa Bushrod be goin' to Richmond for a few months. I gots to help him with his packin' and he gots to tell me what he want done 'round here while he be gone."

"Can't William take us?" Jane asked.

William was on his way out of the cabin door. No way was he taking his sisters into town, especially for shopping.

Observing William's hasty retreat West asked him, "Son, will you take your sisters and your mama to Alexandria?"

Surrendering to the inevitable, William sighed audibly, "Oh, all right. But Jane, you better not ask me to go in and help you pick out fabric colors."

The girls giggled at his comment before exiting the cabin to let their mother know they were going to Alexandria.

Once his daughters left the room, West walked over to the table and sat down on the stool that Daniel had occupied earlier. "Son, you be keepin' a close eye on your sisters and mama when you be in town. I hear that them patrollers be stoppin' Negroes on the road and their free papers be taken from them. Some of them even been sold deep South. You know Samuel from the Peake plantation don't ya?"

William nodded.

"They take his daughter on her way back from Alexandria. Samuel be thinkin' she be sold to a brothel in New Orleans."

William's brow furrowed. "Why, they wouldn't dare stop us. Everybody knows the Fords of Mount Vernon," he stated with utter confidence. He had traveled with his father unhampered throughout the Alexandria countryside without the worry of patrollers or kidnappers many times and never had anyone even asked to see their free papers. Unless otherwise told, most strangers believed they were white.

The young don't be knowin' nothin' 'bout real life, mused West. "Son, we's got to be careful. You best be takin' all the free papers with you and be sure your sisters always be in your sight." West didn't think he was being too cautious with his request.

Not all blacks had the ability to travel as freely as the Ford family. The fugitive slave law was in effect in the South. It denied an alleged fugitive a hearing before a judge, the right to testify in his own defense or summon witnesses, provided heavy penalties for anyone attempting to help a runaway, and required all citizens to assist federal marshals or deputies in capturing fugitives. No black person was safe from the snares of the slave trade. Even legally freed blacks were in danger from kidnappers and bounty hunters selling them back into slavery.

The drive into Alexandria was uneventful. The city's streets were busy and the excitement of being there coursed through William's veins. Parking the wagon a little ways from Miss Josephine's shop, William secured the brake lever and the reins, then came around to help his mother and sisters down.

"William, we ain't gonna be too long," said his mother.

"Okay, Mama. I'll just go over to the general store." William had saved money for the longest time with the intention of buying new boots. Today he would purchase them.

Julia was becoming bored an hour later as she sat in the dress shop. Her mother was talking with her previous employer and Julia knew their conversation could last another hour. They had several bolts of fabrics spread out on a worktable. They were discussing the dress style Josephine wanted Priscella to make for one of her clients.

"Excuse me, Mama, Missus Josephine." Julia said, interrupting them. "Can I go outside and wait in the wagon with William?"

"Why, I guess that be fine. Tell William I'll be out shortly," her mother said before turning her attention back to her employer.

Julia walked over to the shop's entrance and paused. "Want to come outside with me, Jane?"

"No, I want to stay here with Mama." Jane was too absorbed with the bright colors and textures of the fabrics displayed in front of her and just waved her sister away.

Smiling, Julia turned and left the shop. A whisper of a breeze, arid yet sweet, teased the damp tendrils of hair at her temples. Outside of the dress shop, she stopped and took in all the excitement of the city. People strolled along the byways, and servants and tradesmen were going about their business. Fine carriages and other conveyances filled the streets. The idea of sitting in the wagon now seemed so mundane. A quick glance inside of the dress shop window revealed her mother and Miss Josephine still talking up a storm. Glancing towards their wagon, Julia noticed that William was nowhere in sight. She started towards it, but walked past instead. What would be the harm if she walked along the brick sidewalk for a while?

Julia did just that, glancing at the people and taking in the sights of Alexandria. She had been walking for several minutes when she heard a catcall and a whistle. Footsteps came running up behind her.

"Hey, little lady, what be the big hurry?" A man grasped Julia's arm and turned her around to face him and his two companions. The man holding her had a large scar down the length of one side of his face. He was older than the other two by several decades.

Too shocked to say anything, Julia stood mute. The man studied the frightened girl for a few minutes, then his dull, black eyes widened with some sort of vague recognition.

"Bowes, how long are you gonna stare at her?" one of his cronies hollered out.

"Who you be girl?" Bowes said with such vehemence, that Julia couldn't help wondering why.

"Julia. Julia Ford from the Mount Vernon plantation."

"You any kin to a mulatto woman named Venus?"

"Yes. She's-she's my grandmother."

"Well, well, well," he said mockingly. "Fellows, this be no white woman, but a slave girl. A high yella slut just like her bitch grand-mammy." He continued menacingly, "That grandmammy of hers got me fired from the best job I ever had over at Mount Vernon."

"Well, now I guess that changes things a bit," one of the other men sneered as he yanked her towards him. He was the largest of the three, with a scruffy black beard that hid half of his face. He looked like a wild animal, and smelled no better.

Julia was trapped between two of the three men. Fear swelled her throat. For the first time, it occurred to her just how far she had ventured from the dress shop. *Oh, why didn't I get into the wagon?* she thought with growing alarm.

Bowes' mouth curved in a tight, cruel smile. "There be an alley over there," he said looking to the right of where they were standing. "I say let's have a little fun with this whore."

As they started to drag her towards the secluded area, Julia finally let out a piercing scream. Bowes quickly cut it off by placing his large hand over her mouth? *Oh my God, what's going to happen to me now?* she thought with a sinking heart.

Bowes pressed his meaty hand firmly over her mouth and nose; almost making Julia lose consciousness. Her eyes rolled wildly, searching her surroundings for something or someone who might save her. Once in the alley, Bowes pushed her up against one of the filthy walls of a building. Her head was pressed hard into the brick wall. When he lifted her dress with his free hand, Julia knew that he was going to rape her here, against the wall. *Oh God, please help me?* she prayed frantically.

But before Bowes could do any more harm, a man appeared and said in a cultured but firm voice, "That will be quite enough, gentlemen."

The stranger was well dressed, in black pants, matching coat and a pristine white shirt. He carried a cane and wore a hat. The man's large black servant stood at this side, dressed in a similar fashion.

"Damn!" Bowes swore. This was the second time he had been interrupted from seeking his pleasure when it came to these high yella bitches.

Bowes said threateningly, "Mister, this be no concern of yours. We're just havin' a little fun here with this slave gal. Now why don't you take your fancy-dressed nigger and yourself out of here before you git yourself dirty."

The other two men who had accompanied Bowes into the alley laughed at the comments directed to the stranger.

"I said, step away," the man answered resolutely, not the least put off by Bowes' remarks.

"Boys, I think we'd better show this here gent what we do to anybody who puts their noses in what ain't their business." Stepping away from Julia, he and his friends turned towards the newcomers.

Julia slid towards the ground, her legs too weak to stand, and watched the scene unfold before her. The stranger and his servant removed their fancy jackets. They let them fall to the dirt ground, and faced the three men.

"Corrill, you take those two," the stranger said, pointing at the bearded man and his short comrade. "This one," turning his cool gray gaze towards Bowes, "is mine." He brushed a black curl away from his high forehead and readied his stance.

The servant, Corrill, crouched down to the ground, his long arms hanging loosely at his sides. His actions were like those of a primate. It was a fighting skill he learned in the West Indies before he was shipped to America.

"Well lookee here, Jeb, we gots us a real-life black monkey. I guess he wants us to throw him a banana," the large man retorted.

Jeb laughed, exposing a gap between two of his rotting teeth. The two men then circled around Corrill and charged him. As the men advanced upon the crouched man, he rolled to the side and kicked one in the head, did a back flip, landed on his feet, and struck the other man with a flying side kick. Both men were rendered unconscious in less than twenty seconds.

Bowes pulled a knife from his boot. It flashed evilly as a shaft of sunlight caught its sharp edge. His face purpled with rage and his eyes gleamed with hatred at the well-dressed stranger. The two men circled one another—gauging, testing each other, searching for any weakness on the other's part.

"Mister, you should have minded your own business," Bowes said. Spittle settled on the side of his mouth. "Now I got to cut your nose off for stickin' it in mine."

Then he lunged, but the stranger had been waiting for his move and jumped back. Bowes lashed out again, but before his knife could find its intended target, the stranger, with a stunning blow to Bowes' forearm, knocked the knife from his grasp. He grabbed Bowes' arm in a quick movement, turned and pinned it behind his back.

Bowes started screaming while the stranger pulled and bent his arm until an ugly popping sound came from his elbow. The wounded man fell to the dirt ground, keening in agony.

Looking around, the stranger saw the two downed men and Corrill kneeling in front of the frightened girl.

"How is she, Corrill?" he hollered, as he dusted off his pants and pulled on his discarded waistcoat.

"She be fine. A little shook up, but she be all right," his servant replied as he helped Julia to her feet.

For a moment they were the only two people in the alley as coal black eyes met teary, leaf-green ones. Julia smiled shakily at Corrill, showing a hint of two perfect dimples, and then turned to the stranger.

"I thank you sir, and your servant, for coming to my rescue. I truly don't know what I would have done if you hadn't come along."

"You're welcome, Miss—"

"Julia Ford. I live on the Mount Vernon Plantation. I'm in town with my mama, who is over at Miss Josephine's Dress Shop."

"Well, Miss Julia Ford, my name is Jonathan Tarrant, and this is my friend and servant, Corrill Rogers."

Julia studied Corrill once more. He was a muscular man, standing well over six feet. He also was the handsomest man Julia had ever seen. Corrill was in the process of putting on his waistcoat. After donning it, he glanced again at Julia.

Noticing his servant's obvious interest in the young girl, Jonathan said, "Corrill, why don't you escort Miss Julia here back to her mother."

"It be my pleasure." He then offered Julia his arm in a courtly gesture.

Turning towards Bowes, who was still moaning on the ground, Jonathan growled through gritted teeth, "Don't let me see your face again in Alexandria. I don't hold to rape of women, no matter their race." He turned his back on the downed man and strode towards the main street.

William was sitting in the wagon when he noticed Julia walking in his direction with a tall black man in fancy clothes. He jumped down from the seat and waited for them to approach him.

Spotting her brother, Julia broke from her escort's grasp and ran to him. She told William, how Corrill and his friend, Mr. Tarrant, had saved her from certain disaster. William was upset that he hadn't been around to protect Julia and he profusely thanked Mr. Rogers for his intervention on his sister's behalf. Priscella and Jane came upon the group a few seconds later.

When her mother walked up to the trio, Julia said with a huge smile, "Mama, this is Mr. Corrill Rogers. He helped me with a little problem a while ago and I was just introducing him to William."

Priscella knew there was more to Julia's 'little problem,' but decided to ask her daughter for details on their way back to Mount Vernon.

"It's nice to be meetin' you, Mister Rodgers. You be from 'round here?" Priscella inquired, taking in the fine cut of his clothes.

"Yas'am. I works for Mr. Tarrant who owns a plantation outside of Hampton. I come to Alexandria whenever he gots business here."

Directing his intent gaze from Julia to Priscella, Corrill ventured, "Miz Ford, I-I be askin' to visit your daughter when I be back this way, if'n that be all right with you."

Priscella was impressed with the man's demeanor, but she needed to make certain he was suitable to court her daughter. "William, help your sisters into the wagon," she ordered. "Mister Rodgers, would you step over here so we can talk private-like?" She was pointing to an area near the store-front.

Once they were out of hearing distance from the occupants in the wagon, she said, "Now I be understandin' that you be wantin' to court my daughter, but I gots to ask you a question." Looking directly into the man's intelligent black eyes, she said succinctly, "My daughter be free. You be a *slave* or a free man?"

Corrill was not surprised by her direct question. That these black folk were traveling without a massa in attendance spoke volumes as to their privileged status. Unfortunately, he had to answer truthfully. He didn't bow his head and answered with all the dignity he could muster, "I be a slave, ma'am."

Priscella didn't hesitate and replied, "Well, I be sorry then, Mister Rodgers. Any man who be wantin' to court my daughter, gots to be a free man."

"I understand, Missus Ford," he said quietly.

Priscella couldn't help noticing the disappointed look crossing his features. She hardened her heart anyway. She believed that she was doing the right thing for her daughter. In fact she knew she was.

Corrill walked Priscella back to the wagon and handed her in. He smiled briefly at Jane, who was sitting next to her sister on a blanket in the back of the wagon.

"Well, I guess I'd best be gettin' on back to Mister Tarrant. You all be careful on your way back to Mount Vernon." He nodded towards Julia, then went in the opposite direction.

"Mama, did you give him permission to see me again?" Julia asked hopefully.

"Julia, he be a slave."

Her mother didn't have to explain. Julia knew she would never give her permission to see Corrill again. The father of her children would have to be a free man. She had been told that from the time she was a small girl. She was subdued on the trip back to Mount Vernon.

Julia tearfully recounted her near calamity to her father once back in the safety of their cabin. She also told him that it wasn't William's fault that he had not protected her. West held her at arm's length as he scanned every inch of her.

"You be lookin' all right, but I know that don't mean nothin'," he murmured as he brushed her hair from her cheek.

"I'm fine," she murmured. "Truly I am."

Julia was still such a child. She viewed the world with fresh, naive eyes, West reflected. "Little girl, you be protected on this here plantation. You best 'member to never wander away from your mama or brother again," West admonished. Then he embraced her tightly, thanking God that she was all right.

The next several months remained uneventful until later that fall, in 1828, when West's surrogate father, Billy Lee, died. West, Cate, and William bled him during his illness, but to no avail. George

Washington's favorite servant was buried in the Mount Vernon slave cemetery next to West's grandmother and sister. As West watched the last shovel of dirt being thrown onto Billy Lee's grave, he wondered if he was ever going to become immune to the deaths of those he loved.

A tear rolled down his face and he thought sadly, *Nope, I don't reckin' so.*

Chapter 12

What must be, shall be.

Seneca

Bushrod had been away from the Mount Vernon plantation for several months when West wrote to him. He had been left in charge of the plantation and once a month he detailed in a letter to Bushrod what was happening in his absence.

Dear Master:

I'm goin' on with the house for the books and papers. The man that slate the house put it up for six dollars every ten feet. I have received your letter and will attend to the order. We have sickness in the family, my mother is very sick and old woman Dolly is crazy like she was two or three years past. George at the farm is sick. Mr. Roberts comments seedin' the rye on August 24th. I think that you had better write to him to know what time he will get the rye done. Timothy's seed has not been sewn yet and the grubin' is goin' on with four men. I like to know if I must get the scatllin' from Mr. Davies to prepare the garden. I hear that you intend buying the mules that Mr. Peake has to sell, but hear that they are too old. He been talkin' to me about it for fear I would tell that they were old. Please to yourself know that it would be cheatin' you. West Ford your humble servant.

West was concerned about his mother's health. Venus had caught a severe chest cold the previous winter and never seemed to rally from it. She had developed a persistent cough and her lungs ached with every wheeze. The plantation's healer, Cate, had been dosing her for months, but nothing seemed to help. Venus continued to cough up phlegm and lose weight.

"Mama, you gotta rest and be takin' your medicine," West said one day after witnessing her battle with a fierce fit of coughing. Doll had brought her a cup of Cate's tea to drink.

"I got to be takin' Miz Ann her breakfast," Venus said between coughs.

"I be getting' Jane to take it to her," West replied. He helped her sit down at the warming kitchen's table.

"Venus, you gots to drink your tea now so's you can get better," said Doll.

"I ain't drinkin' that nasty old tea, Doll. You drink it!" Venus' furrowed her forehead and her mouth grimaced with the thought of drinking down the foul brew.

"Ahs may be crazy, but ah's ain't crazy 'enoff to drink dat mess," Doll stated emphatically.

Rolling his eyes heavenward, West took the cup from Doll and handed it to his mother. "Come on now, Mama, drink up."

"Oh, all right, but I ain't gonna drink no more of this for the rest of the day."

Venus drank the liquid as quickly as she could, but the urge to gag was overpowering. She took deep, gasping breaths so she wouldn't throw it up.

Satisfied that his mother had complied with his wishes West said, "Mama, I got to go down to the boat dock to fetch Massa Bushrod. He's su'posed to be comin' back today." Walking towards the door that would take him outdoors he turned and uttered, "You be takin' it easy now, you hear me?"

Venus smiled at her concerned son. Not only was West an honorable man, he was a loving father. Every day Venus thanked the Lord that she was blessed with such a son.

On his way to the river, West thought about his position at Mount Vernon. He had been acting as the main foreman for Bushrod Washington for the past several years. Life was good for him and his family. He held a trusted position few white men had, and his children were free in a land where others of his race were not. West prayed daily that someday all of his people could have what he had. And he often wondered about the vagaries of fate that made some men free and others not. He couldn't change the way things were. But he still didn't like it.

West's major concern this day was for the health of his mother and the restlessness of his son, William. His mother was being cared for, but William was another matter. William was always talking about leaving Virginia and heading North where slavery was not accepted. West wanted what was best for all of his children and if William's decision was to leave Virginia, he would support him. He, however, could never leave the South because he would never leave his mother.

Anyway, no one could tend the Old General's tomb the way he did.

West pulled the wagon to the landing dock. A light mist had settled on the Potomac River, mottling the surface into a dull, brownish gray. As West waited for the boat's arrival, he thought about what he was going to ask Master Bushrod today. West had saved money from the small salary he had been receiving from his overseer's position. With it he was hoping to purchase his mother's freedom.

He watched as the boat came down the river to drop off its passenger. When he spied Bushrod, he waved and got down from the wagon. West noticed that his master was looking haggard and not as hardy as before he left on his trip.

"How is everything, West?" Bushrod watched him load his belongings into the wagon.

"Everything be fine, suh. Miz Ann sure gonna be glad to see you."

"As I will be to see her. How is your wife doing?"

"She be fine and the children be fine too. Mama now, she ain't been feelin' well much lately. Old Cate been dosin' her somethin' awful with her smelly potions and whatnot."

All the pleasantries settled, West climbed into the wagon after Bushrod and headed back to the mansion house. He didn't want to broach the subject of obtaining his mother's freedom while they were in the wagon. He would wait for a more opportune time.

At the mansion house, West said, "Massa Bushrod, I be wantin' to talk private like, when you got a moment."

Bushrod looked tired. "That will be fine, West. But for now, all I wish to do is visit with my wife. We'll talk soon."

Several weeks passed then months, but the timing never seemed quite right to discuss purchasing Venus' freedom. Bushrod had not been feeling well since his return to Mount Vernon and he did not leave his bedchamber much.

Venus' health rallied somewhat during the fall months in 1829. But all was not well with the Washington family. Master Bushrod Washington died that November.

West was at his master's side when he took his last breath. "He gone, Miz Ann," West said gently. Ann Washington's face was gray with grief. For the first time West noticed the webwork of lines that marred the white skin of her face. She looked so old. She had been very ill herself for the last several years.

"Miz Ann, let mama take you to your bedchamber now. I be showin' the doctor out."

Miz Ann nodded and allowed Venus to escort her from the room. Correspondence was sent out later that day informing family members and friends about the death of Judge Bushrod Washington. West was truly saddened by his death.

Bushrod was interred in the family tomb. After the funeral his last will and testament was read. Bushrod's nephew, John Augustine Washington II, was to inherit Mount Vernon after the death of Ann. Later that day, after all the guests had departed, John Augustine sent for West. When he entered the library, John Augustine was sitting behind the mahogany desk. He motioned West towards one of the brocade chairs.

"West, you know our family has appreciated all you have done for Mount Vernon in the past several years, and it seems that my Uncle Bushrod has made sure that your hard work and dedication have not gone unrecognized." John Augustine picked up a formal looking document, and read from it:

"Sixteenth, I give to West Ford the tract of land on Hunting Creek adjoining Mr. George Mason and that occupied by Dr. Peake, which I purchased from Noblet Herbert, deceased, which was conveyed to him by Francis Adams to him the said West Ford and his heirs, whatever appears by my ledger to be due to said West Ford is to be paid to him and it is my request that he will continue in his present situation and employment during the life of my wife, provided she wishes him to do so on the terms he is now living with me."

John Augustine placed the document on the desk and watched West, trying to gauge his reaction to the land grant. "Well, West, it seems you own property now. It looks like the tract is around 160 acres. Now that you have land, what are you going to do with it?"

West was in shock and it registered on his face. He inhaled sharply, trying to suck some air into his lungs. He realized he hadn't taken a breath since he heard the word 'land'. When John Augustine announced that Massa Bushrod had left him property, he experienced a moment of such incredible happiness that he couldn't speak. He didn't know if he wanted to jump up and down or fall to his knees and thank the Lord.

Finally, after several long moments, West remarked, "Massa John, I jes don't know what to be sayin' right 'bout now or what I'm gonna do yet."

"Well, you think about it for a couple of days. You might want to borrow one of the wagons and take your family to see the property. It's about two miles north of here."

"I'll do that; thank you, suh."

"West, we hope that you'll stay on and continue in your position here at Mount Vernon. I know that Miss Ann would like that very much."

"Massa John, this here be my home. I'll be stayin' here as long as Miz Ann wants me to."

John Augustine nodded in approval, stood, and handed West the deed to the property. He then shook West's hand in congratulation.

West ran all the way to his cabin and burst into the door. He spied his wife placing some wood into the fireplace. Quickly walking over to her, he grasped her around the waist, and swung her around and around while his children watched in bewilderment.

"West, put me down. What be the matter with you?" Priscella squealed.

"I gots land! Massa Bushrod done willed me some land!" Breathing with excitement, he went on, "It be 160 acres on Little Hunting Creek."

"Oh, my Lord!" Priscella shouted. Her legs were trembling. She went and sat down in the chair by their fireplace. "Why he give you land?" she said a moment later.

West still had a dumfounded look on his face when he answered. "I don't rightly know. Maybe he be tryin' to do right by me. He knew massa Geoge be my papa."

Julia and Jane went to their father and hugged him. William stood by, waiting for his chance to congratulate his sire. William, of all of the siblings, knew the importance of a black man owning land—especially in the South.

"When can we go see it Papa?" little Daniel asked.

"We be goin' on Sunday, right after church."

West was unable to take his family to view the property because Miz Ann died two days later. Once again the family was contacted and the mistress of Mount Vernon was put to rest in the family tomb.

West also had an uncompleted mission—his mother's freedom. Both Bushrod and now Miz Ann had died before he could purchase it from them. He would now have to negotiate the terms with John Augustine II when he next came to the plantation.

A long, cold winter on the Mount Vernon plantation kept John Augustine away from the estate. He was busy at one of his other properties and left the management of Mount Vernon to the now main overseer, West Ford.

It was spring and the season was a burst with its true colors. The last of the winter snow had melted and spring flowers were already blooming in the massive gardens at the plantation. West decided that it was the perfect time for the Ford family to visit their newly acquired property.

William drove the wagon, with his mother and grandmother sitting beside him. Julia, Jane, and Daniel rode in the back. West rode his horse to lead the way.

Their excitement overflowed when they actually drove onto their land. It was a large tract inland from the Potomac River, then known as

Puscattaway Neck. The Washingtons and other county families frequently traveled on the roads next to the tract, which lay between Alexandria and Richmond.

Jumping down from the wagon, William handed out his mother then his grandmother. His father was already riding the boundary of his property.

Priscella said to her mother-in-law, "I want to build our house over there." She was pointing to a clearing next to the creek. "It be high enough in case of floodin', but close enough to haul water to the house."

Venus nodded agreement. She thought with incredulity that her son was free and that he owned land. Never in all of her born days did she think that he would ever be given land. Deep in her heart she knew that the Ole General had made the gift to West through Bushrod, the same way he secured West's freedom from Hannah. *Thank you, Massa George, thank you,* she thought gratefully.

Venus never had the opportunity to travel around the countryside as West and his children did. She was still a slave. Massa Bushrod had not freed her upon his death. So this outing was a new adventure.

Venus gazed at the wooded glen in the distance. Then she assessed the lush green field she was standing in. This was her son's land. Yes, life was good, she reflected. Walking towards the creek she saw a scattered group of large, rounded boulders near the water's edge. Her sixty-plus-year-old body was exhausted more lately than usual, and those boulders looked like a good place to rest. What fun it would be to put her feet into the cool creek water, she thought with excitement. She untied the laces of her worn boots, took off her socks and eased her dress up her legs. Then she put her feet in the water.

God, it be feelin' so good to be alive, she said inwardly. Never had she felt so free. Cate's herbal medicines were working well and her cough was almost nonexistent. Venus turned her face toward the May sunshine, reveling in the warmth against her cheeks. *Yes, life be good,* she thought again.

The girls were setting out a table linen and placing the food on it when West rode back to the picnic site. He waved and smiled at his mother as he dismounted. He and Priscella then walked hand-in-hand to where they would build their house.

Venus watched her grandchildren, laughing because Daniel was trying to walk on his hands. But he kept falling and rolling. Venus chuckled out loud when William grabbed Daniel's legs and tried to help him stay upright, then flinched when she felt a sharp sting on her left ankle. A snake moved away to the middle of the creek. It had bitten her.

Why now, Lord? she questioned. She picked up her shoes and woolen socks and went to where her family was seated.

"Mama, I be just gettin' you a plate ready," said West.

Not wanting to ruin their good time, Venus said, "Son, I don't be wantin' to be spoilin' the picnic, but I ain't feelin' too well." Her eyes looked haunted when she continued, "I jes gonna go lie down in the back of the wagon for a spell. Walk with me son." She was beginning to get dizzy and she knew she didn't have much time.

"You okay, Grandma?" William asked, concern flashing in his light eyes.

"Yeh, boy. You jes 'member that I love you all and I be so glad I could share this day with you."

"Come on, Mama, let me help you to the wagon," said West as he took her arm. She was trembling, and he immediately knew that something was wrong. *As soon as we get back to Mount Vernon,* he thought, *I be makin' sure that Cate dose her again with those herbs for her chest.*

"Son, I be so proud of you," Venus said as West made her comfortable in the back of the wagon. "'Member…who your papa be. He was a great man and you be his son. Keep tellin' your children. Don't never be lettin' them forget. Promise me." Her thin fingers were digging in his forearm.

"Yes, Mama," West replied tensely. He became even more alarmed when he noticed that she was breathing harshly and that her skin was clammy.

Priscella walked up to the wagon and saw the pallor on her mother-in-law's face. "West, I think we best be gettin' your Mama back to the cabin."

"I was just thinkin' the same thing." He studied his mother's wan face. "Tell the others to come on."

Priscella touched West's shoulder and turned to gather the family.

Climbing into the back of the wagon, West cradled his mother's now-sweating brow onto his lap. Priscella took up the reins, Julia and Jane riding next to her. Daniel rode behind William on the horse.

Venus was almost unconscious when they pulled up to the Mount Vernon stable. West carried her to his cabin and had William fetch Cate.

Cate ministered to Venus for several long minutes before she noticed the swelling on Venus' left ankle. She knew what the red-purplish bruise on her leg meant. A snake had bitten Venus, and most of the snakes around the countryside were poisonous.

"You needs to go get your man, Priscella. Venus ain't got much time left." She pointed to the fang marks that were deep and purpling.

When West entered, Cate quickly told him what had happened to his mother. She went on in a matter-of-fact voice, "West, I be sorry, but your mama be dyin', and there ain't nothin' nobody can do about it."

West's throat tightened up and he was finding it difficult to breathe. *Oh Lord no—not my mama*, he thought with torment. His eyes closed briefly with the shock of Cate's pronouncement. With a shaky hand, he pulled a chair next to the bed and stroked his mother's forehead. "I be here, Mama. Can you hear me?" he asked.

"W-West?" Venus' face was dry and her breathing so labored that her chest almost rose off the pallet with each breath.

"Yes, Mama."

"Say one of them p-prayers you be done learned."

His voice cracking, West began, "The-the Lord be my shepherd. I shall not want. He be makein' me to lie down in the green fields; he be leadin' me beside the still waters. He be restorin' my soul. He be leadin' me in the paths of righteous for his name's sake." Taking his mother in his arms, he cradled her to his chest and continued, "Yea, though I walk through the valley of the shadow of death, I be fearin' no evil, for thou art with me. Thy rod and thy staff they be of comfort to me. Thou be preparin' a table before me in the presence of mine enemies; thou anointest my head with oil and my cup be runnin' over. Surely, goodness and mercy shall follow me all the days of my life, and I be dwellin' in the house of the Lord forever."

West sat for long minutes holding his mother, his last parental link in his arms. He tried to imagine a life without her. She had always been there for him. He held her tight, as if by doing so it would keep her spirit from leaving her frail body.

Venus knew she was dying. In the last convulsion of life she opened her eyes and looked up into the tear-streaked face of her son. Lucid, she reached out to comfort him, but her arms could not respond. Then she felt her soul rise from her body.

"Mama? *Mama!*" West shouted.

West knew she had slipped away where she couldn't hear him, and every instinct within him screamed denial. He shook her lightly at first, and then with growing urgency in his desperation to bring her spirit back into her body. His beautiful, loving, hard-working mother, a woman who had never spoken an unkind word against the white man who had fathered him, was dead.

Priscella, tears spilling down her cheeks in silent misery, left the room. She would tell the other family members about their grandmother. She also wanted to give West some privacy with Venus before she prepared her body for burial.

The Mount Vernon blacks attended the graveside services. They were dressed in simple garments made from rough cotton; their hands callused from a lifetime of hard labor. The servants sang a sad Negro spiritual as an expression of their grief, as Venus was well-liked.

William laid a yellow tulip on the simple, pine box coffin and murmured in an aching voice, "I will always love you, my grandmother."

The other grandchildren followed suit, placing daffodils and tulips on Venus' coffin, until only one person remained. West stood mute as he watched his mother being lowered into the shallow grave in the slave cemetery. He was so remorseful because she was free only in spirit, not in body. West never had the opportunity to inform her about her eventual freedom.

"West," a gentle voice said. Looking up, he saw that it was his wife who had spoken. "I know your mama be wantin' you to be happy for her, happy that she be free at last. She be in heaven now with Jesus and his angels and someday you be meetin' up with her again."

West felt like someone was squeezing his heart and he couldn't form an answer. Priscella took his arm, and with his family gathered around him, they escorted him back to their cabin.

Later that evening, when Priscella and he were alone and comforting one another, West whispered, "Mama told me once that everythin's gotta change. And I wish to God, still to this day, that nothin' else is gonna change in my life. But nothin'—nothin' stays the same. Every day somebody be dyin' and somebody else be born." He took Priscella's warm hand into his and squeezed it tightly. "The only thing that I be sure of, is my love for you."

When his family members were finally asleep and he lay awake, he thought about his mama in that cold, cold grave and he realized that he had the rest of his life to forget the pain of her death.

He also had the rest of his life to remember it.

Chapter 13

Liberty! Liberty! How many crimes are committed in thy name?

Madame Roland

On August 21, 1831, in Southampton County, Virginia, Nat Turner, known as the "Black Prophet," and seventy other slaves went on a two-day rampage in a quest for freedom. The slave 'army' burned everything in their path. Nat Turner's master, Joseph Travis, was killed during the revolt, along with sixty other whites. Turner's ultimate plan was to organize an uprising of all the slaves in Virginia. And to do this, he planned to take over the arsenal in Richmond to arm an army of hundreds of runaway slaves.

From the time Turner was born, his life had been in turmoil. His own mother, transported from Africa to Virginia, had attempted to kill him as a child to save him from the fate of slavery. His father, after countless attempts, eventually escaped back to Africa. All Turner ever prayed for was to be free.

The Turner revolt rocked the South and led to the adoption of even more rigid slave codes. More than a hundred blacks were killed following the insurrection. Many slaves and free blacks would not venture too far outside the boundaries of their plantations for fear of reprisals by vengeful whites.

In spite of the grave danger, West knew that he had to travel off the protected Mount Vernon grounds during those fateful weeks. He and his family were in their cabin, and the subject of their dilemma arose during their conversation.

"We gots to go and register our freedom. Too many of our people done been killed, Cella." A muscle ticked in West's lean jaw before he continued, "The children got to go too."

"I be afraid we be hurt, maybe even killed if'n we go into Alexandria right now," Priscella replied fearfully. Her green eyes were tinged with worry.

West massaged the back of his neck in a weary gesture before replying. "This country be a fearful place to live in and even free Negroes gots to be careful now. And long as there be slavery, there's gonna be insurrections, because all men gots the right to be free. And because we're free, we got to go register."

On October 17, 1831, leery Ford family members went into Alexandria to register their freedom. The trip started uneventfully, as many of the county's citizens recognized the clan and left them in peace. It was those who didn't know them that disquieted West. When they reached the courthouse on that brisk fall afternoon, West took Priscella's warm hand in his large, firm one and together with their children, they entered the red brick building.

"Step on up here to the desk," the clerk said, waving them forward. The desk was cluttered with papers and books. The clerk had brown hair everywhere on his head except for the very front, where only a few sparse hairs stood vigil. His wire-rimmed glasses made his blue eyes take on the appearance of an owl.

West said, "I be here to register my family's freedom."

"Waal, you-all come to the right place." Reaching over a pile of papers, the clerk picked up a large leather-bound book and went on,

"This here book be the Free Black Register. I'm just gonna record some information about each of you here." Looking at the handsome group he asked, "Which one of you all is gonna be first?"

West stepped forward. "My name be West Ford. Here be my free papers," he said handing them to the man.

The clerk read over the documents and then glanced up at West. "You were freed by the Washington family over at Mount Vernon?"

"Yessuh."

The clerk studied West more closely. Then with a knowing glint in his bird-like eyes he ventured, "Boy, did anybody ever tell you who you resemble?"

"Yessuh, I be asked that question all the time." West was not going to give the nosey man any further information.

The clerk shrugged and dipped the point of his long-plumed quill into an inkwell. Then he said in a loud voice as he wrote, "The bearer hereof West Ford a yellow man about forty-years of age, five-feet eight and a half inches, high pleasant countenance, a wrinkle resembling a scar on the left cheek, a scar on the left corner of the upper lip, is a free man emancipated by the last will and testament of Hannah Washington, as appears from an original Register heretofore granted by the County Court of Fairfax."

Next the clerk registered William. In the same sing-song voice he said, "The bearer hereof, William, who calls himself William Ford, a yellow boy about nineteen years of age, five-feet seven and a half inches high, a large scar on the left arm occasioned by a burn, is the son of Priscella, a free woman manumitted by Isaac McPhereson as appears on a certificate of George C. Washington on file in my office. Whereupon, given under my hand on this 17th day of October, 1831."

The same process went on with Priscella, Daniel, Jane and Julia taking account of their physical appearances, height, age, and any distinguishing scars. When they were all registered they left the building in a lighter mood.

Once outside of the courthouse, they encountered an old acquaintance—Corrill Rodgers, the man who helped Julia several years before. He was in Alexandria on business with his master when he saw the Ford family. He immediately came over to them.

"Hello! It be good to see y'all again." The family members could see that he had eyes only for Julia.

"Papa, this is Corrill Rodgers," Julia said brightly. Noting her mother's dour expression, she added, "Mama you remember him, don't you?"

"Yes, I be 'membering Mister Rodgers all right," she said, watching her daughter's animated face.

"Please, just call me Corrill."

"Corrill, I be wantin' to thank you for helpin' my daughter," said West as he shook the man's hand. "I don't know what would have happened to her, if'n you didn't come by when you did."

"You don't have to be thankin' me, suh." Smiling boldly at Julia, he went on: "It be my pleasure."

Clearing her throat, Priscella interjected, "Well, now it be nice seein' you again Mister Rodgers, but we gots a long drive ahead of us."

She purposely called him mister. It was her way of indicating he was still not welcome to court her daughter. Priscella then began shooing her children into the wagon.

Julia lingered for a few extra moments, her heart glowing from her luminous green eyes. "I hope I'll see you again, soon, Corrill."

"I be hopin' that too, Miz Julia."

With the help of Corrill, she climbed back into the wagon. Corrill's heart was heavy as he watched it pull away from him.

A few weeks after the Ford's trip to the Fairfax courthouse, Nat Turner was caught and tried for rebellion. West and William were in Richmond on Mount Vernon business on the day of Nat's trial. They stood in the back of the crowded courtroom, as it was packed inside and out with people who came from all over Virginia to see the Black Prophet tried.

West and his son listened as Turner spoke intelligently to the judge when he was asked about his arraignment.

"I'm not guilty because I felt no guilt for what I did," he said with quiet dignity.

"Hang the nigger!" one angry man shouted after his statement. Another shouted, "No! I say we burn him!"

The courthouse erupted with shouts of violence. The judge banged the cudgel on the dais and shouted, "Order! Order in this court, or I'll clear everyone out!"

No one seemed to listen to the judge's commands.

"Son, we need to get out of here, now!" West said. They elbowed their way out amid the hostile crowd. Once outside they hurried to their wagon and headed back to Mount Vernon and safety.

They learned later in the *Alexandria Gazette* that Nat Turner was found guilty and hanged on November 11th. After his hanging, his body was given to surgeons for dissection. The surgeons skinned him like a rabbit. Later souvenir money pouches were made from his skin.

The family stayed close to the plantation for some time after that.

Because of the Nat Turner rebellion, an elaborately detailed body of laws emerged, known as the 'Black Codes.' These codes were intended to regulate every aspect of a black person's life. The death penalty was imposed on blacks, free or slave, for certain offenses including rebellion. West had heard that some defiant slaves in Richmond had been burned at the stake. Other stories circulated through the slave telegraph of drownings, hangings and starvations.

The codes also stated that blacks could not own property or buy or sell goods, and were denied standing in court. Blacks could not possess firearms. To prevent a system of signaling, slaves were not allowed to beat drums, blow horns, or leave their plantations without written permission. They were forbidden to assemble, learn to read or write, or even worship. In Virginia there were seventy-one crimes for which a black person could be executed.

West was allowed to keep his property, though the new law forbade it. The power behind the Washington family name made sure of that. West enlisted the services of the Mount Vernon field servants to help him and his sons clear his property, plant crops, and build a house. The house had a fireplace large enough to stand in, two rooms, and a loft for sleeping. The abode had two windows and thick, wooden shutters to protect them from bad weather. A small, welcoming front porch ran across its width. On that porch sat a wooden rocker that West had spent months carving. In 1833, West sold his original land grant and purchased a 214-acre tract of land called 'Gum Springs' from one Samuel Coolard. Now he owned property valued at $4,280.00. He was considered a rich man, the richest black man in the county at the time.

Several days after the transaction, West and William traveled to Richmond. It was there that William met his future wife. Her name was Henrietta Bruce and she was one of ten children. Henrietta's father, Daniel, had a position as a pony express mail carrier and his family was fairly well off financially. The Bruce family were members of a segment of the population known as 'free people of color.' Like the Fords, they were able to move freely throughout the South because their racial identity was not evident.

William met Henrietta at a gathering at her family's home during one of their evenings in the city. As William sat across from her at dinner, he could hardly eat the honey-glazed ham, candied yams, corn on the cob, green beans and steaming biscuits that filled his plate. All he could do was stare at Henrietta. Her skin complexion was just a touch darker than his. She possessed skin known in the South as 'high yella'— skin with a hint of yellow or golden glow. Her eyes were a dark brown and they seemed to dance when she smiled, which she was doing now as she asked him a question. For the first time in his life, William was tongue-tied. Henrietta was so beautiful that William couldn't seem to use his brain and tongue at the same time to speak, much less carry on an intelligent conversation. He dared not talk for fear he'd babble.

Henrietta was immediately attracted to William. He was so hand-some. She tried to open him up to a conversation, but he seemed distracted. Since it was difficult to talk with him, she contented herself by studying his features while he ate his dinner. Never had she seen chestnut hair on a black man. Henrietta then noted William's high, broad forehead and his slightly flared nose. His lips were thin, but firm. But his most fascinating feature was his blue-gray eyes, at the moment filled with fiery intensity as he caught her staring at him. Henrietta thought her skin would begin steaming at the look he bestowed on her. She flashed him a shy smile and then stared down at her plate.

After dinner, William was finally able to find his tongue and they conversed for several hours before he left, promising to visit her again on his next trip to Richmond. That evening in her bedchamber Henrietta thought about the young man from Mount Vernon. For all William's attractiveness, there was something lonely about him. Suddenly she didn't want him to be lonely anymore. Later she would realize that what she thought was loneliness in William was really isolation.

Two years later, in 1835, William and Henrietta were married in the same church as West and Priscella. It was truly a love match, as the couple couldn't look away from each other during the ceremony or reception.

Many free Negroes attended their wedding. Among them were the Smiths, a family that had been freed by George Washington and had remained on the plantation. Their son, Porter, had a crush on Jane for several years.

Priscella smiled at the pair as she watched them whispering to one another. This was a union she could accept because Porter was a free man. She sought out her younger daughter and saw her sitting alone.

What could she do about finding Julia a husband? Priscella pondered. Her task would not be easy because Julia had lost her heart to a slave.

Later that evening, in the cabin provided for the newlyweds on the Mount Vernon Plantation, William whispered fervently, "I love you so much, Henrietta. I have been lonesome for you all my life."

Henrietta's eyes blazed with happiness at hearing her husband's declaration. Gazing at him with all the love in her heart, she softly murmured, "William, I promise that you will never be lonesome again."

But fate has a way of breaking promises.

Chapter 14

There are two things to which we never grow accustomed—the ravages of time and the injustice of our fellow-men.

Talleyrand

Disturbing the dead. It was a task he didn't want to do, especially, when it was disturbing the grave of his father. West was asked in 1837 to help George H. Duffey check the coffins in the tomb at Mount Vernon. Duffey had been hired by the Washington family to measure for building a new tomb.

When Duffey first met West Ford, he was a little startled by his physical appearance. West was now white-haired and fashioned his hair as George Washington had. Granted, his features were slightly different and his skin a little darker from his days in the sun, but the resemblance to his sire was evident. But it was his striking gray/blue eyes that startled the younger man most. Once Duffey recovered from the shock of meeting West, the two men headed for the tomb.

"I ain't been in the tomb for years now," West told the man as they walked down the path to the cemetery. "I be keepin' the grounds picked up though and my sons also help with all the flowers we get here."

"Do people still send flowers?" Duffey inquired.

"My Lord, yes. Not a week be goin' by that we don't get some kind of offerin' for the Old General."

When they arrived at the vault door, West was unable to open it because he had hurt his right hand repairing a broken wagon wheel, and he asked Duffey for help. After the tomb door was open, West lit a kerosene lamp and held it high. They found the coffins pretty much decayed. He placed the lantern on one of them.

"This here be Massa Washington's" he said.

The casket's lid was almost rotten in parts. Lifting it, West could see his father's remains, and it hurt his heart.

Duffey, looking over West's shoulder, tried not to shudder at what lay before him. The winding sheet that covered the body had decayed and the facial skin was sunken and a ghastly gray. But the remains were still recognizable as George Washingtons.

West and Duffey recorded the measurements for the new coffins. Since Duffey was going into Alexandria, he offered to take the dimensions to Lawrence Lewis, who was still responsible for managing the Mount Vernon estate.

"I best be gettin' some wood and nail over these here coffins tomorrow 'till the new ones be made and the Old General be moved to the new tomb," West remarked as they left the grave site.

"Yes, I think that will be a good idea. We don't want any more moisture to seek into the coffins. Let's go up to the main house so that I can write a letter to Lewis." Once in the library, Duffey took out pen and paper and wrote:

> "West Ford not being able to open the door of the vault at Mount Vernon employed me to do it for him, and to assist him in executing your order, and requested me to make a correct drawing and send it to you, which I have done to the best of my ability. On the account of a leak in the vault the

coffins are very much decayed some of them entirely so, the case of the general's coffin was nearly gone, the lid of the mahogany coffin and the head part are quite rotten, the upper part of the lid is entirely tumbled to pieces so as to leave the lead coffin naked at part. West has got the plate and would have written to you himself, but it was late in the evening, and as I was coming to Alexandria he thought it might expedite the letter by getting it sooner to the Post Office than he could have sent it. You can rely on the accuracy of the drawing, as West was very particular in the measurement and I stood and set it down."

West took William and Daniel into the tomb the very next morning to help him with the repairs. Daniel didn't like it much—being around the dead. At every imagined noise, he began jumping so, that they sent him back to the cabin. In 1837, George Washington's remains were placed into a marble sarcophagus inside of a new tomb area, along with the other members of his family.

Life went on without any major hitches for a couple more years for West Ford and his family. But it became a time of celebration when William's first child, Constance, was born. A little more than a year later, came Hannah. Constance was fair, Caucasian in features. Hannah was born with a darker skin tone, almost a café au lait shade.

William wished his daughters had been born with a darker skin color. He had always felt that his white skin caused him to live in limbo. He was neither black nor white, but a person of color. This connotation had plagued him since he was a child. The darker blacks on the plantation respected him, but they believed he was more white than black.

They couldn't see past his white skin.

The Washingtons treated him special, but they would never acknowledge him as true family.

They could not see past his black blood.

William felt that he couldn't fit in fully with either race.

He and his father were at the dining table in their house at Gum Springs. William was reading a copy of the *Richmond Enquirer.*

"Papa, this paper is full of ads for runaways. Listen," his deep voice intoned, "Fifty-dollar reward. Ran away from the subscriber, his Negro man, Pauladore, commonly called Paul. I understand General R. Y. Hayne has purchased his wife and children from H. L. Pinckney, Esquire, and has them now on his plantation at Goosecreek, where, no doubt, the fellow is frequently lurking."

William put the newspaper down and looked intently at his father. "I can't live in the South anymore, Papa. I can't stand the injustice of slavery. Henrietta is about to give birth to our third child and I don't want my children growing up in this hate-filled place."

He rose from the chair, the wooden legs scraping loudly against the plank floor. Then he began to pace the small room, his hands jammed in his pants pockets.

Watching his son, West was torn on how to respond. He found it difficult to look upon a face so like his own and see the restlessness reflected there. He knew his son would never be content at Mount Vernon. William was educated and intelligent. Besides, the North was calling to him.

West drew in a very slow, deep breath and shut his eyes for a moment. He exhaled and said, "We ain't hated here, son."

"That's because we live on Mount Vernon! We've been sheltered from the abuse of slavery here." Rubbing the back of his neck in a weary gesture, he continued heatedly, "Julia can't find a man to marry because all the free ones she meets are too young or too old and the one she loves is a slave. Jane won't marry Porter Smith because she feels sorry for Julia. And Daniel has no ambition in life beyond fishing and hunting. Papa, we've got to leave this place and make a new life in the North," he entreated.

"William, son, everybody gots to find their own way in this here life. And you be right about what you be sayin' 'bout your sisters and brother. I'm gonna talk to your mama about Julia and Corrill. I be thinkin' Julia needs to be makin' her own choice on who she be wantin' to marry. Now, Daniel still be young and got some time to be makin' his decision on what he wants to do with his life. As for Jane, she done told me jes this mornin' that she and Porter gonna get married come spring.

Gazing intently at his son he said with feeling, "As for me, my life and my soul be here at Mount Vernon. All who I am be here. I know you don't be feelin' the same way about this place as I do." West's blue-gray eyes were earnest now as he went on, "But *I* own land. Land that some day I'm gonna be dividin' up for you and your brother and sisters. This be our home, but I will understand if you want to make yours somewheres else."

William didn't answer right away. He wanted to take his mother and father away from the hatred of the South. He wanted them all to move to New York. So, he would bide his time for now.

"I know this is my home, Papa. I just don't know what I'm going to do yet," William stated quietly.

William had to travel into Richmond the following week. Henrietta's mother, Hannah, wanted to help with the birth of her daughter's third child and William was bringing her to Mount Vernon.

Traveling on southern roads continued to be dangerous for blacks. Any runaway slave was hunted until caught, because slaves continued to be the main source of the South's economy. A prime field hand was valued anywhere from five hundred to twelve hundred dollars. Because they were financial assets, slave owners lived in perpetual danger of having their capital run away, and took extreme measures to have their slaves returned to them.

A patrol system was set up to catch runaways. The patrollers, had the job of enforcing the black codes in the cities and off the plantation grounds in the rural sections. Their services were procured at the request of slaveholders. The patrollers had the right to jail any black person who could not give a satisfactory account of themselves, and to search slave cabins for books, stolen goods, concealed runaways, incendiary literature, and to enforce the nine o'clock curfew for blacks.

William took his free papers on his trip to Richmond as a precaution, but he was not stopped in route. He was, however, dismayed at a sign that was erected on the Alexandria stagecoach road advertising slave catchers. Stopping his wagon in front of the advertisement, he began to read out loud, noticing the spelling errors as he went along:

No Tis—The undersind taiks this method of makkin it none that he has got the best NIGGER HOUNDS in the state, and is always redy to ketch niggers at the best rates. My hounds is well trained, and I have had 15 yere experience. My rates is 10 dollurs per hed if ketched in the beate where the master lives; 15 dollurs in the country, and 50 dollurs out of the county.
DAN MCCOWAN
N.B. Planters should taik panes to let me know, while the niggers tracks is fresh, if they want quick and a good job.

William sighed and shook his chestnut-colored head. The inhumanity of slavery was eating him alive. How could he live in comfort at Mount Vernon when others of his race were worked like beasts of burden? He felt helpless. Making a clicking sound with his mouth and a snap of the reins, he set the wagon in motion.

Several days later, William was waiting outside the post office in Richmond for his father-in-law. The clerk inside told him that Mr. Bruce would be picking up the mail for his delivery shortly. William took out a kerchief and mopped his damp brow. It was hotter than Hades, he reflected as he looked at the cloudless blue sky then back towards the street. In the distance, he saw a man coming towards the post office, carrying several white sheets of paper that appeared to be some kind of notice. The man had dirty, blond hair that was long and shaggy. A full beard covered the lower half of his face. As he neared William, he handed him one.

"Suh, my name be McCowan, this here be a notice on my services. You ever need one of your niggers ketched, I be the one to call." He then walked on down the road, handing his notices to anyone who would take one.

William felt chilled. The paper in his hand dropped with a flutter to the ground. He continued to watch as the grubbily dressed man walked toward a hitching post where he had tied several hounds. The hounds were barking, snarling and jumping as a black woman walking with a white charge went past.

Daniel Bruce came upon William unawares as he stood outside of the post office. Noticing where William was gazing, he remarked quietly, "It's getting bad, son. The South ain't a fit place for free Negroes. There has even been talk of the South's secession from the Union because of the issue of slavery."

"I know, I have been reading the newspapers whenever I can," William replied as he directed his attention to his father-in-law. He took in Mr. Bruce's keen facial features. It was easy to decipher where his wife had gotten her looks. She and her father shared the same light skin tone and brown eyes.

The men started walking over to the wagon William had come to fetch him in. He told his father-in-law before stepping upon the seat, "I've been thinking about moving North, sir," William ventured.

"If war breaks out, that's probably a safe place to be. You know my older daughter, Mary, lives there with her husband.

"I believe Henrietta mentioned that to me once."

"One of my good friends works for a printing office. I'm sure he can probably give a good word about you with the owner."

"If I go, I'm going to need help in securing a position; thank you sir."

Changing the subject Mr. Bruce said, "My wife is anxious to see Henrietta. What you say we head on home and eat a little something before you head back to Mount Vernon?"

The two went to William's wagon and left for the Bruce home. A couple of weeks later, Henrietta delivered a son at the Mount Vernon estate. It had been a hard birth for her. The baby boy was broad-shouldered, with a large head and weighed over eight pounds. William and Henrietta decided to name him John, after John Augustine Washington the present owner of Mount Vernon. John had a caramel-colored skin complexion and had inherited his Grandmother Venus' dimples. William was a proud father and spent his spare time hovering over the infant.

"That be a fine son you got there," West remarked, as he watched William cradle his child in his arms.

"He sure is that, Papa." *And I'm going to give him a better life up North,*" thought a solemn William.

Someday soon.

Chapter 15

When you find that flowers and shrubs will not endure a certain atmosphere, it is very significant to the human creature to remove them out of that neighborhood.

Mayhew

It was hot, still so sweltering that William had to leave his cabin that July evening to cool off. The humidity from the daylight hours remained high and he couldn't sleep. He sat on the step leading to his home and marveled at the scattering of stars through the trees overhead. It was a bright evening, the full moon casting a silvery glow on the trees and ground. Silence surrounded the plantation, with only an occasional hooting of an owl and the chirping of insects.

His wife and three children were asleep inside. He chuckled to himself, thinking about the mischief those three children could get into. William thanked God everyday for them. The midwife told him after the birth of John that Henrietta would never be able to have another child. Even with that pronouncement, he still felt blessed.

Looking about the quiet grounds, he reviewed events of the last several months. His sister Jane had gotten married in the spring and was expecting a child later in the year. His mother, however, was still being stubborn when it came to allowing Julia to be courted by a slave. It was a shame, because Corrill Rodgers was a good man and couldn't change the circumstances of his life.

William could understand his mother's adamant stand against her children marrying a person who was not free. Priscella knew that Corrill could be sold away from her daughter at a moment's notice, and she didn't want that kind of hurt for Julia. William couldn't help but remember the pain he suffered the day his childhood friend, Little Tom, was sold. But he still felt sorry for Julia. William decided that he would speak to his mother in the morning about his youngest sister. Maybe he could make her change her mind about Corrill.

Looking around at the silent cabins he detected some movement by one that sat alone in the distance. It was Billy Lee's old cabin. William saw the house servant, Rufus, ushering a man he couldn't identify into the vacant structure. William's curiosity was aroused and he decided to go investigate. He crept towards the door and could hear muffled whispers and movement coming from inside. William soundlessly approached the window and peered in. Rufus had lit an old tin kerosene lamp and was in deep conversation with a black man. By the stranger's tattered and dirty clothes, he knew the man was a runaway. William decided he needed to know what was transpiring, and stepped inside.

When the fugitive saw William, he stood mute. William could tell by his frozen facial expression that he thought he was a white man.

"Mr. William…" Rufus began, but then didn't say anymore, at loss for an explanation.

"What's going on here, Rufus?"

"Mr. William, dis man need our help." The slave glanced at the open door, ready to flee.

Noticing the slave was maneuvering toward the room's one window, Rufus said, "Don't be scared none. This man can help you." Rufus knew how William felt about slavery.

The runaway had only one arm, the empty shirt sleeve pinned up at his shoulder. William was aware that the legal punishment for runaway slaves was branding an 'R' for runaway on the offender's cheek, or cutting off a slave's fingers and hands, toes and feet, ears, and arms. Many masters felt that branding or cutting worked as a better deterrent than beatings for the most determined runners. Most beatings one could forget, but how far could a slave get with a brand on the face or a missing foot? This man, it seemed, had already tasted his master's wrath. William knew that if it were in his power, he would not let this man be further punished for wanting his freedom.

He would help him.

William said with quiet authority, "Rufus, run to the cook house and get this man something to eat. Stuff some extra food in a linen napkin and put it in the wagon near the stable. Get yourself back here as soon as you can. And Rufus, don't wake anyone or say anything to anyone."

"Yas'm, Mister William." Rufus left.

To the hunted man, William said, "I'm going to help you. What's your name?"

"My name be Elijah," the man said. He didn't fully trust this white man. He had to stay alert, though he hadn't slept in days.

"Elijah, I'm going to help you get away from this plantation. There are many people in the South who help runaways escape up North." Seeing that the man was still leery, William continued calmly, "First I'm going to take you outside and show you a star, the North Star. Whenever you travel at night, you need to follow it. It will guide you to the North and freedom. Gesturing for the man to follow, he said quietly, "Come."

Stepping outside, William gazed into the blue-black sky arched overhead, its cloudless depths studded with thousands of stars. He searched the night sky until he found the constellation he was looking for. Taking the man by his shoulder, he raised his hand and pointed, "There it is, the brightest star in the sky."

William waited a moment for the man to sight the star. Seeing him nod his head, he went on, "The route to the North will be dangerous. But there are those who will help guide your way, both Negro and white."

They heard rustling noises coming from the trees and William waved the man back into the shadows. Several seconds later the bright moonlight revealed that it was Rufus. He had a cloth napkin in his hand.

"I bring de food, Mister William," he whispered urgently. His black eyes darted around the area, searching for the overseers.

"Good. Feed him, and at first light I'll come around with the wagon. I'm going to take him to Richmond, where I know of people who can help him make his way North."

"It be dangerous, Mister William. The patrollers be lookin' for this man," Rufus said worriedly.

"I know, but it's the only way. He'll never get far from this plantation on foot."

William watched as the two entered the cabin, then he turned back to his. He didn't know how he was going to fall asleep. He had much planning to do.

William knew people who worked with the Underground Railroad in Richmond. The Underground Railroad had reached the grassroots level with the development of thousands of agents in the abolition movement. Many influential white abolitionists denounced slavery and were attacked as traitors because of their refusal to affiliate with any political party. They believed that the U.S. Constitution supported and protected slavery, and this led to the charge that they were disrupters of the Union. There was also an intricate support system of free blacks that was also crucial to the movement.

At dawn, William told Henrietta his plans. "Tell no one what I'm about. Don't even tell papa. That way no one can be blamed if I'm caught. I should be back in three to four days," he said as he packed a small satchel with the items he needed for this trip. He put his free papers into the breast pocket of his best jacket.

Henrietta, who stood mute with alarm while he packed, now shrieked, "Please tell me you aren't going to do this. You'll be caught and hanged!" Poking a finger at her temple she continued, "You can't be thinking straight!"

"Henrietta, I have to do my part for the cause of freedom."

"*The cause*?" Henrietta's voice had risen. Her brow furrowed as she elaborated, "Your *cause* is here—with me and our children."

Clutching her shoulders with his two hands, William looked down into her worried eyes and said with passionate conviction, "How can I live here on this plantation knowing that one of our race will be maimed or killed in his flight for freedom? *Freedom that we have.* This is something I have to do. You know that, don't you?" His eyes beseeched her for understanding.

"I know," Henrietta sighed.

"Tell them up at the big house I had to go to Richmond for supplies for the gardens." Seeing the alarm still registered on her face, he said calmly, "I'll be careful. I promise." Then he kissed her long and hard. Holding her at arms' length for a quiet moment, he fixed her image in his mind, then turned and left the cabin.

William had Elijah lie down in the bottom of the wagon and covered him with several old horse blankets and straw. He then placed several empty barrels next to his prone body to help camouflage his form. William noticed that the field workers were just rising to begin their labors. Driving the wagon slowly away from the stables, he left the plantation. No one took much notice of his departure. They had seen him on many occasions leaving the plantation grounds and naturally assumed he was on business for Mount Vernon.

The day grew hotter and sultrier as the trip progressed; the coolness of early morning had been the only respite. William knew that Elijah had to be suffering from the heat, lying under the blankets and straw, but it couldn't be helped. As he drove he thought how peaceful and quiet the countryside appeared. Only the barest of sounds—the soft breeze flowing through the trees and the flapping wings and chirps of birds—could be heard. The drive became so restful that William found it necessary to remain alert, lest an unguarded moment catch him unawares.

Over the next hillside, he stopped the wagon in a dense strand of cherry, elm, and maple trees. The trees blocked out much of the sun and it was cooler here, with the rich smell of verdant foliage in the air. He climbed down from the wagon and lifted the sweltering confines from Elijah.

Sitting up and looking around him, Elijah visibly relaxed when he realized they were just resting, and not being detained by patrollers.

"We'll rest here for a few moments and give you a chance to cool off." William handed Elijah bread, cheese, and a sip of water.

"Ahs shor's do 'preciate what you's doin' for me, Massa William," Elijah said as he placed a large chunk of cheese in his mouth.

"Elijah, don't call me massa. I know I may not look it, but I'm a Negro, just as you are. Gazing down at the grass-covered ground, William picked a few strands and continued, "If the circumstances of my birth had been different, I could be in the same place as you are today." Gazing back up to Elijah William said, "Please call me William."

"Yas'm, mass—William."

Elijah ate the food quickly, as if he was afraid someone was going to take it from him. The man reminded William of the half-starved dog he had fed that wandered onto the Mount Vernon plantation a few years before. It saddened him to see a human being so starved for nourishment. He then glanced at the man's shoulder where he was missing an arm. William had seen men on the plantation who had lost a portion of their arm. Never had he seen one where the whole appendage was gone. He wondered how the man lost it.

"Elijah, how did you lose your arm?" Seeing an agonized look pass over the man's face, William hurriedly added, "You don't have to tell me if you don't want to."

"No, it jes dat sometimes ah kin still feel de pain of it happenin.'" Elijah closed his eyes for a moment and then took a deep breath and said, "De massa's dogs git me when ahs runs away da first time. Dem dogs leeched onto my arm like ahs was dere dinner." Reaching over his chest he rubbed the stump through his rolled up shirtsleeve. "De massa didn't call dem dogs off'n me. He jes let dem try an' take my arm off. And deys did. Dem dogs bit an' snapped an' tore until my arm come off."

Elijah's eyes were hollow as he continued. "One of dem dogs was actually eatin' it before ahs passed out. When ahs woke up, ahs was back at de plantation. Old massa say, "Next time you runs away, boy, ahs jes let dem dogs kill you." Elijah's black eyes watered as he looked at William and he said with quiet intensity, "But dem dogs jes gotta kill me 'cause ah's gonna be free. If'n dey take my legs, ah jes crawl away. If'n ahs die tryin', den ahs jes gonna haf' ta die."

William couldn't hide the horror on his face. He felt a chill travel up his spine at Elijah's fateful words.

The two men ate in silence for a few more minutes and then Elijah made a quick jaunt into the woods. When he got back into the wagon William covered him once more. Then with a flick of the horses' reins, the wagon moved onward towards Richmond.

William thought about the brave man in the back of the wagon. He kept reliving the horror of how the man had lost his arm. He kept thinking, *would I have the same courage to escape if I were in his place?* He hoped so.

In late afternoon William heard hounds baying and horses' hooves coming from behind them. He reached back and gave a quick double rap on the wagon seat and said urgently, "Riders, be very quiet."

Some minutes later several white men rode up to where he had stopped the wagon. William felt the best course of action was to try and brazen his way out of this dilemma. In his most cultured, white-sounding voice he said, "Good morning gentlemen. What can I do for you?"

"We be lookin' for a runaway. Tall black buck with a missin' arm. You seen anyone on this road fittin' this description?" one hairy man said.

The man looked familiar. In seconds his name registered in William's memory. It was McCowan, Dan McCowan—slave catcher. While William had been busy trying to place the man in front of him, he realized that McCowan was scrutinizing him. He hoped he would be perceived as a well-dressed country squire with curly chestnut hair and blue eyes, on his way to Richmond.

Deciding to throw the man off track, William stated, "Aren't you the famous Dan McCowan?" Not letting the man answer his query, he hurried on, "You gave me one of your notices several months back in Richmond. Many of my business acquaintances told me that you were the best slave catcher this side of the Potomac."

The man puffed his chest out with pride as William mentioned his reputation. Smiling at him and showing surprisingly white teeth he said braggingly, "Yeah, that be me."

William could hear hounds approaching in the distance. They were baying loudly and quickly. He knew he had to get the wagon moving in the next few moments or all was lost.

"Sorry that I have not seen your runaway. I am sure a man with your exceptional talents will find him in no time at all."

"If he be around these here parts, I'll ketchum fer sure."

The slave catcher then spit into the dirt and motioned his riders back towards the man leading his hounds. William quickly flicked his wrists to put the horses into motion. They had traveled only a couple dozen of yards when one of the hounds broke from the pack and ran after the wagon.

McCowan rode back up to William and said, "Mister, it seems my dog here thinks you got somethin' in your wagon."

"I guess the scent of slaves is still lingering back there," William replied calmly. "I'm the main overseer at the Mount Vernon plantation. I had to haul several slaves down to the boat landing this morning to load supplies. I guess that's what your dog smells."

Hearing the name "Mount Vernon" had the desired effect William expected. The man looked at him with respect for a moment and then his eyes narrowed slightly, judging the merit of the explanation he was just given by the stranger.

William said with aplomb, "I will be sure to contact you if we ever have any of our slaves run away. John Augustine Washington has many friends in the county, I'm sure I can even recommend you to them for your services."

I be 'preciating that, Mister—?"

"William Ford," he answered as he watched the man get down from his horse and lead it towards the back of the wagon. The muscles in William's back felt tight and strained, battle-ready as he reached for the rifle under the seat.

"Get on away from the wagon, you no good hound."

William turned and watched as McCowan smacked the sniffing dog in the mouth with his free hand and dragged him and his horse back down the road where the other men in his party had been waiting and watching.

He exhaled when the men finally rode off into the woods on his left. That had been a very close call. "Elijah," he whispered, "Stay still, they may come back." He then urged the horses to a more resolute pace.

As he rode away he had to smile. He did it. He had masqueraded as a white man beneath the very noses of the slave catchers. William knew his diction lent well to his disguise. They didn't even suspect he was anything other than what he portrayed.

He drove on in the darkness until he couldn't see, and then pulled the wagon into a strand of trees. The two men made camp that night, but remained wary. The evening was laden with the sound of tree frogs and chirping crickets, and every other night sound that intruded set them on edge. At the first hint of light in the sky, they continued toward Richmond.

As they neared the city late that evening, William traveled the unused roads and back alleyways until they reached the contact's house. William urged the team onto the lawn to deaden the sound of the horses' hooves. He got out of the wagon, swiftly approached the house, and knocked on the door. Shortly thereafter, Elijah was ushered into a storage room until it was safe for him to continue his journey.

"God bless you," Elijah said to William as they stood in the small hidden room at the abolitionist's house.

"God bless you also, Elijah. You're on your way to freedom now." William clasped Elijah's hand and went outside to his wagon. His mood and step were lighter than they had been in years. He decided that he would sleep in the wagon that night and head back home first thing in the morning.

Two days later he had returned to Mount Vernon. No one seemed too interested that he didn't arrive with supplies. Henrietta was sitting by the fireplace when he entered the cabin. She rose with a cry of happiness and ran into his outstretched arms, raining kisses all over his face.

"Enough, woman," he said in mock gruffness.

"William, I've been so worried! Thank God you are all right!"

Hugging her to his chest, he whispered against her hair, "I've never been better."

Chapter 16

He has, I know not what of greatness in his looks,
and of high fate that almost awes me.

Dryder

It was a miracle from God. After four years, William and Henrietta were blessed with their second son, George William Ford, in 1847. William decided it was time that a Ford male carry the Old General's first and middle name.

George was a gray-eyed, chubby, happy infant with a constant, gurgling laugh. Everyone on the Mount Vernon plantation fell in love with him. When George was five months old, he was baptized at St. Paul's Episcopal Church, the church where the Washingtons worshipped. George's baptism was highly unusual, as Negroes were not openly baptized in white churches.

Little George brought laughter to the Mount Vernon plantation. He was always smiling and his sisters doted on him as if he were a cherished doll.

"Let me hold him Mama, please," begged Constance.

"No, it's my turn," cried Hannah.

Little George would smile, his eyes bright with happiness. He didn't care who held him as long as someone did.

George was also the apple of his Grandfather West's eye. Even as a baby George would toddle after his grandfather, begging to be held in his arms.

William wasn't the only Ford that had something to celebrate. His sister Jane also had a son born within months of his child, and she named him William. His mother finally relented on her stand with his sister Julia courting the slave, Corrill. The couple finally jumped the broom after a short courtship. A church wedding was not possible, because Corrill was a slave.

*   *   *

More and more lighter-skinned blacks were being born in the South. New terms were given to the degrees of skin tone that ranged in the Negro race. Besides mulatto (half-black), these new categories included: quadroon (one-quarter Negro blood), octoroon (one-eighth Negro blood) and quinteroon (one-sixteenth Negro blood—a cross between a white and an octoroon). Several laws had been in effect in the South that stated that octoroons (the last degree of black) who were free, and others who had less than one-fourth Negro blood, were legally defined as a white person.

This didn't sit too well with many of the southern slaveholders, because it threatened regional identity and political stability. The South had to find a way to defend the enslavement of the entire 'hybrid' mulatto race in order to keep the institution of slavery intact, and not allow any part of it to be compromised. This was done with theories that attacked the idea that mulattoes were approaching conformity with whites.

In 1849, the state of Virginia defined the status of Negroes and enacted another code that declared:

"Every person that has one-fourth part or more Negro blood shall be deemed a mulatto, and the word "Negro"…shall be construed to mean mulatto as well as Negro."

William was conversing with his father about the new law while they tended the garden closest to the piazza in back of the mansion house. He hands were resting on the handle of a rake. "Papa, this new law was established to keep any person with Negro blood—a Negro."

West was stooped over some rose bushes, snipping off the dead blooms. The garden was full of them this time of the year; lush, full headed roses in every shade. The fragrance of the flowers filled the morning air. Several large bumblebees with their black and yellow -bodies buzzed from one bloom to another.

William went on, "The Virginia legislature feels that too many mulattoes might be able to blend in completely and disappear into the white race."

Standing to his full height, West remarked, "You and I both know that be happenin'. Who can blame them that be wantin' to pass? Being a Negro be hard. Being white be so much easier. Some want it, easier."

William drew in a very slow, deep breath, and then exhaled. "Sometimes, Papa, that's just what I wish I could do. To just leave here and go live where nobody knows who or what race I am." His blue eyes took on a pensive look. "But then I remember that others in my race don't have that option. They're slaves. I may have white skin, but I am a Negro. I can't forget it or deny it. And I can't pretend to be anything else. I just want people not to be so blinded by color."

Glancing off in the distance with a thoughtful look, William elaborated, "I want my children to be more than you or me. I want them to do something with their lives, besides living on this plantation. One day I want one of our offspring to become the president of this country—just like their grandfather."

"Now you are askin' for the impossible, son. Ain't no Negro ever gonna be a president of this here country," West replied, lifting a skeptical gray eyebrow.

William remarked, "I don't expect it to happen in my lifetime or my children's. But one day. One day it won't matter in this country what kind of blood you carry or the color of your skin. I have to believe that there is goodness in people, and goodness will prevail."

"I pray that you be right, son. I jes pray that you be right," murmured West.

Several more years would pass with West and his offspring taking care of the mansion house and grounds for Mount Vernon. Even the youngest Ford, George, now six, began to help his brother, father and grandfather tend the gardens and tomb area. Little George would watch his grandfather West painstakingly pick leaves, weeds, and flower debris from the area of the tomb, talking out loud to someone called the "Old General."

"Who is the Old General, and why are you always talkin' to him, Grandpa?" George asked. West looked over at William who was working nearby, and a silent communication passed between them. It was time to tell George about his heritage.

"George, you be named after your great grandpapa, George Washington. We call him the Old General. He be a white man and my papa," West explained.

Cocking his head to the side, George inquired, "Is that why you and papa's skin is whiter than mine?"

"Yes. But son, you be more than the color of your skin 'cause skin color don't mean nothin', but to those who think it do. My skin may be white, but I gots Negro blood—the blood of my mama. Havin' white skin don't mean nothin' if you gots Negro blood in you 'cause in this here land, it makes you a slave. Slaves belong to massas. The massas owns them. Tells them what to do, when to sleep, when to eat and where they can go. I be a slave once, but I be free now. Thats why you and your papa be free."

Putting his work-worn hand on the boy's shoulder, West added, "I know all I be tellin' you now be hard to understand. And you gonna hear me tell many stories 'bout my papa and about my mama. The onlyest thing you gots to remember is that your great grandpa was George Washington. He was a great general and the overseer of this whole country we live in." Tapping his finger against George's temple he said, "Just 'member that."

Then he said in a more serious tone, "George, you must never tell no white person what I just told you. It be dangerous. Do you understand me?"

George was too young to understand the danger of relaying to anyone what he had just learned, but he understood the somber tone of his grandfather's voice and nodded in acknowledgement.

Still wanting to ask questions, George said, "Why do you keep talkin' to the Old General if he's dead?"

West answered with a chuckle, "'Cause now he gots to listen." Gazing up at the overcast gray sky he added, "Now, we best get this here place tidied up before it rains."

That day would not be the first time George would hear about his family's history. West would tell his grandchildren stories about his life as a slave, as a freeman, his mother Venus, and about their relationship to George Washington. West felt that it was important for his grandchildren to know of their heritage. "Tell your children, tell them about the Old General. But don't be tellin' nobody else 'cause white folks won't be likin' it," he would say.

Young George loved to hear his grandfather's stories about his boyhood, the Old General, and Venus. He would listen for hours to the tales. When West finished with one of his stories, George instantly pleaded for him to repeat it. What did it matter that he had heard them countless times until he had them memorized? He never tired of hearing them repeated. West would just grin, his blue-gray eyes twinkling with good humor and begin his tales again.

George would also besiege his grandfather with questions about George Washington's military life.

"Tell me, Grandpa. Tell me how many soldiers the Old General had in his army?" George asked while sitting with his grandfather on the step of West's house.

"I don't be knowin' for sure. Old Billy Lee told me there be hundreds in the camp that they be stayin' in. Them soldiers snapped to attention whenever the Old General came by them, though. Billy Lee said he felt proud to be 'round such an important man."

"And did he have a sword?" George's gray eyes were wide with wonder.

"Yes, he had a sword."

"Did he stick anyone with it?"

"I don't rightly know," West said, his lips turning up with a twitch.

West was continually amazed with young George's avid interest in the military aspects of George Washington's life. The boy loved to look at the pictures of Washington in his military uniforms and was fascinated by swords. He told West once, "I'm gonna be a soldier just like the Old General."

They were still chatting away on West's porch when he told his grandson, "Hold on, George, I gots to fetch somethin' for you."

George watched as his grandfather stood and entered the house. He came out a few moments later with a wooden sword he had carved for the boy. It was very detailed and had taken West many long hours to complete.

"A sword! Oh, thank you, Grandpa!" George embraced his grandfather. He immediately started his swordplay, arcing the sword overhead and swinging it through the air.

"Careful now, son. Don't go pokin' anythin' that might bleed, like me," West said, ducking from one of the swipes that came too close to his head.

George would take the wooden sword and try and teach himself the rudiments of sword play. Trees and fence posts became his opponents. Many times he would be admonished by his parents when he chased his older siblings around the plantation with his trusty weapon.

The boy and his sword made for a mischievous combination. One such event occurred several days later.

"Look, George," John pointed to Lucy while she rolled out dough for the next day's bread.

The air in the cookhouse was fragrant with the smell of yeast and baking pies. Lucy had her back turned and did not see the boys peeking into the room. George studied his intended target. Lucy was a large woman—almost as large as her mother, Doll, had been. Her breasts were so big they drooped to her waist like two heavy sacks of potatoes.

John's voice broke into his thoughts. "All you have to do is distract her while I swipe one of the sweet potato pies." John's voice held a cajoling tone.

"Why do I have to distract her?" George queried, a furrow marring his smooth brow.

"Because I'm older and you have to do what I say." Like most big brothers, John loved to bait and tease his impressionable younger sibling.

"Oh, all right," George said resignedly.

"Go now while her back is turned," John urged.

"Yes, sir," said George, bringing the sword up towards his chest in acquiescence. He tiptoed quietly up to Lucy. She was humming a song as she rolled out the dough, slapping and then shaping it into a ball. Lucy then picked up a pan of biscuits to put into the brick oven, never missing a note in the song.

Turning and glancing back at John hiding next to the door, George saw that his brother was waving him on. He quickly thought up a plan to divert her attention away from John.

"Auntie Lucy—watch out for the rat by your foot!" George shouted out loudly.

The old woman was so startled she threw the tray straight up into the air, raining biscuits down around her head. She backed up into the tip of George's outstretched sword. The old woman jumped again from the prick to her posterior, her black eyes as round as the skillets she used for cooking the meals.

George stood frozen; the sword still clasped in his hand when she turned towards him rubbing her huge, rear end. One of the airborne biscuits had landed on the white kerchief tied around her head. George's sense of humor kicked in, looking at that biscuit and Lucy's face. He felt the corners of his mouth begin to quiver. John was already laughing and whooping by the door.

"Boy, ah's gonna tan yo' hide!"

Lucy picked up a big wooden spoon from the table and came towards George threateningly. She chased him all around the cook house, but he was faster and wily and threw stools in her way. Finally, she cornered George between the table and the door, blocking his exit.

"If'n ahs catch you, boy, you won't be able to sit down 'til next year," the woman declared, her spoon raised high over her head.

"You've got to catch me first!" George laughed and he quickly dodged left then right, throwing her off direction. Then he sprinted out the door and down the piazza, praying to the Almighty that she wouldn't come after him.

Meantime, John had snatched one of the pies cooling on the sideboard. He was eating it when George showed up several minutes later by the smokehouse. The boys laughed and ate until their bellies felt like they were going to burst.

George stayed away from the cookhouse the rest of the day. He knew he had to apologize to Lucy eventually. The following morning he picked some roses from one of the flower gardens and took them to her as a peace offering. He was a little charmer. No one could stay angry at him for long, including the cook.

The two young brother's antics didn't always lead to mischief. John came up with the idea to help the Negro children on the plantation to learn to read.

"Look, we can teach them," he said to George. "We can hide books under our clothes and take them out to old Billy Lee's cabin. We can teach them there."

"We don't have anything for them to write on," George stated.

"We'll figure it out. What do you say, George?"

George had always worshipped his older brother, and would do whatever he asked. "When do we get started?" he replied a moment later.

The brothers quickly formulated their plans and that very same evening they gave their first lesson. They used a stick in the dirt to write out the letters to the alphabet and simple words. Some of the adults stood as guards in case any of the white overseers' happened by. After the lessons the boys placed the books in a sack cloth and buried it in a hole in the ground so that it would not be detected.

Education was still relatively inaccessible to blacks, slave or free, in Virginia. The slaveholders believed that educated slaves were a source of discontent and that they could destroy the institution of slavery. Most slaves could expect to be whipped if they were found able to read or write. These anti-education laws didn't affect William's children. They were educated on the Mount Vernon plantation, just as he and his siblings had once been. This was because the Fords had the power of the Washington name on their side.

William found out about his sons' clandestine classroom. He followed them one evening after supper to Billey Lee's old cabin. As he entered the clearing, one of the posted guards spotted him. William quickly brought his forefinger to his lips, indicating to him to keep his presence quiet. He then watched in silence as his sons taught the six slave children the alphabet and his heart almost burst from pride. But he was a little disconcerted that they hadn't confided in him about their plans. After the lesson ended, William walked out of the shadows and up to them. The boys were startled to see their father.

"Papa, we…that is…*you* tell him George," said a flustered John.

George's gray eyes widened at his brother's new order. His mouth moved like a fish out of water, but he didn't say a thing.

William smiled and said, "John, George, you make me proud that you want to help others less fortunate, but I wish you would have trusted me to help you. What you are doing is very dangerous, and the consequences could be dire if you are caught."

"Finally finding his voice, George replied, "We've been careful, Papa. That's why we have people lookin' out for the overseers."

"Well, I came upon you unawares, and so can somebody else." Noting their crestfallen faces, he continued, "So, here's what we're going to do. From now own for safety reasons, you will teach the children one day a week. I'll also get you paper and quills for you to write with."

The two boys weren't exactly thrilled to cut out any of their lessons, but agreed to their father's request. The lessons continued only for a few short weeks because once again, the Virginia legislature enacted another one of its many codes to keep blacks in their supposed proper place. The Virginia Constitution now stated:

"If any emancipated slave (infants excepted) shall remain within the state more than twelve months after his or her right to freedom shall have accrued, he or she shall forfeit all such right, and may be apprehended and sold by the overseer of the poor, &c. for the benefit of the literary fund."

The Fords now had to be concerned about being sold to benefit the literary fund.

Chapter 17

Nothing that is can pause or stay; the moon will wax, the moon will wane. The mist and clouds will turn to rain, the rain to mist and clouds again, tomorrow will be today.

Henry Wadsworth Longfellow

Providence continued to rain down on the Ford family and they were able to remain safely within the state of Virginia. It was now being bandied around the country that blacks and whites were separate species. A well-known physician from New Orleans, a Dr. Samuel A. Cartwright, wrote an article in 1851 that appeared in several newspapers, stating that blacks even had particular mental diseases. Cartwright identified one as drapetomania—the disease causing Negroes to run away.

The other disease was known as dyaesthesia athiopica, which was defined as follows: "when he (Negro) performs the task assigned to him in a headlong, careless manner, treading down with his feet or cutting with his hoe the plants he is put to cultivate—breaking the tools he works with and spoiling everything he touches that can be injured by careless handling. Hence, the overseers call it 'rascality,' supposing that the mischief is intentionally done. But there is no premeditated mischief in the case." These new theories on separatism helped the slaveholders hold to their beliefs that blacks were of an inferior race.

Unnerved by the ongoing degradation and labeling of the Negro race, William decided to send his daughters up North. There they would stay with Henrietta's older sister, Mary, who managed a prominent boarding house on Broome Street in New York City. The girls would attend the African Free School that was founded by the New York Manumission Society in 1787. William's brother, Daniel, would accompany the girls on their journey to New York.

Daniel, William, Hannah, and Constance were at the train station when the conductor called that it was time to board. William embraced his daughters, kissed their brows, and watched as Daniel led them up into the train.

"Bye, Papa!" shouted Constance.

She was so excited to be going to New York, that her face literally shone with it. Constance had grown up into an ivory-skinned beauty, with gray eyes and auburn hair. Wherever she went she turned male heads. William asked Daniel to keep a close eye on her during the trip to New York. The little minx didn't realize how her good looks might generate unwanted attention.

Now little Hannah was waving and crying at the same time to William. She was his little angel, with her black hair and hazel eyes. Going up North meant that Hannah could pursue her wish to become a teacher, it was all she ever talked about.

With a heavy, but glad heart, William turned away and headed toward his wagon as the train pulled away. At least he had been able to relocate some of his family up North. *Now if I can only find a way to get my parents to leave the South*, he contemplated, as he climbed into the wagon and headed back to the estate.

*   *   *

Several years after William's daughters had been sent north he was still not able to convince his parents that New York held all their dreams. He continued with his position as one of the caretakers at the estate. Unfortunately, the plantation was becoming run-down. The present owner, John Augustine Washington III, wasn't able to maintain the plantation as well as his predecessors, as he had obligations elsewhere in the county. Many land speculators had approached John Augustine through the years about purchasing Mount Vernon, but he wanted the plantation to be remembered for its importance in American history.

William convinced his father that it was only a matter of time before Mount Vernon was sold, and took steps to make sure that his family wouldn't become unemployed and homeless. He purchased the Peake house, not far from the estate. Then in 1857, his father divided his 255-acre estate into four equal parts for his children—William, Daniel, Jane, and Julia. They were deeded the land for $20 on a yearly rental basis. Upon his death, West told them, he would return the money to them as an inheritance.

As for William's siblings, Jane was presently living with her husband, Porter, and their son William, in one of the slave cabins on Mount Vernon. Julia and her son, West, stayed with their parents on Little Hunting Creek. Julia's husband, Corrill, was still a slave and lived on another plantation and visited whenever he was allowed. Daniel was still residing in New York, along with William's two daughters and had no immediate plans to return to Virginia.

William's belief about Mount Vernon's eventual sale came to fruition. In 1858, John Augustine sold the plantation to the Mount Vernon Ladies' Association for the Union. He retained one-quarter acre of land that contained the tomb of George Washington. The women of the organization promised John Augustine that the Mount Vernon estate would be brought back to its former glory. They also pledged that they would open the estate for anyone who wanted to learn more about American history.

William and his father were talking with one of the members of the association after giving her a tour of the property.

"We would like you to stay on, West, and help us renovate the mansion house and grounds," said Ann Pamela Cunningham, president of the association. "Our hope is that we can bring the plantation back to its original state when President Washington lived here.

"Miz Cunningham, I been on this here plantation since I was a boy. I can 'member just how it looked. I be glad to help you."

Miz Cunningham was staring at West while he spoke, studying him. He had experienced this type examination a hundred times before when people first met him. Now, at seventy-three, he was the spitting image, albeit a little darker, of his sire. Miz Cunningham to her credit, never ventured to ask him about his parentage.

"Good, good," she said after a moment's pause. "Mister Nobel Herbert, who I have hired as my superintendent, will discuss your salary and duties." She took her leave of the two men, bringing an end to the interview.

Several days later, West, William, and Porter began the renovation of the Mount Vernon mansion house. Furniture was repaired and walls painted to their original colors during the days of George Washington's occupancy.

West was making a plow near the conservatory several months later when Benson Lossing, a historian and personal friend of George Washington Parke Custis, came to visit the estate.

"Suh, the mansion house be open to visitors," West said and pointed toward the house. "Ain't really nothin' down this way 'ceptin' the stable and barns."

The man scrutinized West from the bottom of his worn black boots to his white hair that was clubbed in the back with a piece of string.

"You're West Ford, aren't you?" the man asked.

"Yas, suh, I be him."

"My name is Benson Lossing. I'm a historian and I would like to interview you."

"Why?"

"Because I have been told that you have lived on this plantation most of your life, and being a historian, I want to know more."

The man was now openly examining West's facial features and made him a little disconcerted.

West queried, "Well, what ya be wantin' to know?"

"*Everything.*" The historian's eyes held a speculative look. Then he clarified, "Everything you can remember about Mount Vernon, that is."

West was aware that Lossing wanted more than information about the estate. He could see the question forming in the man's eyes, "Are you the son of George Washington?" But West wasn't going to indulge the man. Who fathered him would remain a secret.

Benson Lossing interviewed West for several hours, and at the end of their conversation, Lossing asked if he could draw his picture. West knew then. He knew this man wanted to draw him because he looked liked George Washington, so he agreed.

"That be fine with me. How 'bout I meet you in the morning up at the mansion house, say 'bout eight o'clock?"

"Tomorrow morning it is," Lossing agreed.

West excused himself and went back to his plow-making. The next morning he dressed meticulously in a pristine white shirt, a black satin vest and black trousers. He tied a white silk cravat and groomed his curly, silver hair to perfection.

When West entered the library for his sitting, Lossing was startled at the rich cut of his clothes. West looked like a gentleman of the plantation and a Washington. In fact, Lossing kept referring to him as the estate's patriarch.

As West settled down for his drawing he remarked, "I want to make sure this comes out right. Most artists make colored folks look bad enough anyhow." When the sketch was finished, West signed his name with Lossing's pencil at the bottom of it. Lossing seemed impressed that West knew how to write. The article was printed in the New Harper's Monthly Magazine the following spring.

As Mount Vernon became a tourist attraction, the Ford grand-children sold pictures at the entrance to the plantation. George, now eleven, was intent on being involved in everything that was happening around him. He mingled with the visitors and would offer information to them about General George Washington.

"Sir, did you know that I once saw the Old General's sword? The president's tomb is over that way, Missus. Ma'am, my papa and me was born on this plantation. Sir, its true, my papa knew the Old General!"

This last admission had many visitors wanting to meet West to ask him questions about the life of the first president. Upon meeting him, these same visitors would stare—their mouths hanging open like fish out of water. After a while, West decided it was best not to meet many tourists.

Even with the tranquility that had settled over Mount Vernon, times were troubled in the united American states, with the major quarrel revolving around preserving the Union.

The issue of slavery was secondary. Many Americans in the North and even in the southern states felt it was morally wrong to own human beings, but preserving the Union was the key concern of the day. As more northerners joined anti-slavery groups the Republican Party was organized with the aim of keeping the United States united and the territories free from slavery. Tensions began to mount between the North and the South.

On October 16, 1859, a white abolitionist named John Brown decided to take over an arsenal at Harper's Ferry, where he hoped to procure weapons to arm the slaves for revolt. John Brown and his force of twenty-two men bundled their guns and hatchets into a wagon, and two-by-two marched down the gloomy road to Harper's Ferry Bridge.

They crossed into Virginia around midnight and seized the U.S. armory. He then dispatched a raiding party to the nearby plantation of the grandnephew of George Washington, Colonel Lewis W. Washington, to take him as a hostage. Brown wanted his raiding party to procure the pistol and sword presented to General Washington by the Marquis de Lafayette and Frederick the Great. These trophies would in turn be handed over by the hostage to a black confederate, Osborn Anderson, as a "symbolic gesture." The revolt failed, as Colonel Robert E. Lee moved in with U.S. troops and overpowered the insurrectionists. John Brown and eleven other men were captured and sent to Charles Town to stand trial.

West and William heard about the revolt from Lewis Washington. Later that evening, they had a family meeting to discuss the failed insurrection.

"God knows I don't want to see innocent people killed. But the only insurrection that's going to make a difference when it comes to abolishing slavery will have to be decided by the United States' government. It's the only way for all the people to accept it," remarked William.

"I be agreeing, son. I jes pray somethin' be decided soon," said Priscella.

"We gots to be keepin' an eye on the Old General's tomb," West said. "How do we know that Lee's troops be done caught all the insurrectionists? We don't want no one to be thinkin' they can use the Old General's body as no trophy."

"You think someone would do that?" uttered William.

"These be sick times and there be a lot of sick people out there," said West. "We best set about protectin' the tomb."

For the next several weeks William, West, and Porter took turns guarding the burial site. They weren't just protecting the nation's first hero—they were protecting one of their family member's final resting-place. But all remained quiet on the plantation.

John Brown's trial was held in Charles Town and he was condemned to hang. William had been to Alexandria on Mount Vernon business when news of John Brown's hanging was printed in the newspaper. William brought the newspaper home and on Sunday after church he read an excerpt from the article that quoted John Brown in the face of his hanging:

> "You may dispose of me easily, but this question is still to be settled—the Negro question—and the end of that is not yet! Now, if it is deemed necessary that I should forfeit my life for the furtherance of the ends of justice, and mingle my blood further with the blood of my children and with the blood of the millions of slaves in this country whose rights are disregarded by the wicked, cruel, and unjust enactments, I say let it be done!"

"I be prayin' to God that they wouldn't hang that man," murmured Priscella. "I jes know that one day all he be tryin' to do will happin' for the Negro race. I jes pray to God I be 'round to see it."

Priscella became ill shortly after the execution of John Brown. She had lost considerable weight during the previous year. She was always thirsty and couldn't seem to drink enough water. Some days her vision was so blurry she couldn't see a couple of feet. Her family members became concerned when her ankles swelled to the size of small tree trunks. All they could do was keep her feet elevated.

One morning West woke earlier than usual and reached to shake his wife awake. Usually, Priscella rose before him. Her body felt stiff and so, so cold when he touched her. *Too cold.* Priscella's face appeared waxen—like skin emptied of the soul. He didn't want to believe she was dead and placed an ear to her chest, praying that he was wrong.

There was no heartbeat.

West gathered her into his arms and shouted out in anguish, "Oh, God, no, not Priscella! Why didn't you take me first?"

Julia burst into her parents' room. She had risen from her cot when she heard her father's grief-stricken outburst. Walking closer to her father's weeping form, she immediately knew that her beloved mother was dead. Her legs collapsed from under her and she sat crying on the edge of their bed. She watched tearfully as her father rocked her mother in his arms and kissed her brow, and telling her that he would always love her.

A day later, Priscella Ford's funeral was held at the Mount Vernon slave cemetery. She was to be buried next to West's mother, Venus and his sister, Betty. William stood quietly by as his young son, George, sang a final song for his grandmother. His beautiful tenor voice brought tears to everyone's eyes at the words:

> "Steal away, steal away, steal away to Jesus, Steal away, steal away, steal away home, I ain't got long to stay here. My Lord he calls me, he calls me by the thunder, the trumpets sound within my soul, I ain't got long to stay here. Steal away, steal away, steal away to Jesus."

West had seen death many times, but one never became immune to it. His blue-gray eyes were as barren as a desert that had survived centuries without even the hope of rain as he stood and watched dirt being tossed on his wife's wooden coffin. Priscella had been his anchor so many times when he thought he would drown in life's miry depths. He prayed to God that he would not sink now that she was gone.

"Come on, Papa," said Julia. "Let me take you home."

Julia so much resembled her Grandmother Venus that West's heart wrenched painfully, doubling his grief. His heart was cold—as cold inside as an empty tomb.

Shaking his white head, he said quietly, "You all go on and leave me here for awhile. I got some talkin' to do."

Chapter 18

The wheels of nature are not made to roll backward, everything presses on toward Eternity.

Robert Hall

For the next several months after Priscella's death, conversations of possible secession, war, and slavery dominated the lives of the southern populace. The tourist trade dwindled at Mount Vernon and work became scarce for the Ford family. William decided to look for extra employment in Alexandria.

William had always loved Alexandria, its red, brick buildings and dignified people. But Alexandria was different this day. The city's graciousness was degraded because a slave auction was being held.

William, ever sensitive to the selling of his best friend as a young boy, had the misfortune to view a slave girl being auctioned. He couldn't look away. She looked to be of the same age as his daughter, Constance. William almost gagged as the old feeling of bile rose up into his throat, threatening to choke him.

But he was tougher and stronger now and fought down the old panic.

Two planters were walking past his wagon when he overheard their conversation. They were discussing the woman's unbarred breasts. "I say, wouldn't you like to lay your head on those pillows on a cold winter night?" the younger of the two men said.

"Maybe I'll buy her for Elizabeth to help out in the house," the older man laughed and winked at his friend.

William couldn't make out the rest of their conversation as they walked closer to the platform for a better look at the girl, but he could still hear their continued shared laughter. His pulse rioted and anger seethed from every pore in his body. He vowed that he had had enough of the South. He was going to move the rest of his family up North. William had a dream of a different kind of freedom, a freedom of something better and fairer, away from the South's rigid, unyielding laws that kept blacks in the place of servitude and hatred. New York was the repository of his dreams and aspirations.

William had to make his move within the next few months as the unrest between the North and the South concerning the issues of slavery and secession were becoming more heated. Many people in the North were complaining of the treatment of the slaves, and the South was closing ranks against their outrage.

West understood William's decision to move to New York, but wouldn't accompany him. "Son, I be stayin' here. I can't be leavin' this plantation. My whole family be buried here in the slave cemetery. This be my home."

"Papa, I can't leave you here," murmured William, his blue eyes full of entreaty.

"Son, you got to do what you be thinkin' be best for your family. You been sacrificin' your dreams of livin' up North, always stayin' by my side. It be time for you to go."

William did not want to leave his father now that his mother was dead. It was the most difficult decision he had ever had to make, but as his papa said, he had his children's future to think of. If war broke out, they would be safer in the North. Besides, many people said that if there was a war, it wouldn't last more than a few months, and he prayed that that would be the case. Now he had to convince his other siblings to move with him.

"I won't leave Papa alone," said Julia when William asked her to go to New York. "He's too old, and someone needs to stay with him. Anyway, I can't leave here without Corrill."

"I understand, Julia," William said. "Once I get the family settled in, I'll come back and check on you and Papa whenever I can. I'm leaving you with enough money to last for several months until I can get back down here. Porter and Jane will also be here to help you with Papa."

On the day William and his family left the Mount Vernon plantation, a sudden chill shook him as a thousand fears sprang into his mind. *Would his papa and sisters be all right? How soon could he get back down here? Was he making the right decision?* He prayed that he was. Reality set in as William came to the conclusion that he would be leaving the only home he had ever known.

Seeing the flicker of doubt registering on his son's noble face, West said, "William, you be makin' the right decision. I be proud of you and love you. 'Member who you be. Walk with your head upright and stand proud—stand tall."

With a lump in his throat, William hugged his father. Next came John and then George.

When fifteen-year-old George embraced his grandfather he told him, "I love you, Grandpa." Then he handed his wooden sword to him and said, "Take care of this for me until I come back."

Amid hugs and kisses, tearful good-byes and last-minute admonitions, William and his family left the Mount Vernon plantation.

On May 16, 1860, one month after they left Virginia, Abraham Lincoln was nominated as the presidential candidate of the Republican Party. A congressional resolution was adopted on May 24th and 25th which stipulated that:

"Slavery is lawful in all territories under the Constitution; neither Congress nor a local legislature can abolish it there; the federal government is in duty bound to protect slave owners as well as the holders of other forms of property in the territories."

Horace Greeley, a New York Times editor, wrote an open letter to President Lincoln, known as the "The Prayer of Twenty Millions," which berated Lincoln for catering to the slaveholders. President Lincoln responded:

"My paramount object in this struggle is to save the Union, and is not whether to save or destroy slavery. If I could save the Union without freeing any slaves, I would do it; if I could save the Union by freeing some and leaving others alone, I would do that. What I do about slavery and the colored races, I do because I believe it helps to save the Union."

*   *   *

Once William and his family arrived in New York, they moved in with his wife's sister, Mary, and her husband, James Bell.

"Papa! Mama!" Constance and Hannah screamed in unison as they rushed to embrace their parents when they entered the Bell home. It had been seven years since they'd last been together as a family.

"Mama! Oh, I missed you so much!" cried Hannah. Then came Constance, hugging her mother so tight Henrietta had to gasp for air.

"My baby girls, I can't believe I'm holding you again!" said Henrietta, tears of joy running down her smooth cheeks.

William approached his daughters and enveloped them in a warm, hard embrace. "I can't call you my little girls anymore," he said. "You're all grown up now." He and his wife had missed so much of their girls' adolescence, but he knew they had made the right decision in moving them away from the South.

After all the commotion of seeing their parents tapered off somewhat, Constance chimed, "Papa, mama, I'm engaged to be married. I can't wait for you to meet Herbert," she went on breathlessly.

"*Married?*" When did this all come about?" said Henrietta.

Hannah cleared her throat and said, "Mama let's get you settled in before talking about the wedding."

Looking curiously at her younger daughter, Henrietta said, "Hannah, you can show me where we'll be sleeping. William, why don't you and Constance wait here for John and George? They should be here any minute with the rest of our bags." Henrietta knew Hannah would supply the needed information about Constance's plans.

Once Henrietta and her daughter were ensconced in the guest bedroom, she asked, "Hannah, what do you want to say about Constance's intended?"

"Mama, her fiancé is *white*," replied Hannah, without trying to soften the blow.

"What?" Henrietta's eyes were bright with shock. She sat down on the edge of the bed.

"He's white, Mama. Constance told him she was Creole. He has no idea she lied to him about her race."

"How can this have happened?"

"Constance met him at the mission where she goes once a week to help the poor. He's a doctor. She's been seeing him for several months, and they got engaged a week ago," said Hannah.

"Hasn't Daniel or Mary been keeping an eye on her?"

"Uncle Daniel hasn't been around much since he moved to Staten Island. He comes by about once a month. Aunt Mary has been so busy with the abolitionist movement she's hardly home anymore. She won't even be home today until late this evening. I just didn't know how to tell them about Constance." Wringing her hands, she paused. "Oh, Mama, I'm so glad you and Papa are here. I've missed you so much."

"And we've missed you." Henrietta hugged her daughter, patting her back in comfort. Yes, William and she were here, but what they were going to do about Constance was another matter. Henrietta was afraid that her oldest daughter was going to be terribly hurt.

Later that evening, Henrietta discussed the situation with her husband. "What are we going to do about Constance, lying to that young man of hers, William?"

"I don't rightly know, Henrietta," he replied with a deep sigh. "We'll try and talk to her about it tomorrow."

The next day after supper, William and Henrietta confronted Constance in the sitting room of the Bell house. "Honey, Hannah told us your fiancé is white," Henrietta stated in a matter-of-fact voice.

"Does that make a difference?" Constance's voice was cool as she stood defiantly in front of her parents in the small room next to the dining area. She had clearly drawn a battle line with her stance and tone.

"You know we don't care about the color of someone's skin, but if that one's skin comes in the form of another race, well that's a different matter," her mother replied gravely.

"Why? You and Papa have always said that you would accept whoever I wanted to marry." Constance directed her attention to her father.

William explained, "Now you know that's not what we are talking about here. Trying to pass yourself off as something you're not is what we mean. You can't build a marriage on a lie." Softening his tone, he went on, "Little girl, you've got to tell your fiancé the truth about your race. If he truly loves you he will accept you no matter what."

Constance put her hands over her ears for a few seconds, then said in a tight voice, "Tell Herbert that I am a Negro? *Never!* Negroes are despised here just as they are in the South. I don't want to be a Negro. People think I'm Creole and Creole I'll be."

"We didn't raise you that way, daughter," stated Henrietta.

"No…you didn't raise me at all. You and Papa left that up to Aunt Mary and Uncle Daniel. Well up here, in the North, I've found out how it feels to be white. If you're white you're accepted. Gentlemen hold doors open for you or stand when you enter a room. People smile at you as you past them on the street."

She spat out her next words, her voice rising shrilly, "Being white means you can feel like a human being, not some piece of offal that you sidestep when you see it in your path. And I won't tell Herbert the truth. I won't tell him—*ever!*" Constance ran from the room, tears streaming down her face.

William and Henrietta exchanged pained looks. Henrietta, rising slowly from the sofa, released a long-pent-up breath. "I'll go after her."

"No. Leave her alone for awhile. She'll come around."

"I pray that she does," added Henrietta.

Around bedtime, Constance came to her parents' room and apologized for her cruel words and behavior.

"We know you love your young man, Constance," said William. "Your mother and I have decided to leave it up to you to tell him the truth when you are ready. But you *must* tell him."

Constance's face clouded for a moment then she replied, "I will tell him, Papa. I promise."

During the next several weeks William and his reunited family moved into their rental house in a black, but affluent neighborhood. It didn't take long before William realized that even free blacks were reviled and despised as anywhere in the South. Moreover, the white worker in the North looked at them as a job threat. Some of the free blacks had done well for themselves, but they were the exception. Most lived in enclaves of their own, worked as domestic servants to wealthy whites, as field hands on farms, or in factories.

But the one redeeming factor that held them together was that they were free.

William was also introduced to several prominent Negro families and abolitionists in New York by Henrietta's relatives. He met with Frederick Douglass, William Lloyd Garrison and several others to discuss what the free Negro could do for the abolition movement. Along with his fellow abolitionists, William prodded political leaders about freeing slaves.

"Henrietta, you should have seen their faces when they looked at me. Before I even left the room, I could hear their whispers. Are you sure you didn't tell anyone about my relationship to George Washington?"

Henrietta was in their bedroom, unpacking the last of the clothes from their trunks. She knew she had to tell William the truth. Never had she deliberately lied to him in any form and she wouldn't do so now.

"William I-I told my sister that your father was the illegitimate son of George Washington." She hurriedly added, "Now don't look at me that way. I just wanted them to respect you, to realize that you are an important man."

William's tense face relaxed somewhat as he said, "Henrietta, a man is respected by his deeds and what makes a man important is the quality of his deeds." Taking her two small hands into his, he said softly, "I know you wanted to help us, but we can't let on about our heritage. It's too dangerous. There are those who would rather see us dead than lay a formal claim to the Old General. There are white folks who could not accept the fact that my grandfather had no children with his wife and that his only descendants are Negro."

Henrietta nodded. She silently prayed that she hadn't placed the family in danger.

William's friends found him a position at an abolitionist newspaper. He learned how to set type and assisted with proofreading the submitted articles. In his spare time he helped raise funds and solicited subscriptions for *Frederick Douglass' Paper,* formerly the *North Star.*

George and John sold the newspapers on the street corners of New York City. They hawked the newspapers as they did the pictures they sold on the Mount Vernon plantation. As the young men stood on the street corner of Wall and Broadway, George kept turning his head, trying to take in the sights around him.

"John, I've never seen so many tall buildings crowded together."

"Yeah, and look at all these people," John answered in wonder.

The streets were filled with people of different nationalities, all walking, talking, and hurrying about their business. It was a fact that the cities in the East were becoming more crowded, bursting from the continual influx of newcomers. New York was no exception.

For the first several months, William fought down the nostalgia for his previous tranquil way of life. The city was crowded, dirty, and presented a much faster lifestyle than he and his family were accustomed to. He could remember the slow, easy days in Virginia when there was little even to disturb the way the Potomac River rippled. He thought of the father and sisters he had left behind. Soon he would go back there, but in the meantime he would write to them.

A couple of months passed and Constance knew that it was time to tell her fiancé she was a Negro. True to their word, her parents did not bring up her promise about informing Herbert of her racial status. In fact, they went out of their way not to mention it. It was Herbert. He had been badgering her about their respective parents meeting one another. Constance knew she could no longer hide the truth from him.

"Mama, Papa, I have decided it's time to tell Herbert the truth," she said one night after supper. "He wants to meet my family, and I just can't lie anymore."

Constance burst into tears and William took her trembling body into his supportive embrace. "It's going to be all right, sweetheart, it's going to be all right," he whispered near her ear.

"It's never going to be all right, Papa. I love him and I know he'll never accept me once he knows that I'm a Negro," Constance sobbed.

"Little girl, I know it won't be easy. But you know I'd move heaven and earth to make things right for you. I'll go with you to tell him."

"No! No, I couldn't bear having you there watching me, listening to our conversation. I'll take George or John."

George went with Constance. Herbert was sitting at his desk in the office of the small clinic, reviewing patient charts when Constance entered. George came in after her and stood to the side of the door.

"Herbert I, ah, I need to tell you something," Constance began, her voice wavering. "First of all, I want you to know that I love you more than anything."

"That's wonderful, Darling, because I love you." He smiled as he stood. "I told my mother just this morning that she was going to meet the girl of my dreams."

Herbert was a slightly built young man with hazel eyes and light brown hair. He sported a trim mustache and long sideburns that molded to the curves of his lean cheeks. Herbert put the chart down on a stack of others and then looked curiously over at George.

Constance's eyes misted. There was no sense dodging the inevitable she thought, and said, "I lied to you, Herbert. I'm a Negro, not Creole." Constance took George's hand and pulled him forward. Pausing for a moment to gain her courage, she went on, "This is my brother, George."

There was no way Herbert could mistake George for anything but a Negro. He had gray eyes and reddish brown, curly hair, but his skin color was the true giveaway. It was light bronze.

Sister and brother watched the varied emotions that played over Herbert's face. First disbelief, then hurt, and last a blank look came into his light brown eyes. He didn't speak, but stared at Constance as if he'd never seen her before.

"Please forgive me, Herbert. I love you."

After several long seconds, Herbert moved from around the desk, brushed brusquely past Constance and George, and walked out of the clinic.

Constance closed her eyes against the pain welling inside her, her tears falling freely now. "Take me home, George. T-take me h-home now," she cried brokenly. George felt like crying himself, his sister's pain was so tangible.

Constance never went back to the clinic, believing she'd never see her young man again. Herbert wrote her, stating that he still loved her, but his parents would never accept their only child marrying a Negro.

William took Constance into his arms after the letter she read dropped from her fingertips. "Little girl, take it one day, one step at a time. You will forget, forgive, and heal."

Chapter 19

Brave spirits are a balsam to themselves; there is a nobleness of mind that heals wounds beyond salves.

Cartwright

The North and the South continued to disagree about the rights of succession and slavery. President Lincoln was inaugurated on March 4, 1861, almost the same time Jefferson Davis became president of the Confederate States of America. One month later, the Confederate army fired upon the Union-held Fort Sumter in Charleston, South Carolina. This initiated the Civil War.

The bombardment of Fort Sumter was hailed by abolitionists as a step toward nation-wide emancipation for the slaves. President Abraham Lincoln and the Congress now had to focus on the problems of warfare. Congress put the entire manpower of the country at the president's command, and under these acts he issued new calls for volunteers to enlist and serve in the Union Army. Many free blacks wanted to join as soldiers in the Civil War, but during the initial stages of the conflict, they were only allowed to serve in labor battalions. Blacks served in a variety of support services such as cooks, barbers and teamsters, helping build fortifications, and burying the dead. Daniel Ford served as a teamster.

On September 22, 1862, Lincoln signed the Emancipation Proclamation, effective January 1863, "as a fit and necessary war measure for suppressing said rebellion." The proclamation decreed that all persons held as slaves in states in rebellion were to be free, and those of "suitable condition were to be received in the armed services of the United States."

William was elated when he heard the news because finally the government was making a stand against slavery. Negroes in the North were in a jubilant mood and many victory celebrations were held throughout the city.

The Emancipation Proclamation did not free even one slave when it went into effect, as it was considered a war measure and not an abolition issue. It affected only those slaves under Confederate control. At first the proclamation was more symbolic than substantial, as the South attempted to suppress it. But word swept down the slave telegraph and echoed in every plantation cabin: "Massa Lincum done free us slaves!"

The raging conflict separated the Ford family from home, family, friends, and their way of life. Unknown to William, his father had not received any of his correspondence since the beginning of the war. His letters went unanswered and William became concerned. Many a day Henrietta would notice her husband sitting in a chair, just staring at nothing in particular, his mind far away from New York. She knew that he worried about the welfare of those he had left behind, but to travel through the South to check on them would be extremely dangerous now.

Federal troops had been dispersed very early in the war to protect the Mount Vernon plantation, but William was not aware of this fact. Even though the plantation was safe, West and Julia were struggling to survive. West was too frail to work anymore for the Mount Vernon Ladies' Association, and Porter and Jane had taken up his duties. The salary the couple received barely fed their own family, so Julia had taken in sewing to help keep food on the table for her, her father and her son.

"Little girl, you can't be goin' into Alexandria right now. There be too many soldiers travelin' the roads, and you might come to harm." West's tired blue-gray eyes looked grave. "Wait 'til Porter can be takin' you."

He watched his daughter gather the newly mended garments and place them into a reed basket. Looking up from the clothes she remarked, "Papa, I can't wait for Porter to get well. Why, he's still got a fever. Besides, we need the money. We need food, Papa." Sighing, she said, "Look, I'll take the rifle William left with us. Now why don't you take little West and go fishing."

West knew his daughter had to go into Alexandria and he felt help-less for the first time in his seventy-nine years. His old bones just didn't want to move him around anymore. He was so stiff in the mornings; he could barely lift himself from his bed. He also had been experiencing pain and numbness in his left arm.

Touching her shoulder, he stated, "Be careful, child, I don't think I could live if somethin' bad happened to you."

"I'll be careful, Papa," Julia said and kissed his leathery cheek. "But first, I have to finish hanging the last of the laundry to dry before I can leave."

Julia was putting the last of the clean clothes on the rope that had been strung from the side of the house to an elm tree when she saw a homeless-looking black man walking towards her. Her eyes narrowed and she debated whether she should run and retrieve the rifle that she had left propped next to the wagon or stand there until the stranger neared. Suddenly, the man began running towards her. Julia reacted. She ran to the wagon and hoisted the rifle on her shoulder, pointing the barrel at the stranger's chest as he entered the yard.

"Hold it right there, mister, this here is private property."

The man stopped, startled at her terse command, and then slowly took off his dirty, worn hat. Smiling, he said, "Now why would'ya go and shoot your po' husband, girl?"

Julia stood in shock, her legs unable to respond. She hadn't seen her husband in over two years. On wobbly legs she ran to him, dropping the rifle. Corrill lifted her and spun her in circles. Both were laughing and crying at the same time.

"Corrill, oh Corrill! What are you doing here?" Tears of happiness were running down her face.

"President Lincoln done freed the slaves several months ago. My Massa tell me I could leave or stay on the plantation. I left. I've been walkin' for days to get back to you and our boy."

"No one around here was acting any different, so I thought it was just another rumor," exclaimed the overwhelmed woman as she framed her hands along the sides of her husband's face. "Thank God, Corrill. Thank God for President Lincoln. Thank God we're finally together."

They stood for a few moments more hugging each other. Corrill rubbed the side of his face into her palm. Taking her hands into his, he murmured, "Have you heard from William?"

"No, not since before the war."

"Well, I be sure they all right, being up North and all." Gazing around the deserted yard he asked, "Where be my boy and your papa?"

"They went to the river to try and catch some fish for supper."

"We be alone?"

No longer could Corrill contain his hunger for her. It was there in the slow blaze in his dark eyes and the subtle flaring of his nostrils. It had been too long since they had last been together. For two long years he had thought of nothing but her.

Julia smiled brightly. "Yep, we're alone."

Picking her up in his strong arms, Corrill carried her into the house. Later that evening, the reunited family celebrated the return of one of their own and the freedom of their race.

The Emancipation Proclamation outraged the South and restimulated her greatest anxiety—visions of insurrection. In fact, there was no need for slave violence. As Union forces appeared, they simply walked away—just as Corrill had done. Conversations around supper tables returned to battles, slavery, and politics throughout the country.

In March 1863, President Lincoln signed the inevitable Draft Law. The Draft Law had a conscription act stipulating that all white males between the ages of twenty and forty-six were compelled to serve. The act made the Civil War a war of the poor, because wealthier males could buy their way out of serving for about three hundred dollars. Demonstrations against the law popped up all over New York City. White men were eager to fight and die to save the Union, but were not so moved to sacrifice their lives to free the slaves. Eventually, riots broke out in protest of the new law.

William was leaving his place of work early the day the riots started. He was just about to lock up the newspaper office when one of his close abolitionist friends stopped by. Henry told him that he had arranged for federal soldiers to be sent to his home to protect his family.

"Why place soldiers at my home?"

"We ah, several of us at the movement know who your grandfather was. We feel you need to be protected," Henry replied.

William was taken aback. His associates for the past few years never once spoke of his relationship to George Washington. Now they wanted to protect him. He didn't know how to respond.

Finally he murmured, "I thank you for wanting to keep my family safe."

"Then you'd better high tail it out of here before it gets dark."

The rioting had already begun before William arrived home. Demonstrators chanted in the streets, 'Rich man's war, poor man's fight.' Upon entering his house, he called out loudly to Henrietta. She came hurriedly from the kitchen area, worry registering in her brown eyes.

"What is it William?"

"Henrietta, you and the girls need to stay in the back bedroom where you'll be safe," he directed. "There are rioters all over the city and they're out for blood." Hearing her shocked gasp, he went on, "Where's George and John?"

"We're here, Papa," said John. He and is younger brother had heard their father's remarks as they came into the foyer.

"There are a lot of rioters on the streets and they're angry. I want everyone to stay away from the front of the house. No one is to leave until I give notice," William said gravely.

A loud rap sounded at the front door, interrupting his instructions. "Stay back," said William as he went to answer it.

Three heavily armed federal soldiers were standing on the front porch. The one in charge spoke, "Sir, are you Mister Ford?"

"Yes, I am William Ford."

"Sir, my name is Captain Kelly. I have orders to protect you and your family. With your permission, Sergeants Johnson and Adams here will be stationed inside your home until the riots have ceased."

Of the two men standing behind Captain Kelly. Johnson was older, with a barrel chest and long sideburns. Adams looked to be of the same age as William's brother, Daniel, with sandy blonde hair and brown eyes.

"Thank you, Captain," William replied gratefully. Moving aside, he allowed the two men to enter his home. They stationed themselves in the front area of the home.

On the second day of the riots, young George looked out the front window of the house watching the deserted street. In the distance he could see the smoke of fires that had been set by arsonists. White rioters had surged across the city, hunting down, beating and hanging every Negro in sight, no matter their age or gender.

William wouldn't let any of his family leave the house for fear of them being lynched. To pass the time, George talked to Sergeant

Johnson. Johnson was a big man, standing well over six feet. Even though his size might have been intimidating to some, eighteen-year-old George was not in the least bit put off. Besides, Johnson was a friendly chap, and he even allowed George to handle his saber.

"I've never actually held a real sword in my hands before," George remarked.

"All military personnel have sabers, George. A man has to know how to use one to help defend himself," the sergeant replied.

George took imaginary lunges and repartees that left the Sergeant impressed.

"Where'd you learn to do all those fancy maneuvers?"

"My grandfather carved me a sword out of wood when I was little. I used to practice all the time with it." George handed the saber back to the soldier and said, "I really miss my grandfather. He and my two aunts are in Virginia. We haven't heard from them in a long time."

Noting the sadness on the young man's face, the sergeant said, "I also have family down South, Tennessee in fact. I hope that they're still alive when this damn war is over."

On the third day of the unrest the rioters approached the street where the Fords lived. George, at his usual place near the front window, watched in horror as several houses across and down the street from theirs was torched. Bellowing for his comrade, Sergeant Johnson ran out onto the front porch. A few moments later, William followed Sergeant Adams outside.

"Mr. Ford, please go back into the house. We can't promise to protect you out here," Sergeant Johnson said.

"I thank you sergeant, but this is my family and I aim to help protect it," William replied gravely. He had his rifle loaded and ready.

Johnson nodded and turned and faced the angry crowd.

When the rioters stopped in front of the Ford house, Sergeant Johnson hollered, "This property is under the protection of the federal government!"

"Only Negroes live in this part of the city, and we're going to torch every one of these houses!" one of the men shouted back.

"I suggest, sirs, that you leave now," Johnson said, again more forcefully. He wasn't about to back down from this crowd, though they were outnumbered ten to one.

One rioter started to throw a torch, but Sergeant Adams was ready and shot the man in the arm. The men stopped shouting for a minute, assessing the situation.

"I will again warn you. This house and its occupants are under the protection of the federal government. I'll not hesitate to put a bullet into the head of the next man who disobeys my orders." Johnson brought his rifle up.

The angry group eyed the three men on the porch. All were armed with rifles and pistols. For the first time the protestors noticed that John and George had rifles aimed at them through the open upstairs windows.

"Ah, let's go. These Negroes ain't worth getting killed over," one rioter exclaimed.

The others quickly agreed, and helping their wounded comrade, moved away from the house. The soldiers stood guard outside the entire night.

The rioting went on for four terror-filled days before federal soldiers finally put down the insurrection. Property valued at more than two million dollars had been destroyed. Nearly four thousand persons, white and black, had been killed. A thousand people had been wounded. Many homes of the Unionists were burned down; the residence of the mayor of the city was attacked; and a black neighborhood crowded with poverty-stricken people, was burned to the ground. It took months before the city gained some of its normalcy.

The war was still waging in the South and the Union Army eventually allowed black soldiers to join their ranks. These men were called collectively the 'Black Phalanx,' and were organized into a variety of regiments—engineers, artillery, cavalry, and infantry.

Many blacks gave their lives in battle and saw action in every theater of operations. Twenty black men won medals of honor from Congress for their bravery. Said President Lincoln:

> "Take from us and give to the enemy, the hundred and thirty, forty or fifty thousand colored persons now serving as soldiers, seamen, and laborers and we cannot long maintain the contest."

As to the Ford family, they had survived the worst incident of violence they had ever been privy too. And William couldn't help but contemplate if being away from the protection of Mount Vernon at a time like this had been a wise decision on his part. But he also knew that he couldn't undo what was done and had to live with the choices he made.

The family would just have to watch each other's backs.

Chapter 20

There is a kind of greatness, which does not depend upon fortune. It is a certain manner that distinguishes us, and which seems to destine us for great things.

La Rochefoucauld

In 1863, Western Virginia broke away from Virginia and stayed with the Union. In June of that same year, seventy-nine-year-old West Ford became very ill. Julia was alarmed by the signs of her father's failing health. Recently he'd been having recurring chest pains, shortness of breath, and dizzy spells. He had not risen from his bed this morning and he looked paler than usual.

Doing her best to conceal her anxiety, Julia said, "Papa, you have to eat something. It's the only way to get your strength back."

"Julia, I ain't got much time now on this here earth," West replied calmly.

"Don't say that, Papa. I'll send a message over to Mount Vernon. They can get a doctor to help you." A glassy sheen appeared in her leaf-colored eyes at her father's dire words.

"Little girl, can't no doctor be helpin' me now." The tone of his voice was resigned. "We got to be facin' the facts. I'm dyin'." His faded blue eyes held a faraway expression, as if he were seeing another time, another place.

"Papa, *please* eat just a little for me," she coaxed, trying not to give credence to what he'd just told her.

He opened his mouth slightly and Julia was able to get him to swallow a few spoonfuls of the cooked oats. He fell asleep on his third spoonful. Julia carefully tucked the loose covers around her father's frail form and left the bedroom. She closed the door and leaned on the wall to steady her trembling limbs, her eyes locked shut in suppressed heartache.

Julia sent Corrill with a message to the Mount Vernon superintendent, telling him that West lay at death's door. She knew that he would have a doctor come to examine her father. The very next day, Miss Tracy, secretary to Miss Cunningham of the Mount Vernon Ladies' Association, and Upton Herbert came to West's property on Little Hunting Creek. Finding him extremely ill, they brought him back to Mount Vernon where they could tend to him. Miss Tracy wrote to Miss Cunningham, who was in Alexandria, that:

> "…after finding him feeble and fearing all the excitement might hurt him, we have had him brought here, where we could take better care of him. I felt it was our duty to see that he should want for nothing in his old age."

Julia and Corrill moved into one of the slave cabins that still stood on the Mount Vernon estate, while West was put in his old bedroom on the top floor to convalesce. Unfortunately, West never regained his health. His daughters were with him when he breathed his last.

"Julia, J-Jane come closer," West croaked. His voice was almost gone.

"Yes, Papa?" both girls spoke.

"Give me your hands."

When they complied he squeezed them lightly and said in a whisper as thin as a shadow, "Very tired, my girls. *So tired.* I love you. T-tell William that he be head of the family now. Tell him to stand proud, stand tall, always."

"Papa!" cried Jane. *"Ohh, Papa, Papa."*

She began to weep. Porter placed a comforting arm across his wife's shoulders.

West squeezed his daughter Julia's hand before saying, "Julia, I had me a good, long life, but it be lonely without my Cella." His blue eyes teared momentarily.

He stopped talking for a moment and breathed erratically, as though he had been climbing a flight of stairs. When he finally spoke again his voice was weaker. A few minutes later his face crumbled up and he clutched his left arm. He took a couple of short painful breaths, closed his eyes and then went still.

"Wait! *Pleeease,* Papa! Don't go yet! Please do something, Corrill!" sobbed a hysterical Julia.

Corrill placed a small piece of mirror under West's nostrils. The mirror stayed clear. Then he laid his ear to his father-in-law's chest for a moment. When he lifted his head he said solemnly, "I'm sorry Julia, he's dead. He be with Jesus now."

West Ford's spirit had flown away like a bird that was once caged then given its freedom.

"Oh, God, not my Papa! No, no, no!" cried Julia as she hugged her father's body. Her sobs were heart-wrenching. Corrill kneeled and put his arms around her in comfort.

West Ford died on July 20, 1863, at the Mount Vernon Plantation, the home of his father. Miss Tracy and Julia sent word of his death to the *Alexandria Gazette*. A notice appeared a few days later that read:

West Ford, an aged colored man, who has lived on the Mount Vernon estate the greater portion of his life, died yesterday afternoon at his home on the estate. He was, we hear, in the 79th year of his age. He was well known to most of our older citizens."

West's body was placed in the old tomb of his father. There he would lie until his eldest son came home to decide where his final resting place would be. Unfortunately, his family up North never received a message about his passing.

The war ground inexorably on. Several important events occurred in the month of April, 1865. On April 9, General Robert E. Lee met General Ulysses S. Grant at Appomattox Courthouse to surrender the Northern Virginia Army, thereby ending the Civil War. Slavery became illegal in the United States with the passage of the Thirteenth Amendment to the Constitution. It stated that "neither slave nor involuntary servitude...shall...exist..."

John Wilkes Booth shot and killed Abraham Lincoln at Ford's Theatre five days after Lee's surrender to Grant. Both the white and black populaces were truly stricken by the senseless death of President Lincoln.

After the war ended, William was finally able to travel back to Mount Vernon. As William approached the plantation, a flood of memories and emotions swam through this mind. Some were good, some were bad, but none of them mattered because he was home. He frowned slightly and studied the plantation spread out before him. Mount Vernon was again run down. The fields hadn't been worked and the mansion house and yard looked uncared for. William's heart began to pound with foreboding.

Julia had seen the wagon pull up and stop at the front of the mansion house. She'd been visiting Jane and was on her way back to Little Hunting Creek. When she realized that the wagon contained William and his family she ran up to them screaming and crying out their names. Julia raced into William's outstretched arms, where she was rewarded with a bear hug that almost bruised her ribs. Jane, who had heard the excited shouts, came running up the path leading to the mansion house and was now receiving William's welcoming arms.

After several moments William asked, "Where's Papa?"

Julia looked stunned for a moment then said calmly, "He, he died a couple of years ago, William. I wrote to you, but I guess you didn't get my letter."

William couldn't speak. He staggered as if hit by a physical blow, and sat on steps leading up to the mansion house.

"*Dead? He's gone?*" His voice was stark with grief.

Julia nodded. Her green eyes clouded with the remembered anguish of their father's death.

Something was wrong with William's eyes, a blurring and stinging sensation was affecting them. *Were they tears?* he wondered. He hadn't cried since the day Little Tom was sold, and the urge he felt now was all but choking him. Someone gently touched his shoulder; glancing up he saw that it was Julia.

"Papa told me to tell you, William, that you are responsible for the family now. He also said to tell you to always stand proud, to stand tall."

Trying to compose himself, William rose slowly to his feet. His family members were waiting to take their cue from him. *What am I to do?* he asked himself. *Where are we to go?* William prayed silently to God to give him the strength and wisdom to lead his family. He forced himself to take a steadying breath. He had been reared to assume responsibility, to fulfill his duties, to rise to difficult challenges.

And he would do so now.

"We will go on. We will take care of our children. And we will keep our heritage alive for our children and our children's children."

With stern resolution, he turned his thoughts forward, trusting in God to guide him along the way.

But he couldn't help crying inside.

PART TWO

New Beginnings

Freedom cries…with courage Go!
Give of your heart's rich overflow,
for at the end all struggles cease,
in low, sweet accents whispering peace.

Janet Allen

Chapter 21

*Here lie my ancestors. They were the ones that bore
the brunt of plantation life, through misery, broken
hearts and strife.*

Dr. Judy Saunders-Burton

William had been gone for so long that the family became concerned. It
had been over an hour since he conveyed to them that he needed some
time alone to visit his father's grave. The anxious family members sent
Porter to check on him. Porter met his brother-in-law walking along the
dirt path leading from the Old General's first tomb where West Ford
was interred.

"We need to shore up the tomb door," William said, when he saw
Jane's husband coming towards him. He was concerned that the door of
the tomb was somewhat decayed, although his father's coffin was still in
place and air-tight.

"There are some old boards in the stable that we can use," Porter said,
as he walked beside him back to the mansion house. "Are you going to
leave your papa there?"

"I think it's the best place for right now. With the Virginia countryside in such turmoil, I don't really know where to place his body yet."

Rubbing a hand over his jaw with several slow repetitions, William continued, "I guess the whole South is experiencing the after-effects of the war. All the way down here we saw hundreds of freed slaves wandering along the roads. They were begging for food and medical treatment. They don't have homes—no chance to find jobs. Porter, if most of the white southern populace can't survive without money after this cursed war, then how can the ex-slaves?"

"I really don't know. Not many would want to remain on their plantations once they were freed and all. I know I wouldn't have."

"But freedom isn't enough," said William. "The majority of them can't read or write and are ill-equipped to handle life, now that they're free."

"William, I know you're concerned, but the first thing you have to do is take care of your own family's interests."

William replied, "Let's head on back to the mansion house. I want to get to Papa's property before nightfall."

Over the next several days, William secured positions for John, George, and himself, working on refurbishing the Mount Vernon mansion house and gardens. His sons were also hired to guard the Old General's tomb, a duty they had done before. William wasn't in any financial trouble yet as he had enough savings to keep the family afloat for a while. But the money wouldn't last forever.

The U.S. Army of Transportation set up operations about five miles from West Ford's property near Gum Springs. The government was providing food, shelter, and health care, and thousands of blacks migrated to the area. Some camped out on the Ford property. William had no problem with them settling on their land, as they had no other place to go.

Constance and Hannah donated their spare time to the Freedmen's Bureau to assist the newly freed slaves to read and write. The Freedmen's Bureau was established to aid the many former slaves with tools to help them survive, such as land grants, food, and clothing.

The two sisters were just about to enter the bureau office, but Hannah was waiting for Constance to catch up with her. She was standing with her hands on her hips, watching the slow, sluggish steps Constance was taking. For some reason, the girl had been dragging her feet all morning.

"Come on, Constance. What's the matter with you?"

As she neared her sister, Constance said determinedly, "I can't go in there again Hannah. There're just too many people coming and going; it makes me nervous. And the men—they stare at me and…I just don't want them thinking I'm available."

Hannah studied her sister's appearance. Constance's hands were pale and soft-looking, the nails neatly trimmed. She was also dressed better than any white woman living in the area and she didn't have her reddish-brown hair tied up in a tignon like the one adorning her own. Constance looked white. She still wanted to be white.

Hannah glanced at her own hands, which bore the labors of hard work, her nails ragged and broken. The sisters were as different as sunlight and moonlight.

"Constance, the men stare at you because you're beautiful. They won't harm you. But if you don't want to help out at the bureau, I think Mama and Papa will understand."

"Do you think so? I mean, they're really so adamant that we help out."

"Don't worry. I'll think of something to tell them so you won't have to come here anymore."

Hannah smoothed the frown line on her sister's brow. Constance had never really recovered from her fiancé's rejection. In fact, she had written to Herbert a month before, asking about his welfare. He had written back, telling her he was doing well, but that he still loved her. Constance's next letter asked him to reconsider their engagement. She was waiting for his reply. Hannah wanted to tell their mother what was occurring, but Constance swore her to secrecy.

Breaking into to Hannah's musings, Constance said, "I knew I could count on you." Looking beyond her sister, Constance saw their older brother, John, emerging from the crowd gathered around a food depot. He had come to offer his services and then to walk the girls home. "Here comes John now," Constance said a moment later.

But John wasn't looking at his sisters. He was watching a stately, dark-skinned girl handing out food sacks to a group of families. The girl felt John's avid gaze on her, looked in his direction, and smiled. She had a beautiful smile. He forgot to breathe for a moment and shot her an easy, lop-sided grin, showing even, white teeth.

Walking over to her with his hat in his hands he said, "Here miss, let me help you pass these out." He handed out the last of the food sacks, dusted his hands on his brown pants, and turned towards the girl. "My name is John Ford, and you are?"

"Charlotte Willis. My family be workin' over at the Snowden plantation."

"Do you come here often?" He wasn't going to let this girl get away without being able to find her again.

"Yes, I do. I be volunteering most days."

They both stared at each other. Something magical was happening. Their eyes met with surprised awareness.

"Well, I guess I'll be seeing you around, Miss Charlotte Willis," John said, and he joined his sisters.

Later that evening over supper, William discussed the land grants promised to freed slaves with his family members. Many people in the North believed that ex-slaves should be given a fair portion of the land they tilled in slavery. During the Civil War, Congress had provided for the confiscation of all property owned by men in the Confederate armies. These estates were to be divided into farms of forty acres and handed over to adult freedmen, along with a mule and $50 toward the cost of a home.

"Do you think the government will give out these land grants?" Henrietta inquired.

Shrugging, William replied, "I don't really know."

"Many of the people over at the Freedmen's Bureau aren't even looking for work. They say they are waiting to receive the land the government promised them," John said.

"Son, I pray the government comes through, but I'll tell you, I just don't know," said William.

His doubts rang true, for reparation never came to pass. 'Forty acres and a mule' was the first casualty of reconciliation between the North and the South.

More freedmen during the next year settled onto the Ford property, now called Gum Springs. The area also became a depot for the newly freed to search for their missing family members.

On April 9, 1866, the Civil Rights Bill was passed, which granted blacks the rights and privileges of American citizenship. The act was passed over the veto of President Andrew Johnson. Two months later Congress passed the Fourteenth Amendment. This measure declared that all persons born in the United States were citizens. No state could abridge the rights of such citizens or deprive any person within its jurisdiction the equal protection of the laws. It was unfortunate that many of the southern populace refused to acknowledge the new act and amendment.

It seemed that whatever the southerner had surrendered at Appomattox, they had not surrendered their belief that blacks were inferior to whites.

Chapter 22

Advise well before you begin, and when you have maturely considered, then act with promptitude.

Sallust

William wished he could hear his father's voice just once more. He missed the quiet conversations between them. He'd always known that someday he would become the family patriarch. He had been groomed for it. But Mount Vernon wasn't the same without the noble old gentleman, West Ford.

A year after the Fords returned to Virginia, a black Union soldier rode up to where George Ford was working in one of the flower gardens on the Mount Vernon plantation.

"I'm looking for a man named William Ford," stated the soldier. "He be 'round here anymore?"

George was excited to see a Negro in uniform and hurriedly told the soldier what he wanted to know. "William is my father." Pointing to where William was working on the side of the mansion house, repairing a broken board, he continued. "I'll take your horse for you sir."

"Thank ye kindly."

The man dismounted and handed the reins to George. Ever curious, George followed him after securing the horse.

The soldier stopped a few feet from George's father and called out, "William?"

William turned to face the soldier. "Yes, I'm William." Narrowing his eyes at the stranger, William continued, "Can I help you?"

The soldier didn't answer. Instead he slowly undid the button at the wrist of his faded blue shirt and rolled it back. Then he lifted up the arm, revealing a scar on his forearm.

William's blue eyes widened. His expression changed from shock to amazement to joy as he realized who this stranger was. "My God, is it really you, Little Tom?"

"Yes, little brother, it be me."

William came up to the man and stood for a moment, not knowing how to greet his long lost friend. But Little Tom took it into his own hands and gave William a great bear hug, lifting his feet off the ground.

George watched the reunion of his father and his childhood friend. He wondered how Little Tom received his name, as the man towered over his father by a good six inches.

Little Tom stayed for several days with the Ford family. He told them about what had happened to him after he was sold away from Mount Vernon.

"I cried those first few days as we traveled to our new plantation," he said. "But mama tol' me that cryin' wasn't gonna solve nothin'. She say be strong, Little Tom. I had to be every day 'cause our new massa was a mean one. He didn't like slaves to look him in the eye. We had to always bow our heads in his presence. He sold my mama after a couple months to a plantation in Tennessee."

A haunted look entered Little Tom's brown eyes as he continued, "After a while, I didn't care no more what be happenin' to me and I gots the scars on my back to prove it. Many a time I be thinkin' I was gonna die from those beatins'. But I didn't. When the war come we heard that if'n a slave could get to the Union soldiers, he'd be set free. One day some Union soldiers rode up to the massa's plantation and I just joined up with them." Smiling at William, he said, "Now I aim to see if'n I can find my mama."

Tom wasn't alone in his search. Many ex-slaves were trying to reassemble their families, desperately seeking sons, daughters, mothers and fathers sold as slaves throughout the South.

Tom pulled out a wrinkled piece of newspaper clipping and handed it to William. "I ain't so good at reading yet. But one of them soldiers give me this paper. He say it be from a colored newspaper. He say that people put notices in it for findin' their families. Can you read it for me?"

William glanced at the newspaper. It wasn't the first such notice he had seen. Newly formed black newspapers frequently ran advertisements seeking lost family members. Taking a deep breath, he read, "Information wanted of Caroline Dodson, who was sold from Nashville, November 1, 1862, by James Lumsden to Warwick (a trader then in human beings), who carried her to Atlanta, Georgia, and she was last heard of in the sale pen of Robert Clarke, (human trader in that place), from which she was sold. Any information of her whereabouts will be thankfully received and rewarded by her mother. Lucinda Lowery, Nashville."

He read the dozen more listings. Unfortunately, there was no information on Little Tom's mother.

"I'm sorry, Little Tom," said William after handing him the paper. "These newspapers come out all the time; maybe one day you'll see her name in one."

"I guess I kinda knew that her name wouldn't be in no newspaper. But I gots to keep hopin' and prayin'."

"One must always keep hope alive, Little Tom. I know if your mother is in Tennessee, you'll find her," William replied solemnly.

Later that evening, George begged Little Tom to tell him about his life as a soldier. George asked so many questions that Little Tom said with a chuckle, "Boy, that tongue of yours is gonna dry up for lack of moisture."

When Little Tom left the following day, George became restless. He knew he would never be satisfied tending the tomb of George Washington or working as a gardener. He felt the stinging yearning for something, anything, for going, doing, for something to change. So he decided to join the army. He relayed his plans to his brother while he was weeding the garden next to the house.

"Sign up with me, John," said George. "We'll make the best soldiers. We can become officers someday, just like the Old General!"

"I can't say being a soldier is in my blood, like yours, George. Besides, Papa and I are going into the farming business. Many of the plantations around here are making money from farming and selling their produce in Alexandria. And I'm going to ask Charlotte to marry me."

"Congratulations, John," George said, shaking his brother's hand. "I guess then I'll have to join by myself."

Later that evening, George broke the news to his family. "Mama, Papa, I've decided to join the army." Noting the alarm on his mother's face, he quickly added, "Now listen before you say anything. The government has made provisions for colored troops to serve in the regular army and I'm going to sign up."

"Oh, George you can't!" cried his mother. She rose from the settee she was relaxing on and then dropped back down onto it.

"Now, Henrietta, the boy's old enough to make his own decisions. If he wants to become a soldier, then that's what he will do," William stated calmly.

George's sisters crowded around him, fussing and crying. Henrietta was openly weeping now. William stood back and watched the scene taking place in his home. He wasn't as calm as he let on. He was afraid.

He was afraid for his youngest son. But he also knew that a man had to make his own way in this life, just as he had done.

Walking over to George, William clasped him on the shoulder with his hand and said, "Son, are you sure you want to do this?"

"Papa, I've wanted to be a soldier since I was five years old. I'm sure," George replied earnestly.

"Then we'll support you."

In 1867, at the tender age of twenty-one, George William Ford enlisted in the United States Army. His military unit was the 10th Calvary. George would put away his wooden sword and trade it in for one made of steel.

Since the Civil War, George Ford had aspired to become a soldier. Like most black men who enlisted in the Army, he saw it as a way to attain true freedom in a land where Negroes were still considered as second-class citizens. In 1866, despite objections from white military leaders and southern politicians, Congress formed six all-black regiments, two cavalry and four infantry, headed by white officers. The black soldiers were to serve a five-year term for thirteen dollars a month.

On the day George left Mount Vernon to head out west, he went into the mansion house and looked at a picture of George Washington. With conviction ringing in his voice he said aloud, "I'll wear my uniform with the same pride and dedication that you once wore yours."

A few moments later, he said goodbye to his father as they stood on the wooden steps leading up to the mansion house. William embraced him and said, "Stand proud, stand tall and remember your heritage."

"I'll always remember, Papa."

George realized at that moment that not only did he love his father, he admired him very much. His father's opinions had definitely influenced much of his own thinking. Now it was time for George to follow his own beliefs and his heart. Filled with the wanderlust and adventure he believed the military and the frontier held for him, the young man mounted his horse and left the place of his birth.

But would the military be ready for George?

Chapter 23

And here I stand; judge, my masters.

Shakespeare

It wasn't what he expected. Upon arriving at Fort Leavenworth, Kansas, George Ford was surprised to see that the fort was no more than a group of whitewashed wooden buildings sitting on the prairie. It seemed rather unimposing here in the middle of such a grand wilderness.

There were hundreds of black men assembled at the fort. Many were farmers, servants, cooks, and former field laborers, all looking for adventure, steady pay, and a place to belong in the white man's world. George gazed around him as he tried to find his barracks. It was almost dusk and the area was not well lit.

"Look out, country boy!" A bald, colored soldier hollered when George accidentally bumped into him.

George had been staring at the tall, scar-faced soldier who had ridden up in front of the officer's barracks and dismounted. The man tied his horse to a hitching rail and directed his attention to them.

"Ateenshut." The soldier that George had bumped into immediately stood at attention and saluted the scarred man.

George quickly followed suit and brought his hand up to his head. The officer then walked past them and went into the wooden building.

"Where you be from, boy?" the bald soldier asked him a few seconds later.

"I'm from Virginia. My name's George Ford."

"My name's Charlie Creek and I've been 'round here for two months now. Come on and follow me. I'll show you where you su'posed to bunk down. Charlie stopped in mid-stride and George almost bumped into him again. "Oh, and Ford, that man be Colonel Benjamin Grierson. He's in charge of the 10th Calvary. Ain't a soldier 'round here like the colonel. He be a fair and just man," added Charlie.

"Charlie, how did the colonel's cheek get scarred like that?" George inquired as they started walking towards the colored soldier's quarters.

"Heard tell a horse kicked him when he was a youngin'."

George became concerned a few moments later as he saw where they were being housed. The quarters were located in a low, swampy area of the fort. It was so muddy he almost slipped and fell twice. Finally they stopped in front of the bunkhouse that he would call home for the next several months. It didn't look fit for hogs to live in. Charlie entered and George followed close behind him.

"Soldiers meet your new bunk mate," Charlie stated. "This here be George Ford from Virginia."

Several men were already bunked down for the night and nodded in his direction without rising. Two other men who were standing by their bunks walked over to George and Charlie.

A tall, dark-skinned man sporting a neatly trimmed beard came forward with his right hand outstretched. "My name's John Wright and this is John Jones," he said pointing to a man wearing wire-rimmed glasses. "Since we both got the same name, you can call me J. J.," he added amicably.

"Well, I'll be leavin' you tenderfoots alone now," said Charlie. "We gets up pretty early in the morning so it's best you get some shut-eye." He then turned and left the bunkhouse.

George took the one empty bunk left in the room and placed his small valise down next to it. The two Johns were already stretched out on their bunks and had extinguished their lamps. The bunkhouse was now dark except for the lone lantern next to George's cot. He sat down on the thin mattress, then reached over and turned down the wick on the kerosene lamp. He didn't move for a few minutes as his eyes adjusted to the darkness, then he finally pulled off his boots, and lay down. He lay there for a long time wondering just what he had gotten himself into. Eventually he fell asleep.

The next day Colonel Grierson assembled the newly signed colored troops. Colonel Grierson insisted on a very high standard for enlisted men, and he kept a watchful eye on the new recruits as they arrived at Leavenworth. Assignments were given out to the officers. The new soldiers were to learn to follow orders and perform complicated drills. They were also to practice several hours a day handling their horses and weapons.

"You, soldier," an officer called out to George after conversing with Colonel Grierson. "You seem to know horses. I want you to take these two men," he pointed over to the men known as Eli and Henry, "and teach them how to ride."

George had ridden horses all of his life and was quite familiar with horseflesh. The horses given to the colored troops looked like they were ready for the glue factory, they were so worn out. He'd never seen horses look so poorly. Most of them were over a dozen years old, others were cripples left over from the Civil War. But not one to shirk his duty, George showed the men how to properly mount, hold the reins, and guide the horse's direction.

Eli caught on quickly, but it wasn't so easy for Henry. Henry was a large man and extremely heavy. Already the colored troops were calling him "lard bucket." The first time the horse threw Henry he rolled like a barrel and stopped at George's booted feet. The man rose awkwardly and half-stumbled back to his mount. Henry stuck his left foot in the stirrup, gripped the saddle, and tried to mount—on the wrong side.

George's lips twitched as he called out, "Switch sides."

Then he watched as Henry slowly went to the other side of the mount. After several attempts, Henry managed to climb upon the steed.

"Now tighten your knees on the horse and move your body with him as he moves. It will keep you from bouncing off," George instructed.

After several exasperating hours, Henry learned how to ride.

This was not the last time George was singled out by the officers. He helped to teach the soldiers to shoot, and wield sabers, and in his spare time he taught those who needed to learn to read and write.

After about two weeks into their training, one of the officers asked if anyone was musically inclined in George's group.

"We need a man to play the trumpet. Any of you soldiers know how to play a musical instrument?" Sergeant Mills asked the men as they stood at attention in front of the officer's barracks.

"I do sir," said Private Foster. "My ole massa taught me how to play the harpsichord."

"Good. Anyone else?" asked the sergeant.

The men were shuffling their feet. No one was willing to volunteer. The trumpeter had to lead the troops into battle. It was hard enough trying to focus on staying on a horse and firing rifles without blowing a bugle in the heat of combat.

"I have a little knowledge about music, that is, I got an ear for music sir," said George.

"Well, you and Foster come along with me over to the officer's quarters. We'll get you started on learning how to play reveille."

It didn't take long for George to learn how to play the bugle. He played reveille at 5:20 every morning for his company. Less than twenty minutes later the soldiers fed their horses, then went to breakfast.

Beginning at 6:40 they spent the day on guard duty, practicing military drills or grooming and exercising their horses. The colored troops put in long, tiring days.

After several long arduous weeks the troops of the 10th Cavalry were ready to defend the West. Their shared duty would be to try and keep the peace between the settlers and the confederated tribes that consisted of the Southern Cheyenne, Kiowas, Comanches, Apaches and Arapahos.

Out of the eight companies of the 10th Cavalry; D, E, and L were assigned to the Indian Territory while the others were stationed at posts and camps along the Kansas Pacific Railroad. The Indian Territory encompassed the states of New Mexico, Kansas, Arizona, and Texas. George and his two best friends, J. J. and Henry, were all assigned to the 10th Cavalry, Company L.

Hundreds of soldiers stood at attention in long, straight, neat rows on the day they were to leave Fort Leavenworth and report to other western forts. The heat and the glare of the sun were merciless on the assembled men. Already the soldiers were beginning to perspire under their heavy, blue uniform jackets.

The colored troops were upset because they were ordered not to march in parade past the commander of Fort Leavenworth, General William Hoffman. The 10th Cavalry stood at parade rest, their feet apart and their hands clasped behind their backs as they watched the other companies march by. George was outraged, but schooled his features to show no emotion.

"I guess ole Hoffman don't think we're good enough to wear these here uniforms and to defend our country," J. J. scoffed under his breath to George.

"We're good enough all right," admonished George. "We just have to prove to these white officers what the 10th can do. Stand proud, stand tall, soldiers," George said firmly.

Already his unit looked to him as a leader, and each man stood a little taller as his prophetic words were passed along the rows of uniformed soldiers.

General Grierson even sat a little straighter in his saddle as he noticed the troop's stance change from scorn to one of pride. Grierson was proud of his black soldiers. It was common knowledge that General Hoffman was contemptuous of the colored troops and did his best to make the troops feel unwelcome, uncomfortable, and inferior. General Hoffman had quartered the colored troops on low ground that became a swamp whenever it rained. He wouldn't even allow the men to build a walkway so that they could keep their feet dry. Many of the men had come down with pneumonia.

Colonel Grierson complained to the Army about the harsh treatment his men were subjected to, but his protests were ignored. He also objected to the Army's name for his regiment, the 10th Colored Cavalry. Once, a white officer referred to Grierson's regiment as "colored troops," and the colonel took umbrage.

He told the officer, "You will not refer to this regiment as the 10th Colored Cavalry, but as the 10th Cavalry. Regardless of their colored skins, they are soldiers of the U.S. Army."

The officer, duly chastised, never slipped up again. Even on this occasion Colonel Grierson had argued with Hoffman to let his troops march, but Hoffman remained firm. Yet his men did him proud. Never had he seen them stand taller.

Finally, the movement westward began and the 10th Cavalry filed out of Fort Leavenworth. George's unit and two others were headed for Fort Riley in Kansas. The first night out he volunteered for guard duty. He watched the stars and listened to the night sounds of the prairie. He wondered if the occasional mournful howl of a coyote *was* a coyote. He had heard that the Indians were masters at mimicking animal sounds, and he became more vigilant as his alert eyes swept the occasional patch of brush. Nothing seemed to move, but George was not the least bit assured. The plains Indians were trained as warriors and fighting was their way of life. Fortunately for the 10th, it remained a quiet and uneventful night.

The journey to Fort Riley progressed without incident during the next several days, and at last the journey was drawing to a close.

"My backside ain't never gonna feel the same again," complained Henry. "I ain't got no feelin' left in it. Damn it's so hot out here; you can fry an egg on me!" Sighing loudly, he continued, "Whys I joined the army I don't rightly know. Oh Lordy, Lordy, I gots an itch I can't scratch."

"Will you stop your complainin'!" shouted an exasperated J. J. "For the last hundred miles all you done is whine, whine, whine!"

"Well 'least I don't yell every time I hear a coyote screech," countered Henry.

"I ain't never yelled from no coyote! Anyways, that coyote was too close for comfort. A man can't take a leak now days without some critter or other jumpin' out 'round him." J. J.'s face took on an offended expression.

Henry laughed outright. "You ran back to the camp screamin' like a chicken with its head cut off." He continued with a smirk, "'Sides, everybody heard you."

"I did not."

"Did so."

George smiled as he listened to the banter between his friends. It had been a long ride to the fort and he was just as saddle-sore and fatigued as they were. Trickles of sweat ran from his forehead into his eyes. He blinked at the burning sensation and swiped his jacket sleeve over his face.

The mood of the soldiers brightened as Fort Riley came into sight. The tired troops entered the fort covered in dust and utterly exhausted. Despite the constant pounding of the southwest wind, the stinging sand and dirt, and the blast-furnace heat of the Kansas summer, George noted with pride that not a single trooper slumped in his saddle. They were not willing to look weak in front of the white soldiers now gathered around to watch them ride in.

George eased his lathered horse to a stop in front of another group of run-down barracks set aside for them. He wiped a hand across his eyes, feeling the sting of the small grains of sand that had lodged in them. Shrugging off his exhaustion, he dismounted and took care of his horse before finding his bunk. As George lay stretched out on his cot, he closed his eyes, but was not sleeping. His mind flittered, restless as he contemplated what he could expect on the morrow. Was he ready to fight for his country and possibly be killed or injured?

He hoped he was prepared for battle as he was bound to find out within the next few days.

Upon reaching Fort Riley, Colonel Grierson was told by the fort commander of the dangerous situation that had escalated on the Platte River on the north and to the Rio Grande on the south. More troops were needed to strengthen the military presence. George's company L and companies D, and E were assigned there for their first tour of duty. Two days later the three companies left Fort Riley to join in the peace-keeping process.

Once on the plains, George's company fanned out to protect rail-road-working crews, to escort stages and trains, and to scout out Indian strongholds. During one of their first skirmishes they had fired too quickly, missing their targets, but they had shown no panic when they confronted their first battle with the Comanches. Private George Ford blew the notes to the charge on his bugle as he guided his horse for-ward. He then pulled out his rifle and fired at the retreating Comanche. Battles like this one went on for several months. Company L was doing well for raw recruits.

George would experience the terror of battle after battle during the next several months. Once under the command of Captain Henry Alvord, over one hundred wild-riding Cheyenne chased George's

Company L and Company M. The men were forced to halt and take cover. Crouched behind some boulders, they waited for the attack.

"George, I think I'm gonna die today," said J. J. "If'n I do, don't let them scalp me." Sweat was pouring out of every pore on J.J.'s body. His shirt was drenched and sticking to his skin.

"Shut up, J. J. You aren't gonna die," George said. He pulled his Bowie knife from his boot and stuck it in his pants near his waist. He then made sure his rifle was loaded and ready.

J. J. wasn't the only one nervous. Big Henry stammered, "Oh Lord, Jesus, help us! I jes know we all gonna die. We gonna die, die, die! Them Injuns is gonna take our hair. I jes know they are." Henry was making the other soldiers nervous with his outbursts.

"Get a hold of yourself, soldier," ordered George. "You have to get control of yourself before you can control anything else. Stay calm."

The morning air exploded with the sound of gunfire a few moments later. Soon arrows were flying and several of the soldiers were hit. The fighting raged on until dark and was renewed at daybreak the next morning. That morning the troops had to fight the enemy in hand-to-hand combat. The troops fought hard.

George fought hard.

His knife blade slashed in the air and he jumped back as one of the Indian's blades almost pierced his stomach. Chest heaving from the exertion, and adrenaline pumping through his veins like a powerful drug, he crouched low, his knife poised and ready. George felt his blade slide into the soft area of the brave's belly a few seconds later.

He didn't like killing, but when faced with a life or death situation, he had no choice. He continued to fight and even saved J. J.'s life as he was reloading his gun. An Indian had his tomahawk in the air, ready to bury it in J. J.'s skull when George shot him.

"I owe you, George," J. J. hollered as he saw the Indian fall next to him.

"Just watch my back, J. J.!" George shouted in reply. He just managed to duck an arrow launched his way a moment later.

The Comanche were surprised at the fierce way the black soldiers fought, and finally withdrew. As suddenly as it had begun, the fight came to an end. George's chest was heaving with exertion. Slowly the fact registered in his consciousness that he and his friends were still alive. The 10th had suffered a dozen men wounded, but no fatalities. After the battle, George was promoted to corporal and he resigned from the position of bugler.

It was about this time that the Confederated Indian Tribes began to refer to the black troops as "Buffalo Soldiers." How the name arose is only a guess. Many believed that the Indians saw a similarity between the hair of the black soldier and that of the buffalo. The buffalo was considered a sacred animal to the Indians. It was a fact, however, that the Indians considered the black troops as courageous. The 10th Cavalry accepted their new name with pride and included a buffalo as part of the regimental crest on their uniforms.

The Buffalo Soldiers didn't acquire all their lessons on the battlefield. Their pride of self grew as they learned about the iron discipline of the frontier Army. They learned to accept danger and death as constant companions.

But not all of the Buffalo Soldiers could handle the rigors of military life. Some of the new troopers developed a quick aversion for the Army and took off without a 'by your leave.' Others deserted after minor infractions brought about immediate and harsh punishment.

Corporal George Ford would write to his parents about Private Filmore Roberts, who was detailed to carry the mail to Fort Gibson. He never reported there and was listed as a deserter. George never believed Private Roberts had deserted; he was sure that something had to have happened to the loyal soldier. His surmise proved correct many months later when Private Robert's decomposing body was found lodged between some rocks and willows on the Canadian River. It was presumed that Private Roberts had tried to cross a swollen stream and drowned. The mail pouch was still strapped to his back.

George hardly had time to cool in his saddle during his first year of duty. His unit was constantly being deployed to help escort the hordes of people traveling westward and to scout along the Red River. The 10th was sent to Fort Arbuckle in the early spring of 1868. He and his company erected crude picket shelters for themselves and roofed several crumbling adobe structures to protect the supplies. A few months later, George's unit was sent to Fort Cobb, Texas, when reinforcements were needed to help ward off the Cheyenne and Arapahoe along the Washita River.

J.J. watched a large contingent of the 7th Calvary ride into Fort Cobb after one of their patrols. Looking over at George he asked, "Do you think it's him?"

"I believe it is; he's got long hair, but it ain't exactly blond. It's more reddish blond," George answered.

The man they were discussing was Colonel George Custer. His exploits had inflicted a severe blow to the Cheyenne at the Washita the previous winter.

"Is it true what they say, that he won't serve with colored troops?" J. J. continued.

"Yeah, he refuses to serve with us."

George and J. J. saluted the colonel as he sauntered past them into the fort's headquarters. He had an Indian guide walking beside him. The men found out later that the Indian's name was Bloody Knife.

The next day Colonel Grierson walked up to George and ordered, "Mount your troops up, Corporal Ford. We're headed to Medicine Bluff Creek to scout for a new fort location."

"Yes, sir," George replied as he shouted to the troops who were waiting for their orders. George had learned that General Philip Sheridan, commander of the Gulf Division, disliked the location of Fort Cobb. Sheridan felt that it was ill situated with respect to the Kiowa-Comanche reservation and too far removed to afford effective protection for the Texas frontier.

When the detail reached Medicine Bluff, George helped scout the terrain. A rich blanket of grass and a pure water source covered the whole area. Wild game was seen everywhere. The next day Grierson made his report to Sheridan. Sheridan decided to move immediately to the new site, Camp Wichita, and wanted the 10th to construct a permanent post there.

Torrential rains delayed the move for another week, and even then the movement of troops was tedious as they sloshed through a river of mud and water. The one-day trip took the tired and damp troops four days. When they finally arrived, work began immediately on the new post.

"Here we go again," said a weary Henry as he started clearing an area of underbrush. This was the second time in a year that they'd had to construct a living space out of the wilderness.

Henry continued, "I'm workin' harder here than I did on my ole plantation."

J. J. scoffed, "But at least we ain't got no whip hangin' over our heads."

George's brow was furrowed as he confronted the task assigned to him. He was to take the condemned tentage, newly cut logs, and brush and make some sort of living space out of them. *How am I to accomplish this?* he wondered as he stared at the hodgepodge of materials at his disposal.

Shrugging, he muttered, "Mater artium necessitas."

Looking over his shoulder at George, J. J. asked, "What does that gibberish mean?"

George replied, "It means necessity is the mother of invention."

For the next several months, Grierson and his troopers continued their construction work and spent time preparing for field duty when the need arose. Scouting detachments were in the saddle from dawn to dusk. And in August 1869, the newly completed post was named Fort Sill.

The regimental band did much to soften the rough work and loneliness at Fort Sill. There were concerts in the evenings that were enjoyed by both officers and troops. George would sing, his rich tenor voice lulling the men into thinking of home and family.

The 10th regiment was ill-prepared to cope with the large-scale Indian crisis that arose in 1870-71. Indian war parties grew bolder. Colonel Grierson received word that a band of Kiowas and Comanches had struck heavily along the north Texas border, killing settlers and attacking the troops whenever the occasion was in their favor. The regiment's bugler, Larkin Foster, had been killed. Also, a large contingent of Cheyenne had left their reservation and it was feared that they had joined with the Kiowa.

All summer long, George and his company ran patrols along the Red River. But no matter how diligent they were, they could not intercept the bands of Indians. The Indians were too crafty and they could cross in dozens of locations along the many miles of the river's boundary.

George was with a detachment of troops at the mouth of Cache Creek on a reconnaissance patrol in late summer. He had been ordered to scout ahead of the main body of troops, and J. J. and Henry volunteered to ride with him as backup.

"We ain't never gonna catch 'em," stated Henry to no one in particular as he rode along side of J. J. and George. "Theys be *too* tricky."

"Well, you best be glad we ain't run into no Injuns 'cause they would just love to get your scalp," quipped J. J.

Henry had a lot of hair. It was so full and high that it was hard to stuff all of it under his hat. Self-consciously, Henry started pulling his hat more tightly over his head.

"Quiet," interjected George a few moments later. His eyes narrowed as he scanned the hills around them. They were in a ravine as they scouted along the river's mouth. The hairs on the back of his neck were standing up. George had the eerie sensation that they were being watched. He shifted uncomfortably in his saddle.

"What is it?" Henry asked, his eyes as round as the buttons on his uniform jacket.

"I don't know," George whispered. "It's too quiet. I don't have a good feeling about this."

He listened, his body taut, but ready. His horse began sidling nervously in a staccato prancing, sensing his master's tenseness. All of a sudden, a burst of gunfire exploded around them. George heard a whistling past his ear.

"Get to cover!" he shouted as he and his men raced their horses to a strand of boulders and trees next to the riverbank.

George flattened himself against his mount, tucking his head low beside the horse's mane to make himself less of a target.

Henry didn't make it.

His horse was shot from under him and his leg was caught beneath its weight. The dying animal lay on its side, bleeding profusely, its eyes wide with fear and pain, its nostrils flared, saliva pouring from its mouth. Henry was struggling in his efforts to budge the horse's body from his injured leg, but he didn't have the strength.

"Jesus, help me!" screamed Henry.

Bits of dust and dirt flew into the air where the bullets hit the ground around him and his dying mount. George didn't think; he reacted. He ran from his cover, weaving and dodging the bullets being fired at him, as he went to help Henry. George lifted the dead horse's hind-quarters and Henry was able to slide from underneath. As the men were crawling back to cover, George was shot in the leg. The pain was instant. White, hot agony almost paralyzed him. He edged behind a boulder, took a deep breath, steadied himself, and fired back at the hostiles.

The trio kept firing until the rest of their patrol rode up and chased the Indians off. George was promoted to first sergeant after the skirmish. Now his company began to refer to him as "top sergeant."

The bullet in George's leg was never fully removed. A fragment would remain lodged near the thigh muscle for the rest of his life. After spending several weeks recuperating from his wound at Fort Sill, he was discharged from his tour of duty.

As George was leaving the fort's headquarters, J. J. stopped him to say farewell. "Are you coming back, George?"

"Yes, I'm going to re-enlist. Soldiering is in my blood, but it's been too long since I've seen my family. What about you?"

J. J. said in a serious tone, "You know, I be a slave all of my life before I joined the Army. All I ever be thinkin' about, dream about, be my freedom." J. J. paused for a deep breath, then went on. "After the war ended and we was set free, I left that plantation. I ain't never settin' foot on that place again. So, I guess I be re-enlistin' after a short spell."

George understood why J. J. would think like that. J. J. never knew what it felt like to be a free man until he joined the Army. With George it was a different matter—he was born free. And not a day had gone by that he didn't think of his parents and the place of his birth.

Smiling at J. J., George said, "Well, I can't wait to get home to eat some of my mama's golden fried chicken, candied sweet potatoes, and greens."

"Mmm, that be almost making me want to go with you." J. J. said, rubbing his hand in a circular motion over his stomach.

Both men could appreciate the gesture as they thought about the meals they had consumed for the past five years. The menu seldom deviated from coffee, bread, beans, and old jerky. Sometimes they would get beef and molasses with corn bread for their evening meals.

Grasping hands in a firm shake; the best friends parted company.

As he rode out of the fort, George wondered what had been happening in Virginia for the last five years.

He thought with some trepidation, *What am I going to find when I get there?*

Chapter 24

Confusion now hath made his masterpiece.

Shakespeare

In Virginia ex-slaves were enduring the hardships that came with their newfound freedom since George had been gone. Former masters sought to maintain control over their former slaves by keeping them in a condition as close to slavery as possible.

On March 30, 1870, the Fifteenth Amendment was passed granting blacks the right to vote. The Republican Party had championed black rights, and the majority of black voters became Republicans. Many southern blacks were hassled, terrorized, and even lynched by 'undercover' agencies when they tried to exercise their voting rights. The most insidious of these agencies was the Ku Klux Klan. A group of merrymakers bent on a good time formed the organization in 1865 in Pulaski, Tennessee. By the spring of 1867, the Klan had become a highly organized movement that cut across state lines. Their goal was to keep blacks in their place by administering some form of corporal punishment—whipping, tar-and-feathering, or lynching. A similar fate was usually the destiny of whites who fraternized with blacks.

William and his oldest son were discussing the dire situation at his farm on Little Hunting Creek.

"John, you have to be careful going over to Gum Springs. I hear that many colored folks have been harassed on the road," warned William as he watched John hitch two horses to the harness and traces on the wagon.

"I know, Papa, and I'll be careful. But Charlotte expects me to take her to church tonight to talk to the reverend about our wedding."

"I wish your brother was here to see you get married," William said wistfully.

"So do I. Have you gotten any more letters from him yet?"

"Not since his regiment relocated to Fort Cobb. George has been gone for so many years," William sighed. "I hope he's all right."

"Papa, you know George can take care of himself."

John climbed upon the wooden seat of the wagon and waved good-bye to his father. His thoughts were now on Charlotte.

William stood for a few minutes and watched as John rode away from their farm. John was a good son. His oldest boy worked so hard trying to make their land into a working and profitable farm. William's thoughts then drifted to George. He missed his youngest child. He received sporadic letters from him, but he continued to be concerned about his welfare.

Later that evening, John was escorting Charlotte to her home after a visit with Reverend Taylor, the pastor of their local church. They left the church at dusk, and eventually he would have to light the kerosene lamp that he kept in back of the wagon to illuminate their way home. About a mile away from the church, they heard the sound of hoof beats coming from behind them. The rambunctious riders were hooting and hollering, and a nervous Charlotte tightly grasped John's arm.

"Be still and stay calm when they reach us, Charlotte," said John as he gently patted her hand.

A few moments later, three men on horseback surrounded their wagon.

"Boy, didn't anybody ever tell you it ain't healthy to be out on the road this late?" one of the men said in a highly accented southern drawl. He was skeleton thin, with a face like a badger. His black hair was cut shoulder-length. The other men were larger in stature; one had black hair, the other's hair was dirty blond.

The badger-faced man continued, "Now, why don't you get down from that there wagon, boy. We aim to teach you to mind your betters."

The man's statement elicited chuckles from his two friends. John quickly noted that they had not drawn their weapons. Evidently, they thought he would just climb down from the wagon and follow them like a lamb into the woods. They were greatly mistaken if they believed he would be easy pickings for their pleasure.

John was ready for them.

His rifle was under the wagon seat and he whipped it out, pointing it at the sharp-featured man who had done all the talking. He gripped the rifle so hard he wouldn't be surprised to find he'd crushed the barrel.

In a calm, but deadly voice, John said, "Take your weapons and drop them to the ground." His eyes narrowed to slits with this threat.

"Tucker, he wouldn't dare shoot a white man," said one of the men to the leader of the group.

"Yes, I will, Tucker," John said. "So help me God, I'll blow your head clear off your shoulders." John cocked the rifle for emphasis.

"Do as he says," Tucker ordered. "Drop your rifles." The men still hesitated, not willing to bow down to a black man's commands.

John continued, "I'll give you to the count of five. On the count of five your man Tucker here loses his head." He started counting, "One, two, three…" and at four the men dropped their rifles.

"Now I'll give you another five seconds to get out of here before I start shooting."

The man named Tucker gave him a murderous look and said, "I won't forget this."

John didn't say anything. He fired a warning shot over their heads. The shot spooked the men's horses and they had to grasp their reins to bring them under control. Seeing the rifle pointed in their direction the men quickly rode off, not looking back as John fired off another harmless shot in their direction. He then jumped down from the wagon seat and retrieved their weapons. He wasn't about to leave them on the ground in case they decided to backtrack and reclaim them. Walking to the front of the wagon, he placed them under the seat along with his rifle and then climbed back up next to Charlotte.

His fiancée sat quietly through the whole interlude, but she had been scared almost witless. Relief spilling from her, she hugged John and said, "I thought they was goin' to kill you, then me."

"That wasn't going to happen," he replied in somber tone.

Her brown eyes narrowed with speculation as she studied her future husband. His mouth was rigid and he was still so tense with suppressed ire she could feel it rolling away from him in waves.

She said a moment later, "Would you be done shot that man?"

John didn't hesitate with his answer. "Yes, I would have to protect you." He reached out and rubbed a callused hand lightly over the top of hers.

Charlotte didn't say anything for a moment. She had always had an absolute abhorrence for violence of any kind. The idea that John could talk so calmly about killing a man, frightened her. But they lived in frightening times. She was shocked, but accepted his right to protect her and told him so.

John drove her home without further incident. The next morning he told his father what had transpired the night before.

"Son, I'm beginning to think we should move from Virginia. I hear that South Carolina has the largest number of colored office-holders. I hear these politicians are determined to elevate our race. I might even try my hand in politics."

"Papa, you'd make a great politician." John continued after a moment, "But I'm not leaving Virginia. I'd like to continue farming our land."

William studied his first-born son. John's features were hard and masculine, intelligent and compelling. He had grown into an honorable man. He also liked working with the soil.

"I know you love this land, son. But I have to think of Constance and Hannah. If opportunity for Negroes can exist in this country, it will be in South Carolina where our people have some power in the government."

William was right in his assumption about opportunities for blacks existing where the black politicians were. Eventually, the North became weary after the Civil War of talk about the 'Negro problem' and began to abandon blacks as they migrated for better opportunities to their cities. This was especially true for many of the ex-slaves who were bewildered after gaining their freedom. The fighting spirit of the abolitionists before the Civil War began to ebb. This abandonment was a trend that formed slowly but inexorably, and the status of blacks steadily declined.

William's son, John, married in late 1870, and the couple moved into a house they built on the Ford property. Nine months later their first child, John Jr., was born. In the spring of 1871, William decided the time had come to move his family to South Carolina. He would leave John in charge of farming their plot of land near Gum Springs. But before William could relocate his family, he got two shocking surprises.

"Mama, Papa, I'm going back to New York," Constance announced one week before their designated move. "I am going to marry Herbert."

"What do you mean, you're going back to New York? And you say you're marrying *Herbert*? How did this all come about?" Henrietta exclaimed, a look of puzzlement on her face. She was sitting on a settee in their small living room repairing a tear in her husband's work pants. William was next to her, reading a passage from the Bible.

"I've been corresponding with him since we came back to Virginia. He still loves me and wants me to come back to New York and meet his parents."

"Well, I am surprised," said William. His forehead creased a moment perplexedly. "I didn't think his parents would allow him to marry a Negro girl."

"Well, they still don't know I'm a Negro. We, that is Herbert and I, decided it would be best not to tell them," Constance volunteered. She couldn't seem to look her parents in the face and gazed at the floor instead.

"Did you ever stop to think of how you're going to be able to keep it a secret when we show up at your wedding?" said an exasperated Henrietta. "I know your father looks white, but the rest of us don't!"

That statement caught Constance's attention and she glanced first at her mother then at her father. "Mama, Papa please understand. You can't come to our wedding. Herbert told them that my family was killed in a fire after our return to Virginia. They think I'm an orphan." Constance started wringing her hands in agitation.

"Oh, no he didn't! Tell me you didn't go along with him on this?" Henrietta cried out.

When Constance nodded her head in the affirmative, William sighed and uttered a silent prayer for deliverance. *What is Constance thinking?* he thought bewilderedly.

As if she could read her father's mind, she said, "Look, I'll be all right, and Herbert promised me that I could come and visit you from time to time."

"Oh, he did, did he," her mother answered sarcastically. She was standing now, her hands settled on her hips in outrage.

It was time for William to voice his concerns. He rose from the settee and walked over to Constance. "Daughter, what has gotten into you?

What happened to all of our conversations about standing proud and standing tall because of our heritage? Did all of those conversations go in one ear and out the other? Oh, no, *you* will not do this! I will not have you living your life as a lie!"

It became a screaming match then with Constance yelling back, "What? Papa, I think *you* should reconsider what you just said. Ha! You've been living a lie all of your life! You're a Washington, yet you're content to hide the fact from everyone. And now you want *me* not to pretend to be white. Come on, Papa, why don't you take your own advice? Besides, you can't stop me from being with Herbert, because I'll just run away! And I promise you if I have to run away, you'll never see me again!"

The hurtful words were said and couldn't be taken back. Henrietta burst into tears and William wrapped his arms around his wife. Then he stared at the daughter he didn't know anymore. Hannah, who was sitting in a nearby chair and witness to the tirade, left the room.

Constance was sorry that she hurt her parents, but it would not stop her from living the life she wanted. "Mama, Papa, I know you love me. And if you love me, please let me go. *Please*. I'll never be comfortable being a Negro—begging and scratching to be accepted," she said. "I want to live as a white person so that my children will have an easier life. As white they can be and do anything they want in this country. Being a Negro will only hold them back, and I won't be one and neither will they." Constance's look was defiant.

His attention directed at his daughter's mutinous face, William knew she meant what she said. As much as it hurt to hear his daughter's words, he understood. Having light skin put those of mulatto heritage in an elite place after the Civil War. It promoted distinctions of color in the Negro race that suggested that opportunities for life, liberty and the pursuit of happiness in the United States depended upon one's complexion. If one had white or light skin, the better off one was.

Sometimes William couldn't blame Constance or others for choosing the more fortuitous route and crossing the color line.

"Daughter, we love you." Glancing at his wife's stricken face then back to Constance's, he said resignedly, "I know we need to let you go."

Constance's face lit up at his words. But William wasn't through. He could feel his face burning with ire before he continued tersely, "But let's be very clear about the choice you've allowed Herbert to make for you. Not only will it separate you from your family, it will sever any ties we may have with your children, our grandchildren. Herbert is not a man; for a man stands up for what is right no matter the consequences. You both have made a cowardly decision and there is no honor in it."

One week later, William and Henrietta put their daughter on a train North with a family friend traveling to see relatives in New York. Constance promised to keep in touch with them, and her parents told her that she'd better, or they'd come up to surprise her without hesitation. William and Henrietta didn't even have the chance to deal with Constance's departure. Hannah, their one sensible daughter, dropped another bomb shell a couple days after.

"Mama, Papa...I don't want to hurt you, but I can't leave Gum Springs. I've fallen in love with someone. His name is John Quander. We want to get married."

William took in his wife's stricken face. Then Henrietta did something he didn't expect. She chuckled and said with resolve, "Daughters get married, William, let's plan our baby girl's wedding. And this is one wedding the whole family will be attending."

After Hannah's wedding, William was finally able to move to the farm he bought in South Carolina. He felt alone. His children were gone. But he had his wife, and her welfare would always remain his first priority.

*   *   *

George rode up to his father's property in Gum Springs in the late summer of 1871. The leaves on the trees surrounding the one-story farm house were just beginning to show faint hints of color; red, yellow and orange. It wouldn't be long now before the leaves scattered with the winds, covering the ground in thick, blanket-like clusters over their property.

Jumping down from his mount, he tied the reins to a hitching post in the yard. Then he walked towards the house, leaped up the three rickety steps, and over to the front door. He paused a moment before bringing up his gloved fist to rap loudly on it. When he received no answer, he opened the door and entered. *Where is everybody?* he thought anxiously. He couldn't help but feel edgy, as he had not heard from them in over eight months. He stepped back outside and ran his eyes over the terrain in front of him. Not a person was in sight.

Army life was drilled into him and the first thing a soldier learned early on was to take care of his horses. So he walked back to his and took it into the barn, where he rubbed it down and gave it some grain. Then he headed back to the farmhouse.

He found John coming from the fields a few minutes later. The two men hugged each other fiercely, patting each other on the back in great affection.

"God, George, I didn't think you were ever coming home!" said a jubilant John.

"Yeh, it's been awhile. I thought about all of you every day. His eyes took on a merry twinkle when he said, "I heard you got married, congratulations."

"Yes, I did, to Charlotte Willis. She's over at the Freedman's Bureau and I'm going hitch the wagon a little later and go get her. Do you want to come with me?"

"Yeah, I'll go, but first I want to visit with Mama and Papa. Where are they, in town?"

John took off his hat and wiped his sweaty brow with the back of his hand before answering. "No, they moved to South Carolina about a year ago."

"What! Papa left Gum Springs. Why?" George stared hard at his brother, his brow furrowed as he waited for his answer.

"He just up and got the notion into his head that he wanted to go somewhere else, maybe even try getting into politics, so he moved to Beaufort, where a lot of colored folk are making some headway in the government."

"Politics?" George was beginning to sound like a parrot. "Did Jane and Constance go too?"

"Naw, Jane married one of the Quander boys. You know, the youngest one, John. They have a baby on the way." Then he said quietly, "Did Papa tell you about Constance?" John could see the questions forming in George's gray eyes and went on, "I guess he didn't."

"What about her?"

"Come with me into the house, it's going to take some time to explain what Constance has done, and we might as well be comfortable." John filled him in once they were settled in the house.

George stayed with his brother for a few days and then headed for South Carolina. It had been too long since he had seen his parents. Several days after he left Gum Springs, he walked into the small farm kitchen of his parent's home. William was eating breakfast at the table and his mother was standing near the stove. His father put down the warm, buttered biscuit and rose to his feet. Henrietta was already greeting her youngest offspring.

"My Lord, my baby's come home, my baby's home," Henrietta cried as she clutched her youngest to her breast.

William stood mute and waited while George hugged his mother, lifting her off her feet in the process.

"Mama, please stop calling me a baby," he said good naturedly. "I'm a grown man, Mama. The men in my troop would never let me live it down if they heard you calling me that."

"He's right, Henrietta, the boy, I mean George, is definitely no longer our baby."

George directed his attention to his father, while he embraced his mother. Then he dropped his hands away from her and stood proud and tall before his father.

William took in a deep breath and exhaled slowly. He then let his eyes wander over his son. George had hardened. The hardness was in his eyes, and the eyes never lie. Gone was the young boy who always wanted to be a soldier. Before him stood a man, a man confident in his abilities. William also noticed that the days in the hot western sun had darkened George's skin to a reddish-bronze shade. He now resembled the Native Americans he was commissioned to fight, except for the auburn tint to his hair and his gray eyes.

"Papa," George said and shook his father's hand. William grasped it and then pulled him into his tight embrace.

"It's good to see you, son. How did you know where to find us?"

"I stopped at our farm. John told me where to find you. By the way, his boy looks just like him."

George's voice took on a pained tone. "It was a surprise to hear about Constance. Have you heard from her?"

Henrietta answered, "Not lately. I swear if that girl doesn't write soon, I'm going to go to New York and visit her white family."

William chuckled at her comment because he knew she would. He then asked his son, "Did you see Hannah?"

"Yes. She's grown into a beautiful young woman. She told me to tell you she'll be coming here at the end of the month so we can have a family reunion."

Clucking like the mother hen she was, Henrietta said, "You two sit down in the parlor and continue talking while I go and I'll fix my ba…George something to eat." Smiling brightly at her youngest child, she continued, "I bet you haven't had a good meal since you've been gone."

"No, I haven't, Mama. I've been thinking about your fried chicken, yams, and greens the whole way here."

"Well, that's just what I'm going to fix for you," she replied as she put on her apron.

Walking into the parlor William noticed George's slight limp. *Had he been wounded?* he thought worriedly. He knew his son would tell him about it in his own good time and inquired instead, "Tell me son, is being a soldier what you expected it to be?"

George replied, "Papa, even out West Negroes are still treated with disdain. Some of the white officers don't respect us. Many of the officers even shun duty with our regiments. I've been fortunate to serve under fair commanders. They've asked my opinion about battle strategies and let me help govern the men in my company."

George proudly displayed his sergeant stripes to his father. He showed him the buffalo emblem sewn onto his uniform and told him what it meant. George then went on to tell his father how he had been wounded.

After talking for over an hour, George said, "I'm going back, Papa."

"I figured that, son. You have the Old General's blood in your veins. How long are you going to stay?"

"I'll be here for about six months."

William knew those six months would fly by all too quickly for him.

Chapter 25

Who ever loved that loved not at first sight?

Marlowe

It was at church that Sergeant George Ford fell in love with the minister's daughter. Harriet Blythewood had black hair and flashing dark eyes, and was diminutive in stature. Her skin was the color of warm honey and she had a black tiny mole, a beauty mark next to her generous mouth. A tingle of anticipation curled up George's spine as they made eye contact. She was a member of the church choir and had just been asked to sing a solo. *A fellow singer and a beautiful one at that,* George thought with pleasure. He leaned forward anxiously from his seat on the front pew of the church to better hear her sing.

Harriet had spied the young man in his army-blue, soldier's uniform the first moment he came through the chapel door of her father's church. He was so handsome in his military attire. He was broad-shouldered and had a trim waist. There wasn't a spare once of fat on his muscular frame. The soldier had a firm chin, thin sensuous lips, and eyes the color of gun metal. Harriet broke eye contact from him as she walked over and stood next to her father's podium. Taking a deep breath she started to sing the words:

"Amazing grace, how sweet the sound,
that saved a wretch like me.
I once was lost, but now I'm found,
was blind, but now I see."

George sat in shock for a moment. He stuck his forefinger in his right ear and began moving it in a circular motion, making sure there was nothing in it to impair his hearing. But still the girl's shrill voice bounced off his eardrums in clanging discord. *How can someone who looks like an angel—sing like the devil?* He thought in disbelief. Her voice sounded like a cat's screech every time she hit a high note. Not only was she loud, she couldn't carry the tune.

George looked questioningly around at the rest of the congregation. No one else seemed to be surprised at the girl's terrible voice. On one particularly high note, which she totally destroyed, George could no longer suppress the urge to laugh and his shoulders starting shaking.

William, sensing his son's mirth, nudged him with his shoulder. Then his lips began to twitch as George's mirth became contagious. Henrietta elbowed William and he straightened his face, somewhat. The louder Harriet sang the more George's desire to laugh welled up in him. Finally, he put his hand to his mouth, coughed to cover his snickers, and got up and left the church. Once outside he let loose the laughter that he could no longer contain.

George's laughter, loud and unrestrained, could be heard inside the church. It was so infectious that a chorus of muffled coughs continued to erupt until Harriet finished singing. Weak from laughing so hard, George collapsed on the church steps to regain his breath. He couldn't trust himself to go back in after the song was finished and waited there until the services were over.

An hour later, the minister and his wife stood outside of the church, speaking to their parishioners as they left the chapel. Harriet stood stiffly next to her father. She was so angry she could spit fire. How dare that young man laugh at her! Harriet glared at George, her black eyes shooting daggers at him as he waited with his parents to greet her father and mother. Why even now he was smiling, his even white teeth flashing her a lazy grin. Finally the Fords approached the pastor.

After giving Mrs. Blythewood a hug, Henrietta said, "I enjoyed your sermon, Reverend." Pulling George forward, she stated proudly, "This is our youngest, George. He's on leave from the United States Army for a few months before heading back to Texas."

After exchanging pleasantries with the minister and his wife, George turned his piercing gaze towards Harriet. The Reverend Blythewood had an amused look on his face as he noticed George's interest in her. Turning towards Harriet, he said, "George, this is Harriet, one of my daughters."

George already new her name. He had asked his mother who she was when he first noticed her walking with the other choir members as they gathered on the platform behind the minister's podium. George couldn't help but notice Harriet's rigid posture after the introduction. He took her slender hand into his large one and brought it to his lips in a gallant gesture.

Harriet was momentarily surprised and some of her anger drained away as she gazed into George's eyes. They held her captive with a virile, unflinching directness.

"Miss Harriet, it's a pleasure to meet you," George said in a husky voice as he released her hand.

Something was happening between the two young people. Even their parents were aware of the subtle current in the air that seemed to surround them.

Coughing lightly to break the couple's spell over each other, the pastor said, "We hope to see you at the picnic later on this afternoon, George."

George's intent stare never left Harriet's eyes as he replied, "I wouldn't miss it for the world, sir."

Two hours later, George was pursuing Harriet. She was still upset at his laughter during her song, and kept dodging him whenever he approached her. She circulated, stopping to talk and laugh with her friends, but never with the man with the merry gray eyes. Finally, George cornered her by the dessert table.

"Miss Harriet, would you do me the honor of walking with me. I want to apologize for my rude behavior this morning."

Harriet looked askance at him. George tried to stop his mirth from moving to his lips, but his eyes, those dark gray eyes, couldn't hide it.

Why, he has the nerve to still be laughing at me, she thought heatedly. Before she could open her mouth to vent her anger, he grabbed her hand and was walking her away from the picnic towards a quiet wooded area.

"Mister Ford, you let loose my hand."

George immediately complied.

"You, you laughed at me," Harriet stammered in outrage, suddenly and unaccountably so angry it was all she could do not to slap that smug look off his face.

"Oh, I admit it," George agreed good-naturedly between rumbles of laughter. "But I want you to know that you are the most beautiful girl I have ever seen." All traces of humor left his face as he gave her a soulful look. "You look like an angel."

Then he ruined it by saying, "But you can't sing a lick."

"Oh!" Harriet snorted.

George grinned at her, a disarming grin that made him look young and handsome.

Harriet felt as if a bolt of lighting struck her. She found it hard to breathe. She admitted to herself that George was right about her singing. Even her mother winced when she hit some of her higher notes.

"Well, I must say, you are the first to tell me to my face," chuckled Harriet. "Father refuses to believe that one of his children can't sing."

"Miss Harriet, you may not be able to carry a tune, but then angels only have to smile and bless the world with their beauty."

George had never thought himself to be a poet. Or at least he never had been before. He paused for a moment and looked deep into her eyes.

Harriet couldn't look away. It was as if some invisible force held her spellbound. She had never met anyone like him before. He was a man, not a boy like the ones she met in church, and everything about him said so. And she had never been susceptible to flattery. Nevertheless, she smiled with pleasure at his words.

George grabbed her hand and they walked back to the others at the picnic. He remained in the young woman's shadow for the rest of the day.

George rose early the next morning to begin the day's chores with his father, but his thoughts were on Harriet. William had to repeat his questions and directions more than once. He couldn't help but notice the preoccupied expression on his son's face. William suppressed a chuckle when George handed him a milk bucket instead of the pitchfork he requested. *Ahh, first love,* William thought with a sigh.

They worked for several hours, feeding the horses, cows, goats and chickens, and then cleaned the manure from the cattle barn and other animal pens. By that time, George's silent musings over Harriet had grown to monumental proportions.

"Papa," George finally said, sinking the tines of his pitchfork into the straw next to the stable door. "Did you know mama was the 'one' the first time you looked at her?"

William smiled. "I knew the moment I laid eyes on her. Why, I couldn't even speak the first time I was in her presence."

"Papa, I think I'm in love with Harriet Blythewood."

Gazing at his son's doleful eyes William replied, "We Fords have a way of falling in love at first sight. We seem to know immediately who our soul's partners are. So, I guess you haven't got much time to convince Harriet to love you back."

George grinned broadly. That's just what he planned to do. During the next few weeks George courted Harriet with a patience and determination that he didn't know he possessed. Just before he had to report back to Texas, they became engaged.

"I'll miss you," Harriet said, tilting her head back for a goodbye kiss.

George obliged her with a firm; searing kiss that left no doubt that he would miss her as well. "I'll write to you as much as I can. I'll have some leave time in about six months, so I'll be home in plenty of time for the wedding."

"You're sure?"

"I'm sure," he replied, kissing her once more before mounting his horse.

George rode away from his father's farm and wondered if he was making the right decision in leaving his fiancée and family to once again join the ranks of a soldier.

Why couldn't he seem to shake the feeling that he was making a big mistake?

Chapter 26

Wisdom inspires confidence and prepares us for the
most difficult times.

James Allen Jr.

A different regime was in place at Fort Sill when George arrived for his second tour of duty as a sergeant with the 10th Calvary. Colonel Grierson had been ordered temporarily to St. Louis where he would serve as superintendent of the Mounted Recruiting Service, and Lieutenant Colonel Davidson was now in command of the 10th.

Colonel Davidson was not the commander Colonel Grierson had been. He was highly capable, but he was an erratic officer. The colonel was also a strict disciplinarian, which did not endear him to those in his command. Fortunately for George, his company was transferred to Fort Richardson in Texas under the command of Colonel W. H. Wood. Their orders were to subdue hostile Indians wherever they might be found.

The town of Jacksboro was adjacent to Fort Richardson. The day the 10th rode through the town to enter to the fort, George found out just how unwelcome the black troops were. He should have expected the town's reaction to them. After all, Texas was a former slave state.

"Hey, you niggers ain't wanted in our town!" shouted one mean-looking cowboy as he leaned against a pillar in front of a dance hall.

"You tell'm, Drapper!" another voice hollered out. A chorus of other hateful words were bandied about as the soldiers rode down the main street's thoroughfare.

"Steady, men. Don't let them get you upset," George encouraged them. "You're soldiers. United States soldiers."

The troops settled down somewhat, but the tension could still be felt in the air as they continued their ride.

Jacksboro was typical of the frontier towns that developed in the vicinity of Army forts. The town consisted of a jumble of buildings clustered together on either side of a narrow, muddy track that the citizens referred to as Main Street. The buildings were mostly wood-framed and badly in need of paint. Some seemed to lean against each other for support. Many of the town's denizens consisted of drifters, gamblers, prostitutes and thieves. There were twenty-seven saloons in Jacksboro.

The citizens of the small community disliked the black troops, and altercations between them and the Buffalo Soldiers were frequent. Many a day George acted as a mediator in the disputes.

"Where in the hell is Private Kewconda going?" George asked J. J., who was now a corporal. The men were off-duty and were on their way to one of the general stores when they spotted the private.

"I think he's goin' into the dance hall," said J. J.

Jimmy Dolan's Dance Hall had frequently been the scene of one inquest or another for the last three months. The inquests mostly dealt with fights, as the black troopers of the 9th and 10th tried to assert their rights to frequent the establishment. Now here was Private Kewconda going into the one place that was off-limits to the black troops.

George rode his horse over to the hitching rail in front of the dance hall. He leaped agilely down from his mount and tied the reins securely.

Sheer determination marked every line of his body as he strode towards the entrance.

"Where do you think you're goin', George?" J. J. had dismounted and followed him to the front of the saloon.

"To get Kewconda out of there before someone gets hurt. You stay here with the horses."

"Oh, no you don't. Someone's got to protect your back," replied J. J. as he followed George into the dance hall.

George pushed open the double, wood-slatted swinging doors and entered. Blue-gray smoke wreathed itself into ghostly halos over the heads of the card players seated at the tables. The room vibrated with the sounds of piano music and the laughter and shouts from the winners and losers. The odors of whiskey and unwashed bodies made him crinkle his nose in disgust.

Where is he? George thought as he looked around the crowded room. A few of the gamblers glanced up from their cards as George and J. J. passed by their tables. But the game was more important than seeing two more colored troops enter the dance hall, and they continued with their betting.

George and J. J. finally sighted Kewconda near the bar. Reddy Drapper, the town gunslinger and bully, had the little private by the scuff of his neck. Drapper was waving a knife in the front of the private's bleeding face then moved it down around his genitals, threatening to cut off that particular part of his anatomy. Kewconda was whimpering and begging the man to let him go back to the fort.

"Ah's wants to leave," the private said, his voice tinged with fear. "Ah jes wanted a lil' somepin' to wet my throat. That's all. P-please, jes let me go!"

"You hear that, boys? This piece of nigger shit wants to go back to the fort. Well, black boy, you'll be goin' back, but you'll be missin' a very important piece of yourself."

This comment broke out in raucous laughter from his watching cronies.

George stared at Drapper. Drapper was big, broad as well as tall. He stood several inches over six feet. His hair was carrot-red and he wore it long and shaggy. George watched as a scantily dressed woman walked over to the pair.

"Ah, come on, Reddy, don't hurt him no more!" black-haired Belle cajoled. Belle had been employed by the dance hall for many years, and was one of the favorite attractions. She continued sweetly, "He just wanted to get something to drink, that's all." She sidled up to Drapper, putting her arms around his waist.

Drapper reacted to Belle's request by thrusting her down on the floor with the hand that held the knife and said threateningly, "You keep your nose out of this, you dried up old whore, or I'll carve up that ugly face of yours too."

Cowering, the woman scooted back on the wood floor away from the incensed man. Some of the bystanders who had been watching Drapper muttered to themselves about Belle's rough treatment. They were also disgusted by what Drapper wanted to do to the colored trooper, but didn't have the guts to intervene. The outlaw was not liked, but the men were afraid of him and he used their fear as an aphrodisiac. He was the classic bully.

But George wasn't afraid of Drapper and spoke up. "I suggest you let our man go."

George held his rifle loosely at his side, but his stance led the onlookers to believe that he knew how to use it. Muscles tightened and flexed along the cut of George's jaw. Suddenly chairs were flung back and card games interrupted. The piano player hit a sour note and stopped playing, and the room became quiet as the occupants watched the tableau getting ready to play out before them.

Drapper turned toward the two soldiers. His eyes narrowed on George as he spat a brownish stream of chewing tobacco to the floor near George's booted feet.

"Well, it looks like the cavalry done arrived just in time to save ya, boy," said Drapper.

Drapper was mean, but he was no fool. He could tell this determined black soldier would like nothing better than to put a bullet into him. That other soldier had his hand on his rifle as well. Besides, he knew he couldn't reach his gun in time. He decided he'd put a bullet in their backs when they least expected it. He loosened his hold on Kewconda's neck, letting the bleeding man collapse to the floor.

Over the years a sense of duty had been bred into George. The military training he had received was obvious, as one took in the square set of his shoulders and the self-confidence that had become so much apart of his essence. He had always reserved his outward composure in times of stress. But today, seeing how this outlaw trash had treated Kewconda and Belle, made him see red. His jaw clenched against a wave of pure anger.

Motioning with his rifle at Kewconda, George said, "Get to your feet, soldier, and high-tail it back to the fort."

The private stood and with some semblance of dignity, retrieved his hat and painfully left the saloon.

Drapper couldn't resist taunting George. "That rifle and that uniform don't make you no man. You're still ain't nothin' but a no account nigger."

George inhaled slowly, deeply, refusing to feed the temper riding him. He'd learned years ago that the fastest way to get yourself killed was to get mad. His ability to control his anger saved his hide more times than not. Once a man let his anger take charge of his mind, he didn't think.

Unfortunately, anger blistered inside him.

Anger at Kewconda for putting him in this situation. Anger that the black man was still considered a piece of trash. Anger that he and his men put their lives on the line daily protecting people who didn't appreciate it. And anger that of all the heroic deeds that his unit had accomplished, it could not wipe out the poison of racial prejudice.

Today George couldn't control his anger. George handed his rifle to J. J. His friend said alarmingly, "What you doin', George?"

But George didn't answer him and walked closer to Drapper. He stopped a couple of feet in front of the outlaw. Drapper spit a strain of tobacco juice on George's booted feet and then smiled, showing half of the rotted and brown teeth in his mouth.

"Oh what the hell," George thought nonchalantly before he connected with a deadly right to Drapper's jaw, then a quick, precision left to his nose, knocking him out cold. It was done so fast that the outlaw didn't see it coming. He hit the floor with a resounding thud.

A second later someone threw a punch at George and he instinctively ducked just before driving his own fist into this opponent's soft stomach. Air rushed from the man's lungs and he dropped face-first onto the floor, moaning. The next thing George heard was furious cursing along with the sounds of furniture breaking and the loud, scuffling thuds of fights in progress. It appeared that some of the men in the dance hall were pitching in to help him. The saloon had erupted into a free-for-all, where a man couldn't help but jumping right in and becoming part of it, including J. J.

George fought until there was no one else left to face him. The dance hall looked as if it had been through a cyclone. Shortly thereafter, the sheriff and his deputies came in and arrested George and J. J. Once the men were back at the fort, George faced his commanders at his inquest. He lost one of his stripes and was placed in the guardhouse for a week because, when they asked if he threw the first punch, he answered, "Damn right I did, sir."

George didn't have to worry about Reddy Drapper putting a bullet into his back after their altercation. Draper was arrested by the sheriff a few days later because he was wanted in connection with a murder in Weatherford, Texas. It was ironic that he was escorted by J. J. and two other privates from the 10th ordered to accompany the sheriff who was taking him to the small western town to stand trial.

Several more months passed, and George was unable to take his leave of absence. He wrote to Harriet and let her know that the wedding was going to have to be postponed indefinitely. She wasn't too happy about it, but told him in a return letter that she would wait for him.

A different kind of trouble was brewing in 1874 in the Indian Territory as George's stint with the 10th continued. Throughout the fall and early winter, Indian raiders took scalps, cattle, and horses along the Texas frontier. Colonel Wood complained that he had never known Indians to be so numerous, desperate or persistent. Later that fall, the 4th Cavalry intercepted a party of Indian raiders on the west ford of the Nueces River. In the fight that followed, dozens of Indians were killed, including the son and nephew of the Kiowa chief, Lone Wolf.

When George and his unit rode up to the scene of the battle, Indian bodies were strewn everywhere. George had never seen this many dead men before. Some of the Indian's bodies had been mutilated. Some of the soldiers had taken scalps and other body parts as souvenirs. It was war, and the war had done terrible things to them all.

Sickened by the sight of the carnage, George walked to a nearby strand of trees and boulders. There he saw a young Indian brave, naked except for a breechcloth and moccasins. He was crawling towards a wooded area. The brave had a horrendous gash in his leg from a saber wound. When he spotted George, he tried to stand, but he could not muster the strength. The brave's cold black eyes flashed in defiance, then defeat when he realized he was cornered.

He spoke in his native tongue, "Hemaca. Hemaca huka oyohusi!"

George couldn't understand his words, but he assumed the brave was telling him he wasn't afraid to die. As he continued to gaze down at the brave's rigid face, he knew he could not kill the young man. George was no stranger to hand-to-hand combat, and he had killed men in the heat of battle many a time, but this man was unarmed and helpless. George was also a compassionate man and he made the only decision he felt he could. He decided to help the brave to escape.

There had been enough killing today.

Warily, he knelt beside the Indian and studied him. The brave had three black paint slashes over the bridge of his nose and across both cheeks.

"I just want to check your wound. I want to help you. Can you understand me?"

The young warrior did not understand his words and kept saying sharply, "Hiya, hiya!"

Taking the yellow bandanna slowly from around his neck, George gestured that he wanted to tie it around the injured leg to stop the flow of blood. It took awhile, but finally the brave began to understand what George wanted to do. Reaching out slowly, George carefully wrapped the bandanna around the man's upper thigh. He wasn't surprised that the brave had only a breech cloth on. Most Indians stripped off their clothes for battle so that if they were pierced with a knife or arrow, no cloth would get into the wound to risk the increase of infection. Slowly standing, George, motioned for him to remain quiet by bringing his forefinger to his lips, then he turned and left the area.

Hurrying to his horse, he grabbed his canteen, a satchel of food, and after making sure no one was watching him, returned to the site where he had left the young Indian. George noticed that the brave had crawled into some nearby foliage. Evidently, the man did not trust him to come back alone. Stooping, he gave the man a drink of water from his canteen. The brave drink thirstily and then shoved it away from his mouth when he was finished.

George rose back to his feet. He realized that the man wouldn't be able to leave the area without some kind of support and began looking around for something he could lean his weight on. Spotting a large branch lying nearby, he retrieved it and brought it over to the wounded man. He helped the brave to his feet, propping the branch under his arm. George then put the strap of the satchel and canteen over the young man's neck.

Pointing to George's red-tinted hair the brave commented in his guttural language, "Nehi tahin sa." He then rubbed his free hand over George's red-brown face and continued, "Nehi hasapa." Pointing to his chest he said, "Kangisapa." Then he motioned to George's chest.

George guessed he was telling him that his name was Kangisapa, and wanted to know his. So he told him. "My name is George."

The brave pointed at George's eyes and said, "George Istahota." The brave took an amulet from a pouch near his waist and handed it to him. "Wanapin. Nehi wicasa iyotanyapi. Nehi koda. Nehi danitaga. Nehi tatanka koda."

George took the necklace and studied it for a moment. It was made up of a single eagle feather and two small, arrow-shaped stones tied to leather thongs. Evidently the brave wanted to give him a gift for helping him. Smiling, George put the necklace into his breast pocket.

As the brave made his way slowly from the clearing, he turned once more bringing his fist to his chest, then extended it palm upwards towards George in farewell. "Ka dish day, George Istahota. Ka dish day, tatanka koda."

George brought his fist to his chest then outward, in the same motion as the braves. He watched as the man painfully made his way into the forest.

George didn't know what the Indian said or why he had given him the amulet. He later repeated some of the words to the half-breed scout, Two Birds. Two Birds told him that the words "tatanka koda" meant, *buffalo friend* and "istahota" meant *gray eyes*. "Wicasa iyotanyapi" had to do with *honor* and the amulet was a *"wanapin,"* which declared friend-ship, a shared truce between the two men, that the two men were 'danitagas'—*blood brothers.*

After that day, George Ford came to respect the Native Americans and their futile fight. He could understand the despair that they faced. They were losing their freedom, fighting for the land of their ancestors, and were considered savages just like the black man. He began to loose his taste for the battles to come. But first, George was a soldier, like his great grandfather before him. His job was to fight in the Indian Wars and he would not shirk his duty.

Fortunately, he wasn't involved in too many more heated battles and when it was time for him to reenlist, he opted out of the military. He had seen enough killing.

Quartermaster Sergeant George Ford was honorably discharged on September 11, 1876, from the 10th Calvary. His commanding officer wrote on his discharge papers, "character excellent, good and faithful soldier."

The Sioux brave had summed up George's character correctly when he stated, "Nehi wicasca Iyotanyapi." George was an honorable man.

Chapter 27

Providence has given us hope and sleep, as a compensation for the many cares of life.

Voltaire

George felt naked. It seemed strange for him not to be wearing his cavalry uniform after two stints with the military. He had been in Beaufort, South Carolina, for six months now and found himself missing the life of a soldier. Gone were the days of high adventure. Now all he had to look forward to were the mundane mornings when he fed the livestock. The only excitement he had in months was when his father's bull chased him around the corral. Sighing deeply, he realized that he was not cut out to be a farmer.

While standing near the property's one barn, he let his gaze travel over the spread before him. It was a large farm with 150 acres, too much land for two men to manage successfully. The barn needed painting and the fencing along the front of the house was broken in several locations. His father was unable to keep up the repairs as he had broken his arm a year ago and it never healed correctly. The one bright spot on the property were the roses that grew profusely along the front of the farmhouse. His father had taken cuttings from the roses he had grown at

Mount Vernon and planted them next to the house. They reminded him of the home of his birth.

Why his father left Virginia had puzzled George over the last few months. He knew that his parents loved Mount Vernon as well as he did. George missed the grand old mansion house and the gardens he had tended before he left to join the army. Beaufort was not home to the Fords as far as he was concerned.

George took a long drink from the cool bucket of water his mother brought out while he was chopping logs for the wood-pile, then dumped the remainder over his shirtless torso. Bronzed muscles flexed and rippled, from the width of his shoulders to a lean waist down to narrow hips. Even though he hated farming, life had treated him well, and he really couldn't complain. Besides, he thought with a surge of joy, his Harriet was the main reason he was no longer a soldier. In two weeks he would marry the woman whom had patiently waited for him to return from his second tour of duty.

It was time that he settled down and started a family of his own. His brother John had already fathered seven children. George had a difficult time remembering all of their names. Let's see, he thought amusingly; there was John Jr., George, Martha, David, Catherine, Charlotte, and, ah yes, Elizabeth. He laughed out loud thinking, if he didn't hurry there wouldn't be any names left to give to his own children. Even now John and Charlotte were expecting another child.

The next two weeks flew by and the day of George's wedding was at hand. His brother and he were finishing up with the last touches of their wardrobe.

"I'm so nervous," George stated to John. His brother was helping him tie the black neck cloth around the collar of his white shirt. Doubts swam in his head as he continued to voice his concerns. "What if she changes her mind and doesn't show up at the church? Maybe she just feels obligated to marry me now; after all, I was away for over a year. Do you think she cares that I limp every now and then? Maybe I should speak to her before the wedding starts." George continued to ramble, not letting John answer any of his queries.

"Oh, my God!" George exclaimed suddenly, "Where did I put the ring?" He turned his head aside sharply, pulling one of the ends of the neck cloth from John's hand.

Chuckling softly, John replied, "Relax, little brother, the ring is right here in my pocket." He patted the area for emphasis and said, "And *yes,* Harriet will show up at the church because she loves you. And *no,* I don't think she minds your limp. And *no,* you don't need to see her before the ceremony."

Taking his brother by the shoulders he said pointedly, "You have everything you need, George, because you have love." Slapping his brother on the back, he stated, "Now stand still so I can retie your neck cloth."

George and Harriet were married without a hitch. Two years later, they brought their first child into the world, a boy they named George Jr. He was a beautiful baby with light-brown skin, a slightly flared nose, and silky, black hair. Like his father before him, George prayed that his first-born child wouldn't face the racism that was running rampant throughout the South.

Several weeks after the birth of his son, George went into the small town of Beaufort to buy supplies for the farm. While loading his wagon with the purchased hoe, pitchfork, nails, and lumber, he noticed a strange white woman looking at him. She was standing in front of the town's one boarding house across from the supply store. She brought a gloved hand to her chest, as if seeing him startled her. George thought, *That's all I need, some white woman thinking I offended her.*

It wasn't a belief too far-fetched to comprehend in the small southern town. Just the preceding week a black man had been sentenced to hang. The man had been riding a horse that he had purchased in another county. It turned out that the horse was stolen and sold to him. The accused man had tried to explain how he had obtained the horse, but to no avail. An all-white jury had found him guilty.

George was putting the last of the supplies into the wagon when he noticed the strange woman walking towards him. Taking his hat off his head and wiping the sweat from his brow with his forearm, he watched as she approached. Something was familiar about her. Did he know her from somewhere? His forehead wrinkled with the thought.

She stopped a few feet in front of him and said hesitantly, "Don't you recognize me, George?"

George didn't answer right away. He had recognized her, but was so surprised to see her that he couldn't speak. He opened his mouth and then closed it again. Finally, he gave her a great bear hug.

"My God, Constance! I didn't recognize you at first!" he exclaimed when he found his voice. His spirit soared within his body at seeing his sister again. "How'd you get here? Do Mama and Papa know?" Looking around him he asked, "Where's your husband?"

The smile died on Constance's lips. She took a deep breath and replied, "I've been in town for about a week now, George. And I'm here alone."

"Why didn't you let us know?"

"I was afraid to come home—afraid to face Mama and Papa."

"Why?"

"Oh, George, I've made a mess of my life," she said brokenly. Tears began to roll down her cheeks as she went on, "Herbert never married me. He kept telling me he was waiting for the right time. I never even met his parents."

Shaking her head, she continued, her voice bruised with pain, "He never meant to marry me, you know. He wanted me as a, as his mistress." Her voice had a bitter edge to it. "Just like Papa told me once, Herbert was not the man I thought he was. Herbert told me that I wasn't good enough to become his wife because my blood was tainted."

George stood silent for a few seconds as thoughts of doing bodily harm to Herbert assailed his being. Finally he asked, "What have you been doing all this time?"

Biting her lower lip, Constance looked away from George, and then, swallowing a sob, replied, "I've been living with Herbert. I thought if he could see how good it could be between us, he would change his mind and marry me."

Turning back to George she continued softly, "For several years it was like, like heaven. I was so in love. But Herbert's parents kept pressuring him to marry and produce an heir." Constance's eyes took on a faraway look. "I got pregnant once. I was *so* happy, George. Herbert was so very solicitous to me when I told him I was carrying our child. He even made me a special tea to drink every night for about a week. But I miscarried."

Her eyes turned brittle and her voice sharpened as she continued. "Oh, that Herbert was a clever doctor. You see, he didn't want me to have his child so he gave me that tea so I would lose the baby." Her bottom lip began to tremble and she whispered, "George, I really wanted my baby. I was so melancholy after the miscarriage because I believed that I had caused it somehow. Herbert became concerned when I couldn't eat and finally confessed what he had done. After that, he was very careful and I never conceived again."

Straightening her shoulders she looked back at George and said, "Last year he got married. He swore that nothing would change between us, that I was the wife of his heart. So I stayed. I stayed because I truly loved him and I know he loved me. He still does. But I've, I've finally left him because his wife is pregnant. She's having the baby that should have been mine."

Her eyes flooded with fresh tears. "Oh, George, I'm so ashamed. You don't hate me do you?"

George didn't know what to say. A storm of emotions blew through his soul. Hatred for what Herbert had done to his sister and pain for her plight. He could see that Constance was hurting and he could feel her embarrassment. But hate her? Never. Anyway, who was he to judge her?

Stressing his words with the very softness of his tone, he answered, "Constance, I stood by you when you needed me once and I'll stand by you now. Just know one thing. Mama and Papa love you. Let me take you home."

She smiled and put her hand in his. George helped her into the wagon.

Later that evening, Constance repeated the story to her parents. And as George had promised, they welcomed her back into the family fold. They never again mentioned her ordeal in New York.

A couple of months after Constance's return, George accepted a position as a staff member at the Chickamauga National Cemetery in Chattanooga, Tennessee. He later became the superintendent. When the superintendent of the national cemetery position became available in Beaufort, South Carolina, two years later, he took it.

Thus began his career of taking care of the dead.

During the next several years, the Washington blood would continue to flow in the Ford family. George and Harriet were blessed with four more children: Noel, Irving, Harriet, and Elise. Their children's complexions ranged from the palest ivory to the darkest brown. George's brother, John, now had eleven children with the addition of Polly, Henrietta, Mildred and Cecilia. Their sister Hannah had five children: Nellie, Susie, Harvey, John, and Charles. And Constance Ford, finally over her heartbreak with Herbert, married a black man, Montgomery Kennedy, shortly after her return to Beaufort. They had two children, Montgomery and Florence.

Death doesn't like to be cheated from its due, and after so many births, it called in its marker from the living. It chose William Ford, the patriarch of the family, in 1886. His children and grandchildren gathered at his beside in Beaufort. William was dying from a wasting sickness, and his once-hearty frame had shrunk to half its normal weight.

"I want you to take me back to Mount Vernon when I'm gone," William said to his sons. "I want to go home."

"Papa, you can't mean you want to be buried in the slave cemetery at Mount Vernon, do you?" George asked, his gray eyes burning with unshed tears.

"Son, all my days I wanted to get away from Mount Vernon—away from the injustices of slavery. I wanted to go somewhere, anywhere that Negroes would be treated like human beings. I wanted so much for my children to live in a place where racism didn't exist. Well, I never found that place."

Sighing deeply he continued, "After the war was over and I found out that your grandfather had died, something died in me. There was nothing to keep me at Mount Vernon anymore. The memories hurt too much, and I left."

William's eyes took on a wistful look. "But all these years away from that plantation can't change the fact that it *is* my home. How can I tell you? How can I explain it to you that when you know you're coming to the end of your life, that all you crave is to be buried on familiar ground? Mount Vernon is the place of my birth and that is where I want to lie for the rest of eternity. If I have to be buried in the slave cemetery, so be it. At least I'll be home."

George said, "We'll make sure, Papa."

Grabbing George's hand tightly with his own, William said, "Take care of your mother."

George nodded and squeezed his father's hand. William's voice became stronger as he said, "I have so much more to teach you all, but I know I don't have much time left. Did I tell you, George, to always look a man in his eyes and the truth will reveal itself? That you have to honor God first in all things?"

"Yes, Papa."

William continued, his voice anxious, "Did I tell you, John, that a man keeps his word and protects his family with his life?"

John nodded silently; a lump had lodged in his throat making it difficult for him to breathe.

William became agitated then as he tried to think of all the things that he felt he needed to convey to his children before he passed from his earthy existence. His daughters were crying openly as they came to kiss his hot, dry brow. Then it was Henrietta's turn. She walked as if dead herself to the bed that she shared with her husband and sat down on the mattress near his waist. She took his fevered hand into hers and brought it lovingly to her lips.

"William, shush now, you have taught them. You don't have to worry anymore. Just rest now," she assured him.

"Wait, wait, one last thing," William said quietly, "I want George to be the next chronicler."

"Me? Why me?" George's brow was furrowed at the thought of being given such a monumental task.

"Because you are so much like the Old General. You carry his name-sake, and I want you to keep our legacy alive. Don't let it die." He paused for a moment before saying, "I want all of you to remember who you are. Stand proud, stand tall."

Three days later, William Ford died. His body was brought back to the Mount Vernon plantation where he was buried in the slave cemetery next to his Grandmother Venus. Two years later, his wife, Henrietta, joined him. She was laid to rest next to her husband.

As George stood over his parents' graves the day he buried his mother, he thought about how they had influenced his life. His father had been his educator and his fortress in times of need. His mother had been generous and loving, and had set a firm moral tone for her off-spring. George knew as he walked away from the slave cemetery that he was now the patriarch of the Ford family. That he was now the keeper of the family heritage.

Now what was he supposed to do?

Chapter 28

The wheels of nature are not made to roll backward,
everything presses on toward eternity.

Robert Hall

Although all of his children were receiving an education, George Ford's offspring didn't have the privileges of being taught on the Mount Vernon plantation. The three oldest boys, George Jr., Noel and Irving, attended one of the many colored schools that were springing up in the South to teach the ex-slaves. His daughters, Elise and Harriet, were home-schooled as the small church the boys attended couldn't hold many students in its classroom. Along with their academic education, George would tell his children stories about West Ford, Venus and the Old General. It also became a family ritual to make a yearly pilgrimage to Mount Vernon to visit the graves of their ancestors.

George and Harriet were blessed with their sixth child, Cecil Bruce, in 1893. George was cradling his son in his arms while chatting with his wife in their bedroom. He ran a callused thumb gently over the pulsating, soft spot on the baby's head.

"I hope the chance for some sort of understanding and tolerance for colored people will come in his lifetime," commented George in a rhetorical tone of voice. "Hopefully, all the pain and blood of slavery's past will be forgotten as though it had never been."

Harriet looked up from her child's face to her husband's after his impassioned words. He had spoken from the heart. She prayed silently that his beliefs would come to pass.

But it was not to be.

The South continued to relegate blacks to what they believed was their proper political and social sphere. The political advance began with the issue of voting by legally keeping blacks from the polls, using techniques of disfranchisement, intimidation and violence. Mississippi, followed by South Carolina, established in their constitutions three conditions for voting: a residence requirement, the payment of a poll tax, and the ability to read or to interpret a section of the state constitution. These actions stopped many blacks from going to the polls. Blacks were also forbidden to ride in first-class sections on trains. Other laws required that they be segregated at inns, hotels, restaurants, and theaters.

George knew he had to relocate his family from the continued harassment of his race that existed in the South. So when a position was offered to him as the superintendent of the cemetery at Fort Scott, Kansas, he accepted it. But before he could leave, he decided to visit Mount Vernon. Who knew how long it would be before he was able to do so again?

The Mount Vernon plantation was again opened to visitors in 1897. It seemed that the public was fascinated with the place where the first president had planted his roots. But those roots went more deeply with the Fords. Mount Vernon was their home. It called to them.

When the Ford family pulled onto the estate for a final visit before heading out west, so many carriages and wagons had lined up on the roadside that they had to park theirs down by the stable.

"I don't believe I've ever seen this many people here before," said George as he watched the throngs of visitors waiting outside of the mansion house for their turn to enter.

"Didn't you sell pictures here when you were a boy?" asked George Jr.

His father smiled with remembrance and said, "Yes, I did. Sometimes I got to take the guests through the house to tour the rooms."

"Papa, do you ever wish you still lived here?" asked little Harriet, who went by the nickname of Hallie.

"Sometimes I do. Sometimes I wish that you children could have grown up on this plantation like I did." A nostalgic look crossed his features. "But times change and people change."

George went to the superintendent's house and talked with the current manager of the estate. The superintendent laid out the red carpet for the Fords and made them feel welcome as they visited the grounds. He also made arrangements for them to have some private time in the mansion house after all the visitors had gone.

The Fords had been at Mount Vernon for a few hours when they noticed that four-year-old Brucey was missing. It wasn't the first time the boy had gone off on his on. He was one of those children who wandered. He was always investigating his surroundings, and didn't think he needed adult supervision. The child felt that he was big enough not to have his hand held, and he repeatedly told his family so.

"Brucey, you know you're not supposed to be in here," George Jr. admonished when he found him in the mansion house. He was sitting in one of the ornate chairs in the small parlor staring at the portraits that hung on the walls. Standing over the boy he went on, "We've been looking for you everywhere."

George Jr. looked at the portrait of George Washington. His father told him that his great grandfather, West, had looked just like the Old General. He studied the portrait for a moment, noting that they shared some of the same features. Then stooping down, he picked up his little brother from the chair and left the house.

"I see you've found him," sighed a relieved Harriet as George Jr. came towards her with Brucey. "Where was he this time?" She had her hand on her large stomach—she was pregnant with her seventh child.

"He was in the small parlor," replied George Jr., as he sat his little brother in the back of the wagon with his sisters. With the making of a smile around his mouth, he continued, "He was just staring at the Old General's portrait."

Hallie called out at that moment, pointing her finger behind them, "Look, here comes Papa and the others!"

George Jr. turned from the wagon and spotted his father and two brothers striding along the dirt and gravel walkway that joined the buildings together on the plantation. His father, Irving, and Noel had been down to the old slave cemetery and tomb.

"I don't know why they don't clean up the area," George said, walking up to the wagon. His brows were drawn together in irritation. "I could barely find Mama and Papa's graves with all the weeds growing over them."

Harriet noted the frustration on her husband's face and stated, "The cemetery is important to you because your family is buried there. The new gardeners, they don't care about no slave cemetery."

"I know, I know. But I just can't bear the thought that one day I'm going to come back here and not be able to find their headstones."

"Papa, can we go and pick some flowers for the graves before we leave?" interjected Hallie. She had climbed out of the wagon and was pulling on his hand to get his attention.

Looking down at his youngest daughter, George thought that she was as delicate as a flower petal. She was also the lightest of his children, white-looking with her long, brown hair and blue-gray eyes. She was very tiny and had inherited his dimples. His other daughters, Elise and Vera, were bigger boned and had more of a honey-brown skin color and black hair.

Smiling fondly, George replied, "Yes, you can, but be quick about it. We need to leave here within the next hour."

The girls skipped down the gravel path toward the flower gardens behind the mansion house. Little Brucey tried to follow them.

"Oh, no you don't," his mother said as she grabbed his arm. "You're staying right here where we can keep an eye on you."

He gave his mother a woeful look and then stuck his thumb in his mouth.

The family climbed back into their wagon a short time later and rode out of Mount Vernon. It would be many years before they would visit the plantation again.

Ten days later, the family arrived in Kansas. And three days after that Harriet gave birth to a third daughter that they named Vera. The child was fair-skinned in complexion, with hazel-colored eyes. Vera had also inherited her great-great-grandfather George Washington's patrician nose.

The Fords found out quickly that Kansas wasn't like South Carolina. It was much colder during the winter months and they didn't see as many black folk. They lived in a house that was next to the cemetery at Fort Scott and were virtually isolated from the fort's community. George, however, loved his new position because he was constantly conversing with the soldiers stationed at the fort. It reminded him of the days when he had served as one himself.

The United States entered into a war with Spain less than a year after they moved to Kansas. The U.S. newspapers had been carrying stories of the problems that Cuba was experiencing in trying to overthrow Spain's control. Cuba had been a colony belonging to Spain since 1511 and was struggling to become an independent nation. Many Americans did not like the fact that Spain had control over land and people near their border.

The United States sent a battleship, the *U.S.S. Maine*, to Havana. The War Department hoped the presence of a U.S. battleship would show

American concern for the residents of Cuba. The ship was sunk by an unexplained explosion, killing two hundred sixty crew members, including twenty-two blacks. Spain was blamed for the explosion, and the United States declared war on February 15, 1898.

The Army had no difficulty in securing volunteers for the Spanish-American War. However, the black civilians who wished to enlist were not members of the National Guard and were not eligible for summons to the Army. Many blacks felt that if they fought on foreign soil, it would improve their lot in the eyes of their country.

Under pressure from the black populace, Congress passed an act authorizing the formation of ten colored national regiments. Only four such units were organized. Blacks resented the fact that the War Department stipulated that officers above the grade of second lieutenant had to be white. Many blacks enlisted in the states where there was no ban on black officers. These regiments would be made up wholly or partly of colored troops.

"I'm going to enlist," George said to Harriet without preamble as he put down the newspaper he was reading at their kitchen table. He hadn't even touched his breakfast of fried eggs, grits, bacon and toast because he was so consumed with reading about the war. Their children had already eaten and were working in the garden and completing other chores outside.

Harriet sat immobile, stifling the gasp of dismay that threatened to erupt from her throat. She didn't know what to say. After a moment she spoke, her voice not so firm.

"You—you're going to enlist in the Army?"

"Yes. The enlistments are only for a year, so I won't be gone for long." George rambled on, "This time I want to become an officer, just like the Old General. I can't do that with my old regiment, the 10th, because all the officers have to be white."

Rising from the table he continued, "I've got to talk to my superior to see if you and the children can stay here until I return." His gray eyes glowed with excitement, as if a bright light had been lit behind them.

"No!" she shrieked. "You can't be serious! What can you be thinking of? You're too old to join the Army. You're going to be fifty on your next birthday!"

Shocked at her outburst, Harriet put her hands over her mouth. When she removed them and glanced at her husband, she almost cried. He stood mute. The face he turned to her now seemed older than it had a few minutes before.

Feeling suddenly old and used up, George let out a deep breath. Raking his hands through his short hair, then dropping them to his sides, he said in a voice laced with remorse, "You're right. What am I thinking? I can't leave you and the children. And I am too old. I'm not fit to be a soldier anymore. Why, the leg I took the bullet in is so stiff some mornings, I can hardly bend it."

Hearing the note of self-condemnation in her husband's voice nearly broke her heart. *What have I done?* she thought. Granted, his hair was graying, but he still had the stature of a man decades younger. However, the sparkle in his light eyes had dimmed.

Harriet thought back to when she met George and how proud he was of being a soldier. Soldiering was in his blood. It was who he was. She knew then that she had a difficult decision.

"George, I want you to enlist." Her voice was no longer hysterical as she rushed on before he could comment. She held one of her hands up and said, "Please, don't say anything until I've finished what I need to say. I know you wanted to become an officer when you were a Buffalo Soldier. You gave the Army ten years of your life. If you had been white, you would have at least been promoted to a captain. Now you have a chance to become an officer, and I want you to take it."

She said softly, "Oh, George, I'm sorry I said that you were too old. I was just afraid for you and afraid for me. I don't want to lose you. But I know in my heart that you will make a good officer. I know that the troops you'll command will benefit from your wisdom and strength of character."

He knew that he was one lucky man. She knew him so well. "I love you, Harriet."

"And I love you, too. Taking one of his hands into hers, she said tenderly, "Don't you go off and die on me, George. *Promise me.* Promise that you'll be careful and will come back to me."

"I promise I won't die and that I'll come back to you."

He prayed to God that he would come back alive because he had a lot more living to do.

George Ford enlisted for one year into the Kansas 23rd Infantry the following week with the rank of major. His son, Noel, joined with him, to his mother's dismay. He promised to protect their boy with his life. His oldest son, George Jr., was put in charge of protecting the family while they remained at Fort Scott until their father's return.

Training his battalion in close order drill was the first duty George was assigned. It was necessary for the new recruits to be readied before they left Fort Scott. The colored troops under George's authority had the utmost confidence in his ability to command. They were impressed that he had been one of the original Buffalo Soldiers, knew Indian sign language, and that he was a great shot with a rifle or pistol.

For two weeks he trained the soldiers until they were ordered to Tampa, Florida, where they would be shipped out to Santiago, Cuba. By the time George and Noel's transport reached Cuba, the war was over. The American Navy had destroyed the Spanish fleet in the Caribbean on July 3, 1898. This forced the surrender of the islands on July 16, and an armistice was signed on August 12.

George made friends with a fellow officer named Joseph Morgan on route to Santiago. Joseph was also a major, but in the 8th Illinois Infantry. He had a scattering of large brown freckles on his face and a hawkish nose. On the troop-ship to Cuba, George and Joseph shared their concerns about the war and life in general. The two men were relaxing on the ship's deck, enjoying the cool evening breeze while they chatted. The heat during the day and their continual confinement took its toll on everyone on board. They were relieved that they would reach Cuba the next day.

"I swear, sailing on this ship gives me the willies, George," said Joseph. His body shivered in emphasis. "I keep thinkin' how our ancestors must have felt when they were brought to the States."

"I know what you mean, Joseph," George replied. "We have the freedom to walk around this ship. Slaves were chained, prone for months."

After a moment Charlie changed the subject and asked, "Do you think we'll see any fightin'?"

"I don't know," George answered on a deep sigh. "The war's officially over. We'll probably just keep the peace while the government transitions."

"I'm glad we won't see much fightin', because I ain't never truly had to shoot anyone before. I don't know if I can kill a man." He hesitated and asked, "Have you, I mean, killed anybody?"

Closing his eyes, George replied after a prolonged pause, "Yes, I have. Killing has a way of freezing your soul, Joseph. I didn't relish doing it, but it comes with the territory of being a soldier." Staring fixedly at his friend, he said, "A soldier must defend his country against its enemies, and sometimes that requires taking your enemy's life."

Joseph shivered for a moment at his friend's response. There was much more to George Ford than he thought. He was a seasoned soldier, earning this status through battle and blood. *I'm a babe in arms*, Joseph thought. He decided then and there that George would be his mentor.

The next morning the Cuban coast was sighted. High mountains rose almost from the water's edge, looking enormous across the sea. By late afternoon the ship docked in the Santiago Harbor. After rowing ashore, the men loaded up all the provisions they could carry, packed the mules and headed towards Santiago. They set up camp on a flat area surrounded by jungle on two sides just outside town. George was in command of the 2nd Battalion, and he made sure Noel was in his unit. He didn't coddle Noel or his troops, but guided them with a firm hand. His men respected his cool judgment and fairness.

The colored troops had been ordered to garrison the city and surrounding towns once in Santiago. There Major George Ford met Colonel Theodore Roosevelt. Colonel Roosevelt had been impressed with the fighting ability of the colored troops who had fought next to him at San Juan Hill. When he found that George Ford had been an original member of the 10th Cavalry, he wanted to meet him.

The first time the men met, each took a moment to study the other. George's father taught him to look a man in the eyes and that was what he did after saluting his superior. His first impression of Roosevelt was that he was a toughened soldier—a man's man. The only thing that spoiled Roosevelt's rough image was the round spectacles. They gave him the appearance of an owl, albeit an intelligent one. Roosevelt had tiny lines at the corner of his eyes. So did George. It seemed that Roosevelt also had a sense of humor.

Roosevelt's eyes, when they probed George's, were piercing and sharp. He stood proud, stood tall, as the colonel sized him up. Anyone standing in George's presence couldn't help but feel his strength of character. He was definitely qualified to lead his men; traits that Roosevelt could not help but admire and respect.

George was the first to break the silence. "Colonel Roosevelt, it is an honor and a great pleasure to meet you, sir."

"Thanks for coming, Major. Relax and take a seat." Roosevelt pointed George to an empty rum barrel that was being used for a stool.

The colonel was a little uncomfortable at first, not knowing how to start the conversation. After a long pause he simply said, "You may not know it Major, but I believe we share a common bond with the West. I've worked as a cowboy and I have a passion for hunting." He cocked his head to the side, his eyes bright and continued, "I've even written a book about my experiences on the frontier."

"I've read it, sir, and found it to be pretty accurate," George said as he crossed his arms over his chest. "I spent ten years with the 10th Cavalry during the Indian Wars. Maybe we can compare our experiences." he continued proudly.

Smiling openly now at George, the colonel replied, "I'd like that, Major."

For the next several hours George and Theodore discussed their exploits out West. The two men became fast friends until the colonel was shipped out. They promised to keep in touch with one another once they were stateside.

Shortly after Roosevelt left Cuba, George received orders to move his battalion north and inland to San Luis. The War Department believed it might be healthier for the troops. The march north was excruciating. High temperatures and high humidity brought many to the verge of heat exhaustion.

Whoever the war didn't kill, disease and inadequate supply of food did. By late summer, 1898, some four thousand men were hospitalized with dysentery, yellow fever, typhoid or malaria.

There had been the myth at the beginning of the war that black troops would be "immune" to the diseases of the tropics and capable of more activity in high, humid temperatures. Thus they were dubbed, 'the immune troops.' This proved to be a fallacy, as scores of black soldiers came down with dysentery and malaria. George wrote to his wife about the lack of nourishing food and medicine. There were also no cots for them to sleep on. His troops slept in continually damp tents and on the wet, muddy ground. These conditions helped to foster disease.

George and Noel had been in Cuba for several months during the height of the malaria season, when they contracted the disease in late November. Father and son could not convalesce in the Army hospitals, which were already overcrowded with sick soldiers. George would be ill for a few days and then he would partially recover enough to care for Noel. Then Noel would do the same for him. But a little time would pass, and they would both again be struck down with the recurrent fever.

They were in their camp's quarters off and on for over a month. George felt as if he were dying. Nearly unconscious with fever, he moaned softly, moving listlessly back and forth on his pallet. His eyes were closed, his skin slick with sweat. *I can't die,* he thought with resolve. *I promised Henrietta that I wouldn't.* George struggled to sit up, but fell back listlessly.

"Henrietta!" he called out in delirium. "Henrietta where are you!"

Someone was wiping a cool cloth over his face. God, did it feel good. "I'm here, Papa. Please lie still," said a weary Noel. "Mama made me promise to take care of you."

Noel, with the resilience of youth, was able to fight off the disease and help nurse his father through his worst crisis. George knew in his heart that he would have died if his son hadn't been at his side.

Fewer than four hundred men actually died in combat against the Spanish, whereas tropical conditions, lack of proper nutrition and medical facilities, cost the lives of some five thousand men.

The Treaty of Paris was signed on December 10. Puerto Rico and Guam were ceded to the United States, and the Philippines were surrendered to the U.S. for $20 million. The United States had become an international power.

But the cost of the war was too great for Major George W. Ford. He would return to Kansas weak and sickened with disease. All he could think of on his trip home was, *Will I ever feel well again?*

Chapter 29

Faith is the soul's strongest foundation.

Carol Allen Adams

George and Noel were mustered out of the Army in March of 1899. Upon returning to Kansas, George found himself too weak to resume his duties as superintendent at Fort Scott for several months. He was glad to be home, surrounded by his loving family, but some days he was so ill he wondered if he would ever be healthy again.

"Sometimes I wish I'd never enlisted in the damn war," George said after being sick for over a week. He had never felt so miserable. His body was continually fighting off the malaria bug that would strike him down when he least expected it. The recurring fever almost unmanned him. His wife tended him as if he were an infant. Being so helpless grated on his nerves.

"George, I married you for better or worse and in sickness and health. You will get better," Harriet said with resolve as she placed another cool cloth on his burning forehead.

"Harriet, I don't mean to sound ungrateful at times, but I'm a man. And I feel so useless to you now. I should be the one taking care of you." His gray eyes were dark with frustration.

"George, you have taken care of me since the day we married. Don't begrudge my taking care of you now, especially when you need me the most. Besides, when you get better you can cook for me for a week," she said smugly.

Smiling through his fever, he replied, "I sure will—if you can stand to eat my oatmeal for that long." She grimaced and then laughed. George's oatmeal was so bad that even the pigs turned up their noses at it.

Still chuckling Harriet countered, "Well, maybe I'll think of *something* else you can do for me." She let her fingers skim lightly over his jaw and turned and sashayed from the bedroom. He smiled at her retreating form; suddenly he felt more alive than he had in days.

Closing his eyes, George's thoughts took a different path. He wondered if he, as well as the other black troops who enlisted in the war, had made a difference in the mindset of the country, if all their effort had not been in vain.

If the black troops yearned to garner respect from their value as combat troops, they were sadly disappointed. Segregation, disenfranchisement, lynching and the rhetoric of imperialism were still blatant in the land of the free.

With tender loving care and rest, George began to recover from his debilitating illness. He wasn't a hundred percent, but he was close to it. Along with his job as superintendent, he became active in politics after the war. A new century was dawning, and he wanted to believe it would bring a better day for blacks in the country, and he wanted to be a part of it. When he found out that his friend Theodore Roosevelt, was running for vice president, he sat as a delegate from Kansas in the Philadelphia National Convention in June of 1900. Blacks had flocked to the Republican ticket during Reconstruction. The reason for the tie they felt with this political party was best stated by Frederick Douglass: "The Republican Party was the deck and all else was the sea."

George was feeling good nowadays because he had finally regained his health. He was even able to help secure the black vote for the Republican Party at the convention earlier in the month. He was sitting at his desk, reading the newspaper, when he said out loud, "I don't believe this!" His brow was creased and his expression became befuddled.

Harriet came into the room, wiping her hands on a white cloth. "What's the matter, George?"

He tossed the paper down on the desk. "This article says that Theodore Roosevelt made some disparaging remarks that colored soldiers were dependent upon their white officers during the Spanish-American War."

Scowling, he continued, "It also said that he thought that the colored noncommissioned officers generally lacked the ability to command and handle men as well as their white counterparts." His eyes glittered with ire.

"I don't believe that," Harriet said as she came towards her husband. She touched him lightly on his shoulder. "Why, he's your friend and he respects your military acumen."

"I thought so too," George said, frowning. He put his hand over hers and said, "Theodore even took time out at the convention to talk with me about my health and his upcoming trip out West. There were many men clamoring to sit and talk with him, yet he spoke with me at length. I can't be wrong about him. I'm going to write him a letter about this article."

"You do that, George, you do that," said Harriet.

Turning his head to the side, he kissed her hand before she walked back to their small kitchen to finish dinner. George pulled out pen and paper and started writing:

June 30, 1900—Honorable Theodore Roosevelt, Governor of New York state.

Honorable Sir:

I enclose herewith a newspaper clipping from a colored populist journal published in Topeka, Kansas. We are confronted with this thing on every hand, and would like the authority to refute it. We want to place Kansas this fall where she logically belongs—in the Republican column—and we want the vote of every colored person to do it. The opposition is making capital of this alleged rumor, and it is hurting you with the colored voters. I did not read the article referring to the clippings, but am loath to believe that you have said or written anything derogatory about the colored soldiers as a class. Individual cases of cowardice may be found among all people. There are many ex-soldiers of the 9th and 10th Cavalry living in Kansas, who are justly proved of the achievements of their old regiments. If you will furnish me something to show that you have not maligned or disrespected them, it will be felt for good in the coming election. I am praying for Republican success, George W. Ford Quarter Master Sgt. 10th Cav. later Major 23, Kansas Vols.

George received a letter from Theodore Roosevelt dated July 9th, 1900.

Major George W. Ford, Fort Scott, Kansas

My dear Major Ford:

I thank you for your letter of the 30th that I just received on my return from the west. The attack on me comes from certain demagogues who expect me to speak in the superlative of everybody. I have had similar attacks made upon me because I pointed out the shortcomings of the regular artillery. In my article I mentioned a panic which occurred among some of the colored infantry who had separated from their officers. I stated that, "No troops could have behaved better than the colored soldiers," but added that they were peculiarly dependent upon their officers. I pointed out that some of the colored non-commissioned officers were able to accept responsibility and take the initiative precisely like the very best white non-commissioned officers, but that under the circumstances it was not fair to expect this to be the invariable case; and in conclusion I stated that the Ninth and Tenth Cavalry, who were with their own officers, showed that "Colored troops did as well as any soldiers possibly could do." Finally I dedicated my book "To the Officers and Men of the Five Regular Regiments of the Cavalry Division at Santiago," saying that "I do not believe in any army in the world could be found a more gallant and soldierly body of fighters the officers and men of the 1st, 3rd, 6th, 9th, and 10th U.S. Cavalry," and added that "for my own regiment I was proud to accept the statement that it was on an equality with these regiments." If there is any further information you would like I would be most glad to give it. I may point out that one of the arguments used against me with the National Guard was the statement that I had undervalued them when compared with the regulars of the cavalry division. Of course that was a slander as the present is a slander, but knaves can often persuade fools to go wrong by misquoting or only partially quoting what a man says. A volunteer regiment like the 20th Kansas, when it has had such an experience as that regiment has had, is as good as the best regular regiment in the world. The Ninth and the Tenth Cavalry did so well before Santiago that as I have pointed out in my book, it completely overcame the prejudice even among my south-westerners and to their own phraseology "were delighted to drink out of the same canteen with them."

Faithfully yours,
Theodore Roosevelt

George had been right in his assumption about Theodore Roosevelt. He was an honorable man. He summed up Roosevelt's character the same way an Indian brave once summed up his, he was "Nehi wicasca Iyotanyapi."

Chapter 30

I call upon the Lord, who is worthy to be praised,
and I am saved from my enemies.

Psalms 18 v.3

The Ford family moved to Baton Rouge, Louisiana, in late 1900, when George took a position as the superintendent of the cemetery at Fort Henderson. The family had a house on the outskirts of the cemetery grounds. It was much nicer than the one they shared in Kansas. The rooms were larger and they even had a pump for water in the kitchen. George's job description now called for him to conduct military funerals and he was also responsible for burying the fallen soldiers.

Bruce Ford was eight years old when he first began digging graves with his brothers.

"Why do we always have to live around graveyards?" asked Bruce. He was carrying a shovel over his shoulder as he followed George Jr. They were to meet up with Irving and Noel, who were waiting in the cemetery.

A smile tugged at George Jr.'s mouth at the scowl forming on his little brother's face. Bruce didn't like being in the graveyard, ever since Irving told him the dead walked at night. It had taken their father weeks to convince the youngest Ford that Irving had just been teasing him. And because the youngster was still afraid, their father was giving him a reprieve from the task of digging graves for the day. George Jr. answered his brother's query with the facts as he knew them.

"Bruce, you know our father and our grandfathers took care of the Old General's tomb—I guess that's how it all started."

"But *why* do we have to keep doing it?" Bruce's face took on a bigger scowl.

"It's a job. Jobs for coloreds are hard to come by. When you grow up, you don't have to do this for a living." After a moment he added, "I know I won't, and neither will Irving or Noel."

They sighted their brothers a little farther into the graveyard a few moments later. Irving was relaxing with his back against an old tombstone in the shape of a cross. Noel was standing nearby, his arm resting against the long, wooden handle of a shovel. Irving and Noel looked like their mother; both had walnut-brown skin and black eyes. Irving was the taller of the two, but Noel was more muscular.

"It's about time you two showed up," complained Irving as he rose to his feet. He brushed off some blades of grass that were sticking to his pant legs. He continued, "I was just about to go back to the house to fetch the shovels myself."

"Well, we're here now so let's get started," replied George. Looking at Bruce he said, "You can go play with your friend Isaac now, but—"

Before he could finish, Bruce had thrown down the shovel and was racing back down the path towards the pond.

Cupping his hands over his mouth, George Jr. shouted, "You better be home before dark!"

Bruce waved his hand over his head in acknowledgement. Isaac was waiting for him down by the pond and they had a couple of hours of swimming to get in before dark. Ten minutes later, Bruce spotted his friend lying on a large slab of sandstone. Isaac was letting the summer sunshine warm his body. When Bruce walked up to him, he found Isaac sound asleep. The boy's mouth was so wide open; a chicken could have laid an egg in it.

Bruce noticed how skinny his friend looked without his shirt. The boy's ribs stuck out in sharp angles. He even had bony feet. Isaac was eight years old, the same age as Bruce, but he couldn't read or write.

A mischievous grin split on Bruce's face as a wicked idea popped into his head. He started digging in the dirt, looking for worms. Isaac hated worms. Even when they went fishing, Isaac wouldn't put them on the hook. After Bruce collected a handful of the slimy, wiggly creatures, he put them on Isaac's bare chest. Now all he had to do was wait.

After about five minutes the sinuous movement of the worms woke Isaac. Sleepy black eyes shot open, looking for the source of the sensation on his stomach. He raised his head, gazed down at his chest and screamed. Jumping up he ran into the water, immersed himself, and came up sputtering.

Bruce was laughing so hard tears were pouring from his eyes. He began rolling all over the bank with his mirth. Isaac knew then how the worms had gotten onto him. Scooping up a handful of mud, he came out of the pond and splattered it onto Bruce's smiling face. Both boys started hooting with laughter. They spent the rest of the afternoon swimming and giggling—just enjoying the pleasures of being young.

It was almost dark when the boys decided to head back home.

"Isaac, I'll have George Jr. or Irving walk you home, 'cause its going to be too dark by the time we get to my house," said Bruce. The full moon was visible, which at least cast some light on their walk home. It was his fault they hadn't left earlier. They were having so much fun swimming that he didn't want it to end.

"That be fine with me. Do you think your mama will let me come over tomorrow after church?"

Bruce smiled. His mother went all-out on Sunday's dinner. Isaac had been coming over for the last three of them. He punched Isaac in the arm and said, "Sure you can."

The boys were walking quietly as they neared the cemetery. One path led towards Bruce's house and the other through the graveyard. A noise coming from the wooded area to the left disturbed the silence of the evening. They stopped walking and listened for a minute. A cloud passed over the moon, giving the area an eerie glow.

"W-what's that?" asked Isaac. His eyes were as large as a robin's egg.

"*Shh-shh*," whispered Bruce. He stood very still. Then he looked towards the forested area where they had heard the sound moments before. Apprehension washed over him and he curiously trembled, and it wasn't from the chill in the cool night air. It was more of an imperceptible feeling that tingled up and down his spine.

Bruce spoke in a hushed voice a few seconds later. "I bet it's just Irving, trying to scare us." Then in a louder voice he called out, "You can come on out now, Irving! We're not afraid!"

Suddenly the bushes came alive and three white men stepped out into the fading light. They were about twenty feet away from where the boys stood. One of the men was big, with a large, protruding belly. A black beard covered the whole lower portion of his face. The other two men wore large hats that partly concealed their features. They carried shovels. Bruce knew then that they were grave-robbers.

"You boys out here alone?" said the one with the big belly.

"Y-Yas, suh, we, we be on our way home," Isaac stammered nervously.

A prickling sensation ran up the back of Bruce's neck as he watched the men begin whispering amongst themselves. Something wasn't right. He became frightened. He had a sixth sense that these men meant them harm.

While the men continued with their quiet conversation, Bruce cried, "Run Isaac! Run and hide!"

The boys took off into the cemetery because it was closer than his house. Bruce ran one way and Isaac another. Bruce's feet fell hard on the grass-covered ground as he maneuvered around the tombstones. He ran as if a banshee were after him. The night breeze rushed over his face and his lungs expanded to keep pace with his legs.

Bruce knew the cemetery well and ran towards the area where his brothers had been digging a grave earlier that afternoon. When he got to the open grave, he jumped in, hiding from his pursuers. The impact jolted his small frame for a moment; then he curled up next to the wall of dirt. His ankle throbbed with pain and fear blanketed him. Panic clawed at his throat and he wanted to scream, but he knew that if he did, it would bring those men to him. He shivered, his senses straining for the slightest sound.

An hour passed and still Bruce waited, not moving a muscle, afraid to breathe lest the men hear him. All the while, he prayed that Isaac had gotten away. When he felt it was safe, he tried to climb out of the grave, but couldn't. He couldn't stand on his swollen ankle. He knew then he'd have to wait until someone found him. So he settled down, listening to the night sounds and wondered if the dead walked at night.

"Where could he be? He should have been home hours ago," fretted a disturbed Harriet. The family had gathered in the kitchen, waiting for Bruce to come home. Pot roast, cold mashed potatoes, and sweet peas sat on the table, untouched.

"He's probably on his way home now, Harriet. This isn't the first time we've had to look for him," George assured her.

George was deliberately keeping his voice calm. He didn't want to worry his wife more than she already was. Henrietta had miscarried their eighth child a couple of weeks ago and he didn't want to upset her needlessly. For the first time in his life he felt the sensation of fear settle in the pit of his stomach. He had faced his enemy countless times in the past, undaunted. But tonight he felt helpless because his eight-year-old son was outside, lost in the night. He could be hurt or worse. He shook his head, as if by doing so; he could dislodge the dire thoughts from settling there.

"It's dark out and he can't find his way home in the dark with no light," cried an almost hysterical Harriet.

"Harriet, please go lie down. Vera, you and the girls go help your mama to our room," said George. Turning his attention towards his sons, he continued, "Boys, grab a lantern and we'll go and see if we can find Bruce."

The brothers got spare lanterns from the pantry and followed their father from the house. Once outside their father directed, "George Jr., you and Noel go down the road towards Isaac's house. Take your rifle. Irving, and I will head down to the pond."

Two hours later, there was still no sign of Bruce. George Jr. told his mother that Isaac was also missing.

When George and Irving walked into the house without Bruce, Harriet slumped down onto one of the wooden kitchen chairs. Putting her hands over her face she muttered, *"Oh, God."* Her voice quivered with anguish. "Oh, my God! Where's my little boy? Where's my Brucey? Please God, *please*...I can't lose another child."

George gathered Harriet into his arms and whispered fiercely, "We're not going to lose Brucey. We'll find him, Harriet. We'll find him first-light—I promise you."

He prayed to God it was a promise he could keep.

Bruce was too afraid to fall asleep in the darkened grave. He could smell the damp earth as it surrounded him like a shroud. *What if no one ever finds me?* he thought morosely. Terror tightened his chest, stiffening his limbs.

Papa, Mama, please come get me, he cried inwardly. Then he started to pray out loud, "Please help me, God."

Suddenly, a warm, protective sensation came over him. Bruce sensed a presence—the presence of God and he knew then that he was no longer alone. Finally he closed his eyes and went to sleep.

George Jr. found his little brother early the next morning. The men of the family had split up at first light, looking for the missing boy.

"Bruce! Brucey! It's me, George Jr! Are you all right?" He stood looking down into the grave where his brother lay sleeping.

Bruce sat up and when he saw his brother he screamed out, "George Jr.! Please get me out of here!"

The older brother jumped down into the grave and gave his younger brother a great hug. Bruce was shaking and a little damp, but George Jr. could see that he was okay. He lifted Bruce out of the grave and climbed up after him.

Bruce hung to his brother's long legs, not willing to let him go. "I was so scared at first." Then he reared his head back so he could see George Jr.'s face and said quietly, "You're not gonna believe this, but it felt like God was in the grave with me, protecting me. It was just like Mama said, 'When you are afraid, ask God to help you and he will!'"

George Jr. could tell by Bruce's expression that he believed what he had just said. Who knows, George Jr. thought, maybe God was with him in spirit.

"Come on, let's get you home. Then you can tell us how you got into the grave in the first place," said George Jr. He ruffled his little brother's hair in affection. "Mama will sure be glad to see you!"

George had to hold his wife up by her arms to keep her from crumpling to the floor when George Jr., carrying Bruce, came through the front door of their home. Putting her hands to her mouth, she shook her head rapidly, her eyes welling with tears of happiness.

"Mama!" cried Bruce as he hobbled forward and hugged her around the waist. Harriet blinked her tears away, looked him over carefully and examined his swollen ankle. The rest of the family came forward, each taking turns embracing their brother.

George stood apart from the group, watching his son being greeted, and waited for his turn. He had not slept, and his face showed the lines of strain of his restless night. Finally able to embrace his son, George whispered into his son's hair, "Thank God you're safe."

Bruce told his family what had occurred the previous evening. They were so relieved that he had the sense to run and hide. They all shuddered to think what could have happened if the men had captured him.

"Papa, we need to go and see if Isaac is all right. We lost each other in the cemetery," Bruce said, blinking back tears.

George looked over at his wife. He shook his head slightly for her not to comment that Isaac was missing.

"We'll leave shortly son, just as soon as we get you cleaned up and some hot food in your stomach," replied George.

Later that morning, Bruce watched his sisters as they played tag in the front yard of their home. He was sitting on the front step waiting for his father to take him to see Isaac. His mother had bandaged his ankle and he was using his father's wooden sword for a crutch. The girls stopped their game when several black men on horses galloped up to their house and dismounted. One of the men asked to speak to their father.

"I'll go get him," said Elise, moving quickly towards the front door.

A few moments later, their father came out of the house and walked over to the men. Bruce watched his father's face as they spoke. George bowed his head and slowly shook it. He pinched the bridge of his nose and then looked remorsefully at Bruce. He turned and said something quietly to the strangers. The men mounted up and rode out of the yard as George walked over to his children.

"Hallie, go get George Jr. and tell him to hitch the wagon and bring it to the front of the house. He's out back, working with your brothers in the garden." To Elise, he said, "Take your brother and sister into the house and stay there until I return."

George watched as his children did his bidding. He dreaded telling his wife what the men had just told him. His feet wore leaden boots as he walked up the two steps to the front door of his house. Turning the knob, he went in. Upon entering, he took his wife aside.

Bruce watched as his mother's hand fluttered to her chest. Her eyes were stricken. He knew something was deadly wrong then. He saw his father grab his rifle off the mantle and walk out the door to meet George Jr. Bruce waited a few minutes and then told his mother that he needed to go to the outhouse. He used the back door to leave so he wouldn't bump into his father out front.

I hope I'm not too late, he thought, once he was outside. He peeked around the side of the house and watched as his father and brother drove off down the road. Limping past the vegetable garden, he entered the barn and went to his horse's stall. Bruce pulled the reins over the horse's head and secured the bit in its mouth. He then led the animal over to a bale of hay so that he could climb on its bare back. He didn't take the time to saddle his horse. Nudging his mount forward, he moved quickly and quietly behind his family's wagon.

A few miles down the road George Jr. pulled the wagon into a copse of trees. Bruce rode up near the area, got down off his horse, and tied the reins to a bush. He could hear voices coming from the clearing ahead of him. Some of the voices were raised in cursing, others were crying. Bruce hobbled forward slowly and saw a crowd of people gathered in a small circle. A frown creased his brows while his eyes scanned the group for some sign of what was going on.

Then he saw the reason, and what he saw literally paralyzed him.

It was Isaac's skinny body, dangling from a tree limb. He had been hanged. Several men were gently lowering the young boy to the ground.

Bruce doubled over and dropped to his knees as his stomach lurched. He was overcome by nausea. His anguished scream broke through the cries and moans of Isaac's relatives. George, turning toward the wounded cry, could not believe his eyes when he spotted Bruce vomiting on the ground. He ran over and scooped his son into his arms, rocking him, trying to comfort him.

"Papa, th-that's Isaac! What's happened to him?" Bruce struggled to turn his face back to the area. George pulled him close, tucking his head against his chest so Bruce could no longer see his friend.

"Son, I'm sorry you had to witness this. Someone, someone hanged Isaac," George choked out.

Bruce opened his mouth, but only a sob escaped. When he got his voice to work he cried brokenly, "It w-was those m-men we saw last night, Papa. Th-they killed Isaac. They killed my best friend. Why papa? Why did they kill him?"

George met and held Bruce's grief-stricken gaze. His son's eyes were filled with far more pain than a child should bear. Letting out a deep breath he said sadly, "I don't know, son. I just don't know why someone would hang a child."

Two days later, Isaac was buried. Bruce clung to his father like a shadow at the funeral. He didn't speak to anyone. His brown eyes remained blank until he watched the dirt being thrown on the wooden coffin.

He started shaking uncontrollably and cried, "Papa, the *worms!* The worms will crawl all over Isaac! Don't you know, Isaac is afraid of them!" Bruce's eyes were wild with fear as he asked tearfully, "Will God keep the worms off of Isaac?"

George's throat tightened up. He didn't know what to say. He looked over to his wife for help. Bruce's mother took his trembling hand into hers and led him away from the mourners.

With a soft voice she explained, "Isaac is with God now. Nothing or nobody can ever hurt him again. That body in the grave is not Isaac, it's nothing but an empty shell. The worms can't touch his soul, Bruce."

Bruce continued to cry, but he seemed to understand what his mother was trying to convey to him. The rest of the family walked over to them and they went quietly back to their wagon and home.

It was 1903 and blacks were still being lynched, even though an anti-lynching bill had been introduced to Congress back in 1900. Bills could be written and passed into law, but to those few people who hate, they could not be enforced.

The Fords were very careful after Isaac's funeral, making sure that they were always armed. They also traveled in pairs when they left their home. For Bruce the hanging would continue to be a nightmare within him, waking, sleeping—a nightmare from which he could never seem to shake free. He had lost a friend.

Who else was going to die? he thought.

Bruce didn't have to wonder who was next on the list to meet the grim reaper. Several weeks later, his great Uncle Daniel Ford died. After the Civil War, Daniel had remained in New York, where he had lived as a white man. Shortly thereafter, his great aunts, Jane Porter and Julia Rodgers, passed away.

Chapter 31

*If a race has no history, if it has no worthwhile
tradition, it becomes a negligible factor in the
thought of the world and it stands in danger of being
exterminated.*

Carter G. Woodson

George Ford pursued his ambition in politics and attended the second
annual meeting of the Niagara Movement in 1906. The movement drew
up a manifesto that would establish a program based on the principles
of human brotherhood, freedom of speech and criticism, and the ability to exercise all rights without regard to race. The meeting was held at
Harper's Ferry, where John Brown and his followers had laid down their
lives in an effort to free the slaves.

The speaker of the day was William Edward Burghardt DuBois.
W.E.B. Dubois was a very learned man. He had received three degrees
from Harvard, becoming in 1895 the first African American to receive a
Ph.D. George and William shared the same ideological philosophy. He
also knew he was sitting in the presence of a man destined to make a
mark in history with his ideas concerning equal rights. He was also

impressed by the scholarly attainments of DuBois. He was a man George could respect.

Dubois was standing at the podium in the front of the hall where the meeting was being held. The assembled group was making nominations to the board, and he said to his new friend, "George, we want you to serve as the secretary of the Army and Navy Committee because of your vast military experience. If we are going to make this movement work, we are going to need the talent of men and others of your caliber."

The other delegates in the meeting room were all waiting for George's response to DuBois' nomination. Most were younger than him and all had attended college. George's degree had been earned on the battlefield. Even though he had no advanced educational training, he knew that he had the experience and wisdom they needed to hold the committee chair.

"Gentlemen, I accept your nomination and will gladly serve to the best of my ability," George announced. DuBois came forward and shook George's hand to seal the agreement.

Unfortunately, the Niagara Movement failed early on. The movement couldn't obtain enough members to support its cause and closed it doors four years later. The movement would eventually become known as the National Association for the Advancement of Colored People.

*   *   *

In the early 1900s, blacks began their exodus from the southern states of North Carolina, South Carolina, Mississippi, Tennessee, and Arkansas. Many felt they no longer had any chance for success in their southern home states. They left for greener pastures and better opportunities in the North. This exodus was related to the lien laws, a new system of involuntary servitude that was prevalent throughout the South at the turn of the century.

The flight from the South, unfortunately, caused new racial problems in the North. The systematic reduction of African Americans' status was not confined to suffrage. It extended quickly and efficiently to residential segregation, discrimination in public conveyances, in public institutions, schools, employment and places of entertainment. In spite of being granted freedom from slavery, there were still serious limitations placed on blacks.

African Americans ultimately fell short in their attempts to be free in word as well as deed. The myth of white supremacy had infected the country with the fallacy that the darker-skinned races were naturally inferior. Many newspapers played up crimes in which blacks were involved, and this began the stereotype that blacks were criminal by nature.

George Ford also felt the pull to go North. His wife had just had their eighth child, a boy they named Donald. George wanted a better life for his children, away from the racially motivated atrocities directed at blacks that were occurring almost daily in the South. White supremacist groups in Tennessee were burning black churches and schools, and were whipping, torturing and lynching black men, women and children. The longer they stayed in the South, the greater the chance they could be harmed.

The Ford family was not immune to the atrocities directed at others in their race. A burning cross was lit on their property and their house was set on fire. Luckily, with the help of his sons, they were able to quench the fire before much damage occurred. His family had been targeted. There would be no federal guards to protect his family as in New York.

When the opportunity for a position as superintendent at Camp Butler Cemetery in Springfield, Illinois, was offered to George in 1906, he accepted it. He felt that the only way to secure his family's safety and acquire better economic and social opportunities for them was in the North.

Before the Ford family made its exodus to Illinois, they returned to Mount Vernon. As George and his family visited the graves of their relatives he said aloud, his voice carrying on the wind, "I won't let them forget their heritage, Papa. We'll always stand proud, stand tall."

A month later, the Fords stood in front of their new home. Their house in Springfield was again located on cemetery grounds. But this house eclipsed all the others they had lived in. The two-story brick house had a full basement and was like a mansion to the family of ten. The front of the house contained the office, followed by the parlor, formal dining room, and a spacious kitchen. The bedrooms were on the second floor. A brick fence encircled the entire military burial ground, and a large concrete gazebo sat off to the side of the house. Their closest neighbor lived across a narrow dirt road.

"Oh, I never dreamed we'd live in a house this fine," said a surprised Harriet. She was holding Donald in her arms as she examined her new home.

George hugged her close. "I didn't either."

His gray eyes lit up as he took in the size of the grand house. Hearing his children's laughter, he turned and watched as they raced towards the side of the home to see the columnar gazebo.

Smiling, he turned back to his wife and said, "There's no sense standing around out here. Let's go in and see our new home." Taking Donald from Harriet's arms, he led his wife up the brick porch steps.

The Ford family settled down to a normal as could be expected life in Springfield. Their immediate neighbors knew the Fords were colored, but left them alone because they lived on a cemetery. The boys still helped their father dig graves, and all the children attended Oakhill Public School in Springfield.

The country was still embroiled with race hatred a couple of years later, in 1908. Those blacks who left the South to escape discrimination, found it waiting for them elsewhere. That year was also an extremely difficult one for the Fords.

It was a year that George would remember to his dying day.

One summer afternoon, Hallie came running into the house crying, "P-Papa!" She was breathing hard, and it took her a few seconds to catch her breath. "I-I sa-saw a man—a *white* man down by the creek. He was just staring up at the house. He waved for me to come to him but I ran off."

"He's probably a vagrant, but let's not take any chances," George said. "Get your sisters from the garden and stay in the house with your mother."

Grabbing his shotgun from his office, he went to investigate. The family was gathered in the small living room next to his office when he returned about twenty minutes later. "I didn't see anyone, but I want you girls to keep close to the house for the next couple of days."

Two days after the incident with the strange man, a race riot occurred in Springfield, the home of Abraham Lincoln. It all started when the wife of a streetcar conductor claimed that she had been attacked, dragged from her bed, and raped by a black man. She even identified her black attacker as a George Richardson. The woman later recanted her story when she appeared in front of a special grand jury and admitted that she had been beaten by a white man, whose name she refused to disclose. She cleared Richardson's name during her testimony.

Nonetheless, white rioters ran amuck. Frustrated by George Richardson's protected removal from the local jail to a nearby town, white mobs surged through Springfield, killing, burning and pillaging. An eighty-four-year-old black man, who was married to a white woman for over thirty years, was hanged from a tree within the shadow of the town hall. Five thousand Federal troops were called to restore order, but not before scores of blacks had been killed or wounded.

The Springfield riot was like déjà vu to George. He had been fifteen when the draft riots occurred in New York during the Civil War. This time, they would have to protect themselves. Camp Butler was about twenty miles from the riot zone, but George took precautions and armed his sons.

"Don't take any chances, boys. If someone threatens this house, shoot them," George ordered. He was in military mode. His boys were crack shots and he had the utmost confidence that they could protect their home. Fortunately, the rioters never reached Camp Butler. Over two hundred arrests were made by the federal troops, but not one white person was convicted, not even for disturbing the peace.

The day after the unrest, Bruce approached his father in his office. "Papa, why do white people hate colored people so? We are never going to have a place in America," he continued scornfully. He looked so solemn, as if the weight of the world rested upon his shoulders.

George put down the pen he was writing with, leaned back against the soft cushion of his wingback chair and gazed fixedly at his fifteen-year-old son. Removing his eyeglasses and laying them on the desk, he said, "Sit down, Bruce."

George said simply, "I don't know that all white people hate us. A white person gave me this job. White men fought during the Civil War to help abolish slavery. The majority of the laws passed in this land to help colored folk were put in place by white people. And white blood flows in our veins. In fact, most colored folks living in this country have white blood in them."

George continued, his voice now somber. "But you see, son, there are some white people who just hate. They hate what they don't understand. The racism they feel against coloreds is because they don't understand our history, our culture, and our accomplishments. Colored people have held a subservient place in this country for so long, I guess some white people don't believe it should ever change."

"But Papa, we moved away from the South to get away from racial prejudice. Yet, I've experienced just as much racism here in Illinois than I did in the South." Bruce's eyes blazed with frustration.

"Son, where there is good, there is also evil. All we can do is pray that people's minds change for the better. God will be their ultimate judge and juror."

The next day George made the decision that his children would have the opportunity to gain advanced degrees in school, something he never was able to do. He wanted his children to have a sound educational base so that they could grow economically. Over dinner he told them of his plans for their future.

"You're all going to college," he said, continuing with his meal.

His children stopped eating in surprise. They looked toward the head of the table where their father was sitting calmly after making his statement.

George Jr. asked, "Papa did you just say that we're all going to college?"

"Yes, it's the only way for colored people to gain economic security in this country."

The table erupted in jubilation. It was something they thought they would never be able to do. George directed his attention towards Vera and said, "I know you want to become a teacher, and you shall." Vera was the scholar of the family. Directing his attention to his other daughters, he continued, "Elise, Hallie, I hope you'll want to go too." The girls squealed with excitement and nodded their heads.

George then turned to his four sons. "I want all of you to attend medical school. As physicians you'll reach the pinnacle of success in this country, becoming a credit to our family and to our race."

That night as he lay in bed, George thought with optimism, *Tomorrow will be a better day.*

It was just the quiet before the storm.

The following afternoon, George sat in his office doing paperwork. He had just completed his monthly report when he got a crick in his neck. Reaching up with one hand, he began massaging the ache, trying to relieve the stiffness there. He closed his eyes for a moment and then abruptly opened them when he heard a high-pitched scream. Jumping to his feet he ran outside to the back of the house. Closing his eyes and listening for a split second, he tried to determine where the cries were coming from. At last he heard one particularly pitiful wail that ended on a sharp note, but it gave him the direction. It was coming from the creek that ran behind the back portion of the cemetery.

George ran as fast as his sixty-year-old body could maneuver, adrenaline coursing through his veins. As he neared the creek, what he saw almost caused his heart to stop beating. Donald—his son—his three-year-old boy, was engulfed in flames. George had run across battlefields while bullets and arrows whizzed past his body and plowed into the ground at his feet. The sprint toward his son that day seemed to take longer than his most hellish charge in battle. He yanked off his military jacket as he raced on even faster. When he reached Donald's side, he beat the fire out with the jacket. George wrapped his son in the now-burned garment, picked him up and dashed back towards the house.

Harriet, who had been napping in the hammock, came running towards him. Her eyes became wide with despair when she saw whom he was carrying. She collapsed to her knees. George couldn't stop to console her—not now.

Bruce came sprinting from the garden and George hollered out, "Go see to your Mama."

Once in the house, George placed Donald on the kitchen table. He slowly unwrapped his jacket from his son, his hand trembling like a palsied old man. He winced, looking at the burned flesh all over the boy's small body. In many places the bones could be seen. His little face was unrecognizable. It was blistered and charred. There was no hair left on his head. His hands were shaking so badly that he had to clasp them into fists to stop their movement.

George put his ear to his son's chest. Donald was not breathing. He choked back the bile that had risen to the top of his throat. A deep, hollow ache pulsed through him, making him numb. Donald was dead.

Hearing footsteps running towards the kitchen, he quickly pulled the jacket over his son's body. His daughters rushed into the room and stopped before him.

"Papa, Papa, what happened?" cried Hallie. Vera and Elise were standing behind her, looking at the small, charred bundle on the table. The smell coming from the body was sickening. It was a smell George would never forget.

"It's—It's Donald. He's been burned." His voice broke then. "He's—He's—girls, your baby brother is *dead*."

The wails that assailed him almost made his knees buckle. How was he going to tell his wife that their little boy was dead? How was he to go on living when he couldn't even breathe? He drew in all the air he could as his chest constricted. *God, how am I going to live without my son?*

George had no choice in the matter. A few seconds later his wife came bursting into the kitchen with their other sons. He grabbed his wife by her shoulders, restraining her from removing the jacket from Donald.

"Why is he covered like that?" Harriet asked, her eyes wild with concern. She began shouting out, "Hallie, hurry and bring me my medicine chest. Elise, grab some sheets from the closet. George Jr. boil me some water, quickly."

All these orders were given out as George held her away from the table and their son. But no one moved a muscle to obey her commands.

"Why are you holding me, George?" Harriet was squirming, trying to break his tight restraint. "Let me see to our son!"

His voice hoarse, George said, "He's, he's dead Harriet. There's nothing you can do."

She held up a hand. "*No!*" Her answer was sharp and sudden. "I don't believe you! Let me go to him!"

"Harriet, *no*, I can't let you," muttered George. He closed his eyes momentarily and said, "He's badly burned. I don't want *any* of you to see him like this."

Stiffening her body in her husband's grasp, his wife said calmly, "George Jr., take everyone out to the gazebo." Noting his hesitation, she shouted firmly, "*Now!*"

After the children left the kitchen she turned her face back to her husband's haggard one. He still had her gripped tightly by her shoulders.

"You will let me go, George. *You will let me see my son.*" She stared deep into his eyes. Determination was written over her facial features, and he knew that he could no longer deny her request.

Taking in a shuddering breath, he dropped his arms from her shoulders and watched as she slowly walked to the table and lifted the burned jacket off her youngest child. Harriet started shaking, closed her eyes, and sagged to the kitchen floor as if her bones had melted.

She cried out in her anguish as she shook her head. "*No! No, no, no!* This cannot be my son. This cannot be my son. God, *no!*"

George dropped to his knees beside her and held her tightly. She buried her face deeply against his chest.

"Tell me, George." Harriet whispered, her voice gone soft and ragged. "Tell me that this *is* not Donald. Tell me that this is not *our* son."

"I am so sorry, sweetheart, I can't tell you that." His voice was little more than a tormented croak.

Harriet's shoulders continued to shudder with the force of her sobs as George held her until she went limp in his arms. He scooped her up and carried her to their room. He came back into the kitchen and recovered Donald's body. Saying a prayer for his son, he called his children back inside the house.

"Hallie, I want you to get Donald's best clothes and bring them to me. Elise, you and Vera stay in the room with your mama."

Turning to his sons, he continued, "George, you and Noel go into town and buy a coffin. Take the money from the metal box in my desk drawer. Make sure you stop and report to the authorities what has happened here."

He choked out his next words. "Irving, Bruce, today you will dig a grave for one of our own."

Thirty minutes later, George was trying to peel off the burned clothes from Donald's body, but they had melded to his skin. He realized he had to leave the charred clothes on his body and dress him the way he was. Silent tears coursed down his face at the gruesome thought. George heard a tortured gasp and glanced up to see his wife standing in the kitchen doorway. She had her closed fist to her mouth. A moment later she straightened with resolve, tears glittering in her eyes, and came over to the table.

She said with trembling lips, "George, I'm stronger than you think." She took Donald's shirt from his hands and began dressing him. She crooned words of love the whole time as if the child could hear them. "My sweet, sweet baby boy. *Mama's here.* You just rest now. Your papa and I are just going to dress you in your Sunday clothes. Mama's here...Mama's here now, Donald."

Harriet's soft words broke George's heart. He clenched his jaw tight against his pain.

The funeral was held the next day. Donald was laid to rest in a plot reserved for the Ford family. Harriet stood numb with grief during the ceremony. She had been raised with the word of God, as her father had been a minister. But today she felt as cold as death inside. Her baby son was dead—God had taken him. Why? How could she explain Donald's death to her children when she couldn't understand it herself? Glancing up at the cloudless, blue sky overhead she wondered, *How can the day be so glorious when my son is dead?*

The religious training of a lifetime helped Harriet to finally console her children and herself. For George it was another matter. Harriet had never seen him so eaten with grief. George sat vigil next to his son's grave the day of the burial. He stayed in the cemetery all through the night. He didn't want to leave his son alone in the dark. The next morning he could barely force his legs to move. He wondered mournfully, *How does a son die before his father?* He swallowed the hard knot of despair that had formed in his throat.

George Jr. came upon the small gravesite and sat down next to his father. They were quiet; each lost in their own thoughts.

Finally George Jr. spoke. "Papa, Mama is up and is asking for you. Are—are you coming into the house now?" he choked out.

George saw the tears collecting in his eyes. His oldest son was grieving—his family was grieving—and they needed him. Nodding, he slowly rose to his feet.

Patting George Jr. softly on his back he said, "It's going to be all right, son. Let's go inside now." Glancing sadly once more at Donald's grave they walked towards the house.

The incident of Donald's death was investigated. The neighbors were interrogated. A woman who lived across the road from the Fords said she had seen a stranger walking in the cemetery earlier that morning. Matches were also found where Donald had caught fire, matches that did not come from the Ford home. As to how Donald wound up by the creek; it was surmised by the authorities that he woke from his nap without Harriet being aware of it and wandered away.

The death of Donald Ford was recorded as accidental, caused by a child playing with matches. The Ford family never believed that, but could not prove it otherwise. For George and Harriet, the terrible death of their little boy never completely left them.

It scarred them.

It haunted them.

It was something they could never forget.

Chapter 32

Heaven from all creatures hides the book of fate, all
but the page prescribed, their present fate.

Pope

George Jr. was the first member of the family to graduate from medical college, in the fall of 1911. After graduating, he moved to Chicago to open a pharmacy. But from the very beginning, obstacle after obstacle was thrown in his path. He wasn't able to locate a building in which to open his business because no white landlord would rent to him because of his ethnicity. Finally, George Jr. found a site in a predominately black neighborhood and he hung his shingle on the door for business. Everything was going favorably for a while, until the distributors of the pharmaceuticals discovered that he was black. Unfortunately, they cut off his product line. Without medicines he couldn't keep his doors open. He was unemployed for several months, until he secured a position as a bridge operator.

His brothers, Noel and Irving, graduated from medical school a couple of years later. Noel graduated with a degree in family medicine. He eventually moved to Detroit, set up his practice, and married a woman named Alice Shadd. They had a daughter named Vera. Irving graduated with a degree as a chiropodist and established his practice in Springfield. He had yet to find a wife. George Jr. married Lulu Bowers and secured a position at the city post office.

In 1917, Bruce graduated from Meharry Medical College with a dental degree. But two things marred the excitement of his graduation, the start of World War I in 1914 and the death of his brother, Noel. Noel died from a severe bout with pneumonia and was buried at Camp Butler Cemetery where his father still presided as superintendent. A disheartened Bruce chatted with his father in their home a few months after his brother's death.

"Papa, I really miss Noel. How could he have died so young?" said Bruce as they ate breakfast at their kitchen table.

George placed his fork next to his plate that held his meal of pancakes and sausage and said, "You're right about that. He was a doctor and for the life of me, I can't figure out why he couldn't save himself." His eyes held a pained, puzzled look.

"I've been thinking about that also," murmured Bruce, as he moved his food around his plate with his fork. He hadn't taken a single bite of it. One elbow resting on the table, he rubbed a hand along the bottom of his chin and commented, "You know that if he were still alive he would have joined the Army, don't you?"

"Probably, he loved the idea of being a soldier." George took a sip of coffee before saying, "He would have made a great officer."

"Papa, I'm going to join the Army," Bruce said a moment later.

George sat back in his chair and wiped his mouth on a napkin. In many ways Bruce was like Noel and he, a kindred spirit, he thought. His eyes misted for a moment as he reflected about his son. His beloved Noel had been dead for months now, but the ache of losing another child, stayed with him. The pain was always there, waiting to burst forth at a remembered smile or a cherished memory.

He finally responded, "I know you want to do your part for the cause." Patting his son on the shoulder, he said wistfully, "I wish I wasn't too old to join."

"I know soldiering is in your blood, Papa. I wish you could too."

George commented in a low, sober voice, "To each of us there is a time and our place in that time. I've had my time and place. I spent eleven years serving my country. Take advantage of your time, son. If you choose to join the Army you have my full support."

The United States Army had many social, economic, and educational disparities between the African American and white soldiers when Bruce joined. The Army segregated black and white troops by forming two African-American divisions. The divisions were commanded by white officers to form cavalry, infantry, artillery, medical, veterinary, sanitary, stevedore and engineer corps. No African-Americans were permitted in the aviation corps.

Some blacks who had an education greater than high school felt that they should be trained as officers. But the majority of them were drafted as privates, including Bruce. There was a shortage of black physicians, and the policy not to make them officers, drew sharp criticism from the National Medical Association, a black group with a membership of five thousand.

Many blacks exhibited little enthusiasm for the war. The sympathy of white people for the invaded Belgians was not shared by African-Americans, who knew too well of Belgian atrocities in the Congo. Yet blacks did not lag when the government called for volunteers. More than two million registered under the Selective Service Law, and more than 300,000 were drafted.

The first of the African American troops to arrive on French soil were stevedores. These men became known as Services of Supply (SOS) units and worked day and night to set up docks and warehouses, and to form the core of the supplies logistics system. The War Department felt that blacks were more suited to manual labor because they were familiar with it.

Bruce Ford served as a Private Medical DET in the 370 Infantry, 93rd Division. He was able to practice his dental profession in the Army, but only on the minority troops. Bruce's unit was assigned to General John Pershing, who in turn assigned them to French divisions. The black troops fought with French weapons and under French leadership until the war ended. Approximately 400,000 African Americans served their country during World War I.

When Bruce mustered out of the Army a little over a year later, he headed home to Springfield and to a still-troubled country in regards to race relations. Several days after his return he and his father were chatting about the race problem.

"Read this, son." George handed him a small booklet. "It's a pamphlet I received from the NAACP. You know that I'm serving as secretary of the Springfield branch."

"Papa, I don't know how you have the time or the energy for your position here at Camp Butler and the NAACP."

George smiled. "I'm old, but never too old to fight for our cause."

Looking at the pamphlet Bruce read aloud, "Thirty Years of Lynching in the United States—1889-1918." He arched an eyebrow at his father before continuing. The report stated that 2,522 blacks and 702 whites were lynched because of racial discrimination during 1889-1918.

After Bruce finished reading the pamphlet he shook his head, and then rubbed his hand behind his neck. He asked, "Will things ever get better for our race, Papa? Living in this country is like living in a war zone. When will all the killing stop? What is it going to take for white people to accept us as full citizens with all the rights due to us as citizens?"

George's face was serious and his voice adamant in his response. "What we have to do is to continue educating our children. What we have to do is to continue to vote. What we have to do is to continue on with our legacy."

"Papa, what does our legacy have to do with anything? I mean, *who* really cares that we're related to George Washington? What good does it do? Did it save Donald? It hasn't helped George become the pharmacist he attended college for. Noel wasn't even allowed the military burial that was due him for his service in the Spanish-American War."

Shooting up from his chair, Bruce paced back and forth in front of his father, like a panther in a cage, before stopping and standing in front of him. His father's dark-gray eyes were clouded. Bruce realized that he had caused his father some distress.

"I'm sorry, Papa. But, sometimes I get so angry at the injustices we face that I just can't keep it inside of me."

George answered after a moment, "There isn't a day that goes by that I don't think about what's happening with our race. It rips me apart. There also isn't a day that goes by that I don't think about your dead brothers. I wonder what kind of man Donald would have become if he had lived. I also wonder what's going to happen to Noel's wife and daughter now that he is no longer with them."

George's voice took on a stronger tone, "But our heritage lives on. It lives on in our children and our children's children. You have to care that we're related to the Old General because we are his only blood descendents. And someday, someday that's going to mean something to our descendents and maybe even to this country."

"Then why can't we tell anybody that we're related to George Washington?" Why do we have to keep it a secret?"

"Because people in this country aren't ready to accept us that way yet. There are too many racists groups out there, killing people for being just *colored*. What do you think they would do if they found out about us? We can't take that chance.

"So when do you think we'll be able to tell anyone?"

Sighing, his father replied, "I don't know. It probably won't happen in my or your lifetime. But it will someday."

Bruce eventually agreed with the wisdom of his father's stance on remaining mute on the subject of their secret heritage. How could he not? The racial uprisings occurring almost daily in the country proved that the United States wasn't prepared to hear about the first president's black descendants.

*   *   *

In December 1918, Bruce moved to Peoria, about thirty miles south of Springfield to establish his dental practice. He was the first African-American dentist in the small Midwest town. Bruce had a two-room office located at 321 Main Street, across from the city's courthouse. Destiny was smiling on him the first week his doors opened for business.

"Doctor Ford, my name is Florence Harrison. I have an appointment with you this morning." The woman was standing in the reception area of his office. She placed her small, delicate hand on her swollen face before continuing, "My jaw is paining me something terrible. Can you please take care of me today? I don't think I can go one more hour with this awful pain." Her black eyes beseeched him for help.

She was such a tiny woman, probably no taller than four-feet-nine, Bruce thought. Her hair was not long; it just reached the tips of her shoulders. But he had never seen hair so thick. His ardent examination continued to her smooth skin tone, which was more red than brown.

Finally he spoke. "Follow me, Miss Harrison and have a seat there." *Was that my voice squeaking?* he thought as he pointed to the dental chair.

Bruce was nervous as he asked her to open her mouth. He kept looking at her lips, which were fuller than his own; the bottom one more voluptuous than the top. When she opened her mouth he noticed that she had perfect white teeth. Her jaw was slightly swollen on the left side, and upon further examination, he found the problem. He hated the thought that he would cause her further pain.

"Well, it seems you have an impacted wisdom tooth, Miss Harrison. I'm afraid it will have to come out." At least his voice didn't squeak this time.

Florence's onyx eyes were huge, full of trust. His hands were still at his sides, forgotten in the spell of her gaze. He didn't believe it was possible, but he was just like the rest of the Ford clan. He had fallen in love at first sight. He knew as he stood over her that she was the one he was going to marry.

But how was he going to convince her of the fact?

He succeeded, and the couple's whirlwind romance culminated in marriage in April of 1919.

It was unfortunate that the couple wasn't able to settle down for a life of wedded bliss.

The country's social problems wouldn't allow it.

Chapter 33

*Be not diverted from your duty by any idle reflec-
tions the silly world may make upon you, for their
censures are not in your power to change.*

Epictetus

The rebirth of the Ku Klux Klan in 1919 fanned the fires of racial prejudice against African Americans, Asians, Jews, Catholics, immigrants and
radicals. The new Klan now operated from the east to west coasts of the
country. The Klan's influence inspired race riots that exploded in cities
of the North. Seventy blacks were lynched in 1919 alone, and during a
six-month period of the same year, twenty-odd race riots occurred. The
summer of 1919 was dubbed 'The Red Summer,' for black blood ran in
the gutters of the nation.

One of the worst race riots in the country occurred in Chicago in
July of 1919, only about a hundred and fifty miles from where Bruce
and his new wife resided. The incident was sparked when a young black
boy accidentally drifted too close to a 'whites only' area on a section of
beach on Lake Michigan. The boy had been floating on a homemade
raft and was not aware of how close it had drifted to the shore. He was
pelted with stones until he fell into the water and drowned. Black and

white mobs soon formed, and before order was restored, thirty-eight people had died, and the wounded totaled 537.

Racial tensions occurred throughout the country, and even newspapers pandered to the race bias against blacks. One Chicago newspaper's 1920 headline read, 'Half a Million Darkies from Dixie Swarm to the North to Better Themselves.' By 1920 the African American population had tripled, aggravating problems of crime, health, and housing. African Americans had been stereotyped as criminal and were now labeled as undesirable. There were over 470 thousand more blacks living in the West and North than there had been in 1910.

Bruce tried not to allow the negativities occurring in the country to limit his pursuit of economic stability. He was educated, he was a doctor, and he was going to have his portion come hell or high water. He started his family about the same time as his older brother, George Jr. Bruce and his wife had three children in succession, Florence in 1920, Elise in 1921, and Cecil Bruce in 1922. George Jr. and Lulu had Lena in 1920, Harriet in 1923, and George III in 1924.

As a dentist, Bruce was faring better financially than his brother, George Jr. He was able to move his family into a middle-class neighborhood in Peoria. Many of their white neighbors tolerated them because he was a doctor and his children were fair-skinned. His oldest daughter, Florence, looked Caucasian, with her straight black hair and black eyes. She was as dainty as his sister, Hallie. Elise and her brother, Cecil Bruce, favored their mother's Native-American features. Elise had brown eyes with a hint of amber awash in them and thick brown hair. Little Bruce had straight black hair and brown eyes.

It was a Saturday evening and Bruce had said good night to his children. Their bedtime had become a ritual with him. He was up at five-thirty every morning and arrived home late most evenings. Putting his children to bed was the only time he really was able to converse and play with them.

He and his wife were spending some quiet time in their small living room when he said, "You know that my sisters and Irving don't want children. They believe the country's too troubled to bring a colored child into."

Florence was sitting on a chair across from him, sewing a button onto one of his shirts. She glanced up from her task and replied, "Well, I for one don't care what your brother and sisters believe. As long as people look and think differently from one another, there's going to be problems. And I can't comprehend being married and not having children."

Bruce smiled. "I agree. They don't know what they're missing."

His gaze softened as he reflected on his spitfire of a wife. Florence stood toe to toe with anyone who dared to discriminate against them in any form or fashion. Bruce's mind wandered to an episode that occurred the previous day. Florence had gotten into an altercation with the jeweler who had a shop on the main floor of his office building. He had forgotten his lunch and Florence brought it to him with the children in tow. While waiting for him to come down to the lobby to retrieve it, three-year-old Elise had wandered off into the jewelry store. She had put her mouth onto the jeweler's glass case, looking at the rings that were displayed for their customers' examination. When the jeweler discovered the wet marks Elise's lips had left on the glass, he started screaming at her.

"Whose little pickinninny is this?" The gray-haired man stood rigid, with his arms on his hips. Looking around at his employees he barked, "Somebody get me a clean cloth!"

When a timid female clerk handed him a white piece of linen he muttered, "What's this city coming to, with all these coloreds thinking they can come and go as they please?"

Elise was frightened and started crying as the man continued to rant and rave. She had never been screamed at before. The timid clerk tried to comfort the upset little girl.

Florence, hearing the commotion and Elise's crying, stormed into the store and gave the jeweler a piece of her mind. "Don't you dare yell at my child, you overblown piece of pompous trash! No one screams at my children."

She was livid as she held little Bruce on one hip. Elise was still crying, tugging on her dress while Little Florence was trying to hush her younger sister.

Pointing her finger like a pistol at the man Florence rushed on, "Why, I have a notion to slap that arrogant look right off your face."

The jeweler was furious at what Florence had said to him. He was stammering and sputtering so much he couldn't speak. His face was beet-red with his ire.

Bruce walked into the jewelers at that moment and ushered his wife and children out of the store. Once in the lobby he told her that he would handle the situation.

"Take the children and go home, Florence. I'll go and talk to the manager of the building about what happened here before the jeweler does. The building manager is a fair man and I shouldn't lose my office space over this incident." He leaned down and quieted Elise's whimpers with a finger to her lips.

"Oh, I didn't think about that when I spouted off," said a subdued Florence. Her previously animated face was now sober as she thought about the consequences of speaking her mind. A few seconds later she said, "I couldn't help it, Bruce. That man made me so angry, I just saw red."

"I don't blame you for speaking your mind. But I'll take care of it now." Walking her towards the door to the street Bruce said with a smile, "Please go home before you get the itch to scalp him."

Florence poked him in the arm with her forefinger and he leaned down and kissed her on the forehead. He walked his family over to the trolley car in front of the building and helped them aboard. Yes, his wife was a little spitfire.

Bruce's mind was jogged back to the present at his wife's insistent voice. "Did you hear me, Bruce?" asked Florence. "I've been waiting for you to answer my question."

"I'm sorry, sweetheart. My mind was somewhere else. What is it that you asked me?" He gazed over at her, giving her his full attention.

"I said what we need to do is to shelter the children the best way we can from racial prejudice." Her dark eyes were troubled as she waited for him to comment.

"I don't know how we are going to accomplish that feat." Bruce felt a light tug on his shirtsleeve and turned his head to the source.

"Papa, me no s'eepy," muttered Elise as she rubbed her eyes. She was standing by his chair and he hadn't even heard her approach. She held her baby's blanket tightly, her bare toes sticking out from under her long pink nightgown.

"Me not goin' ta seep tonight." Then her mouth stretched wide in a huge yawn.

Florence scolded, "I bet you better high-tail it back to bed now, young lady." Letting out an exasperated breath she told her husband, "I swear that child is just like you. She acts more like thirteen than three."

Not able to contain his mirth, Bruce laughed aloud, the rich tone of it filling the room with warmth. He rose from the chair, picked up his daughter, and carried her back to bed.

Every weekend Bruce took his family to visit his parents at Camp Butler. He was very devoted to them and he wanted his children to have the opportunity to spend time in their company. During these frequent visits, Major Ford would regale his grandchildren about Mount Vernon and the special heritage they shared with George Washington.

It was during one of the visits that his granddaughter, Elise, asked, "When you gonna take me to Mowth Vermen, Big Papa?"

She was sitting on the floor next to his knee. George had a wool throw covering his legs and watched as she pulled out a loose thread.

Elise was wrapping the thread around and around her finger. The child's finger was turning blue.

"It's *Mount Vernon*," George said, correcting her pronunciation. Taking her hand, he unwound the thread from her little finger before she caused it serious damage.

"That's what I said, Big Papa. When we goin'?" Elise grinned with a gap-toothed smile.

"We'll go soon, child." Grimacing, George moved his stiff leg to a more comfortable position. "Be careful, Lesey, so that you don't bump my sore leg."

Elise, her eyes large with concern, said, "Do you want me to get a knife so you can cut the hurt off?"

George chuckled. "Uh, I don't think that's gonna work, Lesey, but thanks for wanting to help me."

Elise shrugged and started pulling on another loose thread.

Glancing over Elise's shoulder, the doting grandfather noticed little Bruce trying to walk with his brass-handled hickory cane. The cane was taller than he was. His mouth twitched as his grandson started using the cane as a sword. His other granddaughter, Florence played quietly with a doll next to his chair.

These children need to visit Mount Vernon, George thought passionately. They needed to see where their ancestors lived and died. They needed to learn of their heritage first-hand. He hadn't been back to Virginia since 1906, but he knew he would return before his death. Mount Vernon was calling to him, and he felt drawn there like a moth to the light of a flame.

As he sat watching his grandchildren, his mind was heavy with his responsibilities as patriarch of the Ford family. He was the chronicler, the keeper of the family's heritage. He had a legacy to impart to his grandchildren. They had a legacy to continue it. He would tell *no* white person of his heritage. He would trust *no* white person with their secret.

He had lived too long and seen too much race hatred to make that mistake.

It wasn't that George didn't have white friends; he did. But the times he and his family lived in were too troubled to trust them not to speak of the Ford heritage to others, others who may wish to do the family harm. Soon he would choose from among his grandchildren those special ones who would have the fortitude and forbearance to keep their heritage alive. He would recognize deep in his soul which ones to hand the charge over to.

George glanced down at Elise as she tugged on his hand. "Big Papa, can I see your sword? I promise not to stick Brucey with it."

He tried not to chuckle at her comment. "Later, Lesy. I have to get it from the boxes in the basement."

She nodded her head and then went over to play with Bruce.

George doted on all his grandchildren, but it was Elise who was always asking him questions about their heritage. The little imp reminded him of himself as a child. They shared the same spirit of adventure.

It was also George's most earnest wish that his grandchildren get to know each other. Only George Jr. and Bruce had children. George Jr. didn't visit much because of the driving distance from Chicago to Springfield, so George wasn't able to spend time with his grandchildren very often.

In fact, he didn't see much of his own children either and he missed them. His oldest daughter, Hallie, had married a farmer from Texas named Garfield Goins. The couple owned and operated a mortuary in Peoria. Vera lived in Mt. Hope, West Virginia, where she taught at a local high school. She had married Enis Powell, the school's principal in 1921. George's other daughter, Elise, married Douglas Jenkins who had a Ph.D. in education. They lived in Charleston, West Virginia, where Elise also taught at a local high school.

There was only one means to keep the family close to each other and that was to establish annual family reunions. The first one took place in 1928 and was held in the large back yard of the house at Camp Butler in Springfield. George had invited all of his immediate family and close friends. Bruce and his family were running late and were the last to arrive at the outdoor event. George walked over to greet them as they headed towards picnic area. He couldn't help but notice that little Elise was lagging behind the group. She was too busy looking at the people who were in attendance.

There were so many people strolling the grounds that day that seven year-old Elise's head got dizzy looking at everyone. In fact, Big Mama had hired servants to serve the adults refreshments as they conversed in various groups throughout the yard. There were people from all over the country and not all of them were Fords. Some of the local black gentry were also in attendance.

Elise finally had the chance to meet her Uncle George Jr.'s children, Lena, Harriet, and George III. Harriet and Elise were both fair in complexion, but Harriet had dark, almond-shaped eyes. Harriet had also inherited her father's dimples. Lena and George III favored their mother and were darker in complexion. The cousins hit it off right away and began playing hide and seek amongst the tombstones.

As the reunion continued into the late afternoon, Elise became bored listening to all the old people talking about all their old times together. She wanted to search for tadpoles down by the creek, which ran behind the cemetery grounds. But her mother was still a little annoyed with her because of the antics she displayed before the picnic. She told Elise to sit down somewhere and mind her manners. And that was what she was doing as she sat on the picnic bench that harbored the desserts. Her mother was pregnant with her fourth child, and as cranky as a swarm of disturbed bees ever since their altercation this morning. And it was all because Elise didn't want to wear a dress to the reunion. Elise's mind replayed the situation in detail.

"Oh, let her wear what she wants, Florence. She's still a little girl," Bruce stated wearily. He had worked very late the evening before, trying to finish several sets of dentures. Elise's whining was wearing on his nerves.

"She's seven years old, Bruce, and it's high time she starts dressing like a little girl instead of a ragamuffin," said his ruffled wife. "Do you want the whole family to think we can't dress her properly?"

"I don't care what the rest of the family thinks about how my children dress," Bruce answered indignantly. His tone changed to a cajoling one when he realized how harsh his voice had sounded. "Anyway Florence, no matter what you put on her, she'll have it dirty or torn before the reunion is over. You know what I'm saying is true, so you might as well let her wear the overalls."

Elise had gotten her way with her clothing choice. A moment later, little Bruce walked up to the table and started stuffing his mouth with chocolate cake. It was a miracle he hadn't choked to death. She watched him cram yet another piece into his already full mouth.

"Brucey, I'm going down by the creek to catch tadpoles. Meet me there when you get done eating," stated Elise. She was tired of sitting and minding her manners. She didn't wait for a reply, but sprinted away from the gathering. When she got to the creek, she took off her shoes and socks and laid them on the bank. Then, rolling up the overalls to her ankles, she waded into the shallow water.

Ten minutes later, little Bruce joined her. He wasn't alone. There were two little girls accompanying him. When he spotted his sister he said, "Mama asked me to show Elizabeth and Mary the creek." Brucey was scowling. Elise deduced that he hadn't wanted to bring the girls with him.

Elizabeth was the older of the two, probably eight or nine years old. The other girl must have been around six. Both were arrayed in frilly, yellow dresses with white anklet socks and black patent-leather shoes. Elizabeth had light brown hair and blue eyes. The other girl had red hair, and freckles dotted her piquant face. The two girls were colored, but looked Caucasian.

Elise trudged out of the water and came over to them. She wiped her wet, muddy hands on the front of her overalls, and then held out her right one towards Elizabeth in a friendly gesture. "Hi. My name's Elise."

Elizabeth wrinkled her nose in distaste and ignored the outstretched hand. She acted as if Elise were offering her a dead fish. She then started examining Elise from her dirty, wet feet up to the unruly cap of hair that adorned her head. Elise's hair just reached past the middle of her neck, and as usual, it needed a good brushing. The humidity had also given it a wooly appearance.

After a few moments the girl said in a snooty voice, "Are you a girl or a boy? 'Cause if you're a girl, you should be ashamed of yourself." She then fluffed her hair back from her face with her dainty fingers. Each strand had been artfully curled, and not one was out of place.

Elizabeth continued with a smirk, "Girls should be pretty—like me. It's too bad you're not. Besides, with hair like yours, you'll never be pretty."

"Uh oh," said Bruce backing away from the three. He recognized the devilish look on his sister's face. She had bristled like an enraged porcupine.

Elise smiled slyly, her eyes shining with mischief. Then within a blink of an eye, she grabbed the girl suddenly by her arm and dragged her towards the creek. With a mighty shove, she pushed the girl into the water. She held her sides and laughed derisively as the sopping girl emerged a moment later from the creek. Elizabeth resembled a wet seal with her hair plastered to her head. Cakes of mud clung to her yellow dress.

She came out of the water crying and stood in front of her antagonist stammering out, "Just wait 'till I tell my mother on you, you...you..."

"I wouldn't say anything if I were you," warned Elise, waving her doubled fist in front of the girl's face. Elizabeth began crying louder. She grabbed her sister's arm and they raced back to the picnic area, screaming like the devil was after them.

Bruce spoke in a dire voice, "You'd better go hide, 'cause Mama is gonna give you the whippin' of your life." He started to absently kick the ground under his shoe.

"Well, it won't be the first time," Elise said apathetically. She shrugged her slim shoulders, picked up her shoes and socks, and started walking back towards the gathering. *I might as well get this over with,* she thought dismally. Bruce followed her like a puppy at her heels.

Elise had to make amends with Elizabeth about her rude behavior less than an hour later. Her mother was making sure of it. Florence stood stiffly at her daughter's side as Elise apologized to the now-smirking Elizabeth and her doubly snooty mother.

"I, uh, I'm sorry I pushed you in the creek, Elizabeth, and got your *pretty* dress all wet," Elise said contritely. She appeared convincing, with her honey-brown colored eyes wide and innocent. But anyone looking at Elise could have seen that she had her fingers crossed behind her back.

During the next several years, the family reunions continued and the Ford brood continued to multiply. George's sister, Vera, and her husband adopted two girls that they named Vera Leone and Ruth Elise. His other siblings, Hallie, Elise, and Irving still remained childless. His son, Bruce, and his wife had another child that they named Harrison.

The family reunions were George Ford's most favorite time of the year. This was where he could regal his grandchildren about his days as a Buffalo Soldier. He told them he had met the famous General George Custer, Buffalo Bill, and General Nelson Miles. The children would sit in anticipation as they listened to his stories about the great herds of buffalo, roving bands of hostile Native-Americans, battles, and the wagon trains that headed out West. Then he would show them were he had been shot. When his leg wasn't too sore to touch, he let them run their hands over the old scar.

Not one family reunion would go by, however, without George Ford informing his grandchildren about their shared heritage with the first president of the United States. This he would do with the admonition not to speak to anyone outside of the family about their ancestry. Someday the world would know of their heritage, but not now.

It was not the time.

Chapter 34

Difficulty makes for a severe instructor.

Norman B. Allen

Elise was a spirited tomboy from the minute she learned how to walk. She liked to run, play baseball, and climb trees as much as any boy. Her tomboy ways proved useful one May afternoon. School had been dismissed for the day and she had spotted her little brother, Bruce, standing on the playground near the tether ball pole with a crowd of his classmates surrounding him. She quickly headed in his direction.

"Well, you're in trouble now, Alex, 'cause here comes my big sister," said Bruce, who was standing with a group of third graders. Triumph gleaming in his eyes, he began hopping on one foot to the other in his excitement about the upcoming confrontation.

Alex Cryer was a blond-haired, blue-eyed bully of the worst sort. He was grossly overweight and used that weight to push kids smaller than him around. Alex especially didn't like blacks or girls. He had taken Bruce's math notebook and was tearing sheets of paper from it.

"Come on, Bruce, we need to get on home," commented Elise as she walked up to the group.

"Lese, Alex tore up my notebook. Now I gotta do my homework all over again," he complained.

Elise took in the situation at a glance. She didn't like bullies, especially ones who picked on her little brother. Alex was smirking at her. As she continued to watch him, he tore another page from her little brother's book and stuffed it into his mouth. Now he looked like a blonde squirrel with nuts in its jaw. Alex then spit out the paper and held up his middle finger at Elise.

That does it, Elise thought, angrily. She put her books on the cement ground and then took off her pink sweater with the yellow flowers embroidered on it. The sweater landed a moment later on top of her history book. She wore a girly, matching pink jumper that came just below her knees. The dress wasn't a good choice of clothes to fight in, so it was a good thing that she had a pair of Bruce's shorts on under it.

Elise put her hands on her small hips and said tauntingly, "Come and get me, tubby."

The boy's face was infused with blood, turning it bright red. He put his head down and charged at her like an enraged bull. Elise sidestepped him, like a master matador and as he ran past she turned and kicked him in his rear. He fell to the ground and Elise jumped on top of him. When the altercation was over, Alex had a black eye and Elise had a split lip. But she had won the fight. She was a little scrapper.

When they arrived home, Elise tried to sneak upstairs to her bedroom so her mama wouldn't see her torn jumper. Unfortunately, her sister, Florence, was coming down the steps and the two girls stopped in front of each other on the stairs.

"What happened to your lip?" asked little Florence her brow creasing. Then her keen gaze took in Elise's torn jumper. "You're gonna get into trouble when Mama sees your dress."

"Don't tell her and she won't find out," Elise said smartly. She added the threat, "And if you do tell her, I'll put holes in your Sunday school clothes!"

Her older sister opened her mouth then closed it with a smack. "If you do that, I'll take your marbles, especially the blue boulders, and hide them where you'll never find them." She didn't like threats.

The girls were at a stalemate. Elise sighed and said, "Look Florence, I had to fight 'cause Alex was tearing up Brucey's notebook. What was I 'posed do, let him keep pestering him?" Crossing her arms over her small chest, she said, "So I blacked his eye."

"You didn't." Florence's eyes were wide with wonder.

"I sure did, just with my little old fist here." Elise waved it in front of her sibling's nose.

"Okay, I won't tell Mama," she agreed and then grabbed Elise's arm and hurried her up the steps. When they entered their bedroom a few moments later, Florence stated, "I'll sew the tear on your jumper and it will look as good as new."

The two girls were as close as sisters could be, and just as opposite in appearance and temperament. Little Florence had straight, white-people's hair. Elise's hair was coarse and thick. It took their mother twice as long to tame it every day. It didn't help that she was tender-headed. Little Florence was dainty and feminine. Elise was bony, with stick-like legs and their mother fretted every day about her tomboyish daughter's state of dress. Little Florence liked to bake and sew, whereas Elise burned every item she tried to cook. She also couldn't sew a straight line, even if her mother stood over her and guided her hand.

*   *   *

In the summer of 1929, Elise's father and her grandfather George went to Mount Vernon. They learned that the slave cemetery was being turned into one mass burial site, and they wanted to visit the graves of the family before that occurred. Elise wanted to accompany them, but was informed that the trip was to secure the location of the family plots.

Her father promised to take her to the plantation the following year during their summer vacation.

When Bruce and his father arrived at Mount Vernon they immediately walked down the path to the slave cemetery. The old man leaned heavily on his brass-handled hickory cane as they traversed the weed-strewn area. Bruce wanted to reach out with a helping hand, but knew better. Though all but crippled by the old military wound, his father steadfastly refused assistance. He remained the proud soldier.

When they arrived at the old burial site, there were no longer any headstones or markers to distinguish the individual graves. George knew that there were at least a hundred and fifty bodies buried in the now mass gravesite.

There were two men in the cemetery, and they had just finished placing a concrete tablet, in the center of the area. The tablet was a marker, denoting the location of the slave burial ground. The two men rose from their labors when George and Bruce approached them.

"Hello, my name is George Ford and this is my son, Bruce. I was born on this plantation and it was my home for almost twenty years," added George. His eyes were bright with remembrance of those years.

"It's nice to meet you," said the tallest of the two men. "My name is Wilford Neitzey and this is my co-worker, Artie Petit," he said pointing to the man next to him. Petit nodded his head in acknowledgement.

"Mister Neitzey, were any of the remains excavated from the site, and do you know if any of the old markers have been saved?" George asked hopefully.

"We weren't here when the Association had the stones and markers hauled away, and if there were bodies moved from this area, we don't know about that either."

George shook his gray-streaked head from side to side and said sadly, "I have relatives buried here—parents and grandparents."

"Well, we're done here if you two would like to visit for awhile," said Neitzey.

George thanked the two men and watched as they picked up their tools and left the small area. He walked to the middle of the cemetery and stood for a moment. Then he turned in a slow circle. He was trying to pinpoint where his family's graves might be, now that they had no headstones.

"I don't know where they're buried anymore. I think they should have been here," George said walking to a spot near the tablet. Turning back to his son he said, "My memories of this plantation are still as fresh as they were when I was a child growing up here."

Smiling, he closed his eyes for a moment, inhaling deeply. The smells were different. He could smell the Potomac River, but intruding on that smell were the changes technology had wrought, the combustion of engines. In his mind lingered the echoes of long-ago voices.

Bruce studied his father's features more closely than he had done so in a long time. He realized the fragility of his eighty-two year-old patriarch. His father's once-strong body looked gaunt, his face drawn and haggard. Then he saw a glimmer of moisture in his father eyes when he looked over at him. With a pang of sorrow, Bruce had a premonition that his father would not be among the living too much longer.

George gazed sadly at his son. "I can't be buried on Mount Vernon when I die. Everyone who has made me who I am, is buried here. My final resting-place should be here with them. But that can never be. And I know I'll never see this place again."

Ambling over to Bruce and putting his shaking hand on his shoulder he said quietly, "Let's go home, son. There's nothing here but death, and an old man's memories."

Stiffening his back, Major George Ford turned and walked away from the gravesite. They stopped by the old tomb and George noticed that the metal lock appeared rusted, but untouched. At least the final resting place of his great-grandfather, West Ford, had not been disturbed. The two men left the home of their ancestors and boarded a train heading back north.

Later that same year, the stock market crashed and set the Great Depression into motion. African Americans throughout the country were crushed under the depression, and millions were unemployed. Chronic unemployment produced dependency, discrimination, delinquency and disease. Able-bodied men, black and white, unable to support their families by their own toil, turned to petty crime and vice. When a census was taken five years later, there were only 3,805 African American physicians and surgeons in the United States. Bruce and Irving were fortunate that they were still able to practice their professions during the depression years.

Major George Ford retired as superintendent from Camp Butler the following year, in 1930. As a retirement gift, his children bought their parents a house near the city of Springfield, and from this location, the family reunions continued.

The depression of the economy continued its downhill slide and one out of three African-Americans were without jobs in 1931. Some of Bruce Ford's patients were poor black families, and had no money to pay his dental fees. He would treat these patients for free. Other patients paid him with a loaf of bread or a chicken. Sometimes the patients were so financially distraught; he wound up returning the food staples to them on their way out of his office. Because food couldn't pay their bills, Florence had to secure a job as a seamstress to help supplement their income. He and his wife were having a discussion about the matter in their living room after dinner.

"I don't want you to work, Florence," Bruce gritted out. He was upset with the idea of his wife having to help support the family.

Florence wasn't one to mince words. "We don't have much of a choice, Bruce. It's the only way to make ends meet. We can't starve and we can't live on your pride."

Bruce stiffened somewhat; his manhood taking a direct hit. Florence walked over to him and curved her hand around his cheek, trying to take the sting out of her comment. "Don't fight me on this one, Bruce," she said softly. "You know what I say is true. Please let me help."

Turning his head into her warm hand, he said begrudgingly, "I know, but I don't have to like it." A few seconds later he added, "But as soon as we're caught up, I want you to quit."

"I promise," she replied without hesitation. She leaned up and kissed him lightly on his mouth.

Florence's services as a seamstress were in great demand, as her rich, white clientele vied to have their dresses made by her. The money she made assisted with the finances, but she wasn't able to quit working as the year ended.

The following year, in 1932, Bruce' finances took a turn for the better when he put a three-carat diamond in the tooth of an African king. Since the days of piracy, many pirates had gold and silver fillings placed in their teeth, which paid for their burials if they were killed during battle. Gold and silver was later used for filling cavities in the teeth.

The African dignitary paid Bruce very well for this procedure. The extra money allowed Florence to drop her seamstress hours to part-time.

Many people in Peoria had heard about Dr. Ford's unique procedure on the African king, including Diamond Lil. Diamond Lil was a notorious madam. She was an olive-skinned, black woman with an hour-glass figure that could turn the head of any red-blooded male. The infamous madam wore four-carat diamond studs in her ears and diamond rings on each finger. Diamond Lil's clients came as far as Chicago to visit her establishment. In fact, she was a local icon of the city, albeit on the shady side.

"You'll never guess who came to my office this morning," said Bruce to his wife. He picked up a blue spool of thread that was stuck between the cushions and put it into the thread box near her feet.

"Who?" she asked absentmindedly. She was stitching a lace panel along the bodice of a dress she needed to finish by the next morning.

"Diamond Lil." Bruce said simply. He didn't say anything more, patiently waiting for her response.

Florence was intent on intricate work and he could tell that she barely registered what he had said when she replied, "That's nice." Then her head popped up and she quickly glanced over at him. "What? You're not serious are you?"

Now that he had gained her full attention he went on, "I'm dead serious. She waltzed right into my office this morning and told me she wanted eight diamonds put in her teeth. I asked her to come back tomorrow so that I could examine her to see where the diamonds would go."

With a big smile covering his handsome face he continued, "Florence, she offered me three thousand dollars to do the procedure! That's enough money to last us the rest of this year. You can finally quit sewing!"

Florence was flabbergasted. The money would come in handy, and she told him so.

The next day when Diamond Lil came into his office, Bruce asked her to go into the examination room. At least she was dressed a little more conservatively than the day before, he thought. He hadn't mentioned to his wife that Diamond Lil had on a gauzy, red dress that was so low cut, he could almost see clear to her navel. Today she wore another low-cut dress, but at least he could examine her without her breasts falling out. The dress was a shocking orange, with a frilled fringe along the bodice and hem.

When the madam opened her mouth for Bruce's oral examination, all of his hopes about performing the procedure were dashed. Diamond Lil had syphilis. The disease had manifested itself in her mouth with chancres dotting the sides of her cheeks, tongue—even her tonsils. He sent the woman away with a referral to a physician.

Bruce took off his white jacket and put on the one that matched his black pants. He had to go home and tell Florence not to quit her job.

They couldn't afford to lose the extra income.

Chapter 35

All the world's a stage, and all the men and women merely players."

Shakespeare

Varying skin tones among family members in the African-American race are common. Oftentimes a very fair-skinned child is born into a family of a darker complexion, or vice-versa. This was the case with Bruce's wife's family. Florence's siblings, Jenny, Georgia, Foda, Andy, and Ben, were very fair skinned, with blue eyes. All five passed for white and choose to live as such. Florence was the only one born out of the bunch with a copper-colored skin tone and coal black eyes. This color difference sometimes caused problems within their immediate family.

Florence's sister, Georgia, worked as a secretary in Chicago, where she lived as white during the week. On the weekends she would come back to Peoria, where she would live as black. One weekend, Georgia came to visit her younger sister. She strolled into the Ford family living room, flopped down on an easy chair, and kicked off her black pumps.

Her young niece, Elise, was sitting on a nearby sofa. She was struggling with sewing a pocket on a white dress shirt. Unfortunately, she had sewn the pocket on crooked. Her mother would have to rip it out and redo it. She glanced up from the crooked seam and watched as her Aunt took the bobby pins out of her long hair. The titian-red locks fluttered around her shoulders and cascaded half-way down her back.

On a long exhale, she stated, "Lord, let me sit down for a minute so that I can be who I really am."

"Why don't you be who you are all the time, Aunt Georgia?" inquired twelve-year-old Elise.

"Anonymity, Elise, anonymity," Georgia answered shortly. I have the chance to lose myself in a crowd when I live as white. It's *so* much easier to blend in with the white folks and not to have to face prejudice day in and day out."

Georgia studied her niece's even features for a few moments and said assessingly, "Now take you, Elise, for instance. You've got small lips and a narrow nose, and you're light enough to pass maybe as French or Spanish. But what gives your heritage away is your hair, child. You've got colored-people's hair."

Elise absently touched her hair in a smoothing motion. Today her mother had braided it into three thick plaits and as usual, it was a frizzy mess.

Georgia went on, "If you're light and got white people's hair you can pass easily because most people don't pay too much attention to facial features. You see child, it's the hair that is the final test for passing." Georgia ran her fingers through her now loosened tresses. It was satin-smooth in texture and had no curl whatsoever.

Elise laid the needle and the shirt down onto her lap. "Aunt Georgia, why is it that my sister and brothers have white people's hair, and I don't?" Her wide amber-brown eyes held a questioning look as she waited for her aunt to answer.

"You got a piece of the tar brush in you, Elise. You inherited your nappy hair from one of your colored ancestors." Cocking her head to the side she continued, "Take your mother for instance. She inherited our mother's looks. Our mother was Sioux and colored. The rest of us inherited our looks from our white father, who was Irish."

"Is it so important then for coloreds to be white-looking?" asked Elise.

Aunt Georgia hesitated for a moment before she answered. "The lighter your skin is, the easier it is to survive in this racist society. White people seem to treat the lighter coloreds better than they do the darker ones. It's been that way since the days of slavery. It ain't right, but that's the way it is. So I say yes, it helps to be light-skinned."

Rising from the easy chair, Georgia said with a sigh, "At least you can live in one world, Elise, because you can't pass for white. And you don't have to pretend all the time to be something you're not."

Elise watched her aunt walk into the kitchen to see her sister. Then she picked up the shirt from her lap and accidentally pricked her finger with the needle. She quickly placed the wounded digit into her mouth to dull the pain. She couldn't assimilate at the moment everything her aunt had said to her. But one day she would.

Skin color continued to remain an issue for the next couple of years in the Ford family. One Sunday afternoon, Elise's first cousin, Clarence, and his mother, Jenny, stopped by for a visit. Clarence was passing for white at Central High School where Elise would be attending come fall. He didn't want anyone at Central to know that Florence and Elise were his cousins. Clarence was a handsome boy with thick black hair and sky-blue eyes. Anyone standing in his presence would have never guessed that he wasn't what he appeared—Caucasian. The young man was also captain of the football team and extremely popular.

Elise had an altercation with Clarence in her mother's living room that afternoon. She and little Florence were lying on the floor with their younger brother, Harrison. They were drawing pictures in his sketch-book when Clarence came and stood over them.

Clarence glared nastily, then focusing on Elise he spat out, "Don't you dare tell anyone we are related when you come to Central. I want you to act just like Florence does. When she sees me in the halls, she acts like she doesn't know me."

Elise rose from the floor and said succinctly, "Why not, Clarence? We're first cousins and your colored, just like me."

She had had it with her cousin's arrogant attitude. For the last several years he acted as if he were better than she was because he could pass for white.

Clarence grabbed Elise by her bony arm, twisted it and demanded, "You just shut your mouth. I am white. White like my father."

Elise wasn't so easily intimidated. She snorted, "I don't care that your father is white. If you're our cousin, then you have some black blood in you and that makes you colored. And I'm tired of acting like we don't know who you are."

Clarence wrenched Elise's arm further behind her back and said threateningly, "I promise you this, Elise. If you ever tell anyone that I'm colored, I'll kill you." His blue eyes had a fanatical look about them.

She knew he meant what he said. Her cheeks burned with pain, anger, and humiliation. *God, help me,* she thought, because she refused to cry in front of Clarence. She deliberately blinked away the stinging sensation that prickled the backs of her eyes and swallowed uncomfortably. Harrison, noting that Clarence was hurting his sister, came up to him and kicked him in the leg. Clarence pushed him aside to the floor where Florence cuddled him as he cried.

It became a contest of wills then, Clarence applying pressure to Elise's arm and she trying not to cry. But the pain became unbearable. When her emotions were under control she nodded. Clarence smirking, let loose of her arm. Elise swallowing her tears, brushed past him and walked out the front door. She ran down the steps and hurried around to the backyard.

Once there she sat in her favorite spot beneath a pear tree. This was where she did all of her deep thinking. Her thoughts jumped from one subject to another. Why was the color of one's skin so important? Why did some colored people think that they were better because they had light skin? Why did this country have to have all these color rules anyway? Why should it matter? Why couldn't people just be who and what they were?

Elise battled with her frustrated thoughts for the next several minutes. She looked up when she heard the back door to her home slam shut. Her father was standing on the top stair. He had a deep scowl on his handsome face. Spotting her, he walked down the four concrete steps and then towards the tree. Elise quickly wiped the tears from her face with the back of her arm. She didn't want her father to notice that she had been crying.

A moment later, Bruce hunkered down next to his daughter. He didn't say anything right away because he was so incensed. Little Florence had told him what Clarence had said and done to Elise. He had taken the boy by the arm and wrenched it up behind his back as he had done to his cousin. Suffice to say, Jenny and her son left immediately.

"Elise, are you okay?" Her father asked in a soft voice. He took her small, pointed chin into his hand and searched her face. His brown eyes were bright with concern as he noticed her spiky wet lashes and runny nose. Just then, a single tear made a shiny path towards her chin.

"Yes, Papa," she sniffled. "I'm fine. Did Florence tell you what Clarence said?"

"Yes, she did, and you don't have to worry about him threatening you anymore," her father assured her.

Elise sniffed again and wiped her hand across her nose. "Papa, why is being white so important to Clarence?" She stared at him with huge, uncertain eyes.

Bruce heaved a great sigh and replied, "He and his mother live as white people. Your Aunt Jenny wants it that way. Being white in this society is a whole lot easier than being colored. Coloreds are considered as second-hand citizens. So many light-complexioned coloreds who can pass, do. All I can tell you is that if they want to pretend that they don't have colored relatives, then let them."

Massaging the back of his neck with his hand, he added, "I'm ashamed to say that some of my own relatives are color-struck, thinking they are better because they have lighter skin tones. Your Aunt Lulu, your Uncle George Jr.'s wife, was treated so badly by some of our family members at the last reunion, that she has refused to come to any more of them. That's why you don't get to see your cousins from Chicago anymore."

Bruce glanced at the sky overhead and then back at his daughter. "Your fourth great grandfather, West Ford, was right when he said, 'Just because you have a light skin tone, it doesn't make you better.' Remember that always, Elise."

Rising to his feet he added, "Be yourself, daughter, don't let the color of anyone's skin rule your life."

Elise stood, clutched her father tightly around his waist and murmured, "You're the best Papa in the whole wide world."

Bruce patted her on the head and said affectionately, "And you're the best daughter. Now go and help your sister watch Harrison."

Elise skipped towards the back door to her home. Her spirit soared as she thought, *With my father by my side, I can do anything.*

She was invincible.

The following weekend, Elise went over to her white friend, Mary's house. Mary and Elise had been friends for five years. They shared their closest secrets and aspirations with one another. The difference in their racial backgrounds never entered or clouded their friendship.

Mary's favorite activity was swimming, but she could never take Elise with her because the swimming pool was segregated. Colored people could only swim on Friday nights for forty-five minutes. That's because the pool was cleaned and emptied at that time of the week and fresh water put in for Saturday morning.

Elise went with her brother and sister on Friday nights, but never learned to swim. She would just dangle her feet in the water during these sessions. Her brother, Bruce, became an expert swimmer and diver. People would flock around him as he performed dives like the swan, jack knife, and the intricate triple somersault into the water. He had learned to dive from watching the white swimmers on Saturday mornings.

Elise had just come from Mary's house across the street from hers and was skipping up the front steps to her home when she spotted her Aunt Georgia. Her aunt was relaxing on a metal chair on their front porch.

"You're still playing with that white girl, Elise?" asked Georgia. She was fanning herself with a current issue of *Life Magazine*.

"Yes." Elise replied. "We're best friends. We're both starting Central High School this fall. I hope we'll have some of our classes together."

Aunt Georgia slowly shook her head and exhaled. "Elise, be friends with Mary now while you can. Because one day you're being colored is going to get in the way of that friendship."

"Not us, Aunt Georgia. We're like sisters."

"Humph." Georgia smiled cryptically at her niece before opening the magazine and continued reading where she left off.

Her aunt's prophetic words proved true, thought Elise as she walked past her friend Mary in the hallway at Central later that fall. She was now a freshman and the girls were no longer friends. Mary had started dating a boy who was prejudiced against blacks. He forbade her from communicating with her long-time black girlfriend. The defection hurt Elise when she realized that Mary and she would never be close friends again.

Elise watched the emotions playing over her one-time friend's face as their eyes met in passing. She saw some remorse registered in Mary's green eyes, but the girl quickly looked past her and continued on to her class.

Elise now knew that the forces of racial prejudice cut into virtually every aspect of life. Unfortunately, there were two people at the school she had to forget and ignore because of their white skin.

Chapter 36

A man proves himself honorable by his words, thoughts and deeds.

Tim Allen

In 1936, Major Ford received a letter from Lieutenant Colonel N. B. Briscoe, a commander with the Tenth Cavalry, stationed at Fort Leavenworth, Kansas. George had written to him earlier when he had read an article about the Tenth Calvary in a black journal.

"Can you read this letter for me Elise? My eyes don't seem to want to focus today," her grandfather said with a deep sigh. Most of the words blurred together even when he wore his eyeglasses.

"Of course Big Papa," Elise answered. She was sitting in her usual spot on the floor next to his knee. George handed the letter to her and she read in a firm, steady voice:

> "I am most pleased to hear from one of the 'charter members' of the Tenth Cavalry, and am taking the liberty of publishing your letter in the regiment, and of making inquiry through the service papers for other original members. The long and honorable record attained during

the years since 1867 is a great pride to those of us now in the regiment, and I am sure you will be gratified to learn that we hold annually an organization day celebration on July 18th. Among the men in the regiment there are about fifteen whose fathers also served in the Tenth Cavalry. Since you were a trumpeter at one time, you will be interested to know that we believe we have the best field music in the army. It is a great pleasure to hear from you and I assure you that anything you want from the Tenth Cavalry is yours."

Elise glanced up at her grandfather when she finished reading the letter. His eyes held a faraway expression, as if seeing another time and place. She knew he was reminiscing about his days as a Buffalo Soldier. He had been daydreaming and dozing more often lately during her visits with him. During these times, she would sit by his side until he woke up.

Elise would be asked many times in the future to help with her grandfather's correspondence. Even at the age of eighty-nine, Major George Ford was still active in the equal rights movement. He had served ten years as secretary and then president of the Springfield chapter of the NAACP. He would preach to Elise that the colored race had to be active in seeking their civil rights, lest they be taken from them.

Elise was at her grandparent's home for Christmas dinner later that year. She and her grandfather had been discussing what had occurred at the recent symposium on Springfield's economic plan for the year 1937 that had been published in the *Illinois Register*.

They were relaxing in the living room when he said, "Lesey, you must always vote. It is the only way we colored people can have a say in our government. Choose your candidates as if they hold your life in the balance, because they do." Getting up slowly with the aid of his cane he said, "Let's go to my office. I want you to write a letter for me."

Elise patiently walked behind her grandfather as he led the way to his office. She had never seen him so stiff with pain. But she knew better than to assist him. He always told her, 'You have to separate yourself from pain, Lesey. You must not let it win.' She took a seat at the mahogany desk and her grandfather sat wearily down on the worn, black sofa next to it. She took a piece of writing paper from its tray and placed it before her. Next she picked up a pen and waited for her grandfather to begin speaking.

Clearing his throat George spoke out loud, "To the Reverend Gay C. White, Pastor of Laurel M.E. Church:

> "I sometimes wonder if some white persons hope to inherit a different and separate heaven and let us have one such as the one depicted in *The Green Pastures*. I am fully aware of the shortcomings of many of my people, who do not subscribe to the treatment to which we are subjected, but they lack the courage and the interest to come out in the open and protest against it. Many persons think of us as carefree, shiftless characters shown in the theatrical skit of 'Amos n' Andy.' We are so much more than that."

Elise had heard about the book, *The Green Pastures*. It was written by Marc Connelly and opened on Broadway in 1930. *The Green Pastures* was hailed as a great American folk play. The story line was conceived as a farce; laughter was expected upon the entrance of a black man, Richard B. Harrison, playing God. Harrison was a man of great personal dignity, and portrayed the role with such humility that the play emerged as a serious drama.

She continued to write the words as her grandfather dictated them. When she finished she walked outside and placed the letter in the mailbox.

A few days later, the Reverend Gay came to visit George Ford. After conversing with the old major for over an hour, the minister asked if he could submit an article to the *Illinois Register* about George's fascinating life and background. George agreed. A feature article appeared in the newspaper on January 17, 1937, titled: *From Mt. Vernon to Springfield— George W. Ford, Veteran of Indian Wars, Traces Ancestry Back To The Revolutionary Days When Grandfather Was Valued Servant At Mt. Vernon.* He gave them a detailed account of his life and that of his grandfather, West Ford. But he never told his interviewer that West Ford was the son of George Washington. No, he couldn't tell them that, it wasn't the time.

Several more years would pass by, with Elise working as her grand-father's secretarial assistant. During their time together, he instilled in her the importance of acquiring a decent education, how to fight for racial equality, and becoming a responsible, moral, and ethical person. And he always discussed their hidden heritage, that she was to keep it secret, yet ongoing.

Elise had grown into a spirited young lady. That feisty young girl was now in a tug-of-war verbal match with her sister. The girls were in their bedroom on the second floor of their home. The room had oak twin beds, with a large oak dresser separating them. The beds had matching white quilts, with pink and yellow pillows scattered along the headboards.

"Florence, we need you!" Elise exclaimed to her sister. "This game is for the championship. We can't let the lower bluff team beat us."

Elise was sitting on her bed, watching as Florence pulled her long, black hair into a ponytail, securing it with a yellow ribbon. She had just brushed and combed Elise's hair into a thick ponytail before completing her own toilette.

"I don't want to play volleyball today. Chuck is outside with Bruce, and this is the only chance I'll get to see him this week," Florence pouted. She flopped down on her stomach on the bed and faced her sister.

Chuck Pickett was their brother Bruce's best friend. He was a handsome boy with honey-brown skin, curly black hair and an aquiline nose. All the girls at school just about swooned when they were in Chuck's presence, but he only had eyes for the oldest Ford girl.

Elise knew she needed to trick her sister into playing volleyball today. That's why she gave Bruce her best baseball mitt early that morning. The mitt was to be a bribe to get him to the game today.

"Bruce is coming to see us play volleyball and he's bringing Chuck," Elise stated innocently. Now she used her ace in the hole, "This is gonna be the only chance you're gonna get to see Chuck alone. You know Mama won't let any boys talk to us."

Now all Elise had to do was wait. It only took a few seconds as she watched Florence digest her comments.

"Okay, let's go," Florence said quickly. "Just give me a minute to change." Florence put on a white top and black shorts that fell just above the knee. The girls hurriedly exited their room and went downstairs to find their mother.

"Mama, we're getting ready to go to Proctor Center now to the volleyball game. Bruce is coming with us," supplied Elise, as they entered their small kitchen.

Their mother was at the stove, stirring a pot of soup. Her thick, black hair was piled up in a bun at the back of her head and a white apron was tied around her waist. She tapped the spoon she was holding on the edge of the iron pot, turned and said, "Good luck, but you girls come straight home with Bruce afterwards."

"We will," both girls answered in unison.

"I wanna go too, Mama," said nine-year-old Harrison. The rambunctious tyke was eating a piece of cake. The chocolate icing was smeared all over his face.

Elise walked over to him and plunked a kiss on his grubby cheek. She chuckled when he put his hands over his face to keep Florence from trying to wipe off the chocolate.

"You can't go with them today, Harry," their mother said, "but your sisters can take you to the park later." He crunched up his nose for a moment, nodded and went back to eating.

The girls left and walked about two blocks down their street and picked up their friends, Vivian, Dorothy, June, Bessie, Berthela, and Neomie, along the way.

When the eight girls entered the gym at Proctor Center a half hour later, they became giddy when they saw their audience. There were several young men who had come to watch the game, including the four Allen brothers, Jimmy, Altus, Alonzo and Garry. The brothers were an intimidating lot, well-muscled and exuding arrogant self assurance. Their sisters, Mayall, Lanita, Cleta, and Murtle—were members of the lower bluff team. The Allen family was very fair skinned, and many of them could easily pass for white. When Bruce and Chuck spotted the brothers in the auditorium's bleachers, they joined them.

The game was a total disaster for Elise's team a half hour into the game. Every time the ball came over to their side of the net, Elise's team-mates acted like they'd never played volleyball before. They were too busy giggling like ninnies and primping for the handsome young men. Florence couldn't concentrate either because she was making moon-like facial gestures at Chuck.

Elise soon became disgusted and exhausted, running all over the court. She was trying to play everyone else's position. It didn't help any that one Allen brother kept laughing when her team couldn't volley the ball over the net. She swore that if he laughed one more time at them, she would hit him in the head with the volleyball. Unladylike though the thought was, it did give Elise a great deal of pleasure. Thirty minutes later, Elise's upper bluff team lost the game and the championship.

Lanita Allen and one of her brothers sauntered over to where Elise and her friends had gathered to discuss their loss. Elise was wiping her damp face with a small white towel. Glancing at Lanita's brother, she thought irritably that this was the one who kept laughing at her.

Lanita smirked at them and said, "Listen girls, we're sorry you lost." Grinning over at her brother, she continued, "But the best team won, didn't it Jimmy?"

Jimmy, his eyes flashing blue devilment, replied, "They really didn't stand a chance, Lanita. Hey, why don't we throw a party for the losers? It's the least we can do, seein' they can't play a lick." Then he laughed aloud at the outraged look on Elise's face.

"That's it," muttered Elise under her breath and strode angrily over to him.

With her chin tilted up, hands on her hips, she glared at him. Much to her annoyance, her pugilistic stance didn't threaten him in the least. He continued to chuckle at her expense.

Drawing up to her full height of five-feet-four, she spat out, "Why you piece of backwater, from the wrong side of the tracks trash. The only thing that would come to a party you'd throw are the pigs you probably raise for a living."

Then she grabbed the volleyball from Lanita's hands and popped him on the head with it. Eyes blazing with ire, she marched off, leaving him standing there with his mouth agape.

Jimmy stood mute and blinking, in shock as the impact of her words sank in. Then he exploded with laughter. *Why that little spitfire*, he thought delightedly. He had laughed at her antics while she was playing volleyball. She jumped around the court like a rabbit trapped in a box. But he hadn't realized how pretty she was until she told him off. Her eyes were a brilliant shade of caramel, and when he looked into them, something melted inside his chest. She had delicate facial features, finely arched brows, and a small nose turned up at the end. She was magnificent and he was impressed with her fearlessness. This girl wouldn't be easy to intimidate.

"Well, Jimmy, you sure made my sister mad." Bruce broke into his musings. He and Chuck had walked over to them and had over heard Elise's tirade.

"That's your sister?" exclaimed Jimmy. He quickly added, "She sure is pretty. Does she have a boyfriend?"

"Yes, she's my sister, but a lot of good that'll do you." Bruce had a huge smile plastered on his handsome face.

"Why do you say that?" A frown marred Jimmy's brow.

"She'll never have anything to do with you now for laughing at her," answered Bruce as he crossed his arms.

"We'll see about that," Jimmy said as he watched Elise sprint towards the door of the gym. "In fact, we'll see about that tomorrow," he added confidently.

"Don't waste your time, Jim. My Mama won't let my sisters date. Ask Chuck here." Bruce nodded towards his friend. "He's been coming by the house for three months, and the only time he's been alone with Florence was walking over here today."

Chuck didn't comment, but just shrugged.

"Come on Bruce!" hollered Elise. She now stood with her hands on her slim hips, still glaring at Jimmy.

"Well, we'll see you guys later," said Bruce as he hurried over to his sisters.

The next day, true to his word, Jimmy knocked on the Ford's door right after lunch. Elise answered it and when she saw who it was, she tried to slam the door in his face. Jimmy was too quick for her and stuck his foot inside so she couldn't close it. She pushed hard, causing Jimmy to wince from the pressure. Who would have thought this little bit of fluff was so strong? he thought, amazed.

Elise's mother's voice interjected into their pushing contest from the background. "Who is it, Elise?"

"A pig-herder, Mama." Elise retorted.

"What was that?" her mother called back.

"No one of any importance, Mama!" Elise frowned at Jimmy. She let go of the door, stepped out onto the porch with him, and said irritably, "What do you want?"

"I want you," he stated with a roguish smile in a voice smooth as butter. Seeing the questioning look on her face, he went on, "I want to take you out." He eased his bruised foot out of his black loafer, trying not to wince at the pain in his big toe.

Elise stared at the young man before her as if it were the first time. This Allen brother was very fair, as white looking as her mother's relatives. *He sure is handsome, with those electric blue eyes and brownish-blonde hair,* mused Elise. Just looking at him made her heart beat a little faster. She became warm all of a sudden. *Is it possible I'm coming down with a fever?* She thought. Elise placed her hand to her forehead; it felt cool to the touch. She fought the urge to fan herself.

Jimmy was still smiling, showing even white teeth. "Well, what do you say, Elise?"

"I say she doesn't wish to see you, whoever you are," interrupted Elise's mother. She had come to the door and had heard the last part of the couple's conversation. She opened the screen enclosure and stepped out onto the porch.

"Ah, ah, my name's, ah, James O. Allen, ma'am. I just wanted to know if I could visit with Elise," Jimmy stammered. He reached down and was trying to put his shoe back on his sockless foot.

"Well you've seen her and now you can leave," Elise's mother snapped. Then she looked down at his exposed foot and commented dryly, "Mister No Wearing Shoes."

Grabbing her daughter by the arm, she pulled her into the house. Elise couldn't resist looking back at Jimmy, and before the door slammed shut in his face, he shot her a wicked wink.

Jimmy wasn't deterred. He stopped by her house every day for the next month just to get a glimpse of the girl who had stolen his heart. And Elise made it possible as she came outside whenever she could. She was falling hard for her persistent suitor.

Jimmy's perseverance paid off several weeks later. Elise's father wanted to meet the young man he saw lurking outside of their house, and asked him to come in one afternoon. Dr. Ford had an instant rapport with the personable young man. There was strength in the lines of the young man's face—character. His daughter would do well by him if they were to become serious with each other. In fact, he even invited Jimmy and Florence's boyfriend, Chuck, to go to their annual family reunion in Springfield that was being held later that month, to his wife's dismay.

At the reunion, Jimmy met the beloved Ford family patriarch. Major George Ford immediately took a liking to Elise's boyfriend. The young man was extremely polite and a true gentleman. He also liked the fact that Jimmy couldn't keep his eyes off his favorite granddaughter.

Taking Elise aside, her grandfather stated, "I like your young man, Elise. Not only is he a gentleman, he has a good sense of humor. Having humor in a relationship is very important. So, when you marry your young man someday," he paused and winked at her, "he'll surely fill your days with joy and laughter. Now go take a walk. I need to rest a bit before the telling of our family history."

George smiled as his granddaughter literally bounced from his office. Oh, the joy of youth, he reflected. He leaned his head back against the leather, wing-back chair he was sitting on and closed his eyes. Solitude was on his mind this afternoon. Sometimes when he sat alone in his office, time would slip away as if he were held in a trance. He wondered if one could let all the hours slip away, until, blissfully, there would be no more.

Later that afternoon, Jimmy and Chuck were allowed to hear the family story. Jimmy was in awe after learning who the Fords were related too. He swore to Major Ford that he wouldn't tell anyone of their legacy. Jimmy left Camp Butler thinking that Elise's grandfather had the deepest sense of honor and integrity that he had ever known.

Jimmy was walking Elise home from school about five months later. They had their heads close together and were deeply engaged in conversation.

"Mama is never gonna say yes," Elise said to him.

"That's why we have to elope." Jimmy's blue eyes were passionate with his feelings for her. "Once we're married, your parents can't do anything about it."

Smiling, Elise agreed and they finalized their plans.

The next day, Elise skipped math class and met Jimmy outside of Central High School. They drove to the courthouse and were married. Right after the ceremony, he took her back to school with none the wiser.

On Saturday morning, Jimmy knocked on the Ford door bright and early. Elise's mother answered. She had a scowl upon her face; her black eyes were shooting bullets. "Boy, don't you know what time it is?"

"Yes, Mrs. Ford, it's time to come for my wife." He crossed his arms and smiled cockily at her.

"What the hell did you say?" she gritted through clenched teeth.

"I married your daughter yesterday and I've come for her," Jimmy stated arrogantly. The old lady had no choice in the matter now.

Elise's mother picked up the closest object to her, an antique vase. Jimmy realizing her intent, ran off the porch, with Elise's mother chasing him.

Running down the porch steps, she screamed out, "When I catch you, I'm going to snatch you bald-headed!"

She chased Jimmy for about a block before coming to an abrupt halt in front of a six-foot fence. Jimmy climbed and jumped over it, trying to escape her. *She sure is fast,* he thought as he continued to run, almost out of breath.

The next morning Jimmy came to the Ford home again. This time Elise's mother chased him off with a broom. He could almost feel her breath at the back of his neck as he dashed down an alley between Gale and Nebraska streets. *Where did she learn to run so fast?* He marveled as he finally eluded her on a side street.

Monday morning rolled around and Jimmy was again at the Ford's door. This time Elise's father invited him in.

"You're one determined young man," Bruce said, and clasped Jimmy's hand in a firm handshake. His voice took on a warning note. "You take good care of my daughter, because I can run faster than my wife." Looking over his shoulder to where Elise was standing, he said, "Come and greet your husband, girl."

The newly married couple rented a small house on the lower bluff area in Peoria. The basement served as a printing shop. Jimmy and his brothers' Altus, Garry, and Alonzo, ran the printing business from their home.

Two weeks after the nuptials, George Ford became ill. Several of his family members stood vigil around his bedside. But his thoughts were focused on the petite, teenaged girl with eyes the color of warmed brandy who was kneeling beside him. She was clenching one of his frail hands in hers. Every once in a while, when it became difficult for him to grasp a breath, she would grip his hand, forcing him to alertness.

But he was tired, so tired. A number of his family members stood vigil around his bedside—his wife, three sons, three daughters, and several of his grandchildren. But his thoughts were focused on the petite, teenaged girl with eyes the color of warmed brandy who knelt beside him. She clenched one of his gaunt hands. Once in a while, when it became difficult for him to grasp a breath, she would grip his hand, forcing him to alertness.

"Don't die, Big Papa! Please don't die and leave us!" the young girl cried out in anguish. She could sense that her grandfather was slipping away and she couldn't bear the thought of it.

"Everybody dies," he rasped. "It's...a part of life. D-don't cry f-for me, Lesey." He sighed and spoke gently, patting her hand.

"You still have a lot of years left, Big Papa. We need you. Please, I know you can get over this sickness. You just have to!"

Expelling a weary breath, the old man turned towards his grand-daughter and said in a soothing voice, "Lesey...i-it w-will be all right."

His sight was leaving him. It was as if he saw her through a veil, but he needed to look into her eyes and remind her of the task ahead before his voice left him also. He noted that Lesey's eyes were shiny with tears. They pooled in the corners, clinging to her long lashes like raindrops on a leaf before slipping onto her cheeks. She sniffled and rubbed her free hand under her nose.

"C-come c-closer Lesey."

The grief-stricken girl rose and leaned over the bed, resting her hands beside his damp pillow. His hands were skeletal as he gathered his last ounce of strength to frame her face, bringing her closer. He wanted to look into his granddaughter's eyes, needed to see what he knew lurked behind them—strength and fortitude—characteristics she would require for her life-long task. His probing gaze was prolonged and intense. A hint of relief etched his features, as if measuring her and liking what he saw. Then his hands dropped.

A moment later his voice rang out with a surprising burst of strength, "You are the chronicler. The charge is now yours."

He began to cough then gasped for breath. It became a battle for him to regain control from the relentless rattling sound emanating from his overburdened lungs. His will was strong because he couldn't let death claim him yet, not until he finished what he needed to say.

In a much weaker voice he went on, "L-Lesey, d-don't let our h-heritage die."

"I won't Big Papa. I promise."

"I've had a long, good life—ninety-one years. That's more than a lot of people have." His tired gray eyes looked around the bedroom and he inquired, "Where's Harriet?"

Jimmy reached down, pulled Elise to her feet, and put his arms around her as she sobbed into his chest.

Harriet now took Elise's place near her husband's side. She took his hand into hers and brought it to her trembling lips. George's eyes started to glaze over and he said weakly, "I'm going to be with Donald now. He was so little when he left us. I wonder if he'll remember me?"

George's hand felt icy to Harriet. She quickly rubbed it between her own. She was afraid—afraid of a life without him. Gazing down into his dull, gray eyes she said, "Of course he'll remember you." With a soft voice she murmured, "I love you, George. You are my one true love." She watched as his dry, cracked lips whispered, "I love you too."

Several seconds later, George's eyes brightened for a moment, as if he saw something glorious in the room no one else could perceive. Then he said happily, "Oh, Donald, come here, son, come to Big Papa." His eyes closed and his head dropped to the side as he released one long, shuddering last breath.

In a moment he was gone.

Harriet clasped his hand to her chest and whispered, "Wait for me George on the other side. Be there to meet me when my now lonely life is over." Then she let her tears fall.

Major George William Ford was given a full military funeral at Camp Butler Cemetery. His children and grandchildren stood proud, stood tall when the twenty-one-gun salute was fired in his honor. Three empty shell casings were given to his widow along with the United States flag. Harriet gave the flag to Elise. Major Ford's saber was to be given to his firstborn son, George Jr. But his son never received it, as he died a week after his father.

It was an extremely heartbreaking time for the Ford family.

But a new day was dawning. Elise Ford Allen now carried the charge of chronicler.

Chapter 37

A good cause makes a strong arm.
God befriend us, as our cause is just.

Shakespeare

For the second time in history the world would face a devastating war. World War II had commenced. The two African-American Army units, the 92nd and the 93rd, were reactivated from World War I, and the black troops were again segregated from their white counterparts.

Fifty thousand of the minority troops were used in front-line combat. Upon arrival at the front, they were bombarded not by bullets, but with variations of the following leaflet:

> Hello, boys, what are you doing over here? Fighting the Germans? Why? Have they ever done you any harm? Of course some white folks and the lying English-American papers told you that the Germans ought to be wiped out for the sake of Humanity and Democracy. What is Democracy? Personal freedom, all citizens enjoying the same rights as the white people do in America, the land of Freedom and Democracy, or are you rather not treated over there as sec-

ond-class citizens? Can you go into a restaurant where white people dine? Can you get a seat in a theatre where whites sit? Can you get a seat or berth in a railroad car, or can you even ride in the South in the same street car with white people? And how about the law? Is lynching and the most horrible crimes connected therewith a lawful proceeding in a democratic country? Why are you here?

The propaganda had no noticeable effect on the morale of the black troops participating in the armed forces. They were American soldiers and they had a job to accomplish.

Race riots continued to blaze intermittently throughout the U.S. during World War II. Disturbing reports were coming out of the Army camps where African-Americans were stationed. There were riots at Fort Oswego and Camp Davis. Discrimination against blacks were practiced at Fort Devens, murders at Fort Bragg, and the edict, 'not to shake a nigger's hand' at Camp Upton.

Before the black troops went overseas they were stationed at the infamous Fort Huachuca, Arizona, where they were victims of discrimination and ill treatment. This was where Elise's husband, Jimmy Allen, was stationed when he was drafted. African-Americans also clashed with the white townspeople near the fort, and this treatment further devastated morale in the black soldiers. The seriousness of the ill treatment against African-Americans caused the War Department to investigate the situation at Fort Huachuca.

Elise was constantly worried that something dire would happen to her husband when she learned about the racial tensions at the bases. She didn't have to worry over much, as Jimmy was in good hands—his own. His younger brother, Altus, was a prizefighter and had practiced on Jimmy regularly during their formative years.

Jimmy had to prove his prowess while on a three-day leave from Fort Huachuca. He and his friends, Francis and Steven, decided to go to

Phoenix, where Francis had relatives. Francis was tall and muscular, with dark brown skin and processed hair. Steven was short, barely standing five-foot-three, and very dark in complexion. He was also nearsighted and wore the thickest eyeglasses Jimmy had ever seen. The friends were trying to acquire a hotel room for the night, but the clerk at the front desk informed them that they would have to look elsewhere.

"Sorry boys, we're all full up. We ain't got no vacancies," the bald man said, then he continued reading the newspaper spread out before him.

"The sign on the window says that you do," stated Francis. He was pointing to the red and white 'vacancies' sign that had been placed on the window.

The clerk said nastily, "Well, the sign is wrong."

Francis wanted to say something more, but Steven grabbed his arm and was ushering him towards the door. Just as they reached it, two white soldiers came barreling in. One of them almost ran Steven down in the process.

"Look where you're goin', boy," the soldier said as he continued without a by-your-leave.

Steven's eyeglasses had fallen onto the tile stone floor and one of the lenses had cracked from the impact. Jimmy reached down, picked them up, and handed them back to Steven. The friends stood by the door and watched as the hotel clerk issued the two white soldiers room keys.

The clerk's gaze narrowed when he glanced over at the colored soldiers, still standing by the door's entrance. "You boys go on and get out of here! We don't serve your kind at this establishment."

Jimmy stared at the three men by the desk, not caring to conceal the contempt registered on his face. The taller of the two, the man who had bumped into Steven, bristled at his scornful look. He uttered a foul word.

"That's one colored fella you don't want to mess with, Ray," said the smaller of the two men. He had noticed his friend's growing agitation and edged closer to him. He continued, "I saw him knock out two men in a fight outside the mess hall about a month ago."

"Colored? Are you sure, Donny?" questioned Ray. "He looks white."

"He's colored all right," his friend muttered.

"Well, he may be colored, but he don't look all that tough to me," Ray answered. Then he called out contemptuously, "Why don't you jungle bunnies go on down to the colored part of town with the rest of the coons."

Jimmy studied Ray for a moment, then deliberately dismissed him as though he were of no consequence.

Ray didn't like the way the soldier looked at him. His face infused with color. He balled his fists at his sides and took a threatening step in Jimmy's direction.

"Don't do it, Ray," Donny warned. He clasped Ray by his arm and was pulling him back towards the front desk.

Jimmy watched as the man named Donny held his friend at bay. He just smiled, albeit a bit evilly, an intentional taunt to the men. The two white soldiers continued to shoot daggers with their eyes at Jimmy. After a long, tense moment, Jimmy turned and left with his friends.

Ray brushed off Donny's arm and followed them outside.

"Hey, hey you!" he shouted and pointed towards Jimmy.

Jimmy, Steve, and Francis stopped on the steps leading out of the hotel and turned back to the angry soldier.

Noting that he had Jimmy's attention, Ray said boastfully, "Let's see if you can back up that attitude of yours." He then went to an open space on the sidewalk and brought up his fists in a fighting stance.

"Now, Jim, you don't have to fight him," Francis quickly stated. "The last time you got into a fight, you spent two weeks peeling potatoes."

"See you guys in two weeks," Jim answered blithely.

Francis' black eyes rolled upward at the remark.

The altercation didn't last long. Jimmy weaved and bobbed around his opponent with the finesse of a prizefighter. Ray threw a quick, three shot-combination, but Jimmy was able to side-step them. When he had a clear shot, he threw a hard, right uppercut to the man's jaw. Ray staggered backward, clearly stunned by the power of the punch and then his legs buckled beneath him. Shaking his head in a useless effort to clear it, he remained down.

His friend Donny ran over to his friend and kneeled by his side, checking on the incoherent man. Jimmy's friends were slapping him on the shoulder, congratulating him on his fighting acumen.

"Hey man, we need to call you "One Punch," said Francis. His black eyes were round with awe.

Jimmy didn't acknowledge his comment. He was too busy watching to see if Ray was going to rise to his feet. He hoped the man didn't, because he was still simmering.

"Look, I think we need to be gettin' out of here," said a nervous Steven. He was gazing at the crowd of people who were beginning to look like a lynch mob.

"Yeah, you're probably right," said Francis as he noticed where his friend's eyes were fixed.

The three friends started walking away from the hotel, but were picked up a few minutes later by the base MPs. Jimmy had to spend another two weeks in solitary confinement. When he was released, he wrote to his wife, telling her that he had some leave time coming. He left out where he had spent the previous fourteen days.

As Elise read her husband's letter, she made the decision that she would meet up with him while he was on leave. A couple days later, her plans were in motion. "I'm going to visit Jimmy, Mama. He has a week's leave and I can meet him in Macon, Georgia."

Her mother was cutting out woolen material from a paper dress pattern on their dining room table. Looking up at her daughter she asked, "How are you going to get there?"

"Mrs. Bolden is driving down to Atlanta to visit her sister, and she said I could come with her. From Atlanta, I can catch a bus to Macon."

"That's good. You won't have to travel so far by yourself."

Worrying her lower lip with her teeth, Elise said hesitantly, "Mama, I'm a little nervous about traveling so far. I mean, I've never gone anywhere by myself before."

"You'll be all right as long as you keep that smart mouth of yours shut." Her mother put down the cutting shears and looked pointedly at Elise. "Some white people are more prejudiced in the South than they are up here. So you be careful."

"I'll be careful," said Elise. "Well, I guess I'd better go pack some of my clothes. Mrs. Bolden wants to leave the day after tomorrow."

The drive to Atlanta was uneventful. Elise was uncomfortable being cooped up in the car for the three days it took to arrive there. To make matters worse, they couldn't use the white-only public restrooms at the service stations where they stopped for gas. She had to use the bathroom in the great outdoors. Luckily she had some tissues in her satchel. The travelers also had to look for colored eating establishments because the white restaurants would not serve blacks. Finally, they made it to their destination. Elise stayed with Mrs. Bolden's relatives for a day before she caught the bus to Macon.

"Well, here's the bus depot," Mrs. Bolden stated as she drove up to a large, red brick building with two buses parked on the side of it. Her alert eyes scanned the area for a place to park. There were none, so she pulled up as close as she could to the entrance. Stopping the car momentarily she said, "Elise, I'm gonna drop you off here. Wait for me near the front while I go and find a place to put this car."

"Okay," replied Elise as she scooted out of the front seat, taking her cloth suitcase with her. She walked towards the entrance, put her bag down, and waited for Mrs. Bolden to come back. Ten minutes passed and Elise was still waiting for her companion. She became a little uncomfortable when several men began whispering about her. *Where is Mrs. Bolden?* she thought, anxiously. She glanced down at her watch; it was three o'clock. Her bus was scheduled to leave in less than an hour.

Elise decided she could save some time if she went ahead and purchased her ticket. She was unaware of the callous looks directed her way when she entered through the front door of the depot. She walked over to where a short line had formed near the ticket window. After standing in the line for several minutes, she began to hear harsh whispers and knew something was wrong. She just didn't know what it was.

Mrs. Bolden's tall form came running into the bus depot a few seconds later with a frantic look on her face. When she spotted her charge, she rushed over to her. Before she could utter a word to Elise, the loud speaker came on. A disembodied voice barked out, "You niggers get to the back of the station. Be quick about it before we have you thrown out of here."

Never had Elise been so humiliated. She opened her mouth to vent her outrage, but Mrs. Bolden gave her a cautioning look and shook her black-haired head. Elise glanced around the room and noticed the hostile looks directed their way. One heavyset man was striking an umbrella into the palm of his hand as he stared at her. She knew what he was thinking and a nervous shiver passed over her small frame. Several long-nosed women where whispering to each other, not attempting to hide the malice in their eyes. Their hatred was palpable. Angry and disillusioned, Elise squared her shoulders and stood proud, stood tall. She didn't run from the room, but walked like a queen passing through the assemblage of her subjects as she left the building.

Once outside they went to the entrance that was designated for the coloreds. Whispering urgently as they approached the ticket counter Mrs. Bolden said, "Elise, you must learn when to speak and when you can't down here. It ain't like it is up North. These white people would just as soon hang you, as talk to you. Coloreds have to stay in their place down here." When she saw the mutinous look blanket Elise's face she said fervently, "Do you hear me, girl!"

Elise nodded. She was still too upset to reply.

After purchasing her ticket they went outside to wait to board. They were standing some distance from the other passengers when Elise said, "They say "nigger" like it's a normal word."

Shrugging, Mrs. Bolden replied resignedly, "To them it is."

Elise finally was ready to board. When she stepped onto the bus, the driver said, "Find a seat at the back."

Elise pressed her nose to the window of the bus as she absorbed the passing scenery on her journey to Macon. She became disconcerted once again when she saw a prison chain gang. The ankles of the African-American men and women were chained together as they worked along the side of the road. Many of the women had traces of bloodstains on the back of their prison-issued dresses, their feminine time ignored by the armed guards who didn't even acknowledge their dilemma. There was such hopelessness, such despair evident on the prisoners' faces. Tears pooled in Elise's eyes as she felt the humiliation and hardship that those women and men had to endure. *"Dear God, will you please help those people?"* she prayed quietly.

Elise stayed with an African-American officer's family when she finally reached Macon. Captain Charles Brown had gone to college with her father and they had remained close friends. During her stay in Macon, Elise was continually subjected to the blatant racism that existed in the city. She couldn't walk down the main streets, only in the alleyways. She wasn't supposed to look into a white person's face when she addressed them. She must act subservient to whites whenever the occasion arose.

Even with all the negativity she was experiencing, she wasn't going to allow her reunion with her husband to be spoiled because of it. She never mentioned the racial incidents to Jimmy until he left the Army a year later. That's when he told her what had happened to him on his way back from Macon to Camp Polk in Louisiana.

Jimmy had boarded a bus in Macon after his leave. There was only one seat left and it was up front and next to a white soldier. He and another white passenger were the only two without a seat. Jimmy knew that none of the people on the bus would have a problem with him if he sat down. He knew they would not suspect that he was black. Besides, it was a long way to Camp Polk and he didn't relish standing up the entire time. So he sat down. The soldier next to Jimmy was very friendly and struck up a conversation with him.

"This damn war, I'm being sent to Germany next month. How about you?" The blond man said as he rubbed the back of his neck.

Jimmy replied, "I haven't received my orders yet."

"You're lucky. What were you doing in Macon?"

"I'm on leave. My wife joined me there and now I'm on my way back to Camp Polk."

"Oh, yeah? So am I. By the way, my name is Harvey Swenson, originally from Minnesota." He stuck his right hand out for Jimmy to shake.

After clasping hands, Jimmy replied, "My name's Jim Allen. I was born in Carrier Mills, Illinois, and now I live in Peoria."

The men continued their conversation for the next hour until the bus stopped at a spot along the road to pick up one passenger, a middle-aged black woman. She was carrying a worn, cloth valise that she clutched to her chest when she boarded. Jimmy noticed the woman's tired and bleak face when she realized there were no seats available for her.

Jimmy came from a large family, which consisted of five brothers and four sisters. His parents had taught him from an early age that it was not gentlemanly for a man to sit while a lady stood. So, he stood and offered the woman his seat. The woman hesitated for a moment, smiled gratefully, and sat down.

The bus driver shouted out, "Soldier, you can't let that nigger sit there. Get her out of that seat!"

Jimmy ignored the man's outburst. The driver pulled the bus over to the side of the road and parked. The man was around forty, with a belly that protruded over his black leather belt. He came down the aisle and stood in front of Jimmy. Looking over at the woman he said sharply, "Nigger, get out of that seat before I throw you off this bus."

The woman gazed resignedly at Jimmy and started to rise.

Drawing a deep breath, Jimmy said with quiet intensity, "Mister, I'm a nigger. Let's see if you can throw me off this bus." Jimmy seemed to radiate darkness within him, deep and black and dangerous. His icy blue eyes promised much.

The bus driver's brown eyes widened in shock at Jimmy's pronouncement and rigid stance. He slowly backed up a step. He assessed the soldier's strong muscular frame and ham-sized fists. The man knew deep in his being that this soldier could crush him with his bare hands. Sweat began to bead along his brow.

Many passengers noticed the soldier's threatening stare and turned their heads away nervously. One thin man in a tight, checkered business suit made a furtive sign of the cross. He seemed to shrink even more against his window seat.

Now a safer distance from Jimmy, the driver finally recovered his courage and bellowed out, "Are you fellows going to let this…this white-looking nigger get away with this?" He looked over at several of the soldiers sitting towards the front of the bus.

Mumbles could be heard. One of the soldiers spoke up, "Hell no!"

Four of the men stood up from their seats and started shouting obscenities at Jimmy and the old woman. The woman covered her ears and closed her weary eyes. The soldier Jim had struck up a conversation with earlier, maneuvered himself past the woman and into the aisle behind him.

Harvey hollered, "It ain't right for this woman to stand while I sit, so she can have my seat too."

Harvey's comment elicited more shouts, and one of the soldiers took a punch at Jimmy. He swerved just in time and retaliated with a fist that connected with the man's nose. The blow sent the man reeling backward, crashing into one of the passengers in the seat next to the aisle. In a flash, an altercation erupted. Jimmy, Harvey, and the old lady got off the bus after it was all over. They had to walk about two miles to the next town. When they arrived, the MPs were waiting and arrested Jimmy. Harvey was shipped out to Germany soon after.

Jimmy was sentenced to the guardhouse for thirty days, and it wasn't going to be the last time he'd wind up there.

Chapter 38

I am my biggest challenge; the only obstacles lie within me.

Angela Allen

At the end of World War II, following the German surrender, Brigadier General Charles T. Lanham, assistant commander of the 104th Infantry Division, made a comment about the black combat troops: "I have never seen any soldiers who performed better in combat."

Elise's husband, Jimmy, ultimately served two years in the Army and was discharged with the rank of buck sergeant. The couple settled down to a comfortable family life after the war. Their first child, Carol, was born in 1943 in a small community hospital in Peoria. The infant was born with black hair and hazel eyes. She was so light in complexion that the hospital staff mistakenly put down on her birth records that she was Caucasian. It took several hours for Jimmy to straighten out the error the day Elise was released.

Elise was sent home the day after her child's birth and was lying in their bed when her husband remarked, "Our daughter's beautiful, Elise."

She was so tired and responded to his comment by sighing and then falling into a deep sleep. Jimmy smiled at his sleeping wife, he was so proud of her. She never made a fuss during her labor, just popped the baby out and then asked to see her when it was over. *It can't get any better than this,* he thought as he pulled the blanket up to his wife's shoulders.

Tragedy struck the Ford family a year later, in the summer of 1944. Elise's father, Dr. Bruce C. Ford, was dead at age fifty-five from a massive heart attack. Elise watched as the funeral procession filed past her father's open coffin. It had been placed in the middle of her parent's living room so that family and friends could pay their final respects.

Elise was pregnant with her second child. Her aunts, Vera and Big Elise, had forbidden her from viewing her father's body. They were superstitious and believed that looking at a dead person could mark her unborn child. She didn't want to see her father's body as he lay in his coffin anyway. It wasn't a memory she wanted to live with.

She let her eyes wander around the room at her immediate family. Her mother was being consoled by her numerous friends. The look on her face was blank, as if she wasn't cognizant of her surroundings. Elise's brother, Bruce, stood vigil at their mother's side. His brown eyes glistened with unshed tears. Her other two siblings, Florence and Harrison, held hands. Harrison was sixteen and in high school. *What was going to happen to him?* She thought sadly. *What was her mother going to do? How was she going to survive?*

Suddenly, panic struck Elise and she needed to leave the crowded, airless room. Jimmy had taken Carol upstairs to lie down for a nap and hadn't returned. She walked quickly to the front door, opened it, and went out onto the porch. She stood for a moment gasping for breath. Feeling the panic overwhelm her, she darted down the front steps, stumbling on the last one. She grasped at the brick wall banister, scraping the skin off her palms. After righting herself she walked around the side of the house to the backyard.

Once there she headed towards the yard's single pear tree and sat near its trunk. The last time she had been there was when her cousin Clarence had threatened her. Elise remembered how her father had consoled her that day. He had been a wonderful parent. She had always felt that she could go to him when in trouble and that he could solve all of her problems. He'd taught her all the necessary lessons of her life, how to love, how to laugh, how to stand proud, to stand tall. *Maybe if I close my eyes and concentrate really hard, I might be able to hear his soothing voice, she thought.* She put her fingers to her temples and forced her mind to quietness, but the chirping of birds as they played in the branches above her broke into her meditation.

Elise released her grief verbally and called out, "Why did you leave us, Papa? You weren't old. Why didn't you try harder to live? Mama's all-alone and Harrison isn't even out of high school. What's going to happen to them? What's going happen to us all?" She then felt a sense of loneliness that cut so deep, it seemed to settle into her very bones. She sobbed her anguish into the palms of her hands because she would never, never see her father again.

A short while later, she felt a presence. Looking up with a tear-stained face she saw her husband standing over her. She hadn't even heard him come up. She didn't know how long he had been quietly keeping vigil over her. Then he sat down next to her and cradled her in his arms.

"Why did he have to die, Jimmy? I keep thinking that there was something that we could have done to save him. If only I had known he was so sick, that he might die, I could have gone to visit him more." Elise's face was stark with pain as she tried to reason with her father's sudden death.

"Lese, I don't think there was anything you could have done to save him. When it's your time to die, you die."

"But how do we know that? Huh? How do we know that I couldn't have done something? Sometimes I think God gives us the choice to save others. Maybe there is something we can do, if we choose to act on it." She paused for a moment and went on, "But we don't. Sometimes we are too busy, too caught up in our own lives to see what is happening to those around us. We think, oh, I'll go see them tomorrow or I don't have the time to waste talking to them today." She wiped a tear from her cheek with her fingers before going on. "So they die, and we realize that maybe, maybe we should have taken the time. But then it's too late."

"I don't know the answers, Lese. Maybe you're right. Maybe God is trying to teach us to care for others as we care for ourselves. All I know is that we can't change what happened to your father, but we can change how we treat others around us, so we don't have any regrets." Lifting her face to his he said softly, "It's going to be all right Lese. It's going to be all right."

Would it? Elise thought with some doubt. As her husband tightened his hand on hers she thought with a new resolve, Yes, *it would be all right as long as I have Jimmy by my side.*

Elise was melancholy the day she came home from the hospital after giving birth to her second child. She longed for her father to see James Jr., who was born in 1945. Tears misted in her light eyes. Her father would never know his grandchildren, but she knew he would not want her to grieve on account of him.

Then her infant son brought a smile to her lips as he tried to focus on her face. Little Jimmy had light brown skin and eyes that were a dark, greenish gray. He had the look of his great-great grandfather, Major George Ford. *As one life ends…another begins,* Elise thought with understanding. She made up her mind in that instant to heal death's wounds as she admired her newborn.

*   *   *

It was not necessarily a positive thing for African Americans to be prosperous or successful in the 1940s. Many prejudiced whites wanted blacks to remain dependent and as helpless as they were in the days of slavery and Reconstruction. Jimmy and Elise were neither dependent nor helpless. Jimmy started his own printing company in 1946. He became a master printer and Elise became his assistant.

Elise's sister, Florence, had married her long-time boyfriend, Chuck Pickett, and they moved to Canton, Illinois. The couple started their family soon after. Her brother, Bruce, who also served in World War II, took advantage of the G.I. Bill and enrolled into Bradley University, majoring in mathematics. He worked part-time at a local auto shop while he attended classes. Elise's mother continued in her profession as a seamstress to help support herself and her teenage son, Harrison. Her once disliked son-in-law, Jimmy, gave her a portion of his paycheck every month to help her with her finances. Florence finally realized what her husband had seen in James O. Allen.

During the next several years, two more children were born to the Allens, Gregory in 1947 and Linda in 1951. Gregory took after his father in complexion and looks. He had blondish-brown hair, blue eyes, and a strong jutting chin. Linda was her mother's child, with a golden skin tone and eyes the color of peridots. She also inherited twin dimples in her cheeks.

Even though the times were difficult, Elise had married a man who could brighten her days and fill their home with laughter. She had always been attracted to her husband's great sense of humor, as well as his zest for life.

Jimmy displayed his trademark personality during an incident later that summer after Linda was born.

"I can't understand why the city won't pave the street, Jimmy," remarked Elise. She had just brought in the laundry from the clothes-line strung in the backyard and was folding it at their kitchen table. "I can hardly breathe for all the dust," she continued. Then she coughed for good measure.

The couple lived on Kane Street, which was only a dirt road. Cars would drive up and down the street, throwing dirt and dust everywhere, including through the open windows into their house.

"You know, I believe I can get some drums of oil from Caterpillar Tractor Company to coat the street with. The oil would help keep the dust down," said Jimmy. He had been moonlighting at the factory to help with their finances.

Elise folded the last of the bed sheets and towels. She then stacked them in a wicker basket at her feet. Glancing over at her husband she said, "That would help. Will you check on it tomorrow?"

"Sure." Jimmy took the basket from Elise's hands and carried it to the closet where they stored their linens.

That next Saturday he brought two drums of oil home. He placed the barrels in front of their house. He had barricaded the short street by parking his car at one end, and placing four kitchen chairs at the other. He then began poking holes into the lid of one of the oil cans with a screwdriver and a hammer. After he finished putting the holes in the top, he poured the oil out and brushed it onto the street with a long handled broom.

Several of the neighbors came out of their homes and watched as Jimmy whisked the oil over the dirt road. After the first barrel was empty, he retrieved the second one, rolled it into the middle of the street, and again poked holes into the lid. As Jimmy tilted the barrel over the top came completely off, dumping over half its contents into the street. Instead of the expected oil, the can contained paint—bright, yellow tractor paint. Jimmy tried to sweep it up, but it didn't help. He then went and retrieved the water hose from the side of the house to see if he could wash the paint off to the side of the road.

Well, all that sweeping and washing only accomplished the spreading of the neon-yellow paint from one end of the narrow street to the other. Now the street was streaked yellow and black.

"Oh, Mrs. Allen, you better come outside and see what Mr. Allen done, *done*," said ten-year-old Helen Margaret. Helen Margaret lived across the street from the Allens and helped out as a babysitter. She was a pretty little girl with coffee-bean colored skin and shoulder length black hair. All the Allen children adored her.

Elise was scrubbing pots at the sink in the kitchen. Not looking up from her menial task she asked, "What's he doing?"

"It's best you come see for yourself," the young girl answered. Helen Margaret's tone implied that whatever her husband had done, Elise needed to find out what it was as quickly as possible.

Rinsing and then drying her hands on a towel next to the sink, she said, "Helen Margaret, Linda is just waking up from her nap. Would you bring her outside for me while I see what my husband's done, *done?*"

Elise went out her front door and stood on the porch. Her hand flew up to her mouth as she surveyed the catastrophe in front of her.

"Oooh," said Gregory. "Pewtty street, pewtty street." He was standing next to his brother and sister as they watched their father trying to clean up the mess he had created. In fact, all their neighbors had gathered around and were just as awestruck as she was. Helen Margaret in the meantime came outside with Linda and handed her to her mother.

Elise went down the porch steps, walked over to her husband and cried, "Jimmy, what have you done?" She was torn between amusement and shock.

Turning towards his wife, Jimmy said in a calm voice, "Don't worry, Lese. I can clean it up. Get the kids and stay on the front porch. I'm going to try and burn some of it off."

Elise stared hard at her husband, a tiny furrow appearing on her brow. "Do you think that's gonna work?"

"It's the only way to get the yellow paint off." Pointing to a place near his feet he said, "I've got the water hose right here to keep the fire under control."

When the neighbors found out what Jimmy was planning, they scattered in all directions. It was as though they had heard an air raid signal warning them to vacant the area. Some went ducking behind trees, others behind cars. The majority of them went inside their houses and peeked out their front windows. A few minutes later, Jimmy threw a match onto the street. All that oil—all that paint—well the street lit up like the Fourth of July.

Helen Margaret was standing on her porch with her grandmother. Her eyes were wide with wonder at the sight in front of her as she heard her grandmother comment, "That Jim Allen done caught the street on fire."

It took the fire department hours to kill the blaze. But no property was damaged in the fire as the houses sat pretty far back from the road. The following week the city sent a crew out to pave the street.

Elise's husband was always trying to improve and repair things around the house. He thought he could repair anything. As a result of his 'fixing', the family had to go to the second floor to turn on the kitchen light. A screwdriver was modified as a handle to open the oven door. And only cold water came out of the bathtub. But the family didn't mind the inconveniences, because their father kept them laughing.

December rolled in with a frigid blast that winter and the whole city was buried under drifts of snow. Elise was watching from her living room window as her children played in it. Carol, Little Jim, and Gregory were trying to build a snowman. The snowman's head kept sliding off the top and onto the ground. She laughed out loud when the ball of snow slid once again and landed onto Little Jim's head, breaking apart. He just dusted himself off and started rolling another pile of it. Her attention went to Gregory, who was sitting on the ground, eating snow with every pat he made to the snowman's body. His lips were smacking the white stuff off his gloves as if it were a delicacy. Little Jim and Carol were now having a snowball fight.

Elise turned away from the window, the lace curtains falling back into place, and went into the kitchen. Jimmy was at the table where he had taken an old radio apart and was trying to put television tubes into it.

She walked up to him and said, "The kids are out front. Will you bring them in after a few minutes while I start dinner?"

"Yes," he answered absentmindedly. He was trying to figure out how to modify the bottom of the metal tube so it would fit into the socket of the radio's housing. Only the Lord knew why.

Back outside in the front yard, Gregory and Little Jim were attempting to finish the snowman. Carol stood off to the side, watching them. Her feet were freezing and wet even though she had rubber boots on, and she started stamping them in an effort to warm them up. Carol let her hazel gaze wander over to the trash their neighbor had been burning. They had made a bonfire on the ground and all that was left of it were ashes. There were no flames coming from it now, only tendrils of smoke. What harm would it be if she stood in the embers to warm her feet up? she thought. If she went into the house, her mother probably wouldn't let her come back out to play. Making a decision not to go inside, she went over to the now seemingly dead fire and stepped into the smoking remains.

Carol stood still for a few moments, relishing the warmth creeping up her pants legs. A few seconds later that warmth turned into pain; her pants were on fire! She started screaming as the flames ate through the material and burned her skin.

From inside the house her parents heard a tortured cry, "Mama, Daddy, help me! Please help me! I'm burning!"

Jimmy was up and running before Elise could even react. She tore out of the house in his wake, her feet flying over the snow-packed ground.

When she saw her daughter in flames she screamed out, *"Ca-rol!"* The raw shout carried with it every drop of anguish and despair in her heart.

Jimmy took a running dive and tackled his daughter to the snow-packed ground. He quickly rolled her in the wet snow to extinguish the flames. By the time Elise came panting up to them a few seconds later, Carol was safely in his arms.

"Let me have her!" She cried, as she reached for her injured daughter.

"No!" barked Jimmy. "We have to take her to the hospital immediately." Looking down at Elise's bare feet, he said, "Go get on your shoes and coat and I'll meet you at the car."

Helen Margaret's grandmother, having heard Carol's screams, rushed over to Elise as she ran back towards her house. She told her that she and her granddaughter would keep an eye on their other children while they took Carol to the hospital. Elise was back outside within moments.

Jimmy placed his daughter into the back seat of their old Studebaker and settled his wife next to her. He then ran around to the driver's side and hopped in. Carol was whimpering in pain now. Mrs. Crooks, one of their neighbors, brought a wool blanket over to the car and handed it to Jimmy.

He handed it to Elise and said, "Keep her warm; we don't want her to go into shock."

As she covered Carol with the blanket, she caught a visual inspection of her daughter's legs. She couldn't stop the gasp erupting from her throat. It was a horrid sight. The skin on the inside of her calves had mottled into ridged bubbles of transparent sacs. The rims of the burns were charred to dirty black crust and burnt clothing, and the centers of the burns oozed blood and some other liquid.

Hearing her moan, Jimmy shouted out, "W-What is it?" He was frantically trying to maneuver the car through the traffic. He was sounding the horn, trying to keep the other cars and pedestrians from his hurried path.

"Just keep driving, Jimmy!" Elise shrieked as he tried to turn his head to see what was the matter. Her attention dropped down to Carol's legs again and she cried out, "Please hurry."

"Mommy, Mommy, don't cry," said Carol, pain etched on her small features. "When the angels come and get me, I won't be afraid."

Elise almost died herself a moment later when Carol lost consciousness. Putting her shaking hand over her daughter's heart, she sighed in relief as she felt its steady beat. She prayed aloud, "Please God, let my little girl be all right!"

Jimmy, hearing her anguished plea, pressed the accelerator pedal to the floor.

In the hospital waiting room, Elise sat dazed in a metal chair. She was remembering the story Big Papa told her of how her Uncle Donald had died. A few more minutes on fire and Carol may have suffered the same fate.

Elise's mother and sister were also in the waiting room, keeping vigil. Her mother was pacing up and down the carpeted area in front of her. Several long, agonizing hours later, Elise's prayers were answered. Carol would be all right. She had to have skin grafts taken from her upper thighs to replace the damaged, burned skin around both calves, but she would heal with time and bear only a few scars to mark her ordeal.

It would be months before the family settled back down to some semblance of normalcy.

Chapter 39

Love all, trust a few. Do wrong to none; be able for thine enemy.

Shakespeare

The following year, Elise's husband applied for job as a foreman at a newspaper in Tiskawa, Illinois. The town was a small farming community and had no minorities living within its boundaries. Jimmy was standing in the editor's office. The editor had reviewed his application and offered him the position. Jimmy decided he needed to inform the gentleman of his racial identity. If the man didn't want to hire him because he was black, then so be it.

"Mister Davenport, I want to tell you up front that I'm colored." Jimmy stood straight as an arrow and looked the publisher in the eye.

After a slight pause the man said, "Son, I don't care if you're green, as long as you can do the job." He extended his hand and Jimmy returned the handshake.

Jimmy started his job the following morning. Many people in the all-white town didn't believe in extending the olive branch to coloreds the way the owner of the *Tiskawa Chief* did. The residents didn't want the Allens moving into their community. They didn't want the children intermingling with their own and even discussed it at a town meeting. Davenport became perturbed at where the discussion was heading and left without voting.

Because of the town's attitude, Elise's husband thought it best that they not relocate the family. Jimmy drove the forty miles back and forth between Peoria and Tiskawa. He followed this routine for several months until one night he almost drove off the road after falling asleep at the wheel. "We're moving to Tiskawa," Elise stated to him the day after the incident.

The couple rented a small house on the outskirts of the city the following week. The house was owned by Davenport, so they didn't have any problems in that regard. Elise enrolled their two oldest children, Carol and Little Jimmy, in the local public school.

Several weeks into the school year, Carol asked her mother innocently, "Mom, what's a...*nigger*? Her hazel colored eyes were questioning as she added, "Am I one?"

"Who told you about that word?" inquired Elise. Her eyes narrowed as she questioned her young daughter. "Where were you when you heard it?"

"I heard another kid in my class say that they were going to drive by the Allen's house to see the niggers tomorrow morning. Mama, we're the only Allens in the school, so are we the niggers?"

Inhaling and releasing a deep breath Elise answered, "No, we are *not* niggers and I don't want you to use that word again because it's demeaning. It's a word that some white people like to call colored people. Go on and do your homework now."

As her daughter sat down and began her schoolwork, Elise stood with her hands on her hips in the middle of the room. She was furious. *It was time to put these bigoted townspeople in their place,* she thought angrily. A small smile lit her beautiful features a moment later as an idea came upon her. *I've got a lot to accomplish before tomorrow morning,* she contemplated a she finished cooking their dinner.

Elise had acquired a formidable temper in response to racial bigotry, especially if it was directed towards her family. But she was wise enough to know that her anger could cost Jimmy his position at the newspaper or worse. Her husband wouldn't be home until after midnight. He would have to leave again at six in the morning to head back to his position. She decided she wouldn't tell him what she had planned until it was over.

The next morning she kissed Jimmy goodbye and hurriedly worked on her project. After she finished, she smiled down at her neat handiwork. She took one of the metal kitchen chairs outside to the front yard, and sat and waited for the 'visit.' An hour later several cars drove up to her home. When they slowed down and passed Elise sitting in her yard, they couldn't help but read the cardboard sign she held in her hands that read, "Only humans living here…if you want to see something more exotic, visit a zoo." The revelers sped away. Later that evening, Jimmy congratulated his wife on her cunning.

Carol and Little Jim were considered gifted students at the small, rural school. They were more academically advanced than many of the other children in their class. A PTA meeting was held a month after the revelers drove by their home. Carol and Little Jim were to be recognized during the program for their academic achievements. Elise and her husband were discussing the meeting while she prepared his lunch for the day.

"I don't want you to go without me, Lese," Jimmy said as he watched her pack his turkey sandwiches into a silver-toned, metal box. "I'll try to get off early enough to take you."

She closed the top to the lunch box and handed it to him. "The PTA starts at six o'clock. You may not get back in time and we may miss the award's ceremony. I don't want that to happen."

Grabbing his muscled arm and walking him to the door, she continued, "Look, we'll come straight home after I talk to their teacher." She crossed her heart with her forefinger and added, "I promise."

Not fully satisfied, Jimmy asked, "How can you manage with all the kids by yourself?"

"I can manage. Carol and Little Jim can watch the younger ones while I talk to their teacher."

Jimmy knew he couldn't convince her not to attend without him, so he relented. "Okay, but be careful. If I can get off, I'll meet you at the school." He leaned down and kissed her on her nose. Hearing a car horn outside he said, "My ride is here, see you later."

When Elise and her children entered the small auditorium of the school later that evening, she was surprised to see so many people gathered there. It seemed as if the whole community had turned out for the event. The attendees were talking and laughing with each other, but as they noticed Elise's presence, their conversations started to cease.

If a piece of cotton were dropped on the floor it would have been heard in that quiet room. They were all staring at Elise and her children. She held her head high and she could have sworn she heard her grandfather say, "Stand proud, stand tall." She deliberately stared at everyone who stared at her. One by one the hostile and curious faces turned away as they accepted the formidability of this opponent.

A heavy-set woman with a friendly smile plastered on her round face approached Elise a few moments later. Putting out her hand, she said congenially, "You must be Carol and Jim's mother. I'm their teacher, Mrs. Dorothy Hinkley." Mrs. Hinkley was a middle-aged woman with streaks of gray in her auburn hair. She had tiny laugh lines at the corners of her eyes, and her smile was genuine.

"It's nice to meet you, Mrs. Hinkley. I'm Elise Allen, their mother," she answered as she shook the woman's proffered hand.

"Please call me Dorothy, and if you don't mind, I'll call you Elise." The teacher turned to her children. She greeted Carol and Little Jim and smiled at Gregory and Linda. "You have very beautiful children."

"T—thank you." Elise was a little disconcerted. She wasn't expecting this kind of reception.

Taking Elise by the arm as if they were old friends, Mrs. Hinkley walked her towards the refreshment table.

She continued, "I am very excited about having your children in my class. They are extremely intelligent and are the most courteous children I have ever met."

The two women chatted for several long minutes. Elise spoke in a clear, concise matter that showed the breeding of an educated person. The people around her couldn't help noticing her elocution. After a while, several other teachers and parents came over to meet her.

A half hour later the awards were given out. Elise began to relax and was enjoying herself when she felt a prickly sensation at the back of her neck. She glanced around the room for her children. Carol was sitting in a chair feeding a cookie to Linda. Little Jim had Gregory by the hand and they were examining the drawings some of the students had made that adorned the room's walls. The children were okay, but still she sensed something odd. Elise studied the room. Her eyes halted on a tall, gangly man who was staring intently at her from across the auditorium. He had black, short-cropped hair and appeared to be in his mid-thirties. The man had a beak-like nose and sharply cut, sun-baked features. He was very forward in his manner toward her. He stripped her clothes away with his bold eyes. She glanced away from him.

Elise became more uncomfortable when she noticed that the man was moving in her direction. When he neared her person, he deliberately bumped into her and in the process, ran his open hand over her posterior. Before she could react to his boldness, he hastily moved away from her and went back across the room. There he continued to watch her every movement.

Not wanting to cause a scene, Elise said her goodbyes, gathered her children and herded them out of the building. The man followed and caught up with her outside on the steps of the school.

"Hey wait a minute!" he called out. "What's your hurry? I want to talk to you."

The man smelled sweaty, and Elise was sure she caught the odor of alcohol on his breath. He grabbed her by the arm to detain her. She nearly screamed, but jerked her arm free instead, backing away from him. She was carrying Linda on her hip.

Elise brought up her free hand to stop the stranger from grabbing her again and said, "Please don't do that!" She leveled a frosted stare at him and said to Carol, "You and Little Jim take the children to the car."

Carol reached and took Linda from their mother. Little Jim hesitated, glaring at the man who had dared to touch his mama's arm. Elise, noticing his delay said, "Do as I say Jimmy!"

Little Jim reluctantly took Gregory's hand and walked over to the parked vehicle. He kept glancing back over his shoulder at his mother all the way. Elise watched them until they entered their car then turned back towards the stranger.

"That was a good idea, sending your kids away," he said slyly, a leer dancing in his eyes. "We can't work out our arrangement with them standing here." Stepping closer to her he said huskily, "Why don't you take them home and then we can go to someplace more comfortable. I can make it worth your while." He pulled out a wad of bills and asked, "What's your price?"

"I don't know who you think I might be, mister, but you've made a mistake. I'm a married woman." Elise held her chin high in the air.

"What does married have to do with anything? I'm married myself. Anyway, everybody knows that colored women are whores."

Elise was so mad she could have spit bullets. She wanted to rake her short fingernails down the side of his face. She took a deep breath instead and said vehemently, "I am not a whore, and even if I was, you'd never be able to afford me."

The man glared at her as if he couldn't believe she dared speak to him that way. His dark eyes took on a dangerous glint. Then he startled Elise by drawing her to him with a frightening strength. Elise reared back and slapped him hard, snapping his head to the left. The slap was deafening in the quiet of the evening. Before the man could retaliate, Mrs. Hinkley and some others came out of the building.

The stranger drew back from her and hurried into the shadows. Mrs. Hinkley, seeing the man's hasty departure, said with obvious concern, "Are you okay, Elise?"

"Yes, Dorothy. It was all just a misunderstanding. But everything is all right now. Goodnight." Elise walked down the school steps and towards her car. She didn't want to explain anything more to the anxious woman.

When she slid into the driver's seat Little Jim asked, "What did that man want, Mama?"

She answered calmly, "Nothing really important." Smiling, she said, "Let's get you all home now."

Elise drove the five miles back to the house, a frown marring her smooth forehead as she worried about what she was going to tell her husband. She knew Jimmy would hunt the man down like a rabid dog and put him out of his misery. She decided it would be better to keep quiet about the incident to keep the peace.

Some of their neighbors came to make the Allens' acquaintance a few days after the PTA meeting. At first, Elise was a little leery with their belated overtures of friendship. But after a time, the Allens were able to call several of their neighbors close friends, especially Ruth and Fred Steiner. Ruthie would often baby-sit for Elise when she had to run errands. Whenever Fred needed an extra hand at his farm, Jim would be there to lend one.

Several more weeks passed and Carol and Little Jim's classmates were finally accepting them. Elise even helped tutor some of the students in mathematics when she had the spare time.

One evening after her tutoring session, someone followed her home. She saw a truck's headlights in the distance, but as she slowed so did it. It turned off the road just before she reached Ruthie's house to collect her children. She didn't notice the strange vehicle when she left a few minutes later to drive the mile down the road to her home. She was helping Little Jim and Carol with their homework at the kitchen table when she heard three loud raps on her front door about an hour later. She glanced at the clock covered with daisies that was mounted on the wall above her stove. It was eight-thirty. Jimmy wasn't due home for several hours.

"Who is it?" Elise hollered as she stood by the locked door. There was no answer.

It was almost pitch-black outside, as there was only one dim electric-porch light to illuminate the yard. She could usually make out who was at her door by peeking out the window to the side of it. However, the porch was too dimly lit for her to make out anything but a man's tall shape. Blackie, their German Shepard, growled menacingly near her side. The hair on the back of his neck was raised and his teeth were bared for attack.

"Who is it?" Elise asked once more when the knocks came louder.

Her visitor remained silent. She went over to the fireplace, took her shotgun off its brackets from the mantle, and loaded it. She said in a quiet voice, "Little Jimmy, I want you to go to the door and pull back the dead bolt. When I tell you to open it, I want you to do it quickly and drop to the floor." Then she looked over at her shaken daughter and said, "Carol take Gregory and Linda to the back bedroom and stay there until I tell you to come out."

Little Jimmy went silently to the door and slid the bolt back.

"Now!" Elise shouted.

Little Jimmy opened the door, dropped to the floor, and watched as Blackie leaped at the stranger, his body arcing through the air like a well-aimed arrow. The dog struck the man with such force that the two went flying. The stranger landed on his back in the yard. Blackie was emitting frenzied yelps, and the man was yelling, trying to call the canine off. Though the light from the inside of the house was sparse, it shone enough outside that Elise could see who was in her yard. It was the man who had accosted her at the PTA meeting a month earlier. Elise's alert gaze quickly scanned the yard. He was alone.

"Get this damn dog off me!" the man cried.

"Why are you here?" Elise countered.

"I just w-wanted to come in and v-visit for a while, that's all," he whined between gulps of breath. Then he cried in pain as Blackie bit hard into his thigh.

Elise called Blackie off a moment later and pointed the shotgun at the stranger's head as he lay on the ground. She said in a deadly voice, "Get up and get off my property. If you ever come back here again I'll blow your head off." She nudged the weapon against his temple for emphasis.

The man stumbled to his feet and as he limped away she heard him mumble, "Damn nigger bitch."

Her finger's itched to pull the trigger at his comment. Instead she watched him until she could no longer make out his image in the darkness. Once back in the house she made pallets on the floor in her bedroom for the children. Then she sat down in the chair near her bed with the loaded shotgun in her hands. Her ears strained to hear every sound. She could not, would not, allow herself to fall asleep until her husband came home. She was exhausted physically, mentally, and emotionally when he came through the door around midnight.

Elise quickly told him what had transpired. They were standing in the kitchen when she said, "Everything is going to be all right, isn't it?"

Jimmy set an arm around her firmly. The fear in her voice bothered him. "I'll take care of you and the children, Lese," he said soothingly into her hair.

Elise felt protected, even cherished as he held her securely in his arms. She thanked God she had him in her life. He was so much man— big and capable and strong.

Jimmy continued to cradle his wife until she was fast asleep after they had gone to bed. Asleep, she looked fragile and helpless, but he knew her physical appearance to be deceiving. She was tough as nails when she needed to be. But he couldn't rest, as images of what could have happened to his family arose before his eyes. Sleep eluded him throughout the night as he tried to quell his fury. He had not been there to protect his family. This could not be allowed to happen again. Tomorrow he had to find the man who threatened his wife and when he did—a thin smile edged his lips at the thought and finally he drifted off to sleep.

The next morning Elise attempted to detain Jimmy from going after the stranger. His face was taut with his efforts to control the sheer fire of his fury. He had the shotgun in his hands and was heading out the door when she stepped in front of him. She placed her hands on his heaving chest.

"Don't do it, Jimmy," Elise said beseechingly. Her amber eyes were pleading.

He ignored the concern in them. "I won't stand by and let any man try to molest my family." His voice had hardened in a way she had never heard before. It was lethal. Jimmy could be so gentle with those he loved, but he could be deadly with those who threatened them.

Elise wouldn't back down. "And I won't stand by and watch you be put into prison or worse for killing a man."

"He deserves to die."

"God will be his judge and juror."

"God helps those who help themselves." Jimmy's voice was low and matter-of-fact. He reached, moving Elise aside, out of his way.

Grabbing his arm so that he couldn't walk out the door, Elise said quietly, "I'm going to have another baby. If something happens to you, I-I don't know what I'll do."

Her confession stopped him in his tracks. He turned back to her. His volatile emotions warred within him. The instinct to protect what was his was hard to give up immediately. Jimmy clenched his jaw so tightly; Elise could hear his teeth crunching.

Elise said again, "Please, let it be."

Finally her calming voice and the confession that she was pregnant brought him back to sanity. He embraced her and said tersely, "All right Elise, I won't go. But I can promise you *this*, if he shows his face around here again, he's a dead man because no power on this earth will stop me from putting him six feet under. I'll tell the newspaper to put me on the day shift. If they can't, I'll quit. I won't leave you and the children here alone again at night."

It was a very uneasy time for the Allens after that day because Jimmy was waiting for the stranger to show his face once more.

Then all hell would break loose.

Chapter 40

*The most important human quality is having an
excellent character.*

Barbara Allen Foster

The stranger never returned to the Allen home, but the family couldn't
shake the uneasiness of always having to look over their shoulders. They
decided to move back to Peoria, where Jimmy could focus on his printing
company full time. They bought a small four-bedroom house on
Second Street, shortly after the birth of their fifth child in 1953. Joy was
born with sea-green eyes and thick brown hair. She had a small, pert
nose and a pointed chin. Janet came along the following year and
resembled her Washington ancestors. She was also the fairest of the
Allen children, with blue-gray eyes and blond hair.

Many of the Allens' black neighbors thought that Elise and Jimmy
were an interracial couple. Even when they learned of his racial identity,
many of them remained unconvinced. As it was, some of the Allen
children could pass for white. Elise could only pray that they wouldn't
suffer the skin color issues that had plagued her Aunt Georgia and
others in her mother's family.

Elise's husband dedicated all of his time to making his printing business lucrative. He was renting a small storefront building on Third Street for twenty-five dollars a month. The average annual income for African-Americans at this time was around $2,324. This was 59 percent of the average $3,986 received by whites. The Allens weren't rich; they were grossing about $2,700 yearly, and barely had enough money to feed their family. But they were rich in all the ways that mattered.

Jimmy couldn't afford to hire employees for his business, so Elise and the older children helped out. After returning from the print shop every evening, Elise would try to scrub off the ink stains that covered her delicate hands. Sometimes no matter how aggressively she washed, the stubborn stains would remain.

On a hot, July afternoon Elise was working in the back room of the print shop. She was so uncomfortable from the heat and humidity that she had the ends of her white cotton blouse tied up under her breasts. Her hair was done up into a knot at the top of her head. A few damp strands had escaped its confines, curling becomingly around her face. She heard the shop's bell ring, alerting them that a customer had arrived. She rose from the bench where she had been working and peeked around the door jam to see who had entered. A slim, olive-skinned man with wavy, black hair and a mustache came into the building. Two burly, rough-looking men in black suits accompanied him. They stood by the door with their arms crossed over their chests in a relaxed, but guarded manner.

"My name's Martelli," the man said to her husband. "I'm looking for the owner of this establishment."

Jimmy had been washing down the Chandler-Price printing press and wiped his hands on an already inky cloth tucked into his overalls. "I'm the owner, James O. Allen," he answered warily a moment later.

Martelli looked around the small room, taking in the one press and several reams of white paper on the shelves that lined the wall next to it. "Well, Mister Allen, how would you like to make $500 a week?"

Not waiting for Jimmy to answer, he walked over to the printing press and ran his forefinger over the flat, round disc that was the size of a car's hubcap. Noticing the black ink staining his finger, he took a white handkerchief from his breast pocket and wiped it off. Glancing back at Jimmy he went on, "All you have to do is print a little cartoon book for me."

Jimmy's eyes widened in shock at the outrageous sum of money the man had just offered him. It was a fortune. His blue eyes narrowed as he thought, W*hy does this man want me to print for him? There are several large, white printing firms in the city, why didn't he give them the order?*

"Why are you asking me?" He inquired cautiously.

The man paused a second before he answered, his voice deceptively soft, "Because I am a private man Mister Allen. Very private. And I don't like everyone knowing my business. You can appreciate that, can't you?"

Jimmy didn't answer, but nodded his head slightly.

Martelli added, "Look, to make it even easier for you, I'll even supply the paper and the negatives for the cartoons. All you have to do is print them up."

"Can I see a copy of what it is you want me to print?" Jimmy queried.

"Sure." Turning towards the door, Mr. Martelli snapped his fingers and called out, "Gino."

The one named Gino reached into his suit jacket, pulled out a small book, and brought it over to his boss. Mr. Martelli then handed the book over to Jimmy.

Jimmy looked at the cover of the book in his hands. It seemed harmless enough. The cover showed a picture of Dagwood and Blondie. When he opened it, he felt his face burn. The cartoons were pornographic. He closed the book and handed it back to its owner.

"Well, what do you say?" Martelli asked. He had a slight smile on his face after witnessing Jimmy's reaction to the cartoons.

"I think not, Mister Martelli. My children work here sometimes. I wouldn't want them or my wife to see those *cartoons,*" he stated simply.

"I think not," Martelli repeated Jimmy's words. He turned back to the two men by the door and said, "Did you hear that boys? This yokel turned me down."

The two men laughed at their boss's comment. Martelli's black eyes became deadly when he switched them back to Jimmy.

"Mister Allen, I don't think you understand. Nobody tells me no. You *will* print these cartoons and now for a lower price." He fixed him with a hard look that would have caused a lesser man to flinch.

Jimmy stared into the man's eyes, boring into them with a firm intensity and replied, "No sir, I won't." His stance became rigid.

Elise was watching the entire tableau playing out in front of her from her spot by the door. When she heard the stranger threatening her husband, she reached for the shotgun they kept in the back room. Carefully loading it, she went back to the doorway. She gasped when she noticed the two burly men were now holding Jimmy by both his arms. One of them had pushed her husband's elbow up behind his shoulders. Jimmy's lips had thinned and his jaw jutted with anger. Elise knew the look that crossed her husband's face. He was getting ready to fight.

"Now tell me again; you don't want to do this job," Martelli repeated menacingly.

"He doesn't want to do the job, mister," said Elise. She came into the room, pointing the shotgun at him.

"Ah, what do we have here, boys?" Martelli arched an eyebrow at Elise. Amusement tinting his voice he went on, "Now what do you think you're going to do with that shotgun, little lady?"

"I can make it very difficult for you to father children if you don't let my husband go," she answered dryly. She pointed the rifle at the man's groin then met his look unwaveringly.

One of the men slowly reached inside of his suit coat, but Martelli gave him a subtle shake of his head. Jimmy, taking advantage of the man loosing his hold, jerked free of his captors and hurried to stand by his wife.

Martelli assessed Elise's person. She was such a little thing. Didn't she know he could take her and her husband down before she pulled the trigger? Yet, here she stood, as composed as a preacher at his sermon. She wasn't the least bit afraid of him or his men. Martelli started laughing. He found it hilarious that he didn't intimidate this little gal or her husband. One thing he admired was bravery in the face of bad odds. This couple had more 'balls' than most men he dealt with in his business. Besides, he felt magnanimous today. His wife had given birth to his first son a few days before.

With amusement still glittering in his black eyes, Martelli said, "We'll get someone else."

"But b-boss?" Gino stammered.

Martelli turned and gave the man a flinty stare and barked out, "I said, we'll get someone else." Bowing in Elise and Jimmy's direction, he smiled and said to him, "That's one wildcat you have there, Mister Allen."

Still chuckling, he left the print shop and they never saw Martelli again. Jimmy secured a position with Powell Press as a pressman a couple of weeks later, but continued with his own printing business part-time.

It was pretty mundane for the next several months and Easter rolled around. Jimmy thought he would surprise his children and purchased a dozen pink and blue-dyed baby chickens. When he brought them home in a cardboard box and put it down in the living room, Elise stood stupefied.

"Jimmy—*chickens?* What in the world are we going to do with them?" she said as she watched the chirping birds pecking at the sides cf the cardboard box.

"I thought the kids would get a kick out of playing with them." He reached down and picked up a blue one and smiled as it tried to peck at his fingers. He went on, "When they start to grow a little, we'll give them to Hallie."

Elise's Aunt Hallie raised chickens and sold their eggs to local grocery stores. She had a chicken coop in her backyard area and wouldn't mind the new additions. She reached down and picked up a pink chick and thought as it squirmed in her hands, *It's so cute.*

Sighing, she relented and said, "Oh, all right."

That Easter morning the children were so excited to see their new pets. The chicks would now join the family pet menagerie of two dogs, three cats, a turtle and goldfish. A few months later, Elise found herself shooing the pesky birds away from her while she hung the laundry out to dry. The backyard was now a circus of meows, barks, feathers and clucks.

It was time to get rid of the birds, she thought, and told her children. The two youngest siblings put up the biggest fuss.

"Mama, don't give them to Aunt Hallie, we love'em!" cried Linda. Her eyes were tearing at the thought.

"Yeah, Mom, they don't even act like regular chickens," added Greg. "They don't even cluck anymore. They even chased one of my friends who was tryin' to ride my bike."

"They make good watch-chickens, Mama," chimed in Linda.

It was true; the chickens did mimic their dogs and followed the children everywhere they went. Glancing over at her husband, who was looking too amused at the children's deliberations she said, "Okay. But keep them off my clothes line!"

The chickens weren't the only pets the children would receive. Their father bought them a turkey, a goose and a pony. It was against the city's ordinance to have a pony in one's backyard. The authorities turned a blind eye to the 'large dog' kept by the Allens because Jimmy allowed the neighborhood kids to ride it. This was a treat to most of the inner-city children who had never ridden a live horse before.

Elise and her husband were extremely content with the way their life was progressing. The blood ties in their family were unbreakable, forged to steel with loyalty and caring, and their children's days were filled with fun and laughter.

But the times were changing; there was a spirit in the air for African Americans pursuing racial equality that would change the course of history.

Chapter 41

*In the gates of eternity, the black hand and the white
hand hold each other with an equal clasp.*

Mrs. Stowe

The fifties became the decade of justice for African Americans when a
tired black woman named Rosa Parks refused to "move back" on a
crowded bus so that a white person could have her seat. Twenty seven-
year old Martin Luther King led his first boycott for racial equality and
summed up the theme of the day when he stated:

> "But there comes a time to those who have mistreated us for
> so long that we are all tired—and humiliated, tired of being
> kicked about by the brutal feet of oppression. We had no
> alternative but to protest."

On May 17, 1954 the U.S. Supreme Court in the landmark Brown v.
the Board of Education decision declared segregation in public schools
unconstitutional. Chief Justice Warren read the unanimous decision:

"Does segregation of children in public schools solely on the basis of race, even though the physical facilities and other 'tangible' factors may be equal, deprive the children of the minority group of equal educational opportunities? We believe it does. We cannot turn the clock back to 1868 when the 14th Amendment was adopted or even to 1896, when Plessy v. Ferguson was written. We conclude that in the field of public education the doctrine of 'separate but equal' has no place."

Violence exploded in the South as this ruling was announced. Troops were sent there to protect the constitutional rights of the African American school children. The Allen children attended a neighborhood school, and the makeup of the student body was 80 percent minority. They had yet to be bussed to the city's all-white schools.

A year later, Elise had her seventh child. They named the brown-haired, grass-green-eyed boy Norman. The baby favored his fourth great grandfather, West Ford, with a high forehead and slightly flared nostrils.

The Allen family had grown too large for the small, four-bedroom house they were living in and moved to a six-bedroom one on Seventh Street in 1960. The Victorian-style frame home was large and white, on a large corner lot. Elise's husband installed a porch swing that drifted back and forth with the slightest breeze. A row of flowerpots filled with petunias and geraniums graced the porch steps.

During the next three years, two more children were born to the Allens—Angela and Barbara—bringing the total of the brood to nine. When Angela was born, she was mistaken for a Caucasian child, just as her older sister had once been. Her hair was blonde and her eye color was golden, yet not quite hazel. She also had two deep dimples in her cheeks and a beauty mark next to her mouth. Barbara was born two years later. She was golden skinned, like her mother, with curly black hair and eyes a clear shade of gray with just a hint of blue.

The times continued to be troubled when these two children were born. African-Americans were stoned, bombed, clubbed and attacked by police with water hoses and dogs when they stood up for their civil rights in 1963. There were over 10,000 racial demonstrations in that year alone. The assassination of Medgar Evers, the field secretary for the NAACP, in the same year further heightened tensions between the races. His death prompted President John F. Kennedy to alter his policy on civil rights. President Kennedy proposed one of the most aggressive civil rights programs ever enacted by a President at this time. In one of his most powerful speeches he stated:

> "One hundred years of delay have passed since President Lincoln freed the slaves, yet their heirs, their grandsons, are not fully free. They are not yet freed from the bonds, of injustice; they are not yet freed from social and economic oppression. And this nation, for all its hopes and all its boasts, will not be fully free until all its citizens are free."

A march on Washington was organized in 1963 with over 250,000 African Americans and over 60,000 whites participating in the historical event. There were many speakers that day that demanded immediate passage of the Civil Rights Bill implementation of the 13th, 14th, and 15th Amendments of the Declaration of Independence.

"I wish I could participate in the March on Washington," Elise said wistfully to Jimmy. They were sitting at their kitchen table, sharing the morning newspaper. "If Big Papa were still living, he'd have taken a caravan of people with him."

"Lese, I wish you could go too, but we can't afford it," Jimmy replied, not glancing up from reading the classified ads section. He was always looking for better employment opportunities. He was now working at

Powell Press during the day, and printing in his own shop in the evenings and on the weekends.

Elise poured herself another cup of coffee, staring into its black depths as she thought about her life thus far. She was extremely happy in her marriage, but she felt like she had let her grandfather down. For the past twenty years, all she had accomplished as 'chronicler' was to tell her children who their famous ancestor was, warning them not to tell anybody about it. Elise wasn't even active in the local NAACP or any other civil rights organization. While people of her race were dying to further the cause of equality for blacks, she'd been too busy having and raising children to become involved. But that was no excuse, her mind cajoled.

Glancing at her husband's profile, she again marveled how white-looking he was. His hair was still a light, brownish-blond and straight. No hint of his African-American heritage was visible in him. Jimmy didn't understand how it felt to be truly black. He never noticed the furtive looks directed their way when they were out in public. He wasn't cognizant of the racism directed towards others in their race. Even her children didn't really feel the stigma of being black. But passing for white was not an option with her fairer children as far as she was concerned. They were black—and black they would remain.

What am I doing to further the Ford legacy? She thought critically. *Nothing.* That's what bothered her most. But what could she do? She wasn't naïve enough to believe that racial tolerance would come about if the country knew that George Washington had black descendants. No, America's wounds were too deep and raw for that. Anyway, who really cared? An insistent voice in her mind said, *It's your charge, Elise. It takes fortitude to be a chronicler.*

Two centuries of responsibilities as a chosen chronicler had been bred into her. She remembered the words spoken to her by her grandfather, George Ford, to keep the family story alive. She made up her mind at the kitchen table that morning to begin stressing the family heritage to her children. She would relay to them the importance of not allowing it to fade into obscurity. And she would begin the grooming of the next set of chroniclers.

A week later, Elise was combing her daughter, Joy's thick hair. Elise was valiantly attempting to comb her child's locks into three separate braids.

"I'm gonna tell on you!" shouted Janet at Linda as she ran screaming into their parent's bedroom. "Tell her to stop it, Mama!" Janet protested. "I don't look like that old man. I don't. I don't!"

Linda came screeching to a halt beside her a few seconds later. "Yes, you do. You've got his nose." She held up a dollar bill in one hand. She waved it like a flag in the air, then under her sister's nose.

"What old man?" their mother injected.

"George Washington," the girls chimed in unison.

Elise drew a measuring breath. "You know the Old General is one of your grandfathers. I've told you this a hundred times. Janet, you're being teased because you look like him, but you can't change that." Turning to Linda, she continued, "And you look like him too. You may not have his nose, but you look like him, so stop teasing your sister."

Linda, looking contrite, said, "I'm sorry for teasing you, Janet. Here, you can have the dollar." She handed the money to her sister who quickly pocketed it.

Scratching the side of her aquiline nose with her forefinger, Janet lamented, "Mama, when can we tell everybody that George Washington was one of our grandfathers?"

"Oh, Janet honey, this country is too filled with racism to share our family history with outsiders." Seeing Janet's crestfallen face, Elise added, "One day Janet, when the time is right, you'll be able to share our secret with the world."

"Good, 'cause I'm gonna make sure everybody knows about it," she replied assuredly.

"And I'll help you," added Linda.

Elise realized who the next chroniclers would be—Janet and Linda. They were the ones most interested in the family's heritage. Now all she had to do was groom them for the task at hand.

*   *   *

President Kennedy's assassination in 1963 shattered the hearts of many African-Americans. They had come to admire him even though many black leaders criticized him on some of his civil rights policies. A year later, Congress passed the Civil Rights Act in 1964. The act guaranteed African-Americans access to public accommodations such as restaurants, hotels, and amusement areas. The act also authorized the federal government to sue, to desegregate facilities, including schools, and mandated nondiscrimination in federal programs. Equal rights to employment were also established.

A new addition was added to the Allen family in 1964. Elise gave birth to her tenth child, Timothy, and he inherited his mother's caramel-colored eyes and reddish-brown skin tone. He had a curly mop of brown hair and finely chiseled cheekbones and nose. The house was busting at the seams with the large, happy clan, but they made room for yet another family member. Elise's mother, Florence Ford, moved in with them later that year. She could no longer see well enough to work as a seamstress and she went totally blind the following year from glaucoma.

Elise was now volunteering at the local NAACP office whenever she could. She also continued to relay to her children the importance of equality among the races. But it seemed that the United States was unwilling to support all its citizens in equal rights. Frustration at the oversight of African-American equality by the U.S. led to the marked growth of a militant racial sentiment called the Black Power Movement. Malcolm X, formally known as Malcolm Little, was one of the most articulate spokespersons for the Black Power Movement. He preached self-defense against white supremacists and used his organization to encourage militancy regarding equality and civil rights. He was assassinated in 1965.

Martin Luther King led a peaceful march in 1965 from Selma to Montgomery, Alabama, protesting the slaying of Jimmie Lee Jackson, a black demonstrator, and the arrest of almost a thousand others. The march turned violent as police and state troopers attacked the demonstrators with whips, tear gas and billy clubs. The march and its attack were televised and shocked the nation. Throughout the country a flurry of demonstrations erupted. Reports came from the media about riots occurring in many major cities. In 1966, National Guardsmen were brought in to quell riots in Chicago, Omaha, Dayton and Cleveland.

Another group emerged from the movement known as the Black Panthers. The organization was headquartered in Oakland, California and their primary goals included self-defense and revolutionary change in the United Sates. Their platform also included the right of African-Americans to full employment, decent housing, education and an end to police brutality. Local, state, and federal authorities continually harassed the Panthers. Their military image, which consisted of black leather jackets, berets and firearms, troubled many white Americans. The Black Panthers included such notables as: Huey Newton, Bobby Seale, Eldridge Cleaver, Geronimo Pratt, Fred Hampton and Angela Davis.

Elise was worried. She was concerned about her sons, Gregory and Jimmy, becoming involved with the Black Panthers. She didn't want them to join any militant groups because she was concerned for their safety. Besides, she believed strongly in the non-violent approach of Dr. Martin Luther King. Her sons were home on a college break when the discussion of civil rights emerged at their dinner table.

"Why can't we join the Panthers, Mama?" said Gregory. "We have to *force* this country to view us as equal citizens. Even George Washington was a revolutionist, and as his grandson, why can't I stand up for what I think is right?"

Elise glanced at her husband. A silent communication passed between them. Whenever questions involving her Washington ancestors came up during family discussions, they were automatically fielded to her for an answer. She did so now. All of her children's eyes were focused intently on her, waiting for her to answer their brother's queries. She had to make sure that what she said made sense to Gregory, because her words had to make a difference in his thinking—in all her children's thinking.

Trying to force reason into her tone of voice Elise replied, "Gregory, I don't believe violence is the way to solve the problems of inequality that we blacks face in this country. Besides, violence begets only violence." Her voice shook with conviction as she continued, "America's political system doesn't guarantee anybody success. It's what's up here," she had her index finger touching her head, "that will make you or break you in this society. If you use your intellect, then this country will provide you the opportunity to succeed. Because it's going to take a long time before the U.S. can right the wrongs of over two hundred years of slavery, and it sure won't come by force. It has to come by reason, with our race being consistent and persistent in challenging the political powers for change. It will be gradual change, but it will come.

Her voice was full of passion when she said, "The only way to equality is through education. With knowledge comes the understanding and the opportunity for greatness. You have an opportunity to change the perception of how you are viewed by others. You can fight inequality through education."

It took a moment for the children to absorb Elise's inspiring words. When they did, they realized their mother was right. Gregory and Jimmy didn't join the Panthers and went on to graduate from college. The brothers continued their fight for equality by joining non-violent demonstrations.

Unfortunately, the country was taking two steps backward for every one step forward in regard to its black populace and their civil rights.

Chapter 42

*Greatness does not depend upon one's fortune; it is
our manner that distinguishes us, and destines us for
great things.*

Joy Allen Stone

In 1966, Elise was pregnant with her eleventh child. She had the nagging feeling that something was physically wrong with her during the final weeks of the pregnancy. She tried to shake it, but the sensation only strengthened. Elise spoke to her mother about her misgivings.

"I don't feel this child kicking, Mama. Something's not right." Worry lines were etched on her brow and cheeks. Her caramel-colored eyes held a vague appearance in them.

Florence couldn't see her daughter's face, but she could hear the distress in her voice. "Elise, the doctor said that you're not always going to feel the child moving."

"I know what he said. But I've had ten children, Mama, and I know this pregnancy feels different. I feel different." Dark spots danced in front of her eyes for a moment, temporarily blinding her. Steadying herself with a hand against a chair, she said weakly, "In fact, I'm going to lie down for awhile."

Three days later, Elise was in the hospital. The child she had been carrying for the previous nine months had died in her womb. The umbilical cord had become entangled around the fetus' neck. Her physicians had estimated that the baby had been dead for about a week. They also told the family that Elise was in God's hands, because they were not certain they could arrest the poison that was attacking her system. Elise slipped into a coma and the family assembled around her bedside in prayer.

Jimmy stayed by his wife's side for two days and two nights. On the third day, when her vital signs were barely registering, he gripped her hand into his and muttered savagely, "You must live, Lese. *Fight.* Please fight to live. I love you so much; don't leave me alone. You're my life. I can't even breathe without you."

He clasped his hands and bowed his head in prayer. "Please, God, let her live. I love her with all that I am or can be. The children need her. I need her. I know I haven't been praying much to you lately, thanking you for all you've done for me and my family. But I trust in you. *Please.* God, please hear my prayer!" He reached out and shook her form lightly. "Wake up, Lese, wake up!"

Jimmy loved his wife beyond measure, and she had to live or else he would cease to exist. Elise had become his heartbeat. He had never felt so helpless. He was more exhausted than he had ever been in his life and finally fell asleep.

A voice woke Elise. One that was filled with so much pain she knew she couldn't ignore it. It was a weary mumble, its hoarse timbre striking a note of recognition in her subconscious. It was her husband's voice. One minute Elise was lost in a dream state and now she was awake.

She focused on her surroundings and she didn't know where she was for a moment. She was tired, so awfully tired and she ached all over. Her arms and legs felt as if they were anchored to her sides. She turned and saw plastic tubing and a needle inserted in her left arm. Elise realized that she was in the hospital. She saw that her stomach was flat. Evidently, their child had been born, she thought drowsily.

Turning her head, she saw her husband's still form, asleep in a chair next to the bed. He held her right hand. She wanted to speak to him, but her tongue was thick and cottony, and stuck to the roof of her mouth. Removing her hand from his grasp, she lightly stroked his hand with her fingertips. Her touch awakened him and his profile startled her. Haggard lines had been carved around his expressive mouth. His hair was mussed, and he looked like he hadn't shaved in a week.

Jimmy brought her smooth hand to his lips. "Thank God, you're awake," he said softly. "You scared me half to death, Lese."

She finally managed to speak and it came out in a raspy tone. "The b-baby. H-how's the baby?"

A vague sadness appeared in his eyes for a moment, making her uneasy. Something was wrong and her brow wrinkled in concern. Then she glanced again at her stomach and stiffened. She felt Jimmy's hand tighten on her own. She knew then. She knew that their baby was dead.

She felt her heart break into a thousand pieces.

It was touch and go for about a week, but Elise rallied. She told her family that while she was in a coma she had heard their voices calling to her.

"I was in a dark tunnel of sorts and I wasn't alone. People were walking in the shadows, but I couldn't quite make them out, but I could feel their presence. I also knew that they meant me no harm. Never have I felt so at peace with myself or my surroundings."

Her eyes teared for a moment and she blinked them away, "I saw my father in the distance in that tunnel. A bright light illuminated him and he was smiling at me. I screamed out "Daddy" and ran towards him, but as I neared his form he raised his hand up and said, 'Go back, Elise. Your husband is calling for you. Your family needs you.' I said, But Daddy, I miss you so. Please let me talk to you for awhile." Elise sighed deeply before continuing, "But he told me to go back. Go back and one day we'd see each other again. Then I heard Jimmy calling for me and I woke up."

The family members had listened to her eerie but fascinating story in silence.

Her mother's voice broke the quiet. "It's God's will, Elise, it was not your time. God must have things yet for you to accomplish."

"That's good, 'cause I'm hungry," said nine-year-old Norman. The family burst out laughing as Norman's remark drained the tension from the once-dire moment.

Elise remained in the hospital for another week after they stabilized her. She never saw the child they named Matthew. She had been too ill to attend her infant son's funeral the week before. Her Aunt Hallie had taken care of all the burial arrangements. Jimmy told her that Matthew had been born with black hair and dark eyes.

Elise had a long time to contemplate her life while she recuperated at home after her bout in the hospital. Her physicians may have stabilized her body, but it would require a longer time to mend her mind. The death of her child hung around her neck like a heavy weight, causing her most days not to even want to rise from her bed. Someday when the sadness lessened, she would laugh again and feel at peace.

Elise was relaxing in the rocker next to her bed several weeks later. She couldn't lie down another minute. Her mind was so restless. She felt caged and so useless. Her gaze strayed to the scrapbook that housed the family history. Picking it up, she glanced at the yellowed pictures of her ancestors, at those of her father and grandfather. As she focused on the picture of her grandfather she could hear him say, "Take a stand, Lesey." And at that moment she knew what she needed to do. She knew that she could no longer remain a spectator, watching others in the civil rights movement fighting for equality without supporting their efforts. She could no longer remain silent.

Elise Ford Allen was ready to make a stand.

Elise and her husband were enjoying some quiet time in their kitchen later that afternoon. Jimmy was working on a device at the table that would take lint off of printing press ink rollers. She steepled her fingers under her chin and watched quietly for a few minutes, trying to decide how to best approach him with her idea. Well, there wouldn't be a better time than now, she thought and said, "Jimmy, I want to start my own newspaper."

He looked up from the pieces of wire, rubber casings, rollers, and nuts and bolts scattered across the table with a questioning expression on his face. Raising an eyebrow, he parroted, "You want to start your own newspaper?"

"Yes, I do. The black community has no voice in this city. We need a newspaper that focuses on our issues, our concerns, and our accomplishments. I want to write about my thoughts concerning these issues. Maybe by writing my editorials, I might make a difference somehow. Maybe I can open up some closed minds."

Elise's face was animated with her musings. Jimmy didn't want to dampen her enthusiasm, but she had to understand the obstacles that would be placed in her path.

"How are you going to accomplish this? It takes a lot of work to run a newspaper. You have to have advertising, reporters, people to circulate it. And money. Have you thought about all these things?"

"Yes, of course I have thought about all those things," Elise said confidently. "I can start out by writing my editorials on the back of the handbills you print for the Trapps Five and Dime Store. That way we won't have to buy extra paper. And I'm sure that I can get the Trapps' permission. The handbill is already being delivered around the neighborhood so we won't have to worry about circulation, and I won't need reporters for a long time yet."

She smiled brightly at him. "But best of all, I know the printer personally and I'm sure I can work out some sort of payment arrangement with him."

Jimmy lost himself for a moment in her smile and teasing manner. He hadn't seen that smile since before Matthew died. It was pure, unadulterated sunshine. He'd do whatever she asked, as long as he could keep that joyous look on her face.

"Well, I'm sure you can work *something* out with the printer," he answered softly. "But we'd better ask the Trapps if it will be okay with them first."

Later that week, Elise wrote her first editorial and it was printed on the back of the Trapps' handbills. They were circulated throughout the community. Within two months the handbills were requested for her editorials alone.

The Traveler Weekly was established in the fall of 1966. The newspaper started out as a single 8 1/2 x11 sheet with local news items and Elise's editorials. She went to the library weekly to read the U.S. Congressional Record, which kept her politically informed. The teachings of her grandfather, Major George Ford, and W. E. B. Dubois were evident in her written exposés. *The Traveler Weekly* became the first newspaper edited and published by an African American woman in Illinois and grew to tabloid size the following year.

In 1967, Jimmy left Powell Press and officially established the Traveler Printing and Publishing Company. The entire Allen clan now learned the newspaper and printing business from the bottom up.

Fortune continued to smile on the family as Jimmy's tinkering paid off. He patented his first invention, a printing ink, and then his second, a roller he dubbed the "Hickey Picker" that removed lint from printed materials.

The country, however, continued to be troubled and riddled with racial tensions. Dr. Martin Luther King was assassinated in 1968, and his death rocked the African American populace. Black communities erupted in riots, one after another in a hundred and twenty-six cities throughout the country. A committee of inquiry was appointed in response to the domestic crisis. The committee hoped to bring law and order to the chaos of the times.

Boycotts were staged in Peoria to protest King's assassination. One particular boycott called for black students to remain out of school as a form of protest. Elise disagreed with this action. She didn't want the students to suffer the consequences of missing classes, and wanted to hold a peaceful march instead. Elise was sitting in a green armchair located in her living room. Her husband Jimmy was relaxing in a matching chair across from her.

"Jimmy, our community can't afford to have our students not attend school. That's like putting a bullet into an empty gun and handing it to your enemy. I've been fighting all year long with the school board because black students are placed in classes that are not as academically challenging as those of their white counterparts. Black students have also been expelled from school more often than whites for the same offenses."

"I agree that the kids need to go to school, but are you suggesting that we don't go along with the protest?" asked Jimmy as they debated the issue. His brow knitted as he waited for her answer.

"Yes, that's just what I mean—that our children go to school. The school board has issued a statement stipulating that any student who doesn't attend classes will *not* pass to the next grade level."

Hearing a slight movement coming from above her, Elise glanced up and spotted their daughter, Linda. She was sitting on the top step of the long, curving staircase that was adjacent to the living room. Elise motioned for her to come down with a wave of her hand.

She continued her discussion with her husband, "I don't know why a peaceful demonstration can't be held. Nowhere else in the state are students remaining out of school."

"You know the kids will have to cross a picket line." Jimmy's voice held a serious note.

Elise responded wearily, "I know that. But it can't be helped."

Linda was now in the living room by her mother's chair. She was a junior in high school and very popular. "So, Miss Big Ears, you've been listening to our conversation." Cocking her head to the side, she went on, "So, what do you think about going to school tomorrow?"

"I don't want to go, Mama," Linda replied. "All my friends are staying home. Their parent's aren't making them go, so why do I have to?" Her lower lip jutted in a display of pique.

Elise asserted firmly, "I can't speak for your friend's parents because they have to make their own choices when it comes to their children. If you stay out of school, you will not pass this year. You will be held back. And I've always told you that an education is the most important tool an individual can receive."

Her voice lowered in tone and she continued, "I know going to school tomorrow will be the most difficult task you have ever had to do thus far. But it will teach you fortitude and forbearance, qualities you will require when you take on the task as chronicler of the Ford family. Linda, when you attend school tomorrow you will hold your head up high and you will stand proud and stand tall."

Linda and Joy were transported to Manual High School the next day by their parents. A large, virtually black crowd had gathered there with picket signs. They were singing, "We shall overcome some day." Over a dozen police officers were standing near the entrance to keep the demonstration peaceful and to assist students who wanted to enter the school. Those who wished to go into the building had to cross the picket line. Many of the black students who were not participating in the boycott, and who wanted to attend classes, were too intimidated to cross the human chain formed across the entrance. They were standing around in quiet groups.

"I don't want to go in, Mama…please don't make me," blurted out Joy. "None of our friends will ever speak to us anymore if we go in."

"Then you will make new ones, because they're not truly your friends," Elise replied firmly. "You will be a leader not a follower, and to do that you must sometimes stand alone."

The girls and their father exited their station wagon and headed towards the picket line. Elise watched intently from the car. She was proud of her daughters as they stood straight as arrows and walked alongside their father towards friends and foes. Elise remained in their vehicle with Janet, Norman, Angela, Barbara and four-year-old Timothy. All but Timothy would be dropped off at their respective schools after leaving Manuel.

It was the longest walk the girls ever made. The sisters walked proudly beside their father. Taunts of "Tom, Tom, Tom" were chanted at them by members of their own race. The family had to forcefully push their way through the picket line; their father shielded them with his body from the slaps, kicks, and spittle thrown their way. Once they were clear of the crowd, they headed for the entrance of the building.

"Your Mom and I will pick you two up after school," their father told them. He brought his hand up to a long gash near his forehead to wipe away blood that was trickling into his left eye. Someone had evidently struck him with a sign. He went on, "Wait by the office until either I or your mother comes for you." He kissed them on the cheek and turned to walk back to their car.

Linda was the last to enter into the school. She stopped with her hand on the door handle and turned around when she heard several loud jeers. Her heart plummeted to her feet. Her father was on the ground with three, young black men punching and kicking him. Her father had his hands out to the side of his body and was not even trying to defend himself. The crowd was shrieking, "Get that white man! Get that white man!" They thought her father was white!

A red haze covered Linda's vision. With a sound similar to a war whoop, she threw her schoolbooks to the ground and raced back to where her father was pinned to the ground. She took a flying leap and landed on the backs of the boys, knocking two of the attackers off her father. Linda was her parent's child. The boys didn't know what hit them as she pummeled them with her fists. Several police officers ran up to the altercation and within a few moments broke up the scuffle. The young men were immediately taken into custody and the crowd subdued.

Elise, witnessing the incident from the car, came running over to her husband and daughter. "Are you two all right?" she said breathlessly when she reached their sides.

Jimmy smiled and said, "I'm fine." The corner of his bottom lip was bleeding and a bruise smudged the skin beneath his right eye. Directing his gaze to Linda, he said jokingly, "You sure pack a mean punch. That fellow you walloped has a swollen lip and a bloody nose."

Linda was still tense with rage, but a tiny smile tugged her lips at her father's quip.

"Well, what do you expect, Daddy?" she said with a chuckle, her green eyes sparkling. "I've got four brothers to practice on."

Her father hugged her and they walked her to the door of the school.

Many of the people making up the picket line came over to Jimmy and apologized to him as he made his way to their vehicle. After all, it was to have been a non-violent boycott. Some of the black students who had wanted to enter the school earlier, now made their way through the throng as the picket line dispersed.

The black community was stunned by what happened at the high school. Elise received a telephone call from the local leader of the NAACP, John Gwynn, the day after the incident, asking for a meeting. Gwynn told her that they needed to be united in the cause to fight injustice against their race, not each other. Elise was in total agreement.

The black community commended Elise on her courage to stand alone with an unpopular decision when she sent her children to school. The poor and downtrodden of the city's black populace began to besiege Elise for help, and she never turned a soul away. There would be days upon days that the mental fatigue of fighting their battles exhausted her.

One evening Elise was in her home office, working late into the night. Jimmy came into the room and said, "Lese, its late, Honey. Can't you complete what you're doing tomorrow?" He walked over and watched as she took furious notes from one paper and transferred them to another.

"I know it's late, but I just need to finish this information because I have to take it to the school board tomorrow and I need to have my facts in order."

Jimmy watched as she studied the papers on her desk. Her focus was intense as she scrutinized her notes like an attorney preparing for its defense in a murder trial, because what was happening to their race was murder in deed as well as in spirit. He leaned down and kissed her on the cheek and left her alone. An hour later he came back and found her asleep in the chair. He picked her up in his arms.

"I'm still working," she protested sleepily against his shoulder.

"No more work tonight, Lese."

He continued to their bedroom, helped her undress, and tucked her between the bed sheets. She mumbled something incoherently. But he understood her. She said that she loved him. He smiled because he loved her too.

Jimmy was so very proud of her. She was a woman of passion, of intelligence, of commitment. She was headstrong and determined, traits admired in men but scoffed at in women. But his little spitfire ignored the scoffers because Elise was born fighting to control her own destiny.

He also knew her battles were not over.

Chapter 43

Faith exchanges the present for the future.

Greg Allen

It was Sunday afternoon and the family was enjoying a meal of ham, macaroni and cheese, string beans, corn on the cob and cornbread muffins. A double-layered chocolate cake was displayed on the cherry-wood buffet next to the table. When a lull occurred in the conversation, Elise said out of the blue, "I'm going to run for mayor."

Jimmy put his fork down next to his plate and said, "You want to run for mayor?"

"Yes I do. I've been reviewing the qualifications of the other candidates and feel that I can offer just as much as they can in taking this city forward in a positive way."

"Lese, now do you really think you can win?" Jimmy couldn't keep the skepticism out of his voice.

"Honestly, no. But if I can obtain a platform to speak on, maybe I can make a difference to the other candidates and voters. Maybe they will take notice and incorporate some of my ideas into their policies."

Elise's face was shot with determination in her resolve to run. The children were quiet as they waited to hear what their father would say.

"Then run and we'll back you," Jimmy replied seriously a few moments later.

The conversation around the table erupted with shouts of encouragement and the campaign was on. Elise didn't possess the monetary backing the other candidates enjoyed to finance their campaign. She enlisted her best friend, Geraldine Mitchell, as her campaign manager. Geraldine was a petite woman with honey-brown skin. She had flashing black eyes and a heart the size of Texas. No task was too menial or difficult for her to accomplish. She prepared flyers, set up speaking engagements, and answered telephones. The campaign became a family affair as Jimmy printed the flyers and the younger children; Norman, Angela, Barbara and Tim circulated them around the city.

Most of the white populace considered Elise's candidacy a joke. But when she spoke at the debates they changed their tune. The soft-spoken black woman really understood the issues confronting the city and had solid, workable solutions that the others lacked. But it wasn't the time for a black woman to hold a public office in the small, river city. Elise placed fifth among the eight white male candidates who ran.

A week after the election, Elise was relaxing in the leather chair in her office reflecting on what she could accomplish next in her fight for racial equality. She had been extremely busy the last several months campaigning for mayor. A pile of correspondence sat on top of her cherry wood desk. Just as she started sorting the papers in order of importance, her telephone rang.

"Mrs. Allen, I need to see you. Please say you have time for me, it's very important," a woman's voice pleaded. "You're the only one who can help me now. You're the only one with the courage to help me."

"What is it I can do for you?" inquired Elise. The woman had her full attention.

"We can't talk over the phone. I need to talk to you in private, in person," the woman replied.

Two hours later the woman, a Mrs. Garber, knocked on the door to the Allen home. Elise answered it and found a black woman around thirty-five years of age standing on her porch.

"Mrs. Garber?" inquired Elise.

"Yeah, I am," she replied softly, pulling a black wool scarp closer around her throat.

"Come on in and have a seat." She moved aside so that the woman could enter. Then she directed her to an armchair in her living room. As the woman sat, she looked around at the room's tasteful furnishings then back down at her feet.

Elise's first impression of the woman was that she wore too much makeup. Her face was almost clownish in appearance. Elise waited for her to speak and a moment later she did.

"Mrs. Allen, I want you to listen to what I've got to say with an open mind. Please let me finish my story before you make your mind up whether to help me or not."

"Yes, all right." Elise was curious as to why this woman needed her help.

Expelling a long breath, the woman said quietly, "I'm goin' to prison for murderin' my husband. But please believe me, I did it in self-defense." She waited for Elise's reaction and it didn't take long.

Elise sat back fully into her chair. Her eyes widened, but she didn't say anything. She was stunned. *Why did this woman kill her husband*, resounded in her mind. She couldn't possibly help someone who was guilty of committing murder. Elise attempted to keep her expression neutral until the woman resumed telling her story, but wasn't entirely successful.

Mrs. Garber read the emotions flittering across Elise's face. She bowed her head for a moment. Then she looked up with resolve on her features. "Mrs. Allen, may I use your bathroom?"

Elise nodded and showed her where the bathroom was. It was a full, five minutes before Mrs. Garber returned to the living room. Elise noticed right away that she had washed her face. As she sat back down in the chair, Elise could see the remnants of scars. They dotted the woman's face in too many areas to count. Many of them were raised, as if cut by a sharp object. She realized the woman had worn the thick makeup to cover her disfigured face. Mrs. Garber then removed the black wig from her head. There were many bald spots in her short hair. It appeared as if someone had pulled out patches randomly from her skull. The scarf was also gone and the woman's throat area was also scared and bruised. Elise knew that the woman had been battered.

"I killed my husband in self defense," Mrs. Garber said. "It was either *him* or *me*, and I had no choice. He was beatin' me and goin' to kill me in front of my children!"

Her shrill voice increased in volume. "Do you know what it's like to be huddled in a corner while a man beats you until you don't feel the blows no more? Do you know how it feels to hide in your own home from someone day after day, prayin' and beggin' God to let one go by without feelin' the pain of a punch or a kick?"

She looked pointedly into Elise's wan face and answered her own questions. "Mrs. Allen, I can see by the look on your face that you don't know. You don't know that during those beatings that you wish you were dead because then you wouldn't have to feel the pain no more."

Her voice took on a hollow tone. "You know, sometimes God let's us make our own choices. Sometimes the choices are right, sometimes they are wrong." Looking down at her clasped hands she choked out, "I-I tried leaving him, but he threatened to hurt our kids if I didn't come back. I didn't have a job. No money. No one to take me in, so I walked around all night and then finally came home. He beat me for days after that. He put a gun to my head and threatened to blow my brains out in front of our children. *So I fought him.* I kicked and scratched and made him drop the gun on the floor. Well, I got to it first, and then I shot him with it. I shot him with his own gun."

Glancing at Elise with tears in her brown eyes, she said brokenly, "I've got eleven children who need me; some are still babies. "I'm asking—no I'm begging you—to please help me Mrs. Allen. *Please.*"

Elise was barely breathing. She gasped for a moment, bringing the needed oxygen into her lungs. Running a shaking hand down the front of her face, she took a moment to respond, and then answered, "I'll help you."

Aiding Mrs. Garber would become Elise's biggest challenge. It later became her crusade. Elise poured over the police reports, talked to Mrs. Garber's public defender and interviewed the woman's neighbors. When she had enough information, she began writing editorials in her newspaper about Mrs. Garber and domestic violence.

She had her younger sons, Norman and Timmy, deliver the newspapers all over the city. *The Traveler Weekly* could be found in banks, hotels, restaurants, gas stations, anywhere they could leave or sell them. Letters by the hundreds poured into the newspaper from other women suffering from abusive relationships and from those concerned about Mrs. Garber's plight. Elise wrote about the woman's story weekly for over a year and she never tired.

She never gave up.

One day she received a telephone call that changed the course of her life and that of Mrs. Garber.

"Mama, Mama!" cried Barbara and Angela as they met their mother by the front door of their home. Elise had just returned from a meeting with the mayor about repairing potholes in many of the inner city streets.

"What is it?" Elise asked anxiously. Had something happened to one of her children?

"Mama, you're never going to believe what's happened," said Angela. Taking a deep breath, she hurried on, "The governor telephoned and said he's going to pardon Mrs. Garber!"

Elise's legs suddenly wouldn't support her and she dropped into the chair by the door. She listened as Angela continued, "It seems the governor has been following the story from your newspaper. Someone has been sending it to him. He reviewed the case, and now Mrs. Garber is going to go free!"

Barbara chimed in, "Aren't you excited, Mama!" She was sitting on the floor near her mother's feet.

"Yes, I'm excited, girls." Palming her hands and bringing them to her lips, she whispered, "Thank you God."

Elise closed her eyes and leaned her head against the back of the chair. It felt as if an immense weight had been removed from her shoulders. She smiled to herself and said to her daughters, "Sometimes all you can pray for is to make a difference. I wish my grandfather, George Ford, could have experienced this triumph today."

Chapter 44

To every thing there is a season, and a time to every purpose under the heaven; A time to keep silence, and a time to speak.

Ecclesiastes Ch. 3, v. 1,7

Once again life's travails touched the Allen family. Some unknown malady struck Elise's thirteen-year-old daughter, Angela. Angela legs weren't functioning properly. She collapsed at school, at church, and outside playing. Her appendages would give out, as if the muscles had detached from the bones. She was also having a difficult time talking, chewing, and swallowing. Elise took her daughter to one physician after another, but none of them could diagnose her problem.

One day Angela and Barbara were on their way home from school. They were only a couple of blocks from their house, but to Angela, it felt like a couple of miles because it was all uphill.

"Come on Angie, it's just a little farther 'till we get home," insisted twelve-year-old Barbara. She was small in stature, but had the will of a giant as she attempted to carry Angela on her back.

"I can't go any farther, and you can't carry me," said an exhausted Angela. "Leave me here and go on home. Then you can get someone to come back for me."

"Nope," said Barbara crossing her hands over her chest. "I'm staying right here with you 'till someone comes to get us. I'm not leaving you alone." She then helped Angela over to the curb of the street and they both sat down.

"Just let me rest for a moment, Barbara. I'll be okay in a few minutes and then we can start walking again."

Barbara's jewel-toned eyes assessed the fragile appearance of her sister. Angie's light brown hair was damp around the edges of her face and her golden colored eyes had the distinct look of utter weariness. *No, I won't leave her alone,* thought Barbara.

Angela hated being so helpless. Ever since she was a little girl, she had been dubbed "Miss Independent" by her mother. Now she felt as helpless as a newborn babe. When she first started having episodes of weakness, she told her mother, "Mommy, I can't, I can't walk. Just let me crawl and I'll get where I'm going."

Elise heard more than anguish in her daughter's voice. She could hear her frustration, her fear, and her suppressed tears. But she knew that sympathizing with Angela would only make matters worst. Her daughter didn't need her pity; she needed her strength.

Elise's smile was gentle, but firm when she replied, "You will not crawl, Angela. *Never.* Because you have family. We will be your legs when you can't stand. We will be your support."

Angela knew she had to be strong even in the face of her weakness. Besides, her mother never let her doubt for one moment that she would be cured someday.

A few minutes of restful respite on the street curb changed into about a hour. Then with a sure force of will, Angela stood and Barbara placed her arms around her sister's waist in support. The girls had taken a couple of awkward steps when they spotted their brother, Norman, in the distance.

After making sure Angela could stand without her assistance, Barbara started waving her arms in the air and shouted, "Hurry Norman, Angie can't walk!"

Norman had become concerned when his younger sisters hadn't made it home from school in their usual time. He decided he'd better set out and find them. As he jogged along Grove Street, he spotted his sisters and then broke into a full sprint when he heard Barbara's shout.

"You've got to help Angie," said a relieved Barbara, as he stopped at their side.

"I can make it by myself, Norman, just let me hold on to you," said Angela. She put a trembling hand on his arm.

Sensing her weakness, he lifted his sister off her feet and said reassuringly, "I got 'cha now, Angie. Everything is going to be all right. I'll just get you home to Mama and Daddy."

She wrapped her arms around her brother's neck and they went home. Angela, carried by her father or by her brother's Norman and Timmy, became a familiar sight in their small community. Another year would pass before Angela would be diagnosed with Myasthenia Gravis, a form of muscular dystrophy. It was the same illness that afflicted Aristotle Onassis. The disease wasn't curable, but treatable and eventually, Angela began to function as a normal teenage girl.

*   *   *

During the next several years, Elise continued her fight for equality, and her newspaper flourished. But alas, time took its toll on another one of her family members. Her mother died in 1979 from natural causes. Elise was numb as she watched her mother's casket being lowered into the grave of her deceased husband, Bruce Ford, at Camp Butler Cemetery. Florence Ford's coffin would be placed on top of her husband's and the backside of his marker would be engraved with her name.

Elise hated the ritual of burying the dead. That body in the cold metal box wasn't her mother, it had only once housed her soul. She stood with Jimmy at her side in the cool murk of the afternoon air as her youngest children, Angela, Barbara and Timmy took turns reading their grandmother's favorite Bible passages.

Elise didn't listen to the words spoken over her mother's grave because she knew those words of comfort would probably break the tight rein she'd kept on her emotions. She wanted to shout at God, to beg the Almighty to turn back the clock and restore her mother to her. Her usually bright eyes had lost their golden sparkle. They were dry and dull, as if mirroring the dismal shade of the overcast sky.

Timothy stood by his mother's side. He was the youngest sibling and very close to her. Sensing the turmoil erupting within his parent, he placed his hand in hers.

As they walked hand-in-hand from the cemetery, he said soberly, "Mama, I'm here if you need me. Grandma told me that sometimes we have to help you because strong people never lean on anybody. I may not have as big as shoulders as Pop, but you can always lean on me." His eyes were tense with concern.

Elise smiled tremulously at her fifteen-year-old son. Timothy had the appearance of her grandfather, George Ford, but it also seemed that he had inherited his strength and compassion as well.

"Thank you, son," she responded softly. She wouldn't lean on him though. She would not break down in front of her children.

Later that evening, Elise poured out her anguish, her face buried in a pillow to muffle her weeping from her husband. She didn't realize that Jimmy wasn't sleeping. Her sobs caused a painful squeezing inside his chest. He wasn't immune to death. He was present at the deaths of his mother and two of his brothers, Norman and Garry. If he lived as old as Methuselah, he'd never forget how he had held their hands at the end, trying to comfort them, trying to comfort himself. Those haunting images were etched in his mind and he would carry them to his grave.

Jimmy knew the pain his wife was experiencing and continued to let her weep for a few minutes more. Then he took her into his arms. But she was not to be consoled just yet. Her tears fell at a steady pace, coursing down her cheeks, damping her skin. When Elise was able to stop the wracking sobs for a moment she whispered out her anguish to him.

"Oh, God, how much grief can a person take?" Then she fled to a sanctuary deep inside of herself where this most agonizing of all days had never dawned and eventually she slept.

Jimmy did his best to comfort her during the next several days. All he could do was to stand by her side and give his support.

The sneaky tendrils of death continued their assault, claiming Elise's Aunts Hallie, Vera and Elise, her Uncles Irwin and Ben, her brother Harrison's wife, Joyce, and her cousin, Lena. Elise's younger brother, Bruce, died in 1985, and his oldest son, Bruce Jr., died a few years later.

A new decade was approaching and so many loved ones had passed away, but time heals even the most hurtful of pains, and with prayer Elise forged on. She continued her pursuit of justice for minorities with her newspaper.

The U.S. Civil Rights Commission released a report in 1987 that stated that forty-five percent of the nation's minority students still attended segregated schools. This report revealed that only token segregation had been implemented in traditionally segregated areas and that many schools had resisted integration altogether. The unrelenting quest for jobs, housing, fair trials, and equal education continued to dominate her life and the words Elise put to paper.

The Bureau of the Census showed that 12.1 percent of the population of the United States was African-American in 1990. The social conditions showed that about one-quarter of all African-American males were in prison, on probation, or parole. Forty-six percent of all African American children lived in poverty, and blacks were more likely than whites to be victims of rape or aggravated assault. Single-parent house-holds were three times more common among blacks than whites.

Elise's newspaper editorials and articles in the 1990s shifted towards enlightenment, empowerment, responsibility and healing. The fight for equality was taking a different direction in the country, and she wrote her editorials to reflect these changes:

> "We not only want to take part in solving our own problems, but also in making the true principles of democracy a living reality to all Americans, without regard to race, color, or creed. The dignity of the individual, and their civil rights, must be defended always. The real test today is the ability and desire of all of us to meet Americans as Americans and all peoples as equals.

Over breakfast one morning, Elise was reading an article that a close friend had clipped out of the *National Enquirer* and forwarded to her. She was having coffee with her daughter, Joy.

"Joy, listen to this," her brow rose as she read the headline, *"Look Who'd Be on the Throne if Washington Had Been King."* It states here that a Dr. Judith Saunders-Burton, an African-American woman living in Virginia, is claiming to be a descendant of George Washington. It also says that she would be a 'surprise contender' for the Washington throne if George Washington had been named king instead of president of the United States.

"I don't know this woman," Elise stated after reading the article.

"She has to be related to us, if she's claiming George Washington is one of her descendants," Joy said. She picked up the article and glanced at the picture of Dr. Burton. "She kinda looks like George Ford."

"The name Saunders is familiar to me. I want you to try and track her down; then give the information to Janet."

"I'll start with the magazine to see if they can give me a telephone number," said Joy. She went to the office telephone. Two days later, she had the telephone number of Dr. Saunders-Burton and turned it over to Janet. Within a few hours, Janet had the information her mother requested.

"Mom, are you ready for a surprise?" said Janet as she entered into her mother's office. Noting the questioning look on her mother's face, she went on, "Judy is your cousin."

"My cousin?" Elise was sitting in her leather wing-back chair at her desk. She dropped her pencil and waited for her daughter to continue.

"Yep, she's your cousin all right. Judy is the descendant of George Ford's brother, John," Janet told her as she dropped down onto the couch across from her.

"Ahh. I think I met John once when I was about four or five years-old. He died long before Big Papa did. We never met our cousins in Virginia. We barely even spent time with our cousins in Chicago, which is only about a hundred and fifty miles from here."

"Well, now you can. In fact Mama, Judy is also a family chronicler. She's been informing people about West Ford and George Washington for most of her adult life. She wants to get together and share family information."

With the discovery of Judy, another branch of the Ford family tree had been revealed. This branch had also been told the oral history of Venus and George Washington. This discovery served to strengthen the Ford family's claims and the two families began sharing memorabilia and documents on West Ford. Judy had even written a doctoral dissertation in 1986, in which she alluded to the relationship of West Ford and George Washington.

Several months later, Elise was relaxing outdoors on her porch swing, watching cars zoom by on the street in front of her home. She was in deep contemplation about her life and the choices she had made. Her children were adults now and had their own families. Her newspaper was flourishing and her husband's business was lucrative. But she felt that she had let her grandfather down somehow. The new millennium would be upon them in a few more years, and the country still wasn't fully aware of West Ford and his association with the first president.

Her Cousin Judy had been speaking about West Ford and his relationship to George Washington since 1977. Elise's side of the family had followed the edicts of the past chroniclers to keep the story *secret*. The volatile events of slavery, reconstruction, segregation, and the civil rights movement had kept her immediate family from disclosing their heritage in fear of racial reprisals.

The timing never seemed right.

But now the times had changed. Today people could contend with the story about the country's first virtual king fathering an illegitimate son. *So why not make it known to everyone?* she thought with determination. With resolve, she rose from the swing and walked into the house to find her husband.

Jimmy was tinkering on his latest invention, a hospital bed, in the basement when she located him. Once she was able to gain his full attention, she said, "I'm going to take the story of the Ford ancestry public. My grandfather told me that one day the time would be right to let the world know about West Ford and his relationship to George Washington. That time is now. I want the story revealed because it's our children's and their children's heritage. I don't want our legacy swept under a rug anymore and I think the American public is ready to hear the truth."

Letting out a deep breath, Jimmy responded, "I have to agree with you. Why shouldn't you inform the world of your ancestry? What are you planning to do?" He had a speculative look on his face as he waited for his wife's answer.

"Not me, but who. Linda and Janet are the designated chroniclers now. They will be the ones responsible for carrying the charge forward and taking our heritage public."

A few weeks later, Elise read an article from the *Rocky Mountain News* titled, *"George Washington in Their Family Tree, Black Sisters Say."* Putting the newspaper on her desk, she leaned back in her chair and thought about all the past chroniclers who had kept the family secret. Would they be pleased that the family's heritage was finally in the public realm? She sincerely hoped so. She felt so light hearted. Shaking her head, Elise thought bemusedly, that two hundred years was a long time to keep a secret.

She whispered aloud, "Big Papa, the world finally knows of our legacy, and in *my* time."

About the Author

Linda Allen Bryant has spent over twenty years carefully researching her family's genealogy and the surrounding issues. As a result, she has become an expert in early-American history and race relations, including the numerous laws, codes, amendments, and critical players of two hundred years of United States' history.

As one of the official chroniclers of the Ford family heritage, Bryant has appeared on numerous news programs, such as the Today Show, the CBS Morning Show, PBS Frontline, The History Channel and MSNBC. Bryant has also been interviewed by numerous print publications, including NEWSWEEK Magazine, the New York Times, the Chicago Tribune, the Washington Post and the Denver Rocky Mountain News.

Linda Allen Bryant's research is ongoing. Her work focuses on preserving the collective heritage of the family patriarch, West Ford, and his descendants.

Visit the official Ford website at **www.westfordlegacy.com** for a more detailed description of the branches on the Ford Family Tree.

James O. Allen   m.   Elise Ford

Linda Carol James Jr. Gregory Joy Janet Norman Barbara Angela Timothy Matthew

THE FORD FAMILY TREE

GEORGE WASHINGTON (1732-1799)   VENUS (1768?-1830?)
WEST FORD

WEST FORD (1785?-1863)   PRISCELLA BELL
WILLIAM · DANIEL · JANE · JULIA

JANE · PORTER SMITH
PRISCILLA · DANDRIGE · JULIA · ANNIE

WILLIAM · HENRIETTA BRUCE   JULIA · CORRILL RODGERS
GEORGE · JOHN · CONSTANCE · HANNAH   CORRILL JR. · WEST

JOHN · CHARLOTTE WILLIS
DANIEL · JOHN · GEORGE · CATHERINE · CHARLOTTE · ELIZABETH · MILDRED · CELIE · POLLY · HENRIETTA

CATHERINE · GEORGE SAUNDERS
BRUCE · JAMES

BRUCE · MARIE KING
JUDITH · RUBY · BRUCE JR. · JOSEPH KAY

JUDITH · KENNETH BURTON
ROBERT · DANIELLE

GEORGE · HARRIET BLYTHEWOOD
CECIL BRUCE · VERA · IRWIN · BERTRAM · GEORGE JR. · HARRIET · DONALD · ELISE

VERA · JAMES POWELL   GEORGE JR. · LULU BOWERS   ELISE · DOUGLAS JENKINS
VERA · RUTH · ELISE   LENA · HARRIETT · GEORGE III   CAROL

LENA · JAMES CRAIG
SANDRA · JAMES JR. · WENDELL · LOVELLA · GREGORY · JUDITH · JAKIE · DEBRA · CYNTHIA · CHERYL

CECIL BRUCE · FLORENCE HARRISON   HARRISON · JOYCE POST
ELISE · BRUCE · HARRISON · FLORENCE   TERRY · WAYNE · ALISON · CHERYL · KAREN · CRAIG

BRUCE · DOLORES FINLEY
BRUCE JR. · GLENN · CYD · LOIS ANN · CANDY LYNN

ELISE · JAMES O. ALLEN
CAROL · JAMES JR. · GREGORY · LINDA · JOY · JANET · NORMAN · ANGELA · BARBARA · TIMMOTHY · MATTHEW

FLORENCE · CHARLES PICKETT
CECIL · MIKE · BOYD · PATRICIA · LARRY · BEVERLY · DAVID · KAREN · SHARON · DEBBIE

West Ford

Appendix A: West Ford: a Chronology—1785-2001

1785	West Ford, the son of George Washington and Venus, is born in Westmoreland County, VA.
1799	George Washington dies at his Mount Vernon plantation.
1802	West Ford comes to Mount Vernon with new owner, Bushrod Washington. West becomes caretaker of George Washington's tomb and is befriended by Washington's old valet, Billy Lee.
1805	West Ford is freed on his 21st birthday; his portrait is drawn to commemorate the occasion.
1812	West Ford marries Priscilla Bell, a free woman; they have four children; William, Daniel, Jane and Julia. The children are educated on the Mount Vernon plantation.
1829	Bushrod Washington dies and wills 160 acres of land to West Ford. John Augustine Washington II inherits Mount Vernon. West works at Mount Vernon as an overseer. Venus dies a slave before West can buy her freedom.

1833	West Ford sells his land and purchases 214 acres adjacent to it; the area is known today as Gum Springs and is a suburb of Alexandria, Virginia.
1834	William Ford marries Henrietta Bruce, a free woman; they have four children; John, Mildred Constance, Hannah, and George. The children are educated on the Mount Vernon plantation.
1851	West Ford's land increases to 225 acres.
1857	West Ford divides his property into four equal parts, 52 ¾ acres for each of his four children.
1858	John Augustine Washington III, the last private Washington to own the Mount Vernon plantation, sells the estate to the Mount Vernon Ladies' Association for the Union.
1859	William Ford, West Ford's first born son, moves his family to New York before the Civil War. West Ford remains on his property in Virginia and continues working for the Mount Vernon Ladies' Association. Benson Lossing sketches his picture for an article he is writing on Mount Vernon.
1863	West Ford dies at the Mount Vernon plantation where the Mount Vernon Ladies' Association cared him for; his obituary is posted in the Alexandria Gazette. Ford is buried in the old tomb of George Washington.
1863	William Ford returns to Virginia and works as a caretaker on the Mount Vernon plantation.
1867	George Ford, son of William and grandson of West, joins the 10th Cavalry and heads West.

1871	George Ford completes first tour of duty and meets his future wife, Harriet Blythewood.
1872	George Ford re-enlists in the 10th Cavalry as a quartermaster sergeant.
1876	George Ford is wounded, retires as first lieutenant from the 10th Cavalry, and returns to Beaufort, South Carolina. He marries Harriet Blythewood in Beaufort, South Carolina; they have eight children.
1896	William Ford dies and is buried at the Mount Vernon plantation.
1898	George Ford joins the F&S 23rd Regiment, Kansas Infantry, with the rank of major in the Spanish-American War in Cuba; becomes a personal friend of Teddy Roosevelt.
1899	Major George Ford moves to Chattanooga, Tennessee, and takes a position as superintendent of cemeteries.
1906	Major George Ford is elected to serve as the secretary of the Army and Navy Committee for the Niagara Movement; he becomes a close friend with W.E.B. Dubois.
1907	Major George Ford moves his family to Springfield, Illinois, where he becomes superintendent of Camp Butler Cemetery.
1917	Cecil Bruce Ford, youngest son of Major Ford, and his brothers graduate from Meharry Medical School. Cecil Bruce becomes a dentist.
1918	Dr. Cecil Bruce Ford joins the Army as a private medical DET in the 370 Infantry, 93rd Division.

1919	Dr. Cecil Bruce Ford relocates to Peoria, Illinois, and marries Florence Harrison; they have four children: Florence, Elise, Bruce, and Harrison.
1929	Major George Ford visits the Mount Vernon plantation for the last time. The Slave Memorial is erected at the Mount Vernon slave cemetery.
1937	Major George Ford is interviewed by the *Illinois Register* newspaper about his army life, his grandfather, West Ford, and his days at Mount Vernon.
1939	Major George Ford dies at the age of 91 at his home in Springfield, Illinois; His body is buried at Camp Butler Cemetery.
1939	Elise Ford Allen, daughter of Cecil Bruce Ford, becomes the family chronicler. She marries James O. Allen; they have eleven children: Carol, James Jr., Gregory, Linda, Joy, Janet, Norman, Angela, Barbara, Timothy, and Matthew (dies at birth).
1944	Dr. Cecil Bruce Ford dies in Peoria, Illinois.
1945	Elise's husband, James O. Allen, forms the Traveler Printing Company.
1966	Elise Ford Allen becomes the first African-American woman editor and publisher in Illinois. Her newspaper, the *Traveler Weekly,* debuts in Peoria, Illinois. Elise becomes a well-known civil rights activist.
1973	Elise Ford Allen becomes the first African-American female to run for mayor of Peoria, Illinois.

1979	Elise's mother, Florence Ford, dies.
1988	Elise Ford Allen receives over a dozen awards from the Peoria community for her work in civil rights.
1994	A *National Enquirer* article, speculating upon who should be heir to the U.S. 'throne' left vacant by George Washington, results in the Allen/Ford family reuniting with another branch of the Ford family through descendant Dr. Judy Saunders Burton.
1996	The Allen/Ford family goes public with the story of George Washington in their family tree; articles appear in *Newsweek*, *Time*, and *Der Spiegel* magazines, which interviewed Linda Allen Bryant and Janet Allen.
1998	The Washington/Venus story breaks in every major newspaper in the U.S. Feature stories with the chroniclers, Linda Allen Bryant and Janet Allen, are carried in the *Chicago Tribune*, The *Washington Post*, The *Peoria Journal Star*, *Rocky Mountain News*, *Foster's Daily Democrat*, *Newsday*, *Waterloo Courier*, *Boston Globe*, and *USA Today*. The sisters appear on a number of television broadcasts that carry the story as well, including a live debate on MSMBC. Channel 9 Denver, Colorado; mentions on major city networks including CNN, BET, and Saturday Night Live. Linda Allen Bryant is featured on several live feature radio broadcasts, including WGN, Sheridan Broadcasting Network, KACT Los Angeles, and BBC London.

2000	The West Ford story ushers in the new millennium with a new website and media interest continuing to grow. Linda Allen Bryant and Janet Allen appear on the Today Show, CBS Sunday Morning News and MSMBC. The *Chicago Tribune*, The *New York Times*, The *Denver Post*, and The *Rocky Mountain News* do several feature articles. Other print articles and television broadcasts are in the works. In March, a historic meeting took place at Mount Vernon between members of the Ford family and Mount Vernon staff with documentation presented claiming their heritage. In May, PBS broadcasted a documentary featuring the Ford history and posted a mini-documentary called *George and Venus* that still can be seen on the worldwide web.
2001	Ford descendant Linda Allen Bryant publishes, "I Cannot Tell A Lie." The book is the first to explore her family's controversial history. The History Channel features her and the Ford family history in a documentary called *Family Tree* in September. Exploration into the saga of West Ford and the African-American descendants of George Washington is ongoing. And thus, the story continues.

Appendix B: West Ford Mentions in Print

The significance of West Ford being mentioned in many recorded documents attests to his importance in the Washington family. Many of these factual excerpts appeared in the book and are presented here with their references. This section starts with the year 1801 and continues through 1940. All mentions after 1940 are noted in the bibliography, as they are too numerous to list.

1801—Hannah Washington's Last Will and Testament, Bushfield— Westmoreland County Circuit Court:
"...a lad called West, son of Venus, who was born before my husband's will was made and not therein mentioned, I offered to buy him of my dear sons Bushrod and Corbin Washington, but they generously refused to sell him but presented the boy to me as a gift, it is my most earnest wish and desire this lad West be as soon as possible inoculated for the small pox, after which to be bound to a good tradesmen until the age of twenty one years, after which he is to be free the rest of his life..."

Venus and her mother Jenny are also mentioned in Hannah's will:
"...some of my most indifferent things my daughters in law Hannah Washington and granddaughter Anne Aylett Robinson may at their own discretion, give Letty, Jenny, Suck & Venus though the two last mentioned treated me with great disrespect in my last hours..."

"...my dear husband left me in his will the following slaves to dispose of as I chose at my death provided I gave them to our own children the slaves are as follows—Billey who is dead since his wife Jenny, their daughter, Venus who has brought a daughter since called Bettey, these three slaves I give my beloved grandson Richard Henry Lee..."

1812—West Ford marries Priscilla Bell at First Presbyterian Church of Alexandria by Reverend James Muir (Arlington County Court House Marriage Registrar, 1803-1879; Corbin, 1982, Chapter II, p. 8; Robinson, 1981, p. 167).

1826—Bushrod Washington's Last Will and Testament, Fairfax County, Virginia:
"...Sixteenth, I give to West Ford the tract of land on hunting creek (sic) adjoining Mr. George Mason and that occupied by Dr. Peake which I purchased from Noblet Herbert, deceased, which was conveyed by Francis Adams to him, the said West Ford and his heirs, whatever appears by my ledger to be due to said West Ford is to be paid to him and it is my request that he will continue in his present situation and employment during the life of my wife provided she wishes him to do so on the terms he is now living with me.

1829—A letter written on August 27, from West Ford to Bushrod Washington who was visiting the family estate of Blakeley in what is now Jefferson County, West Virginia, (Fairfax Chronicles, May-July 1986, Vol. X. No. 2, Donald Sweig, Ph.d.)

"I'm going on with the house for the books and papers. The man that slate the house put it up for six dollars every ten feet. I have received your letter and will attend to the order. We have sickness in the family, my mother is very sick and old woman Dolly is crazy like she was two or three years past. George at the farm is sick. Mr. Roberts comments seeding the rye on August 24th. I think that you had better write to him to know what time he will get the rye done. Timothy's seed has not been sewn yet and the grubing is going on with four men. I like to know if I must get the scatlling from Mr. Davies to prepare the garden. I hear that you intend buying the mules that Mr. Peake has to sell, but hear that they are too old. He been talking to me about it for fear I would tell that they were old. Please to yourself know that it would be cheating you. West Ford your humble servant."

1830—Tax and property records of West Ford (Fairfax County Deed Book, 1830, Y3-400; Property Records A & B Schedules, 1830-1850; Robinson, 1981, p. 169).

1831—A description of West Ford appears in the Register of Freed Slaves, Fairfax County, Virginia:
"...the bearer hereof West Ford, a yellow man, about forty seven years of age, five feet eight and a half inches high, pleasant countenance, wrinkle resembling a scar on the left cheek, a scar on the left corner of the upper lip, is a free man emancipated by the Last Will and Testament of Hannah Washington as appears from an original Register heretofore granted by the County Court of Fairfax."

1837—A letter from George H. Duffey to Lawrence Lewis, dated April 1, 1837, when they were examining the tomb of George Washington. (Lewis, 1837; Robinson, 1981, p. 17):
"West Ford not being able to open the door of the vault at Mount Vernon employed me to do it for him, and to assist him in executing

your order, and requested me to make a correct drawing and send it to you which I have done to the best of my ability...West has got the plate and would have written to you himself but it was late in the evening and as I was coming to Alexandria he thought it might expedite the letter by getting it sooner in the Post Office than he could have sent it. You can rely on the accuracy of the drawing as West was very particular in the measurement and I stood by and seen and set it down."

1857—A letter from John A. Washington, Jr. April 17, 1857 (Washington, J. A., 1829):
"West will go up in the morning and I sent up by him some bacon and shad that I have had prepared for Cousin Harriet—some fresh fish that we may certainly meet on Monday, and that you my precious wife and friend be restored to health and strength..."

1857—Undated letter of 1857 to John Washington, Eleanor, his wife (Washington, J. A., 1829):
"West has just sent me up your letter, which I am truly glad to get...West has hurried me so much that I must say goodbye my beloved husband and hoping soon to be with you..."

1857—Division of West Ford's land to his children (Corbin, 1982, Chapter II, p. 11; Fairfax County Deed Book, 1857, A3, 331-333; Robinson, 1981,p. 170).

1859—Benson J. Lossing, 1859—interview and sketching of West Ford's picture for the *Harper's New Monthly Magazine*. Benson Lossing stated:
"I found him prepared (West) having on a black satin vest and silk cravat, and his curly gray hair arranged in the best manner."
West states to Lossing: "Artists make colored folks look bad enough anyhow."

West wrote his name on the sketch, a copy of which appears in the original article.

1859—*Harper's New Monthly Magazine*, 1859, Vol. 48 p. 445—Interview of West Ford for a lead article. West spoke about his plantation on Little Hunting Creek where he would retire after the Washington estate was no longer in the Washington family.

1859—A letter from John A. Washington, Jr., dated February 25, 1859 to his wife (Robinson, 1981):
"Tell West to make a strongbox to hold the woodwork of the different ploughs he has made to go to Waveland and to box them all up together with triple, double and single trees for the ploughs."

1863—A letter dated June, 1863, to Pamela Cunningham, founder of the Mount Vernon Ladies' Association from Sarah Tracey, the association's secretary (Muir, 1975, p. 68; Thane, 1977, p. 248):
"We have had old West Ford brought here. Mr. Herbert and myself went to see him Sunday and found him very feeble; and fearing all the excitement might hurt him, we have had him brought here, where we could take better care of him. I felt it was our duty to see that he should want for nothing in his old age."

1863—West Ford's obituary appears in the Alexandria Gazette on July 21, 1863, (Robinson, 1981):
"West Ford, an aged colored man, who has lived on the Mount Vernon estate the greater portion of his life, died yesterday afternoon, at his home on the estate. He was, we hear, in the 79th year of his age. He was well known to most of our older citizens."

1885—A letter from Colonel Harrison Dodge, resident director of the Mount Vernon Ladies' Association from 1885-1936 (Dodge, 1885-1936; Robinson, 1981, p. 164):

"Herbert Upton visited Mt. Vernon last week and I questioned him closely upon many of the Mount Vernon traditions and ancient features upon which I need and wished enlightenment. As to the style of fence and copying on the garden walls he says he followed the description given by old West Ford, Judge Bushrod Washington's servant.

1937—"From Mount Vernon to Springfield," *Illinois State Register,* January 17, 1937, by the Rev. Gay C. White, details the life of West Ford's grandson, George Ford, at Mount Vernon. Story also talks about his grandfather, West Ford.

1940—*Pittsburgh Courier,* "*West Ford Known As The Negro Son Of George Washington.*" Article shows resemblance between West Ford and George Washington (J. A. Rogers, p. 24. Sex and Race).

Appendix C: Documentation on West Ford

Following is a list of responses to several questions posed to the Ford family. This information was gathered and disseminated by Linda Allen Bryant as documentation of West Ford's paternity and presented to the Mount Vernon Ladies' Association in March, 2000. For more information on West Ford and his descendants, visit the official website at www.westfordlegacy.com.

When was West Ford born?

No one is sure of the exact date of West Ford's birth. This is because the birth dates of slaves were generally not recorded. Literature has reported dates from 1784 to 1786. In a register dated October 17, 1831, for free blacks living in Fairfax County, Virginia, there is a reference to West Ford being 47 years of age. That would suggest that he had to be born in 1784. Another entry, dated March 3, 1839, gives his age as 54 and would suggest that West Ford was born in 1785. West Ford's obituary, printed in the *Alexandria Gazette*, stated that he died at the age of

79 in July, 1863, making the year he was born 1784. Historian and reporter, Benson Lossing, wrote an article in 1858 on West Ford, commenting that West was 72 years old, making 1786 as the year he was born.

In the list of John Augustine Washington's Negroes, dated 3 March, 1783, there is no mention of West. Only Billey, Jenny (West's grandparents) and Venus were listed as slaves. (**From J. A. Washington's Ledger C, RM-73, MS-2166**).

Did George Washington know West Ford, or his mother, Venus?

We contend that George Washington did in fact know Venus and West.

Ford oral history states that Venus was a young girl when she was first asked to 'comfort' George Washington. She also met George Washington on his visits to Bushfield before and after the Revolutionary War. Ford oral history further states that after Venus became pregnant with West, Washington no longer had sexual relations with her. When asked by Hannah Washington who the father of her child was, Venus replied, "The Ole General be the father, mistress."

Other references that Venus and George Washington were probably acquainted comes from correspondence dated 2/17/97 **from the MVLA to Linda Bryant:** "The fact that Venus' parents were also singled out in John Augustine's will might suggest that the possible link between the Washingtons and West Ford's family goes back several generations." **John Augustine's June, 11, 1784, Will** states, "Billey, Jenny, & Venus, I give impower my Wife to devise to such of my Children by her as she please." Certain additions were made to this will on November 19, 1785. There was no mention of West in these additions.

An interesting fact is that George Washington played with slave children—Jenny, Joe, Jeremy, Phyllis and Steven. (**Thomas Flexner's, "The Black Mount Vernon"**). Jenny was Venus' mother.

Information that George Washington had known West Ford can be found in the **1937** *Illinois Register* **article titled, "From Mount Vernon to Springfield—George W. Ford, Veteran of Indian Wars, Traces Ancestry Back to Revolutionary Days When Grandfather was Valued Servant at Mount Vernon."** The article quotes Major Ford saying: "He tells us that his grandfather (West Ford) frequently went when a lad, as a personal attendant, with General Washington when he attended church in the more immediate neighborhood of Mount Vernon, Polick Church."

Dr. Judith Saunders-Burton's 1986 Doctoral Dissertation titled, "A History of Gum Springs, Virginia: A Report of a Case Study of Leadership in a Black Enclave" states on page 20: "Oral history connects George Washington and West Ford in several situations. For example, Catherine C. Ford Saunders, the great-granddaughter of West Ford, often told the story of West Ford riding everywhere in the wagon with George Washington (**Saunders, C., 1945**). Bruce A. Saunders, West Ford's great-great-great-grandson, stated that, "George Washington carried West Ford to Christ Church with him, and that a pew was provided for West." (**Saunders, C., 1970**).

Philip D. Morgan's "Slave Counterpoint—Black Culture in the Eighteenth-Century Chesapeak & Lowcountry" 1998, The University of North Carolina Press, on page 356 mentions George Washington and Venus: "George Washington estimated that his servants stole two glasses of wine to every one he consumed. Venus did "everything in her power to provoke" her master to remove her from the household and send her to an outlying quarter, and eventually won her wish." These two sentences in his text occur one after the other, suggesting Venus and George new of each other.

Aren't George Washington's whereabouts well documented through his diaries?

James Thomas Flexner, a biographer of George Washington, stated in his book titled, "**George Washington—The Forge of Experience**" page 232, that: "George Washington's earlier diaries never contained those personal soliloquies in which a man speaks freely to his most intelligent, beloved, and understanding friend—himself." Therefore, it is highly unlikely that Washington would record his dalliances with Venus or their son, West Ford.

There would be other times that George Washington would not enter into his diaries that he had visited his brother's plantation. "He (Washington) dined at Hobb's Hole, now Tappahannock, on the 20th, where he must have crossed the Rappahannock River the same day or the next, though he says nothing about it in his diary account." (**The Washingtons and Their Homes, John W. Wayland**).

When did George Washington have the opportunity to meet Venus?

Washington's diary entries show that his brother John was at Mount Vernon a number of times in the years between 1760 and 1786.

A reference taken from **The Washingtons and Their Homes, by John W. Wayland,** states: "The last week in August of the same year, 1768, Washington spent partly with his brother John at Bushfield. He was at Bushfield two or three days, taking dinner there on Sunday, the 28th, after attending services at Nomini Church."

There is also correspondence available that reports that John Augustine visited his brother in June of 1784, (**Letter from George Washington to John Augustine, June 30, 1784**). Other recorded dates the brothers were in each other's company are June, 1785, October, 1785, and October, 1786. (**The Washingtons and Their Homes, by John W. Wayland**).

One particular reference in Wayland's book includes an excerpt taken from a letter to **George Washington from John Augustine, dated July 17, 1785,** that read: "Previous to my setting off to Mt. Vernon and Alexandria the last time I was up, a great Coat of yours that you had been kind enough to lend my son Corbin when he was last at your House, and a book that my Wife's maid the time before the last that she was there had put up supposing it to be her Mistresses, as she had one in the Chariott to read on the road, but I forgot both and brought them back..."
Venus, being a house servant in a maid's capacity, of course would have accompanied her mistress to Mount Vernon.

One date proposed for George and Venus' initial liaison was after the death of Washington's nephew, Augustine, in 1784. **In a letter dated April 4, 1784, from John Augustine to George Washington,** he states: "Should Bushrod return shortly, as soon as he has spent some days with his Mama and recovered from the fatigue of his Journey, he and Corbin and my Self will do ourselves the pleasure of waiting on you, unless I should hear that you are gone to the northward."

Wasn't George Washington's brother's plantation too far away for him to visit Venus on a regular basis?

The Bushfield plantation was about a day and a half to two days ride from Mount Vernon. George Washington was an expert horseman; a two-day ride would not be that difficult for him to accomplish. Washington's visit to Mount Vernon in September of 1781, as reported in Elswyth Thane's book **"Washington's Lady" on page 188** states that: "It was Humphreys, yes, but only because he had managed to keep up with George, who had ridden the sixty miles from Baltimore in one day to snatch a few precious hours in his home before the rest of the company arrived."

John Fitzpatrick's article, **"The George Washington Scandals, Manuscript Division of the Library of Congress", page 389,** stated that: "Washington's diaries show that his daily ride around his farms was in utter disregard of the weather or season; snow-drifts that stopped his horse did not always stop the rider, who at times abandoned the animal and plunged forward on foot."

The brothers also traveled back and forth from their plantations by schooner via the Potomac River. One reference states: "The last week in August of the same year, 1768, Washington spent partly with his brother John at Bushfield. This time he came down the Potomac from Chotank, in King George County, in his schooner, fishing with a seine in Machodoc Creek, Nomini Bay, and other places thereabout. (**The Washingtons and Their Homes, John W. Wayland**).

Were there any contemporary accounts reporting any relationships between George Washington, other women, Venus and/or West Ford?

There are several known sex scandals associated with George Washington. **John C. Fizpatrick's, "The George Washington Scandals", Manuscript Division of Library of Congress", page 389,** discussed these scandals in a 1927 article. These scandals have not been proven as fact, but have been bandied about for years. The scandals consist of 'Sweet Kate', the mulatto washer-woman's daughter who may have slept with

Washington. George Washington's use of ciphers next to various female slaves listed in several of his diaries have also drawn attention; and his fatal illness of December 13, 1799, was alleged to be the result of an assignation with an overseer's wife.

Many historians will now concede George Washington's love for Sally Fairfax, his best friend's wife. In **Thomas Flexner's book, "George Washington—The Forge of Experience", page 198,** depicts a letter George Washington wrote to Sally Fairfax in which he states his unrequited love for her.

Dr. Judith Burton's 1986 Doctoral Dissertation states on **page 19** that: "Florence Holland and Robert King, both residents of Gum Springs and employees at Mount Vernon during the 1940s, have alleged that on several occasions they read a diary that listed the children sired by George Washington; although it is not known whether West Ford's name was listed in the diary. They further claimed that when they were discovered reading the book by their supervisors at Mount Vernon, the book was confiscated and they never saw it again." (**Holland, 1972; King, 1956**).

Did West Ford live at Mount Vernon?

West Ford moved to the Mount Vernon plantation after the death of Martha Washington. West Ford was freed on his twenty-first birthday and Ford oral history states that a drawing was sketched of him to commemorate the event. The original drawing of West Ford at twenty-one years of age is in the possession of the Mount Vernon Ladies' Association. The ornate-framed sketch was given to the Mount Vernon Association by a descendant of John Augustine Washington.

Benson Lossing, a historian writing an article on West Ford and Mount Vernon in 1858 made a curious reference several times that West

Ford was known as the patriarch of the plantation. Lossing also sketched a picture of Ford in his early 70s for *Harper's New Monthly Magazine*, 1859. In Lossing's own words he states: "Although set free by the will of his master in 1829, he (West Ford) has never left the estate, but remains a resident there, where he is regarded as a patriarch. I saw him when I last visited Mount Vernon, the autumn of 1858, and received from his lips many interesting reminiscences of the place and its surroundings. Just at evening, when returning from a stroll to the ancient entrance to Mount Vernon, I found West Ford (the name of the patriarch) engaged at the shop, near the conservatory, making a plough. He is a mulatto, very intelligent and communicative; and I enjoyed a pleasant and profitable half-hour's conversation with him. He came to Mount Vernon in August, 1802, and when I saw him he was in the seventy-second year of his age.

West Ford well knew Billy, Washington's favorite servant during the war for independence. Billy, with all of his fellow slaves, was made free by his master's will; and he received a liberal pension and a residence for life at Mount Vernon. His means for luxurious living had a bad effect upon him, and Billy became a bon-vivant. Delirium tremens finally seized him, with its terrors. Occasionally West Ford sometimes relieved him of the paroxysms by bleeding. One morning, a little more than thirty years ago, he was sent for to bleed Billy. The blood would not flow. Billy was dead and the last but one of Washington's favorite servants passed from earth forever.

I left West Ford at his plough-making, with an engagement to meet him the next morning before breakfast for the purpose of delineating a pencil sketch of his features. I found him prepared, having on a black satin vest, silk cravat, and his curly gray hair arranged in the best manner, for he said, 'the artists make colored folks look bad enough anyhow.' When my sketch was finished, he wrote his name under it with a pencil."

In 1985 Donald Sweig wrote in the **Fairfax Chronicles** that: "In his role as overseer at Mount Vernon, Ford had considerable independence and responsibility." West Ford was also treated as a privileged servant by the Washington Family. Ford's children were educated at the estate schoolhouse along with the Washington children. (**Correspondence from Washington, J. Jr., 1857**). West Ford's grandson, George Ford, was baptized at the age of five at St. Paul's Episcopal Church, where the Washington's worshipped. (**From "Mount Vernon to Springfield"**).

Washington's old valet, Billy Lee, befriended West Ford. In Elswyth Thane's book titled, **"Mount Vernon is Ours—The Story of its Preservation"** he stated on page 248 that: "Old West Ford was an exceptional Negro who had been one of Judge Bushrod's household, and could remember the stories told in his (Billy Lee's) somewhat boozy old age by Billy Lee, who was General Washington's body servant." Ford oral history states that Billy Lee was like a surrogate father to West Ford and told him many stories about the "Ole General."

West Ford became the first tomb guard for George Washington's gravesite. Three generations of Fords would also hold the title of tomb guard at the Mount Vernon plantation. (*1937 Illinois Register* article titled, **"From Mt. Vernon to Springfield—George W. Ford, Veteran of Indian Wars, Traces Ancestry Back to Revolutionary Days When Grandfather was Valued Servant at Mount Vernon" & George Ford's 1939 obituary**).

Is the Ford oral history a new claim?

The West Ford story is not a new claim. Dr. Judith Saunders-Burton has been in contact with the association since the early 1970s. Linda Bryant contacted the Mount Vernon's Ladies' Association in 1997, requesting information regarding West Ford's body for possible DNA testing.

Is there any documentation to corroborate the Ford family's oral tradition?

Three generations of Fords lived and worked on the Mount Vernon plantation including Major George Ford, son of William, West Ford's first born son. Major George Ford was sixteen years old when West Ford died. Major Ford is cited in a **1937** *Illinois Register* **article titled, "From Mount Vernon to Springfield—George W. Ford, Veteran of Indian Wars, Traces Ancestry Back to Revolutionary Days when Grandfather was Valued Servant at Mount Vernon"** discussing his home and his family life on the plantation.

Ford's 1939 obituary also appeared in the same newspaper. Both articles cite statements made by Major Ford concerning his grandfather and the time he spent at Mount Vernon, which validates and corroborates the family's oral tradition: "He (West Ford) lived at Mount Vernon for nearly sixty years and was raised in the Washington family; Major Ford frequently recalled stories his grandfather told of the Washington family; Major Ford remembers this picturesque old fellow, his grandfather, as a sort of privileged character at Mount Vernon and in the city of Alexandria."

The descendants of Major George Ford did not speak openly to anyone outside of their race about George Washington being in their family tree. The family elders worried that the story of their shared heritage with the first president would spark racial reprisals during the eras of slavery, Reconstruction, segregation, and the civil rights movement. It was only when one of the present-day chroniclers, Elise Ford Allen, decided the time was right to take the heritage public that the sisters Janet Allen and Linda Allen Bryant, started speaking openly to the media.

On the other hand, Dr. Judith Saunders-Burton and the Fords in Virginia have been very open with the story of George Washington being in their family tree. **Historian J.A. Rogers** quotes in his 1940 book titled, **Sex and Race in the New World, page 222,** that "In the District of Columbia is a Negro family, which claims descent from Washington." **A 1940s** *Pittsburgh Courier* article also by J.A. Rogers stated: **"Know Your History: West Ford, known as a Negro son of George Washington."**

Did George Washington bestow special privileges upon West Ford?

West Ford was not mentioned in George Washington's last will and testament. This was probably to be expected as Washington was aware that his will would be made public for generations to come. His reputation would have been demolished if he had laid claim to an illegitimate, slave son.

West Ford did, however, remain the personal attendant of George Washington until he became the first president of the United States. (**From "Mt. Vernon to Springfield"**).

Was West Ford's body entombed in the old family vault at Mount Vernon, and has it been removed?

During the heart of the Civil War in 1863, the Mount Vernon Ladies' Association's secretary, Ms. Sarah Tracy, and Upton Herbert, the first resident superintendent of the estate, took West Ford from his home on Little Hunting Creek to Mount Vernon after finding him ill. Elswyth Thanes book, **"Mount Vernon is Ours",** said on **page 248:** "We (Sarah Tracy and Upton Herbert) have had old West Ford brought here (Mount Vernon). Mr. Herbert and myself went to see him Sunday and found him very feeble, and fearing all the excitement might hurt him, we have had him brought here, where we could take better care of him.

I felt it was our duty to see that he should want for nothing in his old age." West Ford died two months later and his obituary appeared in the *Alexandria Gazette* the next day.

Ford oral history states that West Ford was buried in the old tomb of George Washington. His oldest son, William, was in New York during the Civil War. William was told upon his return to Virginia that his father's body was in the old tomb, and he never had it removed.

In 1997, Linda Allen Bryant asked the Mount Vernon's Ladies' Association if the old tomb could be opened to see if West Ford's body was interred there for DNA tests. She was told that the tomb was a national monument and that it would take a court order to open it. In October 1998 a tour guide told Bryant that the tomb had been opened, that it was empty, and it was going to be renovated for viewing by the public in 1999.

What technology is necessary to test for paternity, and can DNA testing establish West Ford's paternity?

For a 99.9 percent match the DNA from West Ford and DNA from George Washington would be needed. Without West Ford's body, paternity tests cannot be conclusively made at this time.

Linda Bryant contacted Dr. Eugene Foster, the pathologist in the Jefferson/Hemings study, for his recommendation on the Ford case. **Dr. Foster in correspondence dated 11/28/98** stated that: "To do this the way we did the Jefferson study, one would need to have DNA from at least one living male-line descendent of West Ford and one living male-line descendant of one of George Washington's brothers, or other paternal relatives. If the Y chromosomal DNA from these two individuals matched exactly or almost exactly, that would be strong evidence that a Washington, not necessarily George, was West Ford's father. In the event that there was a match, one could conceivably go farther by trying to get a sample of George Washington's DNA. If his Y chromosomal type was exactly the same as that of his paternal relatives, one would still not know whether he or one of his relatives was the father. On the other hand, if George Washington's DNA was slightly different from that of his relatives and if it exactly matched that of the West Ford descendant, it would be strong evidence that George Washington was West Ford's father."

Will the association provide a sample of George Washington's hair for a DNA testing in the future if technology changes?

Yes. The association is committed to providing samples of Washington's hair for DNA analysis, when DNA science concludes that these hair samples can resolve the issue of West Ford's paternity. The association is committed to historical accuracy. (**Mount Vernon Press Release, October 1999**). The Ford family will seek the commitment of the association at the appropriate time DNA testing is initiated.

Was George Washington Sterile?

No one truly knows if George Washington was sterile, including historians. No one examined George Washington to determine the assumption. Washington did have a bout with smallpox and malaria, but there is no medical proof that these diseases cause sterility.

George Washington and Martha did not have children together, but it may have been Martha who was incapable of conception. As stated by the Association's research, forty percent of the time the male is at fault, and that leaves the greater percentage with the female. (**Mount Vernon Press Release, October 1999**).

One must take into consideration that Martha had born four children in succession by her previous husband and may have had complications, which may have caused her not to be able to conceive during her marriage to Washington. In the book, **"George Washington—the Man Behind the Myths", by William Rasmussen and Robert Tilton,** the authors state on **page 90:** "According to a tradition passed down in Masonic circles, Martha Washington would have needed some sort of corrective surgery in order to conceive additional children, after the birth of Patsy."

Martha Washington believed the problem may have been with her, as stated in **Elswyth Thane's** book titled, **"Washington's Lady", page 29:** "She (Martha) wondered if something had gone wrong at Patsy's birth, to leave her last child so frail and herself under a disability. Or was it— Nancy had thought it possible—because she had had measles nearly three years ago?"

George Washington himself did not believe he was sterile. **In Miriam Anne Bourne's book titled, "First Family—George Washington and his Intimate Relations",** page 107, she states, "Would Washington's happiness have been even more genuine and permanent had he children of his own? A remarkable letter written in 1786 (West Ford's birth date is believed to be around 1784-1786) to a nephew reveals that in George's opinion it was not because of himself that he was childless. The letter stated: "If Mrs. Washington should survive me there is moral certainty of my dying without issue, and should I be he longest liver, the matter in my opinion is almost as certain; for whilst I retain the reasoning faculties I shall never marry a girl and it is not probable that I should have children by a woman of an age suitable to my own should I be disposed to enter into a second marriage."

Bibliography

Alexandria Gazette, Obituary of West Ford, July 21, 1863, p. 2.

Alexandria Gazette, Mount Vernon as it Was, June 19, 1950.

Adams, Pam, Washington Father of Country, Slaves, The *Peoria Journal Star,* February 3, 2000.

Allen, Elise Ford, (August, 1960; December, 1966), Oral Interviews, Peoria Illinois.

Allen, Elise Ford, (August 28, 1974; April 12, 1975; August 16, 1976; July 3, 1977; December 20, 1978), Oral Interviews, Peoria, Illinois.

Allen, Elise Ford, (January 16, 1981; May 27, 1982; December 27, 1986), Oral Interviews, Peoria, Illinois.

Allen, Elise Ford, (December 15, 1994), Oral Interview, Peoria, Illinois.

Allen, Elise Ford, (July 29, December, 1996) Oral Interviews, Peoria, Illinois.

Allen, Elise Ford, (January 20, March 16, 17, July 23, 24, August 28, 29, 1997, July 1999, March 2000), Oral Interviews, Peoria, Illinois.

Andrist, Ralph K., The Founding Fathers—George Washington—A Biography in His Own Words, *NEWSWEEK*, New York, 1972.

Aptheker, Herbert, The Negro People in the United States, Citadel Press Book, Published by the Carol Publishing Group.

Aptheker, Herbert, Negro Slave Revolts in the United States, 1526-1860, New York, 1939.

Asimov, Issac, The Genetic Code, The Orion Press, New York, 1962.

Barrett, Walter, Old Merchants of New York City, 1865.

Bennett, Harriette Ford (January 28, 1998, 1999, 2000), Oral Interviews, Chicago, Illlinois.

Bennett, Lerone Jr., Before the Mayflower—A History of Black America, Sixth Edition.

Bourne, Miriam Anne, First Family—George Washington and his Intimate Relations, W. W. Norton & Company, New York.

Briggs, Bill, *Denver Post*, Whose Ancestor—Family Traces Lineage to Washington, April 24, 1997.

Brookhiser, Richard, Founding Father—Rediscovering George Washington, The *Free Press*, 1996.

Bureau of Refugees, Freedman, and Abandoned Lands Records, RG 105, National Archives, Washington, D.C.

Burton, Judith Saunders, A History of Gum Springs, Virginia: A Report of a Case Study of Leadership in a Black Enclave, Ph.D. Dissertation, May 1986.

Bushfield Westmoreland County Circuit Court, (1801). Hannah Washington's Will, (No.20). Mount Vernon Ladies Association Archives, Mount Vernon, VA.

CBS/This Morning, July 7, 1999.

Christian, Charles M., Black Saga—The African American Experience, Houghton Mifflin Company, 1995.

Clarke, John Henrik, William Styron's Nat Turner: Ten Black Writers Respond, Boston, Mass: Beacon Press, 1968. (Reprinted as The Second Crucifixion of Nat Turner. Baltimore, MD: Black Classic Press, 1997).

Conyers, Dwyane, Last Year, Two Female Descendants of George Washington Showed Up, AOL.com., November 9, 1998.

Conway, Moncure Daniel, George Washington and Mount Vernon, Long Island Historical Society, 1889.

Corbin, D., The Father of Gum Springs, Unpublished manuscript, 1982.

Correspondence from Mount Vernon Records on Slave Burial Grounds, 1947.

Cunliffe, Marcus—George Washington and the Making of a Nation, Harper & Row, New York, 1966.

Der Spiegel, Personalien, 48/1996.

DAR Museum, News Release, DAR Museum and FBI—Split Hairs Over George Washington.

Dodge, H. H., Mt. Vernon: Its Owner and its Story, Philadelphia, PA, J. B. Lippincott, 1932.

Dodge, H. H., Harrison Howell Dodge Letterbooks, Mount Vernon Ladies' Association Archives, Mount Vernon, VA, 1894.

Duffy, John, Epidemics in Colonial America, Louisiana State University Press, 1971.

Elkins, Stanley and McKitrick, Eric—The Age of Federalism, Oxford University Press, 1993.

E. Washington to J. A. Washington. Library, Mount Vernon Ladies' Association.

Fairfax Chronicles, Dear Master": A Unique Letter from West Ford Discovered, by Donald M. Sweig, 1986.

Ellis, Joseph J., Jefferson's Legacy, U.S. News & World Report, November 9, 1998.

Fairfax County Courthouse Deed Book, 1819-1850. Nos. A3-332; A5, 554-560: B1; C4, 162-163, C6 451; E3; F4, 445-446; P5, 559-560; U2, 386; X3, 400; Z2, 169.

Fairfax County Land Tax Book, 1819-1850.

Fairfax County Land Records, 1873.

Fairfax County Land Tax Records, Fairfax, VA, Fairfax County Public Library.

Fairfax County Property Tax Records, Fairfax,VA, Fairfax County Public Library.

Federal Census List 1860, Washington, D.C.: National Archives.

Federal Census List 1870, Washington, D.C.: National Archives.

Federal Census List 1880, Washington, D.C.: National Archives.

Fitzpatrick, J. C., The George Washington Scandals, Manuscript Division, Library of Congress, Scribner's Magazine.

Fitzpatrick, J.C. (Ed.). The Diaries of George Washington, 1771-1785 (4 vols.), Boston: Houghton Mifflin Co.

Fleming, Thomas J., Affectionately Yours, George Washington—A Self Portrait in Letters and Friendship, McLeod Limited, 1967.

Flexner, Thomas, George Washington, the Forge of Experience, 1732-1775, Little, Brown, and Company, 1965.

Flexner, Thomas, George Washington—Anguish and Farewell (1793-1799), Little, Brown, and Company.

Flexner, Thomas, George Washington and the New Nation (1783-1793), Little, Brown, and Company.

Flexner, Thomas, Washington the Indispensable Man, Little, Brown, and Company.

Ford, Delores Finley, (February 11, 1997, March 2000,) Oral Interviews, Galesburg, Illinois.

Ford, Harrison, (February 23, 1997, March 2000), Oral Interviews, Northridge, CA.

Forman, James, The Making of Black Revolutionaries, Open Hand Publishing, Inc., 1985.

Foster, Eugene, Personal Correspondence, 1998, 2000.

Free Black Register, No. 121, Book No. 2, Fairfax County, VA.

Free Black Register, No. 122, Book No. 2, Fairfax County, VA.

Free Black Register, No. 123, Book No. 2, Fairfax County, VA.

Freeman, Douglas Southall, George Washington, Vols. I-VI, J.A. Carroll and M. W. Ashworth, Vol. VII, Scribner's, 1948-1957.

Gates, Henry Louis, and Cornel West, The Future of Race, Alfred A. Knopf, 1996.

Gardner, Joseph, George Washington, a Biography in his Own Words, Harper & Row, Publishers, Inc. 1972.

George Washington Papers, Series 2, Vols. 16-19, Reel 7, Library of Congress, Washington, D.C.

Gordon-Reed, Annette, Thomas Jefferson & Sally Hemings: An American Controversy, University of Virginia Press, 1997.

Greenblatt, Augusta, Heredity and You, Coward, McCann & Geogehegan, Inc., 1974.

Guild, J. P., Black Laws of Virginia, New York: Negro Universities Press, Chap. 39, 1969.

Hamilton, Charles V., The Struggle for Political Equality, National Urban League, 1976.

Hannah Washington's Last Will and Testament, 1801.

Illinois State Register, (January 17, 1937), From Mount Vernon to Springfield. (Reprinted in *Northern Virginia Heritage,* 1983).

Irving, Washington, The Life of George Washington, Vols 1-5, G. P. Putnam; Hurd, and Houghton, 1864.

Jackson, L. P., Free Negro Labor and Property Holding in Virginia, 1830-1860. New York: Atheneum, 1906.

Jackson, Robert, *Rocky Mountain News,* George Washington in Their Family Tree, Black Sisters Say, November 4, 1996.

Jackson, Robert, *Rocky Mountain News,* Sisters Want Research on Their DNA History, November 12, 1998.

Jackson, Robert, *Rocky Mountain News,* Women Seek DNA Link to Washington, July 7, 1999.

Jackson, Robert, *Rocky Mountain News,* Two Sisters to Follow Up on Possible Link to Washington, February 3, 2000.

J. A.Washington to Eleanor Washington, Library—Mount Vernon Ladies' Association Mount Vernon,VA.

J. A. Washington to Eleanor Washington, Ibid.

Jenkins, Elise Ford (December 1966), Oral Interview, Peoria, Illinois.

Jeter, Jon, *Washington Post,* Slave Descendants Claim George Washington Tie, November 11, 1998.

J. P. Guild, Black Laws of Virginia, New York: Negro University Press, 1969.

John Augustine Washington's Last Will and Testament, 1784, Mount Vernon Ladies' Association.

John Augustine Washington's List of Slaves on Bushfield Plantation, March 1783.

Kinny, Pat, *The Courier,* True Birthright, November 13, 1998.

Lampton, Christopher, DNA Finger-Printing, An Impact Book, 1991.

Leckie, William H., The Buffalo Soldiers—A Narrative of the Negro Cavalry in the West, University of Oklahoma Press, 1967.

Ledgerwood, I., Gum Springs, *The Washington Post, Potomac,* October 24, 1964. pp.5-8.

Leone, Bruno, Slavery Opposing Viewpoints, Greenhaven Press, Inc., 1992.

Levy, Harlan, And the Blood Cried Out. Basic Books, 1996.

Library of Congress, Manuscript Division, Letter from Major George Ford to Theodore Roosevelt, and Letter From Theodore Roosevelt to Major George Ford, 1900.

Lossing, B., Mount Vernon and Its Associations, *Harper's New Monthly Magazine,* 48 (106) 1859.

Manier, Jeremy, For Father of Our Country, DNA May Spell A Son, *Chicago Tribune,* November 10, 1998.

Manier, Jeremy, Father of Our Country May Have Been Dad, *Chicago Tribune,* May 26, 2000.

Marriage Register, (1803-1879), Alexandria County, D.C., Arlington County Court House, Arlington, VA.

Meltzer, Milton, The Black Americans—A History in Their Own Words, 1619-1983, Harper & Row, Publishers, 1987.

McCall, Nathan, What's Going On, Random House, New York, 1997.

Military Records of George Ford in the 10th Cavalry and the 23rd Kansas Infantry.

Milkovits, Amanda, *Foster's Daily Democrat,* George Washington's Hair Apparent, November 15, 1998.

Mondadori, Arnoldo, The Life and Times of Washington, The Curtis Publishing Company, 1967.

Morgan, Philip D, Slave Counterpoint, University of North Carolina Press, Chapel Hill & London, 1998.

McConnell, J., Negroes and Their Treatment in Virginia from 1865-1867, New York: Negro University Press, 1967.

Mount Vernon—Commemorative Guidebook, George Washington Bicentennial Edition, Text by James C. Rees, 1998.

Mount Vernon Correspondence, Mary Thompson, 1995.

Mount Vernon Gazette, Chronicler of Gum Springs, April 27, 1989, Christa Watters.

Mount Vernon—A Handbook, Mount Vernon Ladies' Association, 1995.

Mount Vernon and Its Associations, New York: W. A. Townsend and Company, 1859.

Mount Vernon Ladies' Association, Annual Report, 1985.

Mount Vernon Ladies' Association of the Union, The Last Will and Testament of George Washington, 1939.

Mount Vernon Press Release, October, 1999.

MSNBC—Brian Williams Show, July 10, 2000.

Muir, D. T. Presence of a Lady: Mount Vernon, 1861-1868, Mount Vernon, VA: Mount Vernon Ladies' Association, 1946.

NBC/Today Show, July 7, 1999.

NEWSWEEK Magazine, Tracing a Familiar Face, November 15, 1996.

Northern Virginia Heritage, Publication of Free Black Registrar, 1983.

Northern Virginia Sun, Free and Black in Northern Virginia Before the Civil War, May 22, 1968.

New York Times, Washington Talk, November 8, 1985.

Osgood, Herbert L., The American Colonies in the Eighteenth Century, Columbia, 1924.

Ottley, Roi., Black Odyssey—The Story of the Negro in America. New York: Charles Scribner's, Sons, 1948.

PBS/Frontline, Jefferson's Blood—George and Venus, March 28, 2000.

Phillips, Ulrich Bonnell, American Negro Slavery, 1918.

Pickett, Florence Ford, (January 30, 1997), Oral Interview, Peoria, Illinois.

Pittsburgh Courier, West Ford: Know Your History, 1940, p. 24.

Powell, Anthony, An Overview: Black Participation In the Spanish-American War, Internet Doc., 1999.

Powell, Vera Ford, (August 1960), Oral Interview, Peoria, Illinois.

Reef, Catherine, Buffalo Soldiers, Twenty-First Century Books, 1993.

Registrations of Free Negroes Commencing September Court 1822, Book #2; edited by Donald Sweig.

Register of Free Blacks, 1835, Book 3, pp. 59, 123; edited by Donald Sweig.

Reuter, Edward Bryon, The American Race Problem, 1927.

Rhodenhamel, J. H., Letter, Mount Vernon Ladies' Association, 1978.

Robinson, H. S., Who Was West Ford? The Journal of Negro History. Washington, D.C.: Association for Study of Negro Life and History, 1981.

Robinson, H. S., Descendants of Daniel and Hannah Bruce. The Negro History Bulletin, 1961.

Robinson, H.S., A Paper on Daniel and Hannah Bruce: Free People of Color—Their Descendants and Achievements, 1779-1988.

Robinson, Wendy, *The Urban Spectrum,* Black Family Seeks Roots Beneath the Cherry Tree, March 1997.

Scates, Darlene, *South Bend Tribune,* By George, She's Related, Woman Says, February 21, 1997.

Sharp, James Roger, American Politics in the Early Republic, Book Crafters, Inc., 1993.

Smith, Jessie Carney, Ethnic Genealogy—A Research Guide, Greenwood Press, 1972.

Smith, John David, Black Voices from Reconstruction 1865-1877, Millbrook Press, 1996.

Smith, Page, The Shaping of America—A People's History of the Young Republic, Vol. 3, Penguin Books, 1980.

Smith, Richard Norton, Patriarch—George Washington and the New American Nation, Houghton Mifflin Company, 1993.

Society for Promoting the Manumission of Slaves—and Protecting Such of Them as Have Been or May be Liberated. Minutes and Reports, 1785-1849, 12 vols.

St. Louis Post-Dispatch, Black Family Would Prove Link to George Washington, November 11, 1998.

Staton, R. L, The Church and the Rebellion, 1864.

Staughton, Lynd, Class Conflict, Slavery, and the United States Constitution, The Library of Congress, Bobbs-Merrill Co., 1967.

Sunday Morning/CBS—Segment on Ford Family, February 27, 2000.

Swiggett, Howard, The Great Man—George Washington as a Human Being, Doubleday & Co., Inc., Garden City, New York, 1953.

Szoke, Anita, *Peoria Journal Star,* Former Peoria Sisters Claim Famous Roots, November 22, 1996.

Thane, E., Mount Vernon is Ours: The Story of its Preservation, New York: Duell, Sloan, & Pearce, 1966.

Tenzer, Lawrence R., The Forgotten Cause of the Civil War: A New Look at the Slavery Issue, Scholars' Publishing House.

The Traveler Weekly, Thesis says George Washington Fathered Their Fourth Great-Grandfather, Vol . 31, No. 22, November 16, 1996.

Thorne, Chistopher, *Peoria Journal Star,* Family Eyes Gene Test of Washington, November 10, 1998.

Thorne, Christopher, Peoria Family Claims Link to Washington, *The Peoria Journal Star,* November 11, 1998.

Time Life Books, The Old West, 1973.

Tindall, George Brown, America: A Narrative History, 1984, W. W. Norton.

The National Enquirer, Look Who'd be on the Throne if Washington Had Been King, 1994.

The New York Public Library—African American Desk Reference, Schomburg Center for Research in Black Culture, The Stonesong Press, Inc. 1999.

The Rosette, A Hairsplitting Matter, Volume 1, Issue 2, Summer, 1994.

The Washington Post, Register of Freed Slaves Bares Fairfax County "Roots", February 8, 1977.

United States Census Office, 1870, Washington, D.C.

USA Today, DNA Tests Sought, November 1, 1998.

USA Today, What's Going on in the Racial Divide, November 3, 1997.

Van Sertima, Ivan, African Presence in Early America, New Brunswick, U.S.A. Transactions Publishers, 1992.

Van Sertima, Ivan, They Came Before Columbus, Random House, 1976.

Wade, Nicholas, *New York Times,* Descendants of Slave's Son Contend That His Father Was George Washington, July 7, 1999.

Washington, John Augustine, Letter to George Washington, April 4, 1784, Library, Mount Vernon Ladies' Association.

Washington, G., Diaries of George Washington, 1748-1799, 4 vols., edited by J. C. Fitzpatrick, Boston: Houghton-Mifflin, 1925.

Washington, George, The Washington Papers, Saul K. Padover, Harper, 1955.

Washington Post, October 1982.

Wayland, John W., The Washingtons and Their Homes, The Virginia Book Company, Berryville, Va., 1944.

West, Cornel, Race Matters, Beacon Press, 1993.

Weyl, Nathaniel and Marina, William, American Statesmen on Slavery and the Negro, Arlington House, 1971.

Wheeler, Major General Joseph, Under Fire with the Tenth U.S. Cavalry, American Publishing House, Chicago, Illinois.

Wiener, Elizabeth, *Washington Post,* Tracing the Washington Blood, February 23, 1984.

Winslow, Eugene, Afro-Americans '76—Black Americans in the Founding of Our Nation, Afro-Am Publishing Co., Inc., Chicago.